PICASSO PRINTMAKER

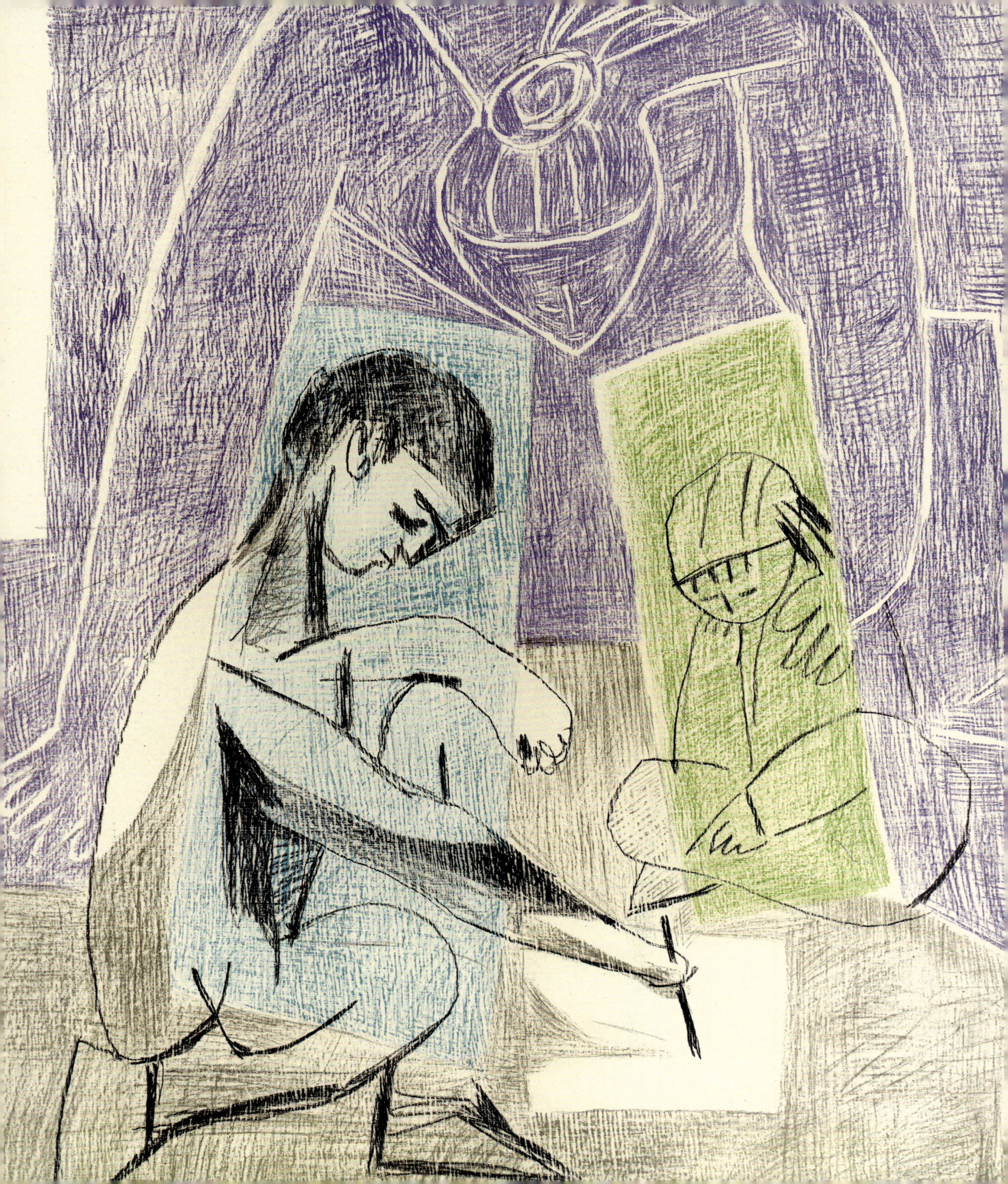

PICASSO PRINTMAKER

CATHERINE DAUNT

The British Museum

Published to accompany the exhibition
Picasso: printmaker at the British Museum from
7 November 2024 to 30 March 2025.

Supported by

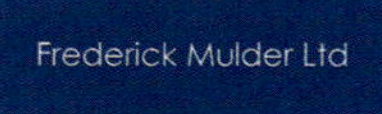

ARTscapades

The Michael Marks Charitable Trust

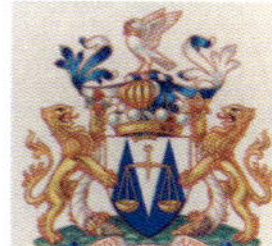

First published in the United Kingdom in 2024
by The British Museum Press

A division of The British Museum Company Ltd
The British Museum
Great Russell Street
London WC1B 3DG
britishmuseum.org/publishing

Picasso: printmaker
© 2024 The Trustees of the British Museum

A catalogue record for this book is available
from the British Library.

ISBN 978-0-7141-2699-9

Designed by Sandra Zellmer
Colour reproduction by Altaimage
Printed in Italy by OGM

Further information about the British Museum
and its collection can be found at
britishmuseum.org.

Front cover: Pablo Picasso, *Still life under
the lamp*, 5th state and definitive form, 1962
Linocut in black over green, red and yellow.
British Museum 2013,7075.9
Funded by Art Fund, Patrons of the British
Museum, James and Béatrice Lupton, the
Vollard Group, Hamish Parker, and Simon and
Virginia Robertson

Back cover: Pablo Picasso,
Women on the beach, 11 May 1947
Transfer lithograph.
British Museum 2006,0929.18
Presented by Gordon and Ursula Bowyer

Frontispiece: Pablo Picasso,
The little artist, 18 May 1964
Colour crayon transfer lithograph.
British Museum 2016,7048.11
Funded by Art Fund (with a contribution from
Art Partners), the Wolfson Foundation, the Vollard
Group, Hamish Parker, Clive Gillmore, Katrin
Bellinger, Margaret Conklin, Anthony Diamond,
Christian Duerckheim, David Lawson, Dr Frederick
Mulder, David Sabel and Daniel Thierry.

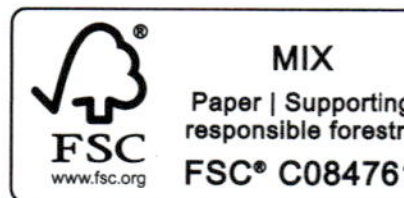

CONTENTS

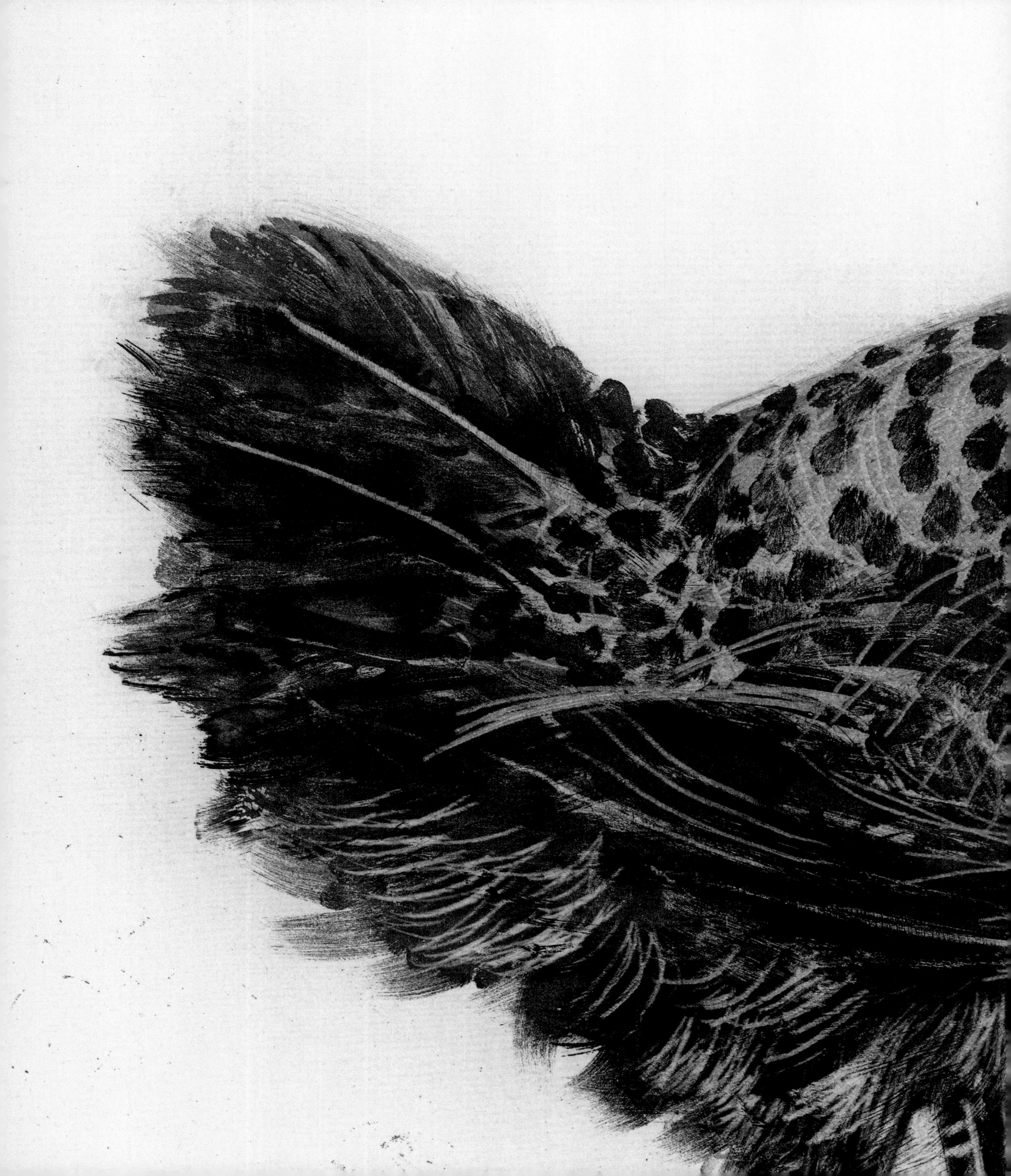

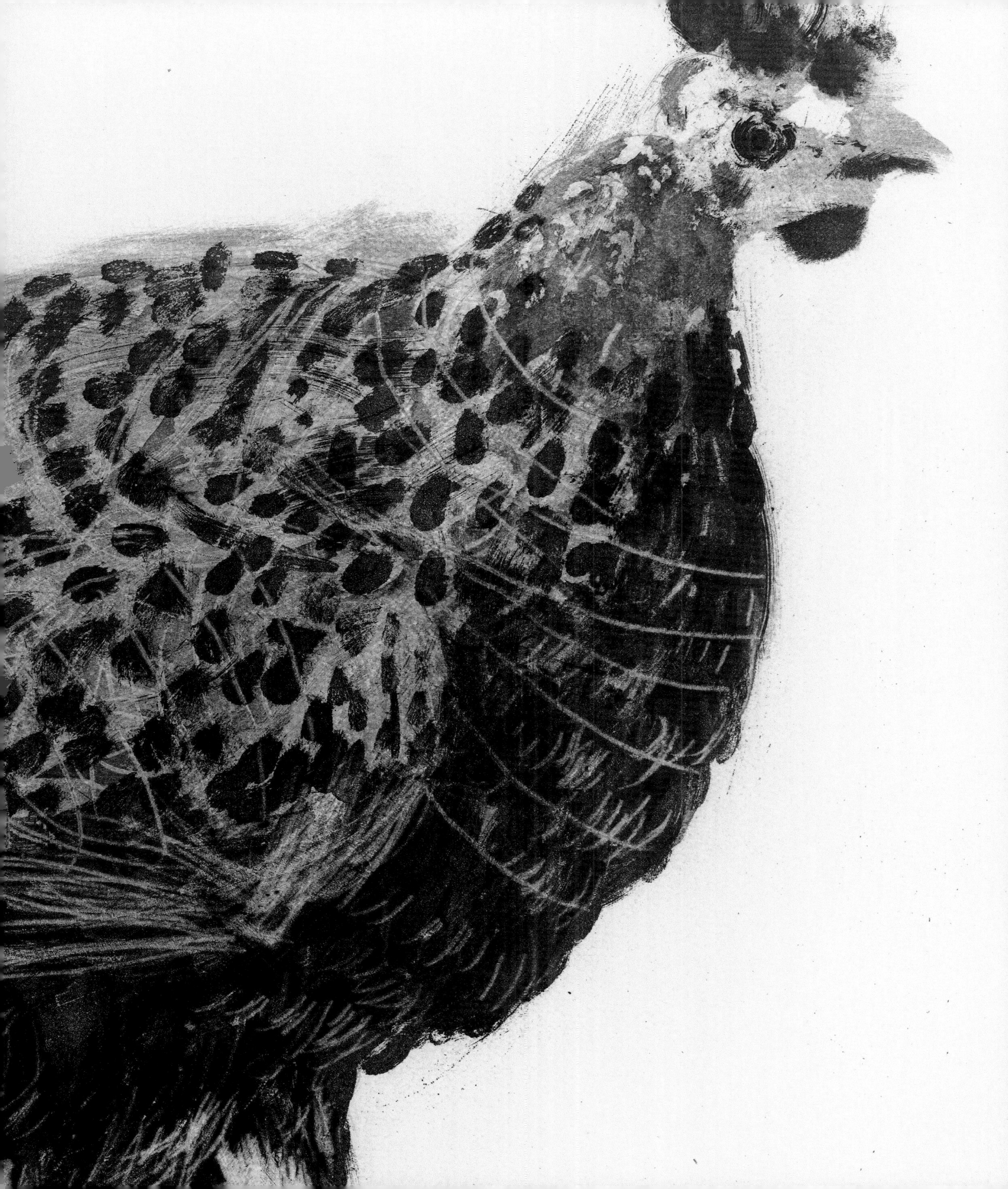

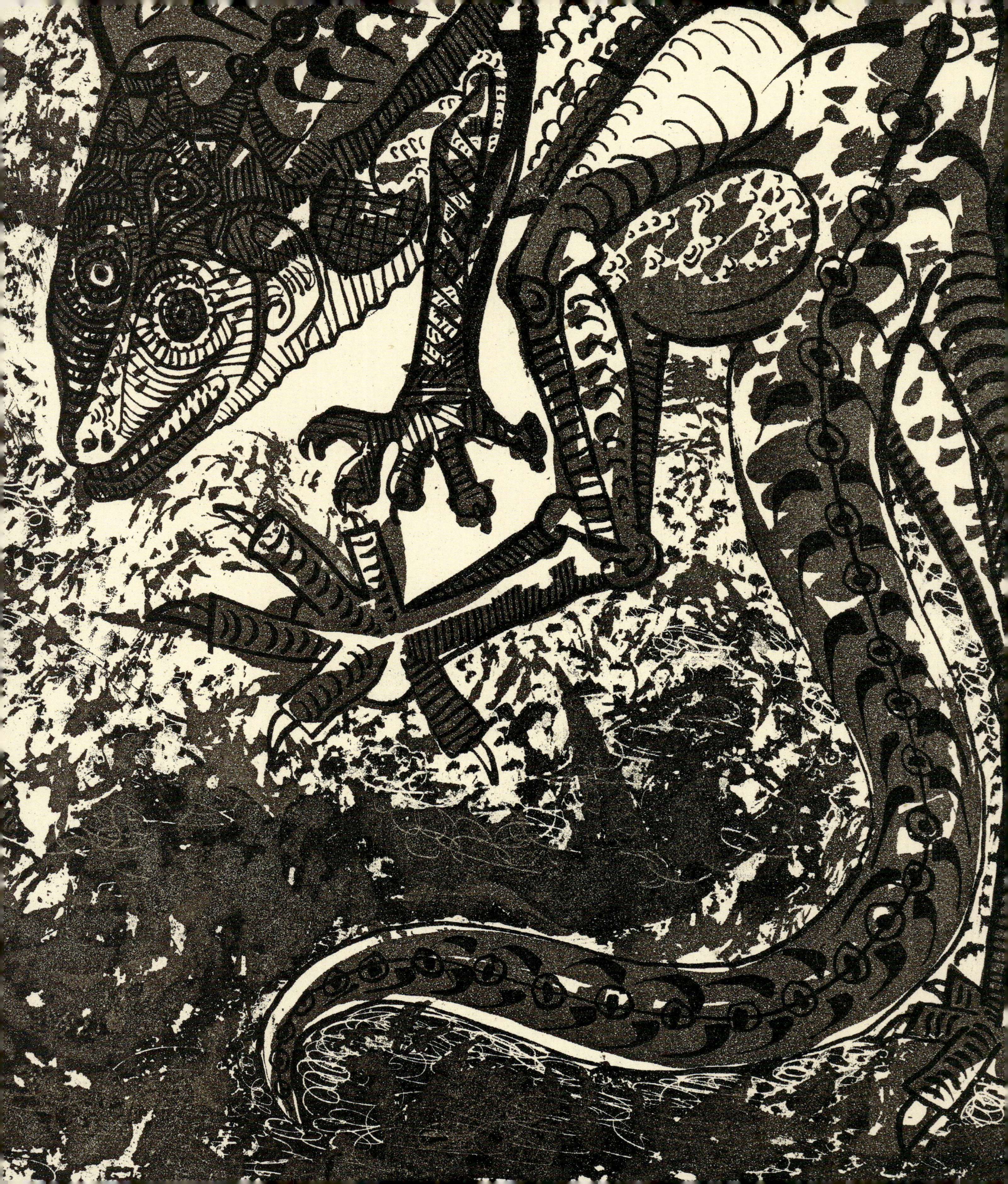

DIRECTOR'S FOREWORD

From its foundation in 1753, the British Museum has been shaped in
large part by the varied tastes and passions of the collectors who have
donated, sold or bequeathed their holdings. The impressive scope of the
present exhibition and book, exploring Picasso's lifelong engagement with
printmaking, is proof that this continues today. Without the generosity of
Hamish Parker, the donor in 2011 of the *Vollard Suite* from the 1930s and
in 2014 of the *347 Suite* (a late outpouring of printmaking named after the
number of works in the set), and the work of Stephen Coppel, the recently
retired curator of modern and contemporary works on paper, *Picasso:
printmaker* would not have been feasible. Thanks to Hamish Parker's
intervention, the Museum can now showcase a key element of Picasso's
printmaking: his gift for freewheeling invention, working through linked
ideas and themes in successive plates of a series, as seen in the *Vollard
Suite* and *347*. Today the Museum owns over 550 prints by Picasso, the
largest collection in the United Kingdom

This book and exhibition highlight Picasso's creativity and technical daring
as a printmaker. His Cubist drypoints (1908–15) show how his prints fed
into and reflected one of the most radical moments in his career, while
prints from the 1930s demonstrate his experimentations with the aquatint
technique. The post-war lithographs and linocuts show Picasso's enthusiasm
for exploring and mastering new techniques. The progressive proofs of *Still
life under the lamp* (1962), for example (see pp. 104–5), reveal the artist's
extraordinary skill in anticipating from the outset how the overlays of colour
would combine to create the finished composition in his head. The curator
Catherine Daunt's selection also includes prints that reflect darker aspects
of Picasso's art – a paradox embodied in the artist's identification with
the Minotaur, a mythical beast with the head of a bull and the body of a
man, whose character in his art switches unpredictably from meekness to
savagery. This book takes us from his youthful days as a struggling artist
in Paris to his 80s, when he still proved restlessly innovative and prolific.
It demonstrates that throughout his final years, Picasso continued to make
prints that were experimental and dynamic.

Dr Nicholas Cullinan OBE

Pages 6–7
The hen (detail), 1952.
Sugar aquatint and scraper.

Opposite
Lizard (detail), 1936.
Sugar aquatint and drypoint.

INTRODUCTION

On 16 March 1968, at the age of 86, Pablo Picasso (1881–1973) began work on a series of etchings that would occupy him until 5 October. In just under seven months he produced 347 prints, made using a variety of intaglio techniques, that as a group offer a profound insight into his life, concerns and creative preoccupations at the time. Printmaking had been an important, if episodic, part of Picasso's output since 1904, when, after moving to Paris from Barcelona, he made the etching *The frugal meal*, his first print as a professional artist (see p. 33). Over the course of his life, he produced around 2,200 published prints and a further 230 that were unpublished, including etchings, drypoints, aquatints, lithographs and linocuts.[1] He made prints in every decade of his career but engaged with the medium more deeply when circumstances and commissions offered creative opportunities that he wished to pursue. Picasso made his first major body of prints between 1904 and 1906, but it was in the 1930s, when he produced the 100 etchings that would later be published as the *Vollard Suite*, that printmaking became for him a medium through which he could investigate a subject or idea in depth, using multiple interrelated images. In 1968 when he found himself largely confined to his home in the South of France, an aged artist confronting both his past and his legacy, it was through printmaking that he chose to process his thoughts and emotions (fig. 1). With printers and a studio close at hand, Picasso worked at a relentless pace, at times on five, six or seven prints a day, exploring his fantasies, reflecting on his experiences and reconnecting with dead artists, friends and lovers. For Picasso, printmaking was the art form through which stories could be told, discoveries could be made and adventures could be had.

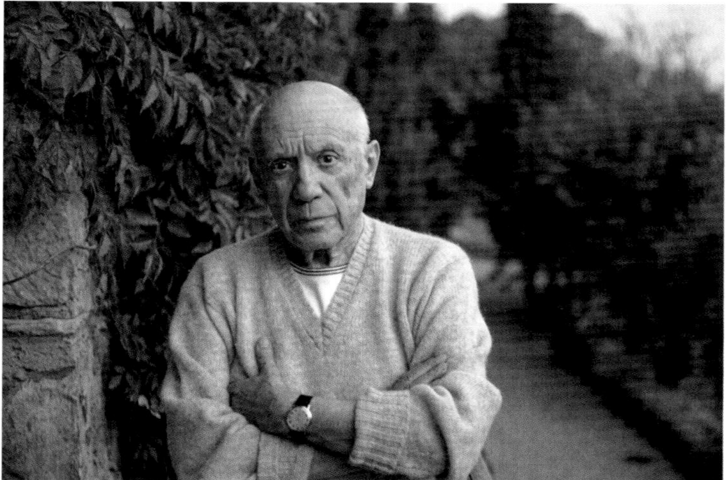

Fig. 1
Pablo Picasso in Mougins, France, 1966.

The saltimbanques

Picasso made his first print in Barcelona in 1899 when he was 17, an etching of a picador (a horse-mounted bullfighter) holding a lance. Forgetting that the image would be reversed, he inadvertently made his hero left-handed and called the print *El Zurdo* (*The Left-Hander*). Although inexperienced in printmaking, Picasso was already an accomplished painter and draughtsman by this point. Born in Málaga on the Spanish coast to Maria Picasso López and José Ruiz Blasco, an art teacher, Picasso was initially taught by his father. He went on to train as an academic painter at art schools in La Coruña, where his family lived from 1891, Barcelona and Madrid. While in the capital, he spent time in the Museo del Prado, where he became familiar with the giants of Spanish art, including El Greco (1541–1614), Diego Velázquez (1599–1660) and Francisco de Goya (1746–1828), artists from whom he would draw inspiration for the rest of his life. In 1899 Picasso moved to Barcelona, where he became part of a group of bohemian artists and writers who met in the Els Quatre Gats tavern, the location of his first professional solo exhibition in 1900. At that time, however, Paris was the centre of avant-garde art in the West, and the draw to the city was strong. After several years of moving back and forth, Picasso settled in the French capital in the 1904, taking a studio in the run-down Bateau-Lavoir building in Montmartre, nicknamed for its resemblance to the laundry boats on the Seine, specifically its tendency to sway in the wind.

It was in Paris that Picasso made his first group of prints, beginning with *The frugal meal*.[2] Paris had become a centre for printmaking in the nineteenth century as Impressionist and Post-Impressionist artists embraced the medium, and dealer-publishers established themselves in the city, working with existing print studios. Artists were able to reach a larger audience through prints, which were more affordable than paintings and sculptures and could be disseminated more widely. Picasso, who lived in relative poverty in 1904, was no doubt drawn to printmaking for these reasons, but he was also aware of the creative possibilities of the medium through his familiarity with great printmakers of the past including Goya and Rembrandt (1606–1669), and the prints of his immediate predecessors such as Édouard Manet (1832–1883) and Henri de Toulouse-Lautrec (1864–1901), whose work had a particular influence on him at the time. Having received no formal training in printmaking and with little money to spend on materials, Picasso made use of the resources around him. He learned etching techniques from Ricard Canals (1876–1931), a Catalan artist in the Bateau-Lavoir whom he had known in Barcelona, and for *The frugal meal*, he recycled a zinc plate that had previously been used for a landscape etching by another compatriot, Joan González (1868–1908).

The frugal meal is a remarkable print. It depicts an emaciated couple at a table in a cheap drinking tavern. An empty bowl sits on the table before them alongside a bottle and two glasses. The pair are physically entwined yet emotionally disconnected. The skeletal fingers of the man's hands frame the thin body of the woman, suggesting a co-dependence based on alcoholism, poverty and survival. Evidently blind, he faces to the left, while

1 These numbers come from Anne-Françoise Gavanon, 'Il n'y pas d'art populaire, seulement de l'art. Picasso et la linogravure', in *Picasso et les arts et traditions populaires: un genie sans piédestal*, ed. Bruno Gaudichon and Joséphine Matamoros, Paris: Gallimard, 2016, pp. 220–35, at p. 222. For a glossary of printmaking terms, see p. 158.
2 After *El Zurdo*, Picasso did not title his prints; the titles used in this essay are taken from the catalogue raisonnés of his prints, translated from the French or Spanish.

her haunted gaze is directed at the viewer. Picasso's skills as a draughtsman are clear, but so too is his affinity with etching. Fluent, assured lines define the figures, their elongated limbs displaying the influence of El Greco, while shadows and a sense of depth are achieved through hatching and cross-hatching. The only indication of Picasso's inexperience is the faint tufts of grass at the upper right, a remnant of González's landscape that Picasso had failed to fully scrape away. After making the image on the plate, Picasso had the printing done at a studio run by the leading Parisian printer Auguste Delâtre (1822–1907) and his son, Eugène (1864–1938). Although he bought his own press in 1907 and experimented with pulling his own prints, for the most part he relied on the services of professional printmakers throughout his career. *The frugal meal* is a key work of what is known as Picasso's Blue Period (1901–4), when his paintings were dominated by blues and greens and his subjects were melancholy in tone. He had been deeply affected by the death by suicide in February 1901 of his close friend Carles Casagemas (1880–1901), a poet and artist with whom he had first visited Paris from Barcelona in 1900, but his art also reflected his life at that time, which brought him into contact with extreme poverty and people living on the margins of society.

Picasso's prints of 1904–6 align closely with his paintings of the period in both style and subject matter. As his Blue Period came to an end, he began to make paintings in a rose palette dominated by itinerant acrobats and clowns (known as 'saltimbanques'), whose performances he witnessed at the Cirque Medrano, one of the few forms of entertainment that he and his friends could afford, and with whom he rubbed shoulders on the streets of Montmartre. His prints of the period follow this shift in subject, although the precarity of a hand-to-mouth existence remains a feature of the Rose Period images (1904–6), making the shift an evolution rather than a dramatic change. Initially, Picasso had the prints editioned in small runs by the Delâtres and they were marketed by the dealer Clovis Sagot (d. 1913). In 1911, however, by which time Picasso was much better known, *The frugal meal* and fourteen other plates were purchased by the dealer Ambroise Vollard (1866–1939), who had them coated in a thin layer of steel to make them more durable (a process known as steel-facing) and published as *La suite des saltimbanques* (*Suite of acrobats*) in 1913. Printed by Louis Fort, each plate was published in an edition of 250 plus a luxury edition of 27 or 29 on Japon paper. Vollard was a towering figure in the Parisian art scene. He had opened his first gallery in the city in 1893 and made his name as a dealer and publisher, championing the work of Paul Cézanne (1839–1906), André Derain (1880–1954) and Henri Matisse (1869–1954), among many others. Vollard had been an early supporter of Picasso, giving him his first exhibition in Paris in 1901, and would play a pivotal role in his printmaking career.[3]

Cubism

In around 1906 Picasso's style changed significantly as his work began to reflect his interest in ancient Iberian art, sparked by a display at the Musée du Louvre of recently excavated objects, and the art of Africa and Oceania.[4] Several of the artists and poets Picasso associated with in Paris had begun

3 On the 1901 exhibition, see Barnaby Wright (ed.), *Becoming Picasso: Paris 1901*, London: Courtauld Gallery, 2013. On Picasso's relationship with Vollard, see Gary Tinterow, with research by Asher Ethan Miller, 'Vollard and Picasso', in *Cézanne to Picasso: Ambroise Vollard, Patron of the Avant-Garde*, ed. Rebecca A. Rabinow, New York: The Metropolitan Museum of Art, New York, 2006, pp. 100–17.
4 On Picasso's engagement with African and Oceanic art, see Peter Stepan, *Picasso's Collection of African and Oceanic Art: Masters of Metamorphosis*, Munich and New York: Prestel, 2006; and Yves Le Fur (ed.), *Through the Eyes of Picasso: Face to Face with African and Oceanic Art*, Paris: Flammarion; Musée du Quai Branly-Jacques Chirac, 2017.

to study and collect African and Oceanic masks and statues, including the painters known as the Fauves – Matisse, Derain and Maurice de Vlaminck (1876–1958) – and Picasso's close friend the poet Guillaume Apollinaire (1880–1918). Attracted by the formal aesthetic qualities and perceived 'spiritual' properties of these objects rather than their ethnographic significance or an interest in their makers, Picasso started his own collection in 1907, beginning with a wooden tiki from the Marquesas Islands. By this point, this interest was already influencing his work, most famously and audaciously in his monumental painting *Les Demoiselles d'Avignon*, which he completed in 1907 after making many preparatory drawings (figs 2–3). The painting depicts five female sex workers, naked 'ladies of Avignon' (a title given to it later, probably in reference to a street in the red-light district in Barcelona), with semi-abstract, mask-like faces against a fragmented background. It is considered a turning point in Picasso's art, not only as an example of the influence on European painting of what would then have been termed 'primitive art', but also as a key work towards Cubism, the stylistic breakthrough that he made the following year in collaboration with the French artist Georges Braque (1882–1963).

Cubism developed from a theory that the mode of representation that had been dominant in Western art since the Renaissance, based on the use of linear perspective and foreshortening to create the illusion of three-dimensional space, did not adequately or accurately reflect the true experience of seeing. Instead Picasso and Braque sought to depict an object from multiple viewpoints simultaneously and disrupt traditional ways of representing space, the movement towards which can be seen in the splintering of the plane in *Les Demoiselles d'Avignon*. The two artists met when Apollinaire took Braque to see the painting in Picasso's studio in 1907.

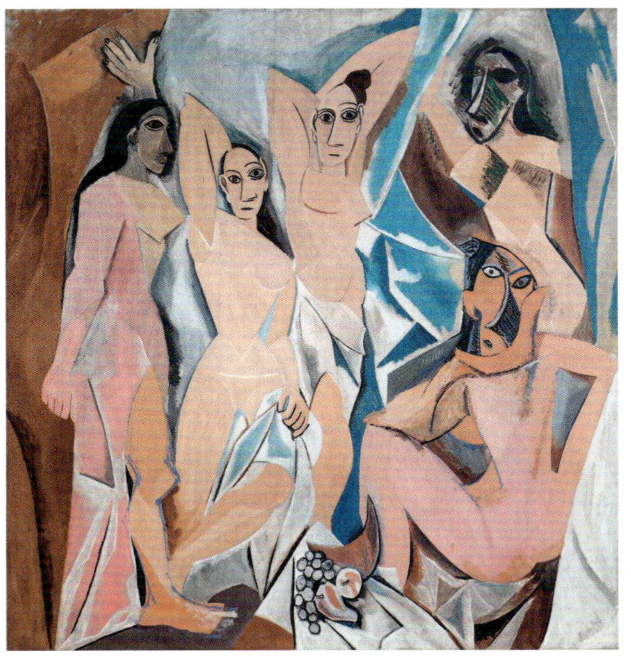

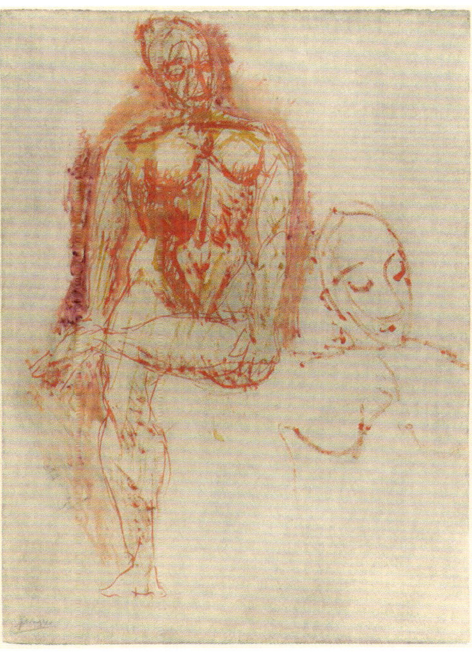

Fig. 2
Pablo Picasso, *Les Demoiselles d'Avignon*, 1907. Oil on canvas. 2439 × 2337 mm. Museum of Modern Art, New York, 333.1939

Fig. 3
Pablo Picasso, Study for *Les Demoiselles d'Avignon*, 1906–7. Red, orange and pink bodycolour and watercolour on paper. 626 × 460 mm. British Museum, 1996,0216.3. Purchased with a contribution from Art Fund (as the National Art Collections Fund).

They were soon in daily contact – 'like two mountain climbers roped together', in the words of Braque – working in parallel on Cubist compositions that could have been made by a single artist.[5] Printmaking played an important role in Cubism, as both artists explored their ideas on the plate as well as the canvas (fig. 4). They were encouraged in this by the German art dealer Daniel-Henry Kahnweiler (1884–1979), who had opened a gallery in Paris in 1907 (fig. 5). Kahnweiler, unlike Vollard, was enthusiastic about this new direction in art and therefore published all of Picasso's Cubist prints.

The drypoint *Still life. Fruit bowl* (see p. 39), which Picasso developed through three states from 1908 to 1909 and which Kahnweiler published in 1912, shows Picasso exploiting the linear qualities of printmaking to experiment with multiple viewpoints. The simple subject – a bowl of fruit on a table with jugs – is portrayed through a combination of naturalist forms and geometric shapes, while the perspective is broken down through a patchwork of parallel lines. Deep lines provide shading to indicate three-dimensionality. There is a strong sense in this print that Picasso is thinking as he draws on the plate, attempting to find an answer to a question that is not yet fully formed. He had solved this problem by the summer of 1911, when he made the drypoint *Still life. Bottle* (see p. 40), probably while staying in Céret in the French Pyrenees with Braque. By this point, he had flattened the picture plane further and abstracted the objects – a bottle of cheap marc brandy and playing cards – to a point almost beyond

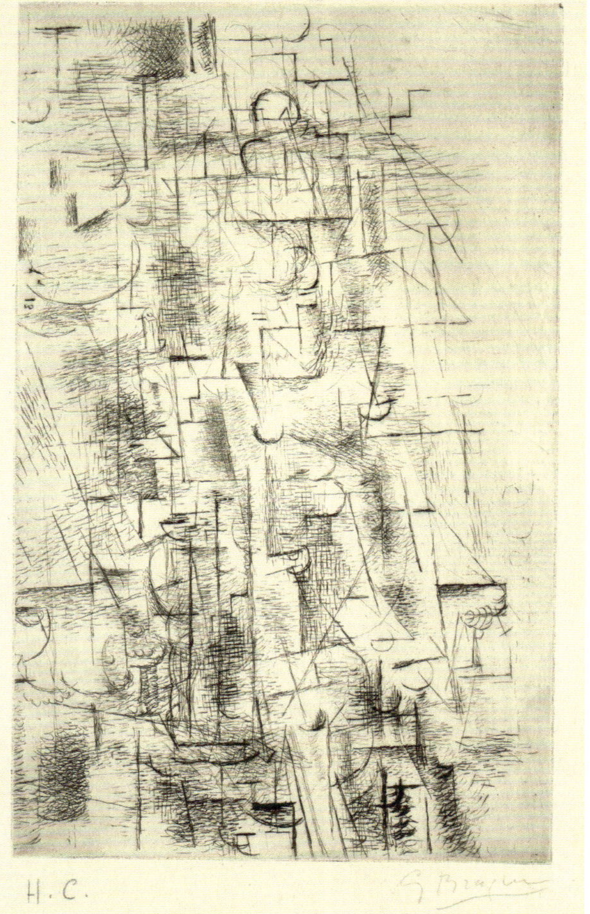

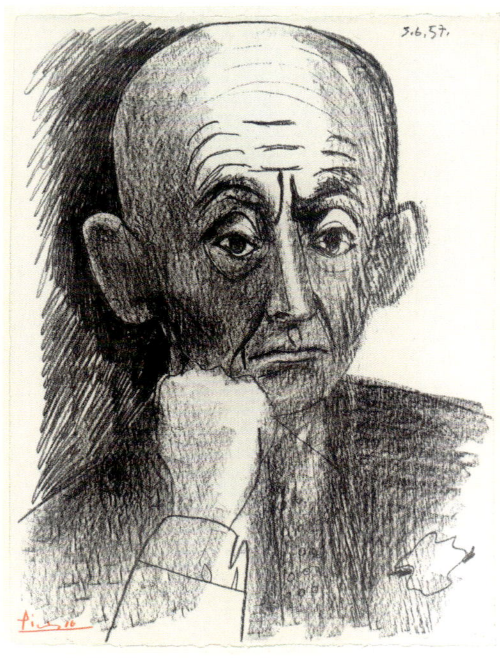

Fig. 4
Georges Braque, *Still life I*, 1911. Drypoint on paper. 346 × 218 mm. British Museum, 1975,1025.4.

Fig. 5
Pablo Picasso, *Portrait of D.H. Kahnweiler II*, 1957. Crayon transfer lithograph. 655 × 506 mm (sheet). British Museum, 2016,7048.14. Funded by Art Fund (with a contribution from Art Partners), the Wolfson Foundation, the Vollard Group, Hamish Parker, Clive Gillmore, Katrin Bellinger, Margaret Conklin, Anthony Diamond, Christian Duerckheim, David Lawson, Dr Frederick Mulder, David Sabel and Daniel Thierry.

Fig. 6
Pablo Picasso, *Portrait of Olga in an Armchair*, 1918. Oil on canvas. 1300 × 880 mm. Musée Picasso Paris, MP55.

recognition. Small patches of parallel lines give the suggestion of surrounding space, replacing the dense, oppressive background of the earlier print. Considered to be Picasso's most important Cubist print, the work was printed by Eugène Delâtre and published by Kahnweiler in an edition of 100 the following year, along with *Fox*, a companion print made by Braque on the same occasion, depicting a bottle of gin with playing cards. Their Cubist prints were not commercially successful, but they played an important role in this radical and highly influential development in modern art. His partnership with Braque came to a definitive end in 1914, when Braque joined the army to fight in the First World War. Picasso had moved on from Cubism by the 1920s.

Classicism

Picasso's engagement with the print medium dwindled during the war: materials were difficult to obtain, and Vollard temporarily closed his gallery, while Kahnweiler was forced to leave Paris.[6] The war years did, however, see significant new influences on Picasso's art that were to transform his printmaking. In 1917 Picasso travelled to Rome to work with the Russian ballet impresario Serge Diaghilev (1872–1929) on the costumes and set designs for the ballet *Parade*, the music for which was composed by Picasso's friend Erik Satie (1866–1925). The classical art that he saw there, and on visits to Naples and Pompeii, sparked a return to a more naturalistic representation of the figure, a development that can be seen in his curtain for *Parade*, which appears to reference Pompeii-style frescos. While in Rome, Picasso also met Olga Khokhlova (1891–1955), a ballerina with Diaghilev's company, the Ballets Russes, who became his first wife in July 1918. Picasso's marriage brought a shift in social status for the artist that is reflected in his beautiful yet polite portraits of Olga, which carry an air of bourgeois respectability (fig. 6). His early images of Olga also show the influence of the French artist Jean-Auguste-Dominique Ingres (1780–1867), who was himself influenced by classical art, as do Picasso's portrait drawings from this time of friends and associates, including Vollard and the poet Max Jacob (1876–1944).

Picasso's prints of the 1920s followed the changes in style and subject matter that these influences brought about. Strong-limbed sculptural figures and groups of standing women, inspired by classical subjects such as the Three Graces

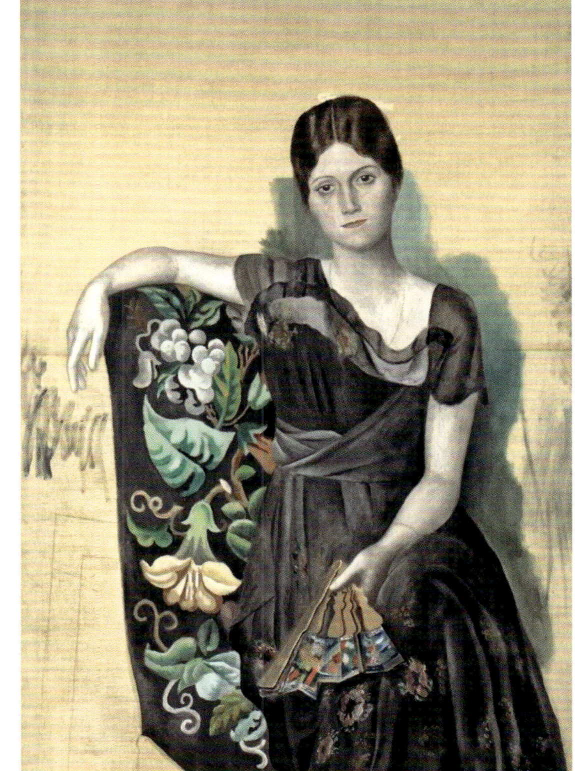

5 Dora Vallier, 'Braque, la peinture et nous', *Cahiers d'art*, vol. 29, no. 1 (October 1954), p. 14, quoted in Donna Stein and Burr Wallen, *The Cubist Print*, Santa Barbara, CA: University Art Museum, University of California, 1981, p. 23.
6 Tinterow 2006, p. 112.

and the Judgement of Paris, began to appear, for example in the etching *Group of three women* from 1923 (see p. 44). Around the same time, Picasso began to make prints and drawings of figures defined through pure line, with no shading or modelling (fig. 7), which recall the linear figures of ancient Greek vase painting and engraved Etruscan bronze mirrors, objects that had also inspired Ingres (figs 8–9). Picasso's departure from Cubism has been viewed by art historians as part of a wider 'return to order' whereby artists abandoned radical movements such as Fauvism and Futurism in a post-traumatic retreat to more conventional modes of representation following the First World War.[7] But throughout the 1920s, Picasso continued to experiment with style and approach, oscillating between 'classical' imagery, Cubist-style compositions and, from 1924, images influenced by Surrealism, a movement with which Picasso was closely associated although never fully aligned.[8] Speaking in 1923, Picasso explained:

> The several manners I have used in my art must not be considered as an evolution, or as steps towards an unknown ideal of painting … If the subjects I have wanted to express have suggested different ways of expression I have never hesitated to adopt them.[9]

In 1927 Picasso received two commissions that were to have a considerable impact on his printmaking. One came from the young Swiss publisher Albert Skira (1904–1973), who persuaded Picasso to provide the images for a luxury edition of Ovid's *Metamorphoses*. Skira had initially proposed a book on Napoleon, a subject in which Picasso had no interest, but they agreed on Ovid, possibly at the artist's own suggestion.[10] Picasso had contributed prints

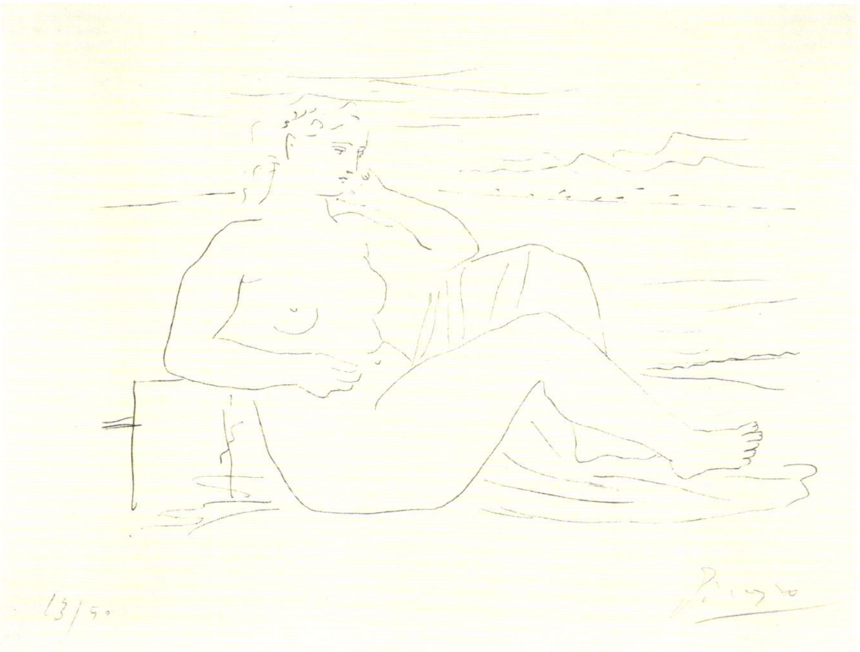

Fig. 7
Pablo Picasso, *Woman beside the sea*, 1923–4. Crayon lithograph. 200 × 310 mm. British Museum, 1949,0411.4640.

7 See Elizabeth Cowling and Jennifer Mundy (eds), *On Classic Ground: Picasso, Léger, de Chirico and the New Classicism, 1910–1930*, London: Tate Publishing, 1990.
8 On his oscillating styles, see Elizabeth Cowling, *Picasso: Style and Meaning*, London and New York: Phaidon Press, 2002.
9 'Picasso Speaks', *The Arts*, New York (May 1923), quoted in Cowling and Mundy 1990, p. 201.
10 Françoise Gilot and Carlton Lake, *Life with Picasso*, London: Virago, 1990, pp. 180–1.

to numerous illustrated books since 1905, sometimes providing a portrait for a frontispiece and at other times a series of narrative images. When required to do the latter, his approach was not to illustrate the story in a literal sense, but to produce a set of images that related more generally to themes, characters and episodes. The thirty etchings that Picasso created for Ovid's *Metamorphoses* include Hercules killing the centaur Nessus, the death of Orpheus and the rape of Philomela by her brother-in-law, Tereus. Tales and characters from Greek and Roman mythology had started to enter Picasso's work in the late 1910s, following his visit to Italy, and this project allowed him to further delve into these stories. The etchings follow the pure linear style that Picasso had used in his prints since the early 1920s, although by this point the lines had become more fluid and the compositions more dynamic.

Around the same time, Picasso received a commission by Vollard to provide etchings for an edition of *Le Chef d'œuvre inconnu* (*The Unknown Masterpiece*) by Honoré de Balzac (1799–1850) (see pp. 46 and 47). Picasso seems to have identified with the story, which is about an old painter called Frenhofer who spends ten years on a potential masterpiece but after finding the perfect model to inspire him to complete it, obliterates the image in a confused mass of lines and colour. The project cemented an important subject in Picasso's printmaking, the artist and model, which appeared

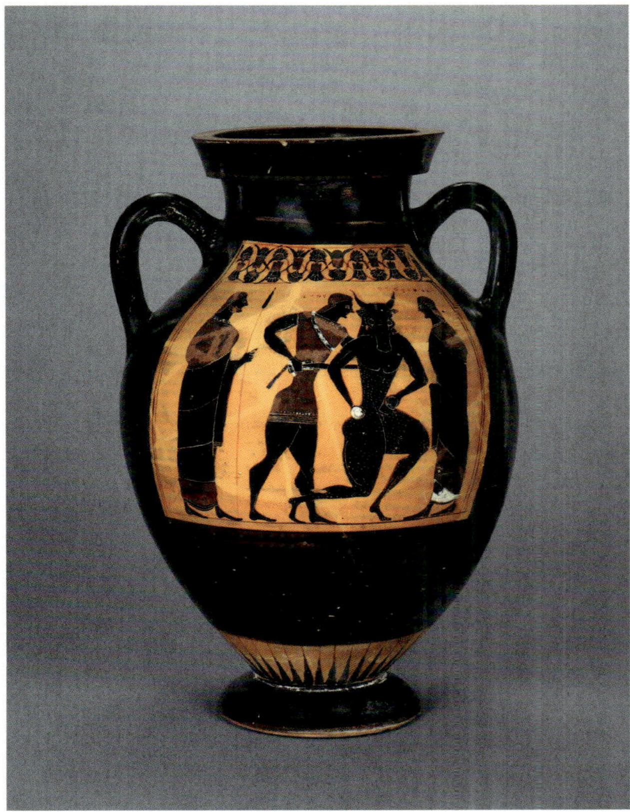

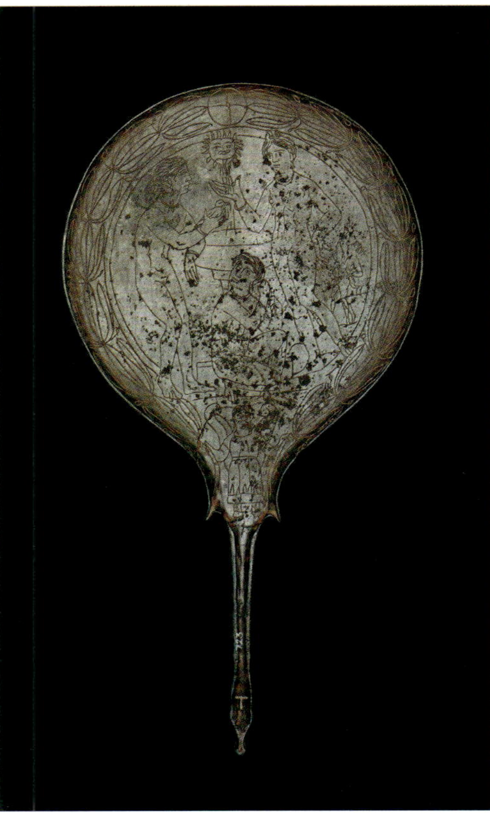

Fig. 8
Amphora depicting Theseus slaying the Minotaur, *c*. 540 BCE. Pottery. 357 × 260 mm. British Museum, 1920,0315.2.

Fig. 9
Etrusco-Latin mirror, 325–300 BCE. Bronze. Diam. 168 mm; H. 313 mm. British Museum, 1814,0704.922.

repeatedly in his work thereafter. In addition, like the *Metamorphoses*, it allowed Picasso to make an interconnected body of narrative prints through which he could explore character, drama and human relationships, and develop the classical style that had come to dominate his graphic work by the late 1920s. By 1931, when both books were published, this interest in printmaking as a narrative medium had firmly taken hold and Picasso had begun work on the 100 etchings that were to make up one of his greatest printmaking achievements: the *Vollard Suite*.

The Vollard Suite

In 1927, when he was 45, Picasso met Marie-Thérèse Walter (1909–1977), a 17-year-old with whom he would soon begin an affair. For several years he continued to live with Olga and their son Paulo, who had been born in 1921, and see Marie-Thérèse in secret, eventually moving her into an apartment close to the family home. Much of their time together was spent in the studio, where she slept or read while he worked, and when he went on family holidays to the coast, she would stay nearby. In 1930 Picasso purchased the Château de Boisgeloup, around 60 kilometres northwest of Paris, where he set up a sculpture studio and began to make plaster heads inspired by Marie-Thérèse. Her bright blonde hair and distinctive profile, shaped by her prominent nose and angular chin, appear repeatedly in Picasso's paintings from this period, while his evident lust for her brought an erotic charge to his work. In 1935 Olga found out about the affair and that Marie-Thérèse was pregnant, and left Picasso, taking Paulo with her. It was within this context that Picasso produced the *Vollard Suite*, 100 etchings made between 16 September 1930 and 4 March 1937, and all is contained within: the infatuation, the excitement, the sex, the power, the turmoil, the fallout and the art.

The etchings were not initially intended as a series and do not follow a sequential narrative structure. It is unclear exactly how they became a suite, but it is thought that Picasso promised to provide Vollard with 100 plates in exchange for two paintings, one by Renoir and one by Cézanne.[11] Forty-six of the prints are on the subject of the sculptor's studio, a development of the painter and model theme from the Balzac prints, reflecting Picasso's own experiences of working in the sculpture studio at Boisgeloup. The images include depictions of the sculptor admiring his art, the sculptor and model reclining and the sculptor and model with various visitors including other women, artists, dancers, horses, athletes and performers. Many of the scenes contain sculptural heads resembling those that Picasso made of Marie-Thérèse. Picasso created this group over a year from spring 1933, sometimes producing several etchings in a single day. The figures are classical in both style and appearance, frequently nude and wearing garlands, while the sculptures often sit on Greek-style columns.

The other major theme in the series is the Minotaur, the legendary half-bull, half-man from Greek mythology. The Minotaur, a creature of interest to the Surrealists as a symbol of a person's dark, animal instincts, first appeared

11 Stephen Coppel, *Picasso Prints: The Vollard Suite*, London: The British Museum Press, 2012, p. 17.
12 On Marie-Thérèse's sexual experiences with Picasso, see John Richardson, *A Life of Picasso: The Triumphant Years, 1917–1932*, London: Pimlico, 2007, p. 329.

in Picasso's work in 1928, but it was in 1933, when Skira asked Picasso to design the cover for his new magazine, *Minotaure*, that a deeper fascination developed. The result of a sexual encounter between Pasiphaë, the wife of King Minos of Crete, and a bull, the Minotaur was kept in a labyrinth by the king, where it was periodically fed young men and women. It was a dangerous, hungry beast, born out of sexual deviance and desire. Picasso had been interested in bulls since he was a child, when he would attend bullfights with his father. His attraction to the Minotaur was clearly an extension of this, but the creature also became for him an alter-ego, a character through which to explore his own primal urges and his sexual dominance of Marie-Thérèse.[12] Fifteen of the plates in the *Vollard Suite* depict the Minotaur, who is variously shown in bed with a young woman, participating in a Bacchic orgy, raping a centaur, wounded in a bullfighting arena, caressing a sleeping woman and finally, in a succession of four plates made between September 1934 and January 1935, blinded and being led by a little girl (see p. 66). The subject of the Minotaur was to reach its climax in Picasso's art in *Minotauromachy* (fig. 10), a large-scale etching and engraving from 1935, which, although not included in the *Vollard Suite*, extended the iconography, depicting a young girl watching a violent encounter between the Minotaur, and a horse carrying a wounded female bullfighter.

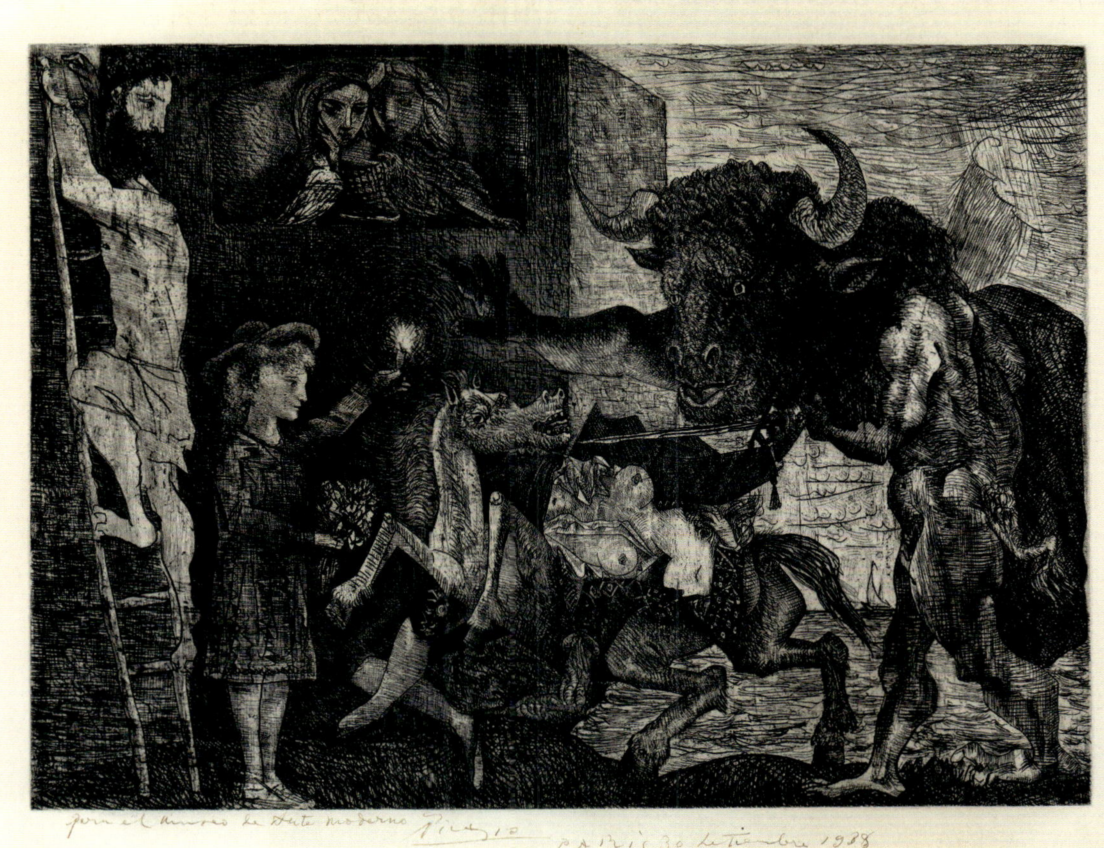

Fig. 10
Pablo Picasso,
Minotauromachy, 1935.
Etching, scraper and burin on copper; printed on Montval laid paper. 570 × 770 mm.
Museu Picasso, Barcelona,
MPB 45.006.

Picasso made the majority of the *Vollard Suite* etchings between September 1930 and December 1934. In 1935, the year in which Olga left him and Marie-Thérèse had their daughter, Maya, he made very little art, concentrating instead on writing poetry. He contributed one print to the suite in 1936, *Faun uncovering a sleeping woman* (see p. 57), a demonstration of the sugar aquatint technique that he had learned from the master printer Roger Lacourière (1892–1966), with whom he had begun to work in 1934, and which allowed him to use a brush on the plate, enabling him to produce more painterly etchings. The composition of the print, which depicts a faun leaning over and uncovering a naked sleeping woman, owes a debt to two etchings by Rembrandt on the subject of Jupiter and Antiope from 1631 and 1659 (fig. 11), representing Antiope's seduction by the god Jupiter in the form of a satyr. Indeed, Rembrandt's influence can be felt throughout the *Vollard Suite*. It has been suggested, for example, that Picasso's portrayal of the Blind Minotaur relates to Rembrandt's etching *The Blindness of Tobit* (1651) and that his sculptor's-studio prints can be compared to Rembrandt's *The Artist Drawing from the Model* (*c.* 1639) (fig. 12).[13] In addition, Picasso's occasional passages of dense cross-hatching seem motivated by his stated desire to achieve blacks like those of the Dutch master.[14] Picasso held Rembrandt in particularly high esteem and was familiar with his prints. That he was on Picasso's mind when he was composing the *Vollard Suite* is made clear by the caricature-like portraits of the Dutch artist that appear in four prints dating from January 1934. Rembrandt appeared spontaneously, Picasso told Kahnweiler, developing out of a scrawl: 'What came out was Rembrandt. I began to like it, and I kept on.'[15]

In 1937 Vollard selected 97 of Picasso's etchings for what was to become the *Vollard Suite* and Picasso fulfilled the agreed 100 with three portraits of Vollard himself, made on 4 March (see p. 67). The following year, Vollard

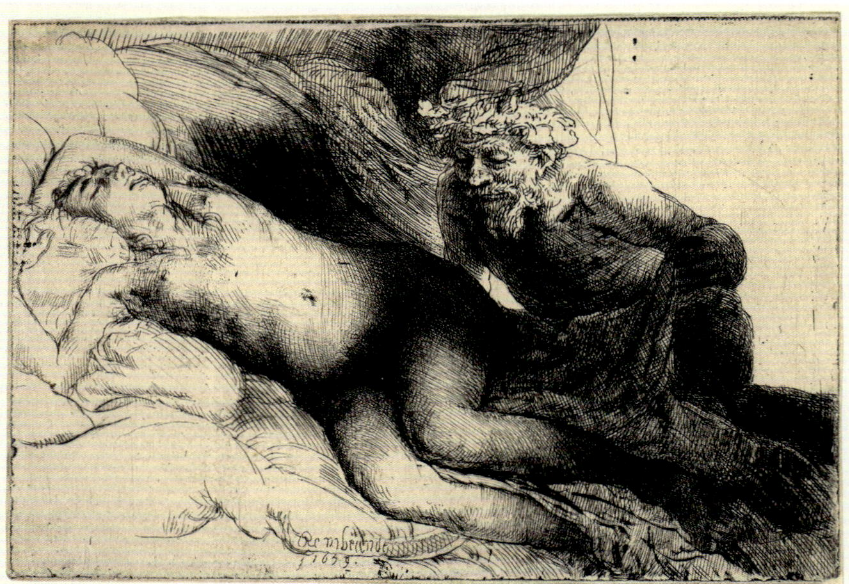

Fig. 11
Rembrandt van Rijn, *Jupiter and Antiope*, 1659. Etching, engraving and drypoint. 140 × 206 mm. British Museum, 1910,0212.368.

13 For a detailed discussion of Picasso's debt to Rembrandt, see Janie Cohen, 'Picasso's Dialogue with Rembrandt's Art', in Janie Cohen and Isadora Rose De Viejo, *Etched on the Memory: The Presence of Rembrandt in the Prints of Goya and Picasso*, London: Lund Humphries, 2000, pp. 80–122.
14 Lisa Florman, *Myth and Metamorphosis: Picasso's Classical Prints of the 1930s*, Cambridge, MA: MIT Press, 2002, p. 125.
15 Daniel-Henry Kahnweiler, translated by Hans Bolliger, quoted in ibid.
16 It has been suggested that Vollard intended to publish at least some of the Minotaur prints as illustrations to poems on the subject by André Suarès (1868–1948): Rebecca A. Rabinow, 'Vollard's *Livres d'Artiste*', in *Cézanne to Picasso*, pp. 197–212, at pp. 206–9.
17 Coppel 2012, p. 21.
18 Hans Bolliger, *Picasso: Suite Vollard*, Stuttgart: Verlag Gerd Hatje, 1956.
19 Daniel-Henry Kahnweiler with Francis Crémieux, *My Galleries and Painters*, trans. Helen Weaver, New York: Viking, 1971 (originally published 1961), p. 108.

commissioned Lacourière to print the suite in an edition of 260 on handmade
Montval paper bearing a 'Picasso' or 'Vollard' watermark, plus an edition of
50 with wider margins on the same paper bearing a 'Montgolfier' watermark
and finally, an edition of 3 on vellum. Lacourière completed the printing,
but Vollard died in a road accident on 22 July 1939 before the suite could
be published.[16] In 1948 the prints were bought along with most of Vollard's
stock by the French dealer Henri Marie Petiet (1894–1980), minus the three
portraits of Vollard, which were sold to another dealer, Marcel Lecomte
(1914–1996). Petiet began to sell the etchings, both as individual prints and
the occasional full set, although he was forced to buy the portraits of Vollard
from Lecomte to complete the group when required.[17] In 1956 the first book
on the series was published, Hans Bolliger's *Picasso's Vollard Suite*, in which
the author organised the prints into the following categories: 'Battle of Love',
'The Sculptor's Studio', 'Rembrandt', 'The Minotaur', 'The Blind Minotaur' and
'Portraits of Vollard', plus a group of miscellaneous images that sit outside
these themes.[18] Although useful in helping to understand the prints, this attempt
to organise and order in some ways misses the point: the free-flowing nature
of the subjects and imagery reflects Picasso's new approach to printmaking,
which had become an art form through which he could explore stories, thoughts
and feelings that were instinctive and of the moment.

Post-war lithographs

Picasso spent most of the Second
World War in Paris with Dora Maar
(1907–1997), the Surrealist photographer
with whom he had begun a relationship
in 1936, and Jaime Sabartés (1881–1968),
an old friend from Barcelona who had
become his personal secretary. In the
1920s Picasso had been described by
Kahnweiler as 'the most apolitical man
I have ever met', but the outbreak of
the Spanish Civil War in 1936 sparked
a political awakening.[19] In 1937 he made
Guernica for the Spanish Pavilion of
the International Exposition in Paris, a
large-scale grisaille painting depicting
the horrifying events of the aerial
bombing of Guernica, a town in the
Basque region of Spain, by German
and Italian forces. In the same year
Picasso produced the two-part etching
and aquatint *The dream and lie of
Franco* (see pp. 72–3), which comprises
an 18-scene narrative across two
sheets that both lampoons Francisco
Franco (1892–1975), the fascist leader
of the Nationalists in Spain, and

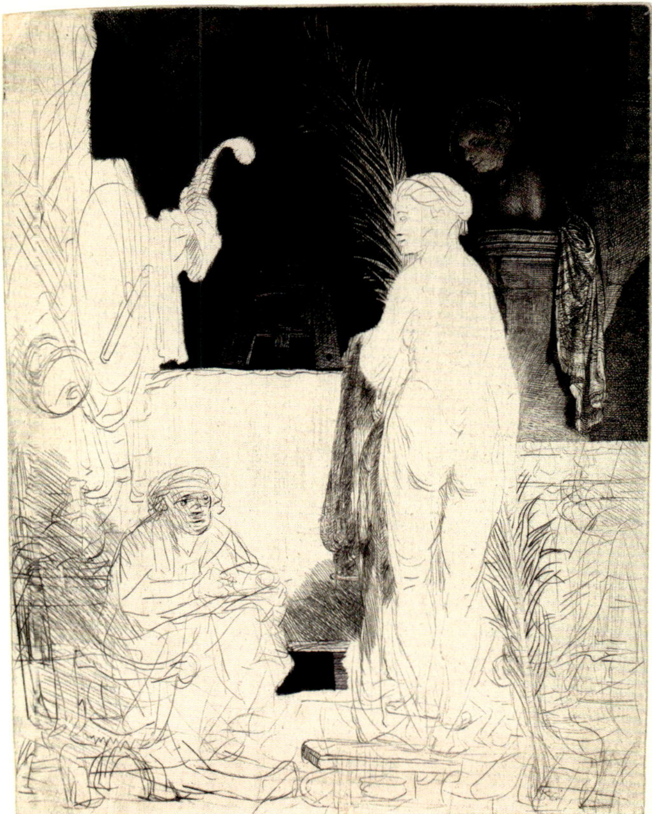

Fig. 12
Rembrandt van Rijn,
*The Artist Drawing from
the Model, c.* 1639.
Etching, engraving and
drypoint. 232 × 185 mm.
British Museum, F,5.140.
Bequeathed by Clayton
Mordaunt Cracherode.

expresses the profound pain and suffering of the people of Guernica. Intended to be cut up to form postcard-sized images, the prints were available for sale in the Spanish Pavilion with proceeds going to help the Republican cause. The bombing of Guernica also inspired a series of drawings, paintings and prints of *The weeping woman*, a figure in the throes of grief, whose image may have been based on Dora Maar. Picasso maintained his anti-fascist stance throughout the Second World War but kept a low profile and avoided making direct references to the subject in his work. He made relatively few prints during this time, concentrating instead on painting, making bronze sculptures and writing poems. When Paris was liberated in 1944, he joined the French Communist Party and was widely feted as a symbol for the resistance. In 1949 his lithograph of a dove was used to illustrate the poster of the Paris Peace Congress and was widely adopted as a symbol of peace beyond France.

As artists, intellectuals, dealers and collectors began to return to Paris at the end of the war, Picasso sought a new creative challenge, as well as refuge from the many visitors eager to see him.[20] He found both at a lithographic studio near the Gare de l'Est run by the printer Fernand Mourlot (1895–1988), which had been recommended by Braque. Picasso had made lithographs since the 1920s as a means of reproducing his drawings in print but had never fully explored the possibilities of the medium. For four months from November 1945, he worked continuously at Mourlot's studio, arriving at around 8.30 or 9 a.m. most days, and often working until after 8 p.m. At night he would sometimes continue work, making an image on transfer paper at home, which would then be transferred onto the lithographic stone in the studio the following day.[21] Mourlot's assistants were impressed by his energy and skill:

> We gave him a stone and, two minutes later, he was at work with crayon and brush … he would scrape and add ink and crayon and change everything! After this sort of treatment the design generally becomes indecipherable and is destroyed. But, with him! Each time it would turn out very well.[22]

Picasso clearly enjoyed the variety of textures and marks that can be achieved with lithography, and he worked relentlessly to first master the technique and then find new and innovative ways of working. In Mourlot's words: 'He looked, he listened, he did the opposite of what he had learnt − and it worked.'[23]

One feature of lithography that Picasso found particularly attractive was the relative ease with which changes could be made to a composition on the lithographic stone or zinc plate, so that his images could be radically altered and their evolution recorded through the printing of progressive states. It was something that could not be achieved with painting, in which changes to a composition inevitably obscured or destroyed the earlier version of the image. This process is exemplified most famously in *The Bull* (1945–6), a series of 11 lithographs in which Picasso progressively reduced the figure of a bull from a naturalistic representation to its most basic linear form (figs 13–14). This metamorphosis of a lithographic image can also be seen in a series inspired by the painting *David and Bathsheba* (1526) by Lucas

20 Pat Gilmour, 'Picasso and his Printers', *The Print Collector's Newsletter*, vol. 18, no. 3 (July–August 1987), pp. 81–90, at p. 85.
21 Hélène Parmelin, 'Picasso's Iron Wall', in Fernand Mourlot, *Picasso Lithographs*, trans. Jean Didry, Boston, MA: Boston Book and Art Publisher, 1970, n.p.
22 Jean Célestin quoted by Parmelin in ibid.
23 Mourlot quoted by Parmelin in ibid.

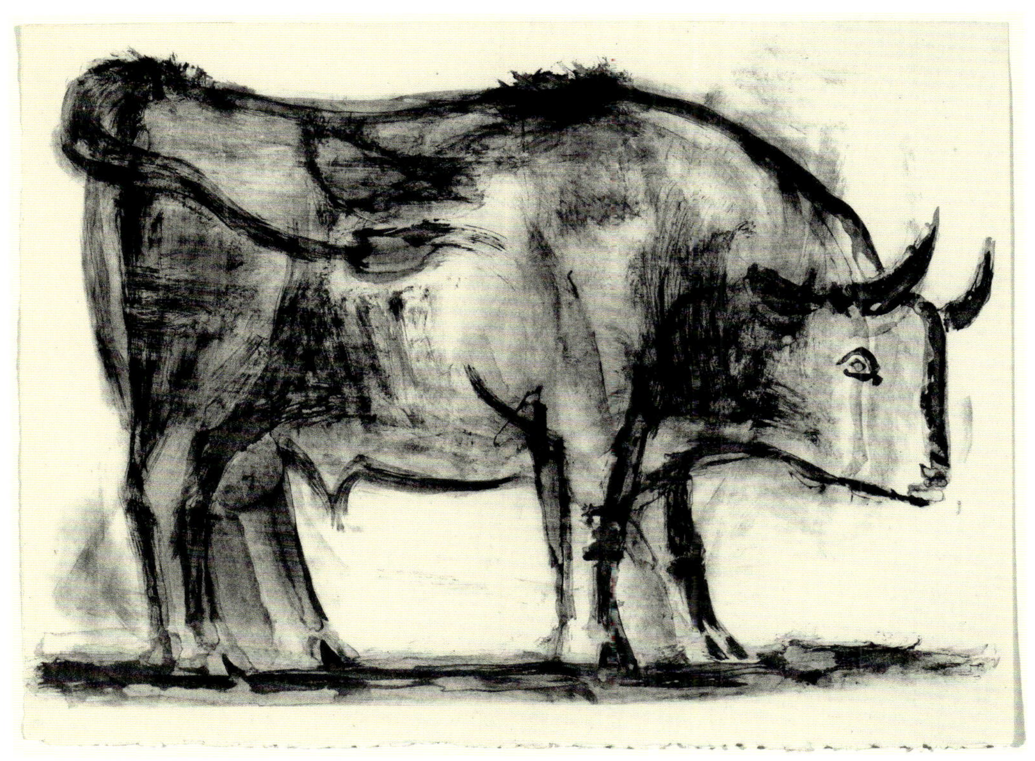

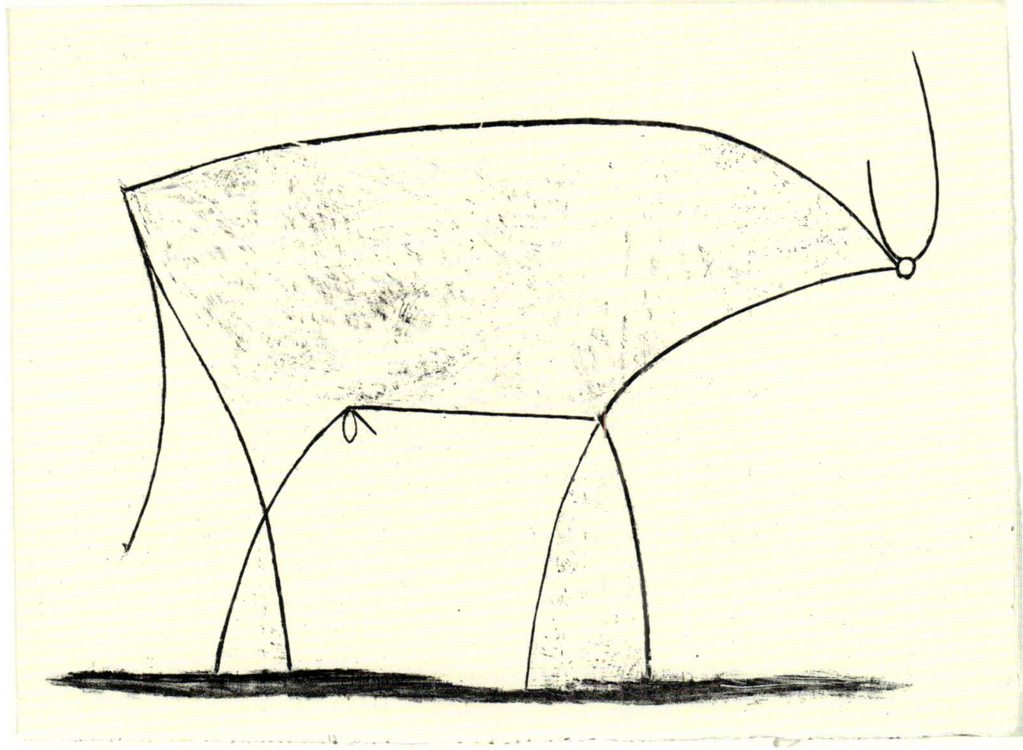

Fig. 13
Pablo Picasso, *The Bull* (1),
1945. Lithograph on Arches
paper. 324 × 442 mm (sheet).
National Gallery of Art,
Washington, 1982.12.1.

Fig. 14
Pablo Picasso, *The Bull* (11),
1945. Lithograph on Arches
paper. 325 × 444 mm (sheet).
National Gallery of Art,
Washington, 1982.12.11.

Cranach the Elder (1472–1553), which Picasso made between 1947 and 1949 in ten states (see pp. 80–81, 83). Although all were printed from the same zinc plate, the image goes through an astonishing transformation from light to dark and back again. From this period on, repetition, variation and seriality became major characteristics of Picasso's work, in both print and painting. From the mid-1950s, for example, he produced several extended painting series inspired by works of art including *The Women of Algiers* by Eugène Delacroix (1834) and *Las Meninas* by Velázquez (1656). Printmaking had induced in Picasso a desire to see where an image could take him. He had reached the stage, he once commented, 'where the movement of my thought interests me more than the thought itself'.[24] Lithography continued to provide a creative outlet for Picasso beyond 1946, and he continued to work with Mourlot for the rest of his career, producing around 400 lithographs.

Linocuts

By the mid-1940s Picasso had long felt the pull of the South of France, spending summers there for many years before he settled in Vallauris, near Antibes, with his partner Françoise Gilot (1921–2023) in 1948. Picasso had met Françoise, who was 40 years his junior, in 1943 when he was still in a relationship with Dora Maar. They had moved in together in 1946 and had their first child, Claude, in 1947. Paloma, their daughter, was to follow two years later. Being on the French Riviera brought Picasso closer to Spain, which he had refused to visit since Franco took power, and the Mediterranean culture with which he felt a deep connection. Mythological subjects began to percolate in his mind once more as he felt closer to the ancient cultures from which they came. Living in Vallauris also brought new possibilities for Picasso's art, notably the opportunity to make ceramics with the Madoura pottery, which was based in the town.

Although Picasso continued to make both etchings and lithographs in the late 1940s and 1950s, printmaking became harder to practise as he relied on printers travelling down from Paris with plates, then waiting while he created the images before returning to the capital to print them and sending proofs back for his approval. In the late 1950s, however, a new printmaking opportunity presented itself. From 1951 Picasso had been involved in creating posters to advertise the annual ceramics exhibitions in Vallauris (fig. 15), which were printed in a local studio run by Hidalgo Arnéra (1922–2007).[25] After several years of working with Arnéra on the posters, Picasso began to investigate linocut printing in a more creative way and made around 200 linocuts between 1954 and 1962, producing most of them in a concentrated burst of activity from 1959. Picasso's previous engagement with relief printing had involved a few experimental woodcuts in 1906 and 1910, a technique that he had found difficult and uninspiring. He found linoleum easier to work with and came to the technique at a time when he was working on ceramics and was therefore disposed to a more artisanal way of making prints. Picasso and Arnéra established a pattern whereby Picasso would work on the blocks late at night, his chauffeur would take them to Arnéra for printing in the morning and Arnéra would take the proofs back to Picasso at 1.30 every afternoon.[26]

24   Quoted in Marie-Laure Bernadac, 'Picasso 1953–1972: Painting as Model', in *Late Picasso: Paintings, Sculpture, Drawings, Prints, 1953–1972*, London: Tate Publishing, 1988, pp. 49–94, at p. 88.
25   Gavanon 2016, p. 222.
26   Patrick Elliott, *Picasso on Paper*, Edinburgh: National Galleries of Scotland, 2007, p. 21. On Picasso's relationship with Arnéra, see Anne-Françoise Gavanon, 'Arnéra, Picasso et la linogravure: "Sans toi je ne peux rien faire et sans moi tu ne peux rien faire"', in *Picasso: Les Années Vallauris*, Paris: Réunion des Musées Nationaux, 2018, pp. 199–211.
27   Gilmour 1987, p. 88.
28   Gavanon 2016, p. 226.

Fig. 15
Pablo Picasso, *Exhibition (19)55 Vallauris*, 1955. Linocut. 661 × 530 mm. British Museum, 2010.7007.2.

Fig. 16
Picasso washing a linocut print in the bath, Notre-Dame-de-Vie, Mougins, 1964.

As with lithography, Picasso was eager to find ways of making linocuts that suited him and his art. Arnéra described the artist's 'aggressive delight in encountering an obstacle and surmounting and conquering it'.[27] One of the methods that Picasso adopted was the reduction linocut technique, taught to him by Arnéra, which allowed them to print multicoloured linocuts from a single block rather than cutting a block for each colour, as was traditional. First Arnéra printed a background colour from an uncut block on the number of sheets needed for the edition, then Picasso would cut part of the composition, which was printed over the background in a different colour, after which the block was cleaned for the next section to be cut and printed in another colour, and so on. The black lines would be printed last. The earlier stages of the image were destroyed in the process, although progressive proofs could chart its evolution, and there was no room for error. Picasso needed to know from the beginning exactly what he was aiming for, which he seemingly achieved without ever making preparatory drawings or plans.[28] The advantage was that only one block needed to be cut and, in Picasso's view, the images had a dynamism and synergy that he felt was missing from linocuts printed from multiple blocks. In addition, Picasso experimented with the 'rinsed linocut' technique, whereby Arnéra printed an image in greasy white ink, which was then rushed to Picasso's home, where he would rinse the paper with Indian ink using a brush and shower hose over the bath (fig. 16). The bare paper would absorb the dark ink and the greasy image would repel it, producing a negative image that was somewhere between a linocut and a drawing (see p. 101).

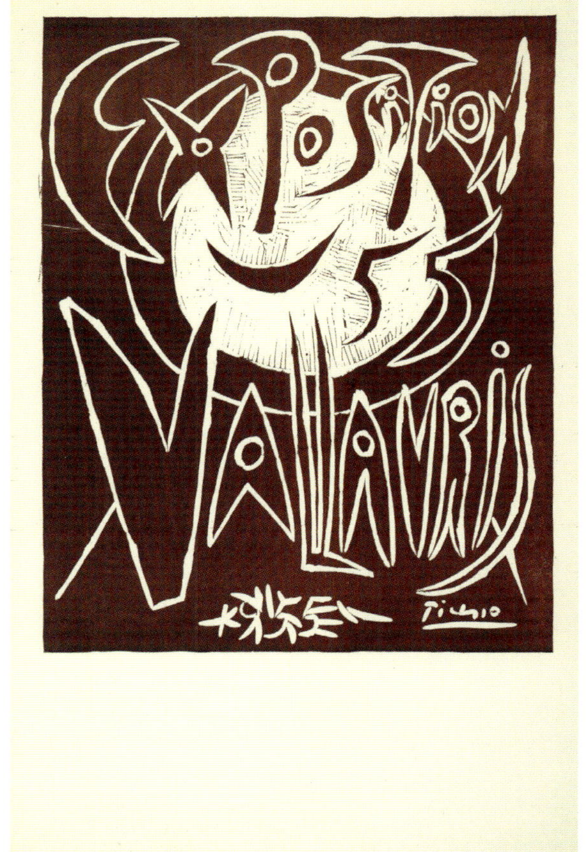

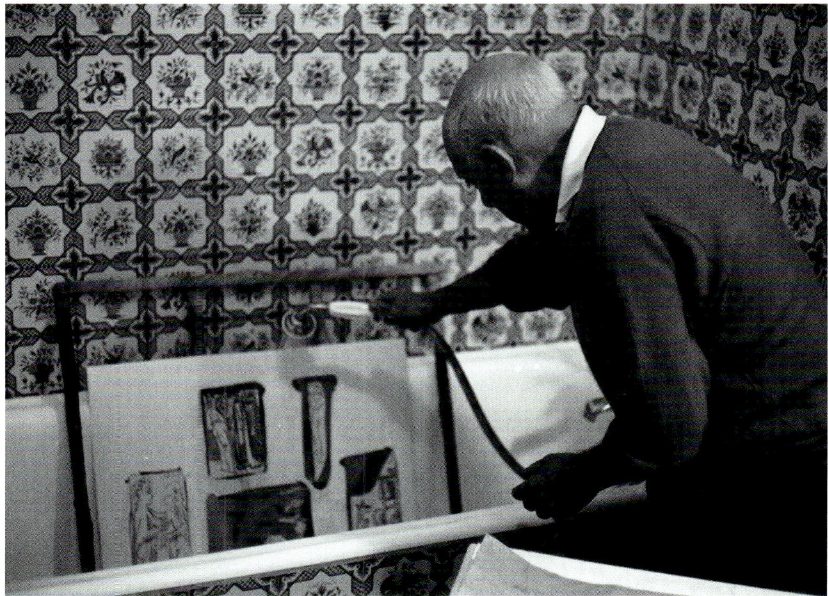

The 347 Suite

By the time Picasso began to work on the *347 Suite* in 1968, he rarely
left Notre-Dame-de-Vie, the home in Mougins, near Cannes, that he
shared with Jacqueline Roque (1927–1986), whom he had married
in 1961. Picasso's relationship with Françoise had ended in 1953 and
he and Jacqueline, whom he had met when she was working in the
shop of the Madoura pottery, had moved in together the following year,
becoming free to marry following the death of Olga in 1955. In 1965 he
had undergone surgery for an ulcer, the recovery from which prevented
him from travelling. He watched the celebrations for his 85th birthday in
1966 from afar, which included a huge retrospective spread between the
Grand Palais and Petit Palais in Paris, and various satellite exhibitions.
His isolation meant that he learned about developments in art and the
world from friends, newspapers and magazines, books and television.
At the same time he found himself out of step with current movements.
He disliked most contemporary art, including Abstract Expressionism,
Pop and New Realism, and in turn was dismissed by young artists, who
were increasingly citing Marcel Duchamp as their creative ancestor rather
than him.[29] In addition, his late work had received a negative response
from some critics, including the influential American Clement Greenberg
(1909–1994), who argued that Picasso's work had long since 'ceased
being indispensable' and that he 'no longer contributed to the ongoing
evolution of major art'.[30] In 1964 his personal reputation had taken a hit
with the publication of Françoise Gilot's book *Life with Picasso*, which
provided the public with embarrassing details about his private life and
portrayed him as an egotistical and often cruel partner. By 1968 Picasso
had grown old. He had a fear of death and had lost many of those to
whom he was closest, including Jaime Sabartés, who died in February
1968, the month before he began the *347* etchings.[31]

When Picasso first returned to printmaking following his operation
in 1965, he made several prints of enormous phalluses with heads,
arms and crowns. Sex was clearly at the forefront of his mind. He once
said he made images of bullfights on Sundays, the day he would usually
attend the bullring, as a kind of substitution for not being able
to experience the real thing.[32] His later prints are full of sex: brothel scenes,
images of intercourse and masturbation, and hundreds of naked figures.
To some viewers the sexual imagery in his work is repugnant, particularly
his objectification of women and images of violence or domination. Since
his death, further revelations have emerged about Picasso's character
and behaviour, adding to Gilot's picture of a self-centred and abusive
misogynist.[33] In addition, Picasso's Eurocentric attitude to non-Western
art, which he was able to see and collect through colonial channels, has
increasingly been criticised. In 2023, the fiftieth anniversary of his death
was marked by multiple exhibitions around the world, but it also sparked
a debate across media about how his art should be viewed.[34] It is unlikely
that Picasso foresaw the controversies that his life and art now engender,
but in 1968, as he made etching after etching, it seems he was thinking
not only about sex, but also about his achievements and his legacy.

29 John Richardson, 'L'Epoque Jacqueline', in *Late Picasso: Paintings, Sculpture, Drawings, Prints, 1953–1972*, London: Tate Publishing, 1988, pp. 17–48, at p. 25; Memory Holloway, *Making Time: Picasso's Suite 347*, New York: Peter Lang, 2006, pp. xvii, 22, 28.
30 Clement Greenberg, 'Picasso since 1945', *Artforum*, vol. 5, no. 2 (October 1966), pp. 28–31, at p. 28.
31 Holloway 2006, p. 72.
32 John Richardson, 'Picasso: The Mediterranean Years', in *Picasso: The Mediterranean Years 1945–1962*, London: Gagosian Gallery, 2010, pp. 11–45, at p. 38.
33 See for example Marina Picasso's *Picasso: My Grandfather*, with Louis Valentin, trans. Catherine Temerson, New York: Riverhead Books, 2001 and Sophie Chauveau, *Picasso, le Minotaure*, Paris: Gallimard, 2020.
34 The recent conversation about his legacy has taken place across media; examples include Claire Dederer's *Monsters: A Fan's Dilemma*, London: Sceptre, 2023; season 3 of the podcast *Legacy*, Wondery, 2024; the BBC's three-part documentary *Picasso: the Beauty and the Beast*, 2023; and the exhibition *It's Pablo-matic: Picasso according to Hannah Gadsby* at the Brooklyn Museum, New York, 2 June–24 September 2023.

The first print in the *347 Suite*, the largest in the series, was worked on by Picasso over a week from 16 to 22 March. It includes a self-portrait, an image of the artist in profile as an old man with wispy hair and wrinkles. A taller figure resembling Picasso's friend, the poet Jean Cocteau (1889–1963), stands behind. Both men, on the left of the image, look towards a strongman on the right, while a nude woman reclines in the space between. At the centre, in the middle ground, a female circus performer rides a horse in an arena. Her costume fails to contain her breasts, and the horse is visibly excited. A sea of spectators watches from the dark behind, multiple sets of eyes directed at the performer, at Picasso and at us. Picasso's theatrical opening to the *347 Suite* encompasses a number of the subjects that recur throughout that series and that were established themes in his art, including self-portraiture, ageing, portraits of friends, the female body, sex and titillation, watching and being watched.

As with the *Vollard Suite*, the *347* etchings do not follow a particular narrative or plan. When discussing his printmaking at this time, Picasso said,

> one never knows what's going to come out, but as soon as the drawing gets underway, a story or an idea is born … I enjoy myself no end inventing these stories, and I spend hour after hour while I draw, observing my creatures and thinking about the mad things they're up to. Basically, it's my way of writing fiction.[35]

The suite covers a wide range of subjects, forming a kind of compendium or review of Picasso's interests both in 1968 and over the course of his career. Saltimbanques make an appearance, as do sex workers, horses, musketeers and Frenhofer's unknown masterpiece from the Balzac tale. Some scenes depict an artist in the studio, while others present well-known characters, including El Greco, Rembrandt and Manet, great artists with whom Picasso wished to be remembered, and friends and lovers including Jacqueline. Sixty-six plates feature Celestina, a character from the dramatic work *Comedia de Calisto y Melibea* attributed to Fernando de Rojas (*c.* 1465–1541), which was first published in 1499 and was well known in Spain. Celestina is an old procuress with magical powers who arranges an affair between the title characters, with tragic consequences. In Picasso's prints, Celestina often lurks in the corner or watches from shadows, always scheming, always seeing. The character, who was also depicted by Goya, had been portrayed by Picasso as early as 1904 in a Blue Period painting, now in the Musée Picasso, Paris, in which her second sight is hinted at through her blinded left eye.[36] Other prints in the *347 Suite* reflect films and television programmes that Picasso had been watching, including a series of Roman chariot scenes and references to the televised Catch wrestling, with which he had become obsessed.[37] The turbulent events in Paris of 1968 are hinted at in one plate through a caricature of the French statesman Charles de Gaulle (1890–1970, see p.115). Sex also features prominently in the suite, not least in a series of prints made in response to Ingres's paintings on the subject of Raphael (1483–1520) and La Fornarina, the first of which was made in 1814, which depict the famous Italian painter with his lover, 'the

35 Robert Otero, *Forever Picasso: An Intimate Look at his Last Years*, trans. Elaine Kerrigan, New York: Harry N. Abrams, 1974, p. 170.
36 On depictions of Celestina by Goya, Picasso and others see Enrique Fernández, *The Image of Celestina: Illustrations, Paintings, and Advertisements*, Toronto, ON, Buffalo, NJ, and London: University of Toronto Press, 2024.
37 Richardson 1988, p. 29; Holloway 2006, pp. 123–5.

baker's daughter', with whom he made love so excessively that, according to his biographer Giorgio Vasari (1511–1574), it contributed to his early death. Picasso's *Fornarina* prints – in which various figures, including Michelangelo and the Pope, watch as Raphael and La Fornarina have sex – are among his most explicit images and were censored in early exhibitions of the suite.[38]

Picasso's extraordinary explosion of printmaking over seven months in 1968 was made possible by his printers, brothers Aldo (1931–2008) and Piero Crommelynck (1934–2001), who had set up a printing studio near Picasso's home in Mougins in 1963. The Crommelyncks had trained with Lacourière and established their own Paris studio in 1955. Both brothers developed a close relationship with Picasso, who came to view them in his final years as members of his family. When in Mougins, the Crommelyncks would call on Picasso in the late afternoon to see if they were needed and, if so, would work with him until late into the night.[39] As ever, Picasso learned from his printers but continued to make his own technical discoveries in the course of working on the prints. He experimented, for example, with applying grease with his fingers to the etching plate before drawing the image, which created interesting smudges and unusual textures. He also used cotton swabs dipped in petrol to rub away the etching ground leaving soft, fuzzy areas that would be exposed to acid and therefore hold ink, a method he put to use, for example, to depict the fur coats of several of the characters that appear in the suite.[40] Picasso's advanced age had diminished neither the enjoyment he got from printmaking nor his eagerness to try new ideas and, as Aldo Crommelynck observed, his lines remained as controlled and as fluid as ever.[41]

Picasso continued to make prints into his final years (fig. 17), producing his last series, the *156 Suite*, with the Crommelyncks between 1970 and 1972. When the British artist and writer Roland Penrose (1900–1984) visited Picasso during those years, he observed 'Engravings absorb him entirely … [Picasso] seems to [feel] greater freedom and scope for experimentation in graphics – more so than with drawing.'[42] Printmaking absorbed Picasso for many hours until 1972, when he made his final print, completing a body of work that has transformed the medium and inspired many other artists to make prints. He died on 8 April 1973 in his 92nd year.

38 Holloway 2006, pp. 158–63.
39 Richardson 1988, pp. 26–8.
40 Holloway 2006, pp. 113–15.
41 Holloway 2006, p. 10.
42 Elizabeth Cowling, *Visiting Picasso: The Notebooks and Letters of Roland Penrose*, London: Thames & Hudson, 2006, pp. 332–3.

Fig. 17
Picasso working on an etching plate at home in 1970.

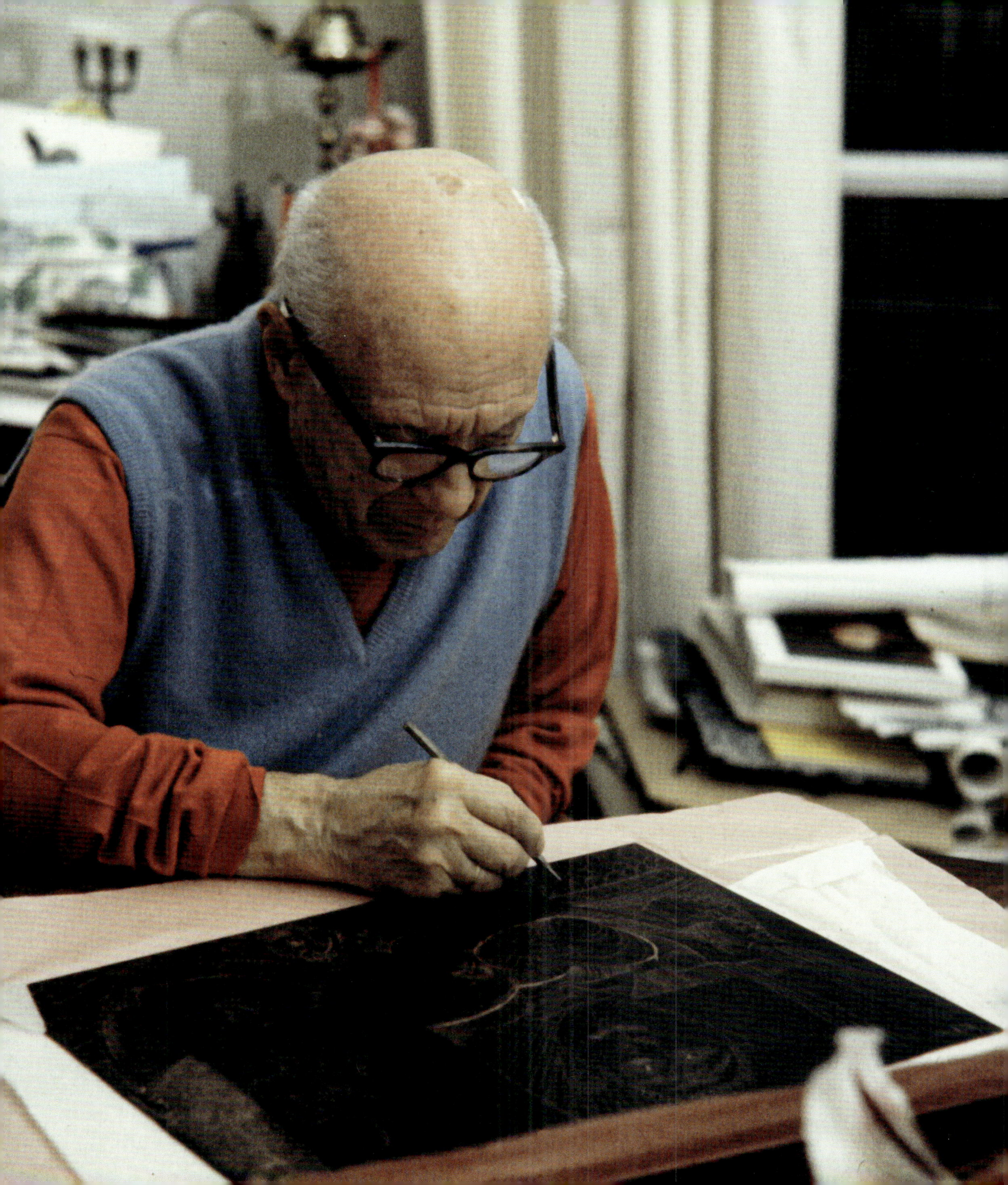

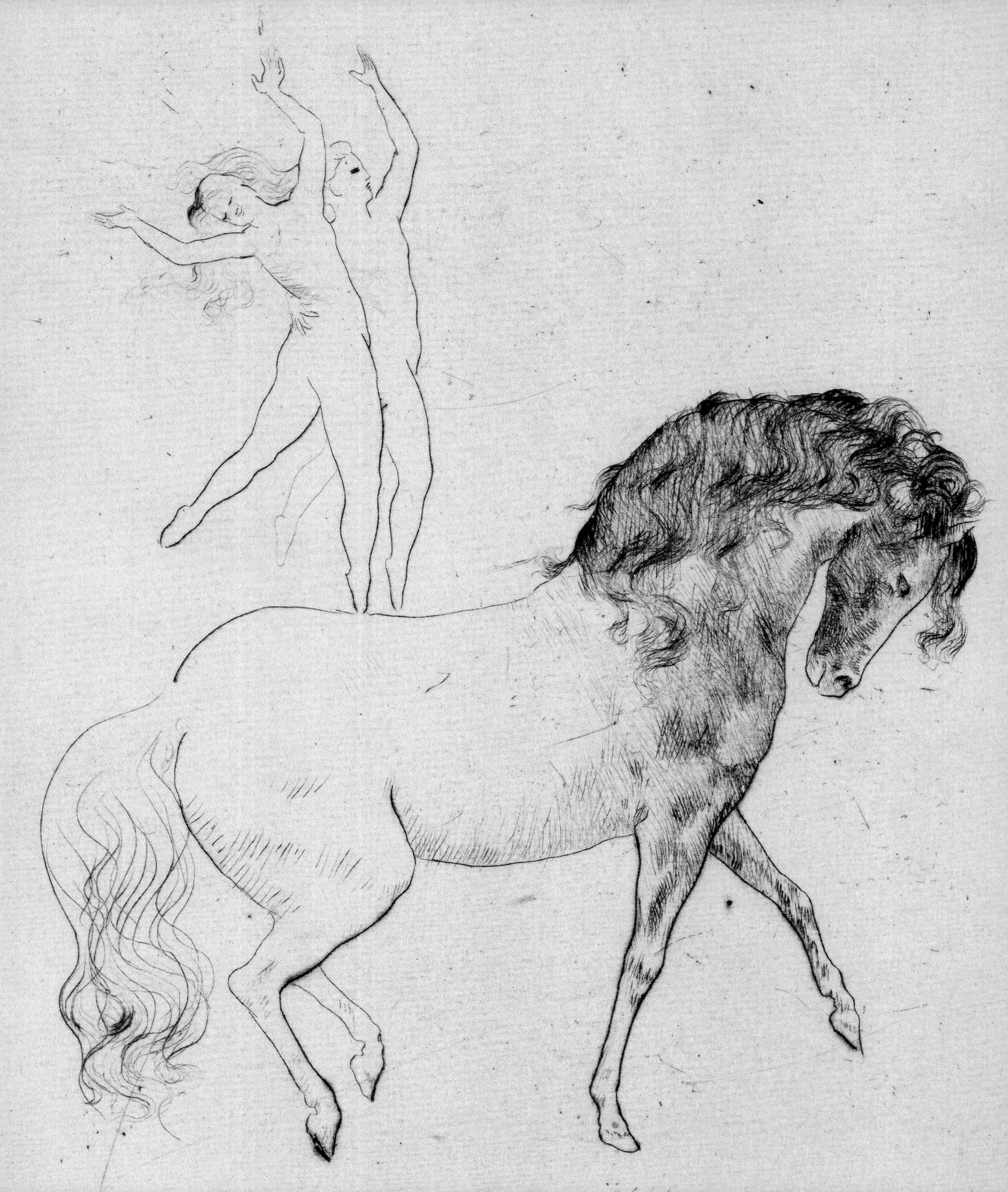

PARIS

We will all return to the Bateau-Lavoir.
We were only truly happy there.

Picasso moved to France permanently in 1904 after several years of living between Paris and Barcelona. The prints in this section were produced during two distinct periods of his life in the French capital. The first, a group of etchings and drypoints from 1904 to 1906, are some of Picasso's earliest prints and were made when he was living and working in a dilapidated building known as the Bateau-Lavoir in Montmartre. Relating closely to his paintings of the time and reflecting the lives that Picasso witnessed around his studio, they depict scenes of poverty, emaciated figures, alcoholics and itinerant circus performers known as 'saltimbanques'. A struggling artist himself, Picasso made his first etching of the group, *The frugal meal* (p. 33), on a zinc plate previously used by Joan González (1868–1908), and his second, *Head of a woman* (probably his lover, Madeleine, whose last name is not known, p. 35), on a tiny plate made from copper, a more expensive material. These early plates were published in 1913 by Ambroise Vollard under the collective title *La suite des saltimbanques*. Most impressions of Picasso's early prints are from Vollard's 1913

editions, including all of the British Museum's group, except for *Bust of a man* (p. 35), which is a rare survival from the 1905 printing.

The second group of works in this section represents Picasso's development of Cubism between 1908 and 1915, alongside the French artist Georges Braque. Picasso's Cubist prints are preceded in the British Museum's collection by a study drawing for his painting *Les Demoiselles d'Avignon* (now in the Museum of Modern Art, New York), which he completed in 1907 (see figs 2–3, p. 13). The painting, and subsequent prints, mark a radical moment in Picasso's art as he sought to depict a subject from multiple perspectives in a way that he felt depicted the true experience of seeing.

The frugal meal, 1904, published 1913
Etching and scraper

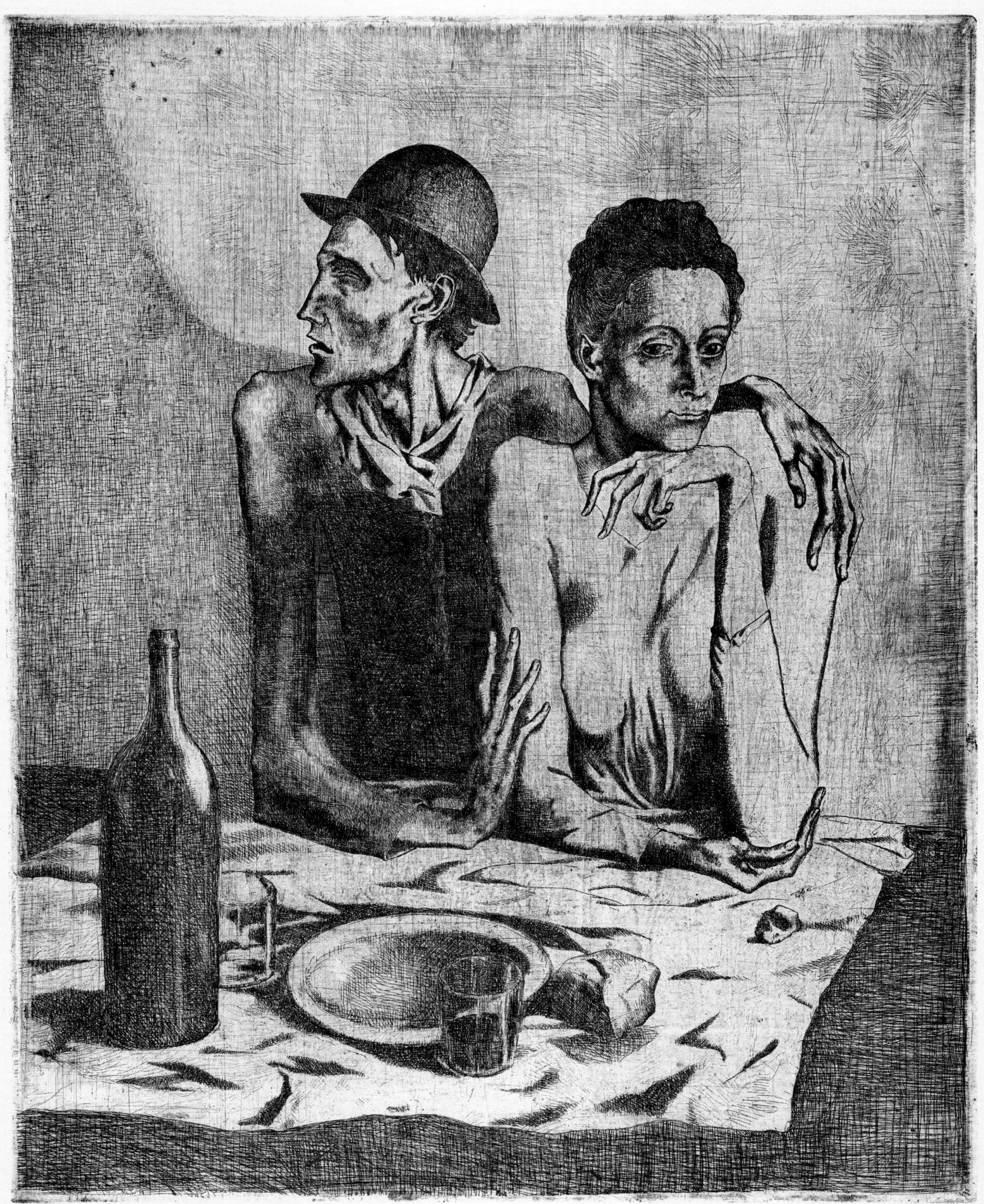

The poor, 1905, published 1913
Etching

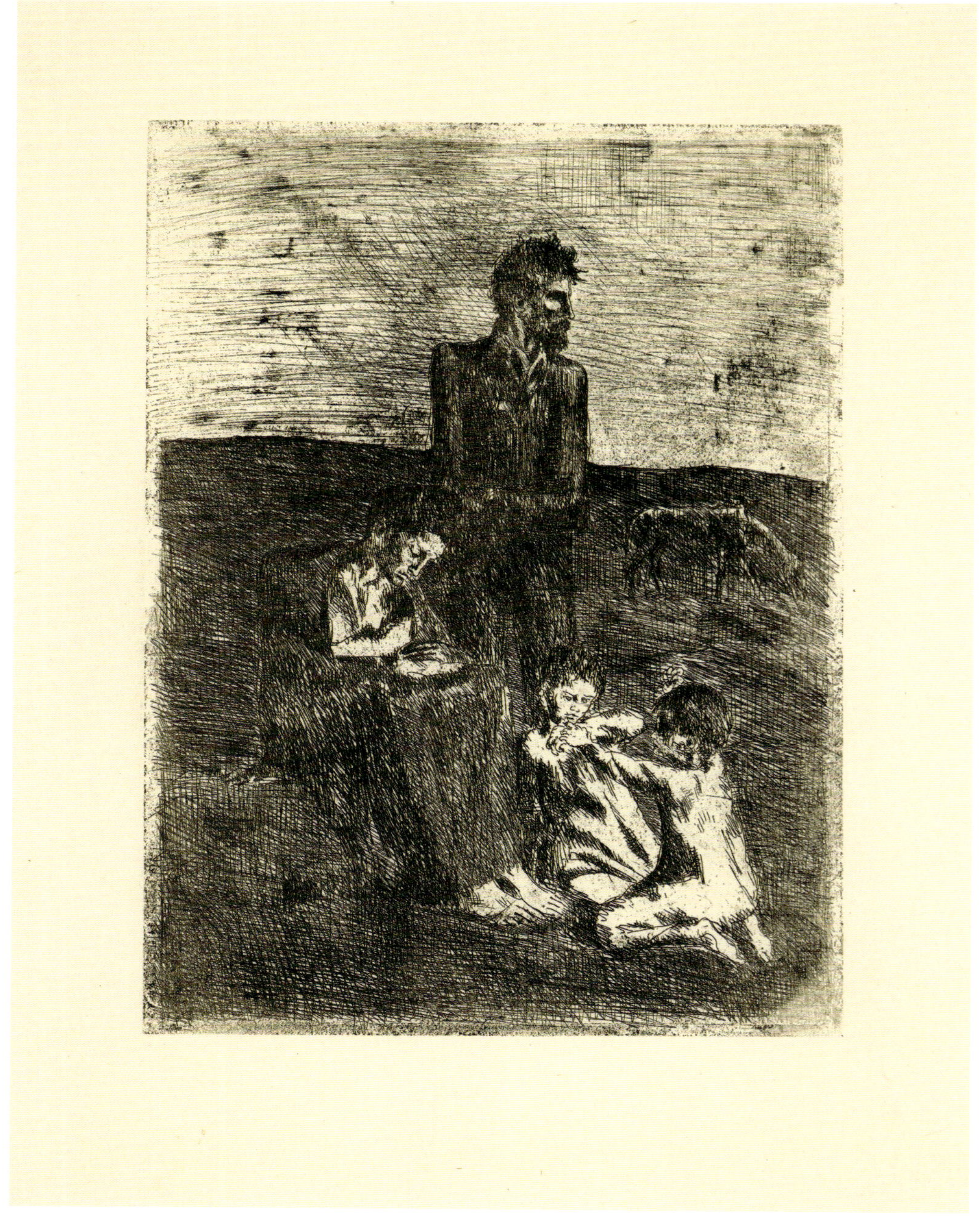

Bust of a man, 1905
Drypoint

Head of a woman, 1905, published 1913
Etching

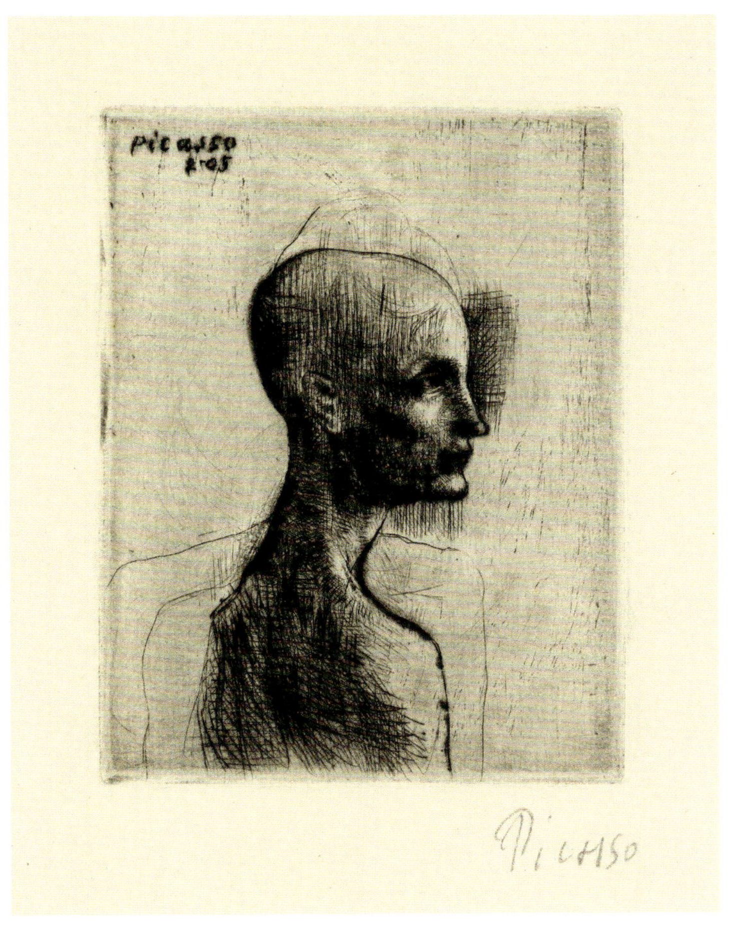

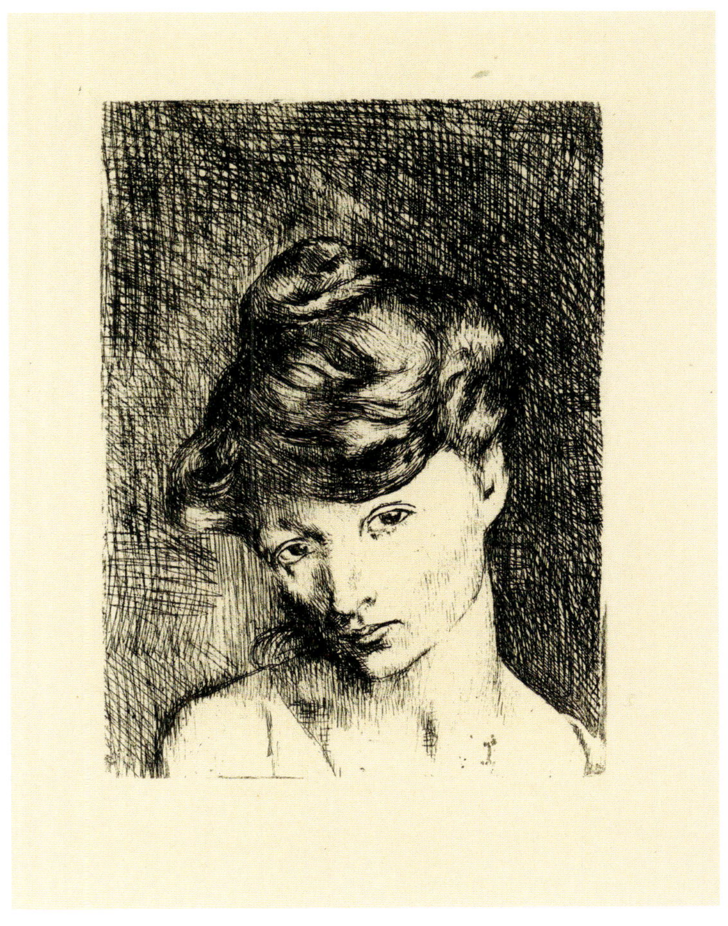

35

At the circus, 1905–6, published 1913
Drypoint

Salomé, 1905, published 1913
Drypoint

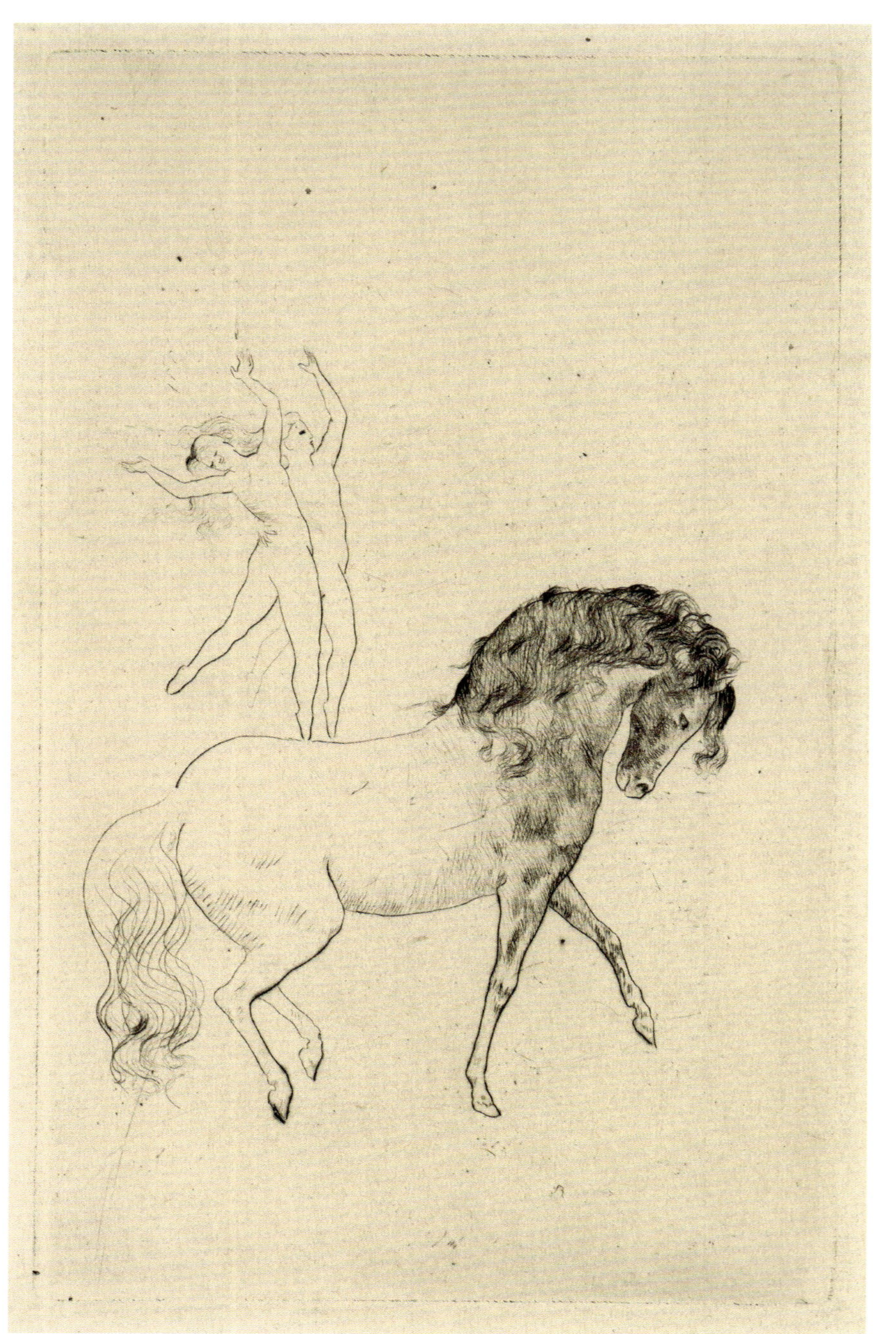

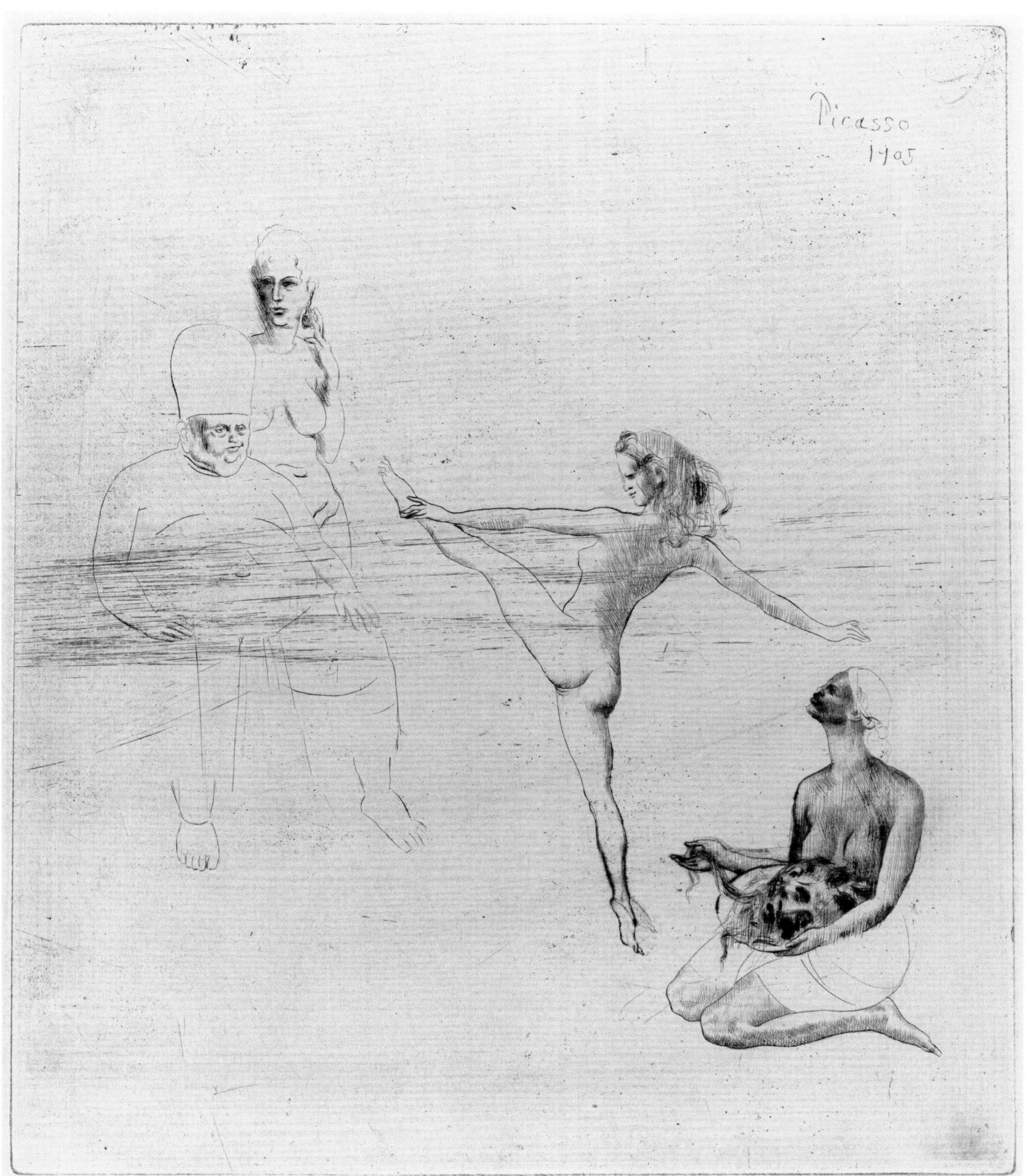
Picasso
1905

Still life. Fruit bowl, 1908–9, published 1912
Drypoint and scraper

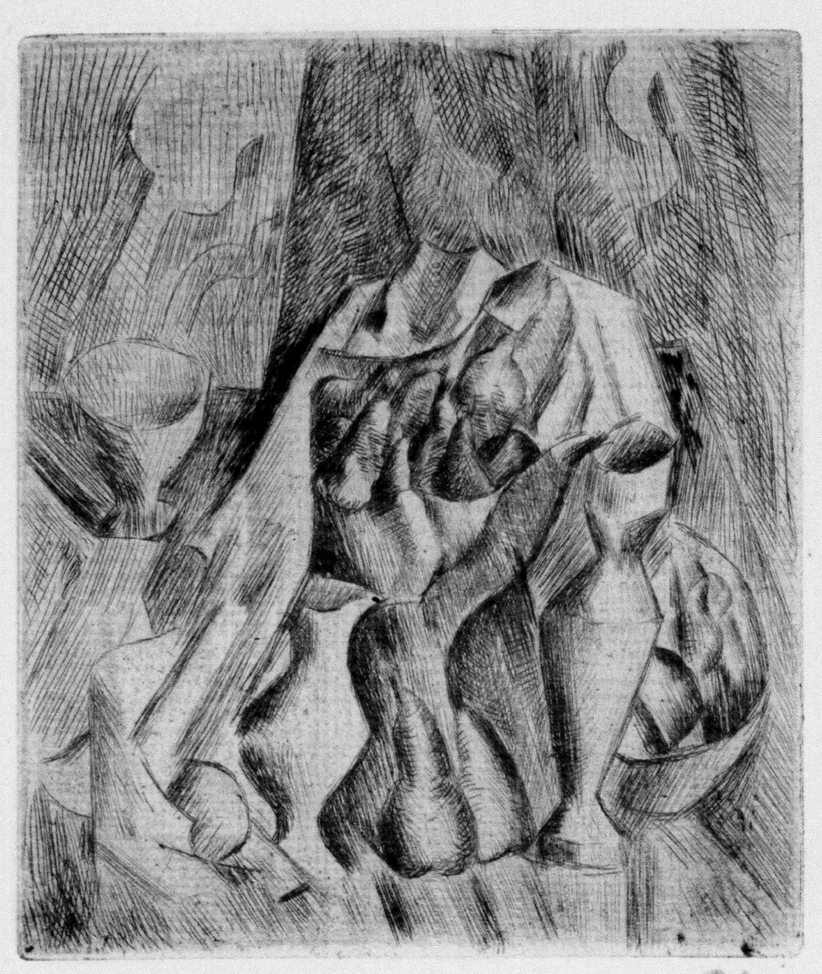

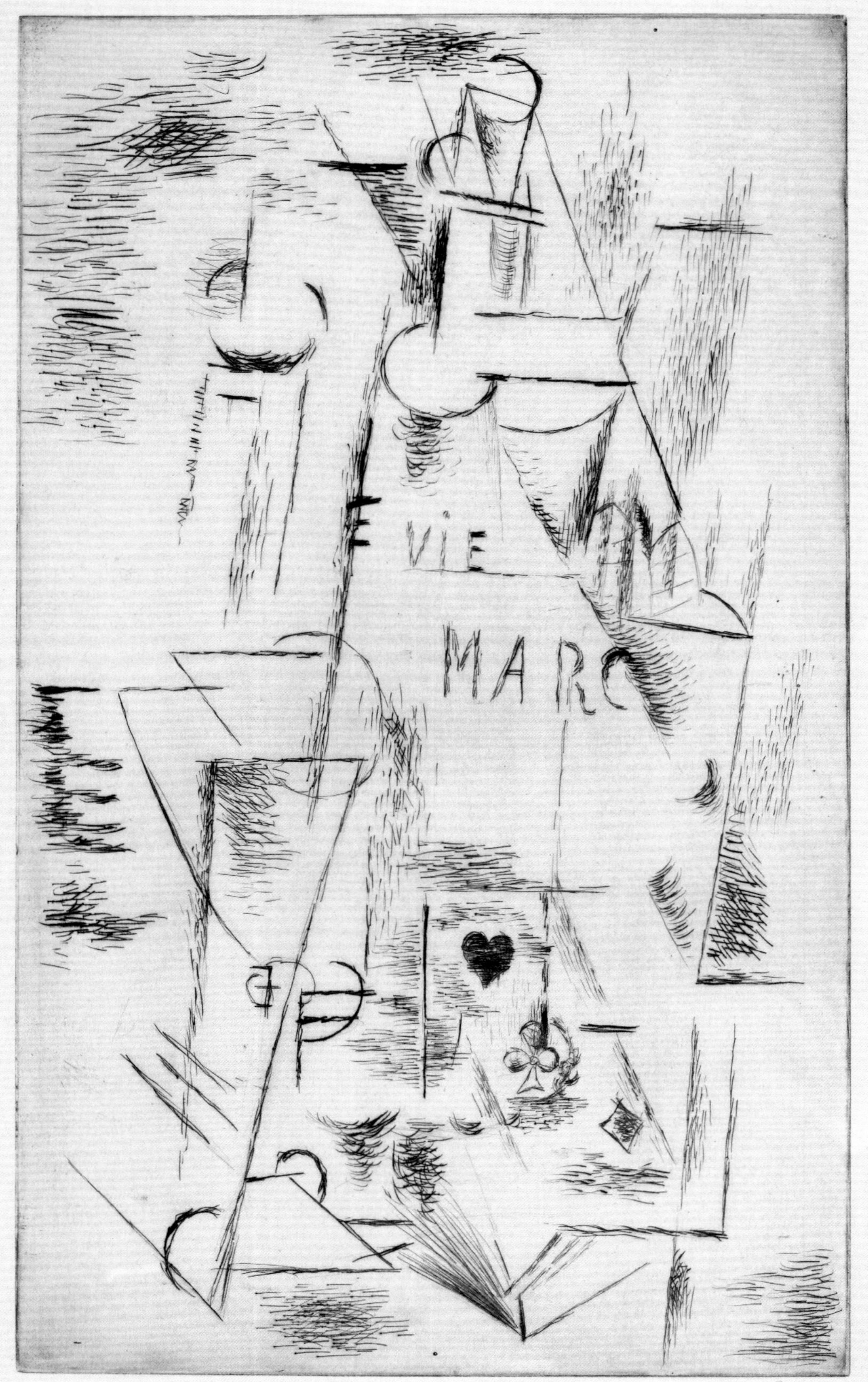
VIE
MARC

Still life. Bottle, 1911, published 1912
Drypoint

Man with dog, 1915 and 1930, published 1947
Etching and scraper

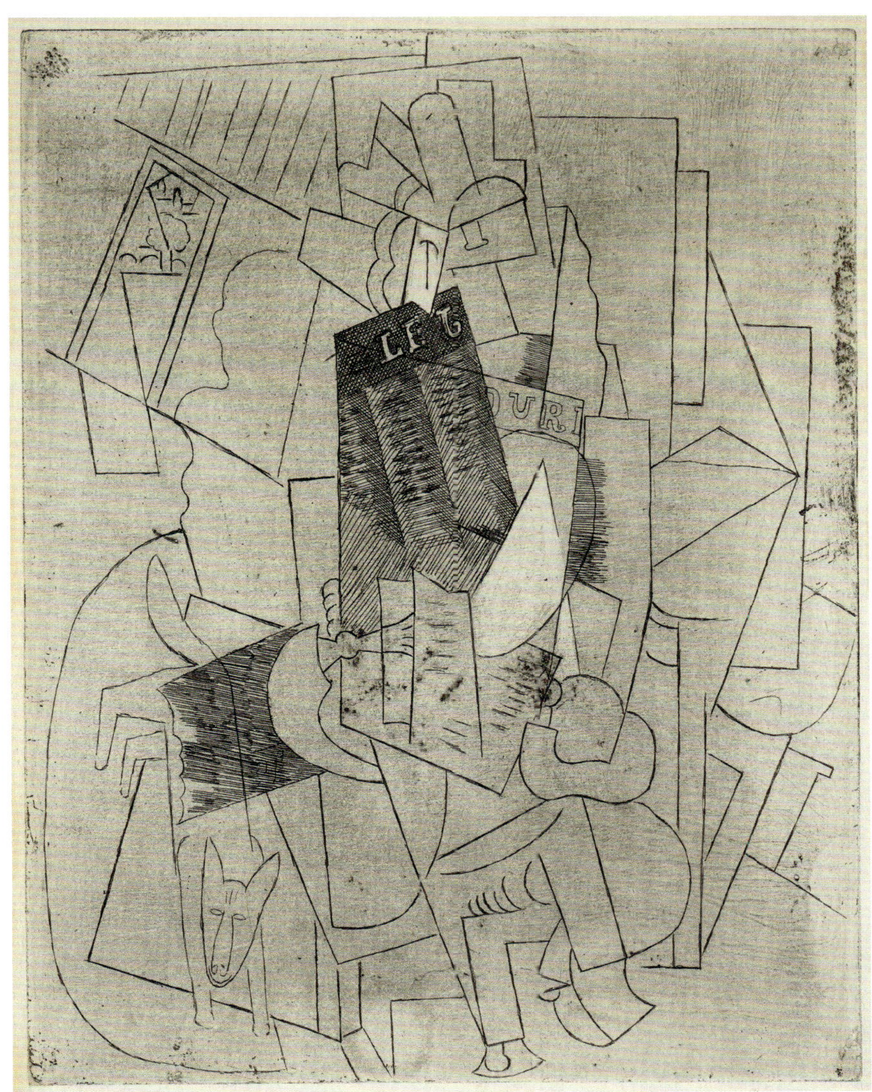

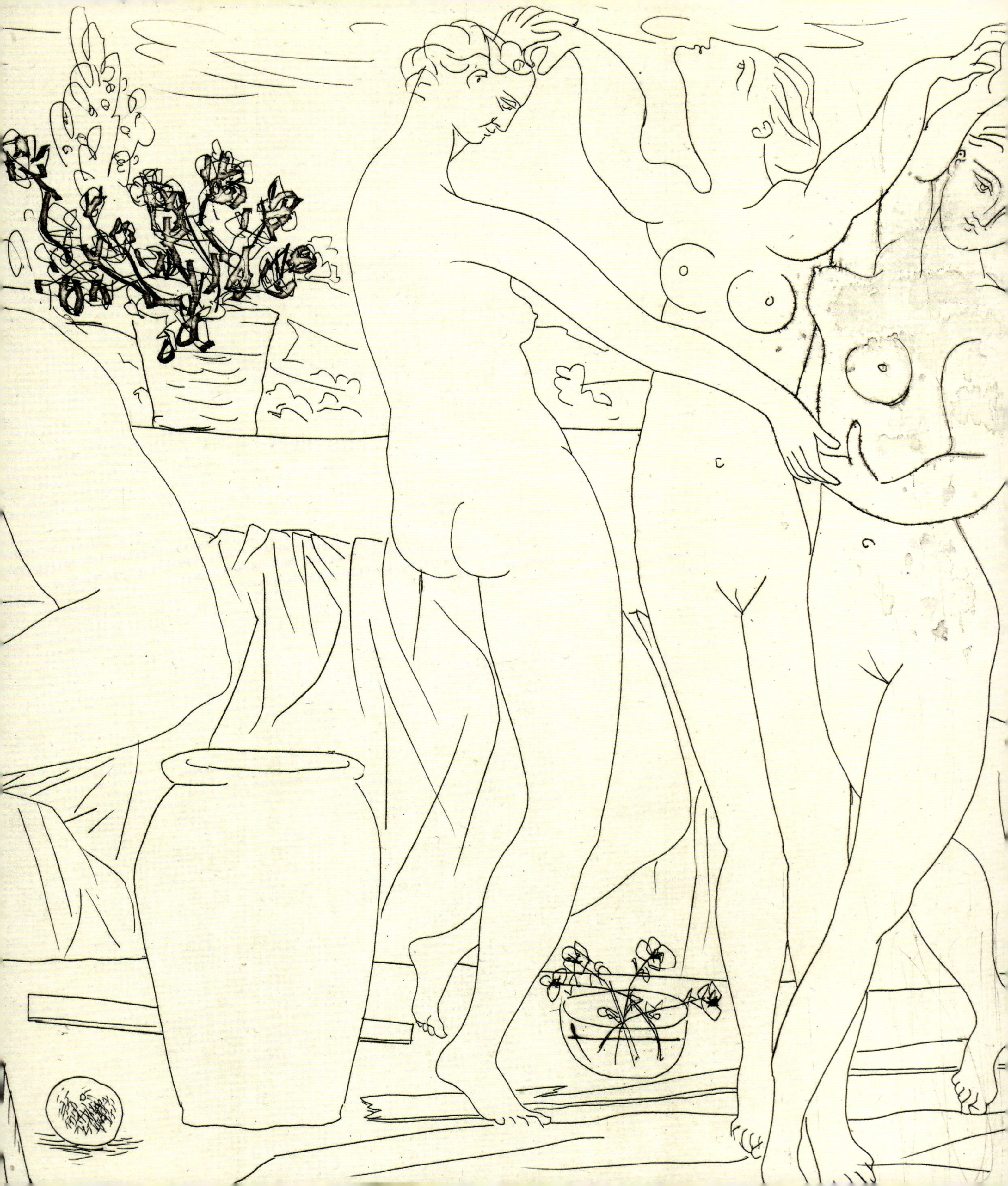

BETWEEN THE WARS

If all the ways I have been along were marked on a map and joined up with a line, it might represent a Minotaur.

After making very few prints during the First World War, Picasso re-engaged with the medium in the early 1920s, by which time he had moved away from Cubism, developing a more naturalistic style inspired by the classical art that he had seen on a visit to Italy in 1917. The prints in this section reflect this new direction in his work. *Group of three women* (1923) is reminiscent of themes in ancient sculpture such as the Three Graces, in which women stand in groups. Pure line figures recall the decoration on ancient Greek pots and Etruscan mirrors, and the neoclassical drawings of the French artist Jean-Auguste-Dominique Ingres. Meanwhile, Surrealism began to influence Picasso's work in around 1924, bringing an increased eroticism and psychological undercurrent to his art, and an alternative approach to representation, as evident here in the semi-abstract lithograph *Figure. Bather in the cabin* from 1929 (p. 45).

Picasso's great printmaking achievement of the 1930s was the *Vollard Suite*, 100 etchings made between 1930 and 1937 for the dealer-publisher Ambroise Vollard. Major themes include the sculptor in his studio and the Minotaur, the mythical half-man, half-bull, who is variously portrayed as tender, lustful, violent and vulnerable. The suite reflects Picasso's life at the time, including his focus on sculpture, an affair with the much younger Marie-Thérèse Walter and the breakdown of his marriage to Olga Khokhlova. From 1934 Picasso worked with the leading printer Roger Lacourière, who expanded his printmaking capabilities, teaching him the sugar aquatint technique, which Picasso used in 1936 for *Faun uncovering a woman* (p. 57) and his illustrations to *Buffon's Natural History*. That same year civil war broke out in Spain. Picasso responded in print with *The dream and lie of Franco* (1937, pp. 72–3), which satirised the Nationalist leader and expressed Picasso's horror at the bombing of the Basque town of Guernica, an event he also depicted in a mural-size painting.

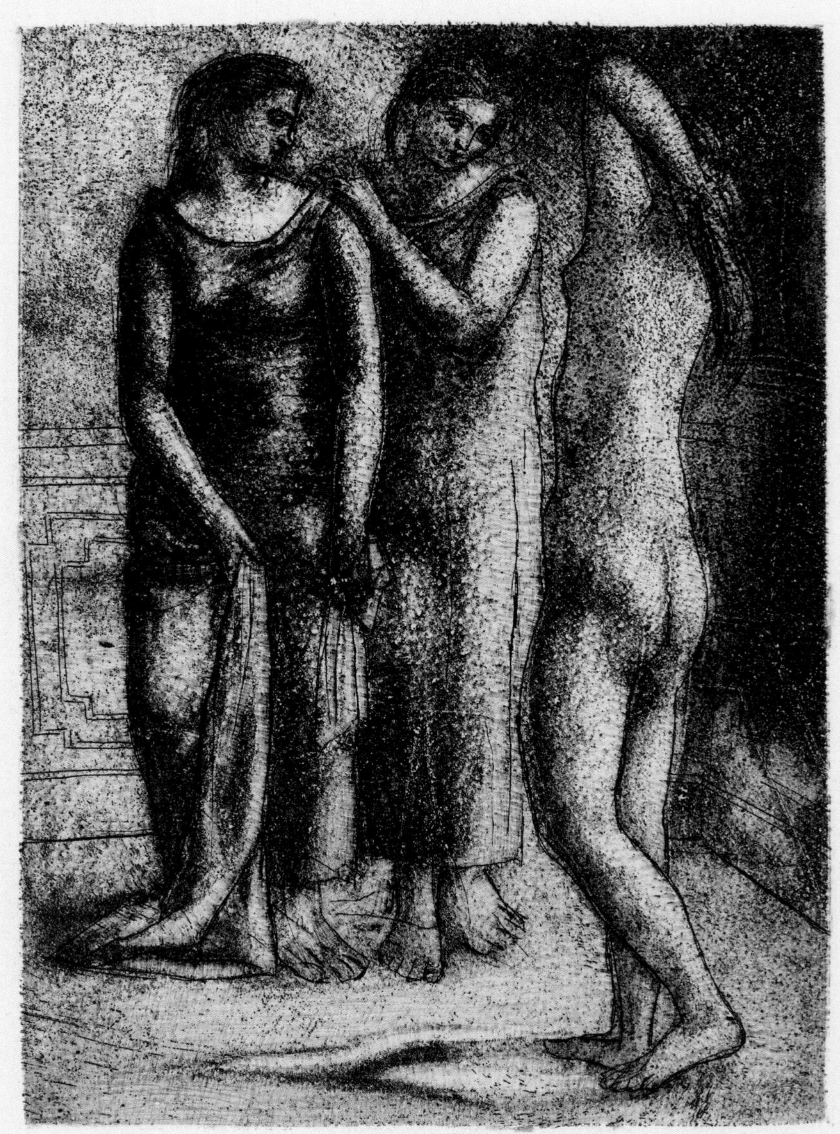

Group of three women, 1923, published 1929
Drypoint, scraper and etching

Figure. Bather in the cabin, 1929
Lithograph

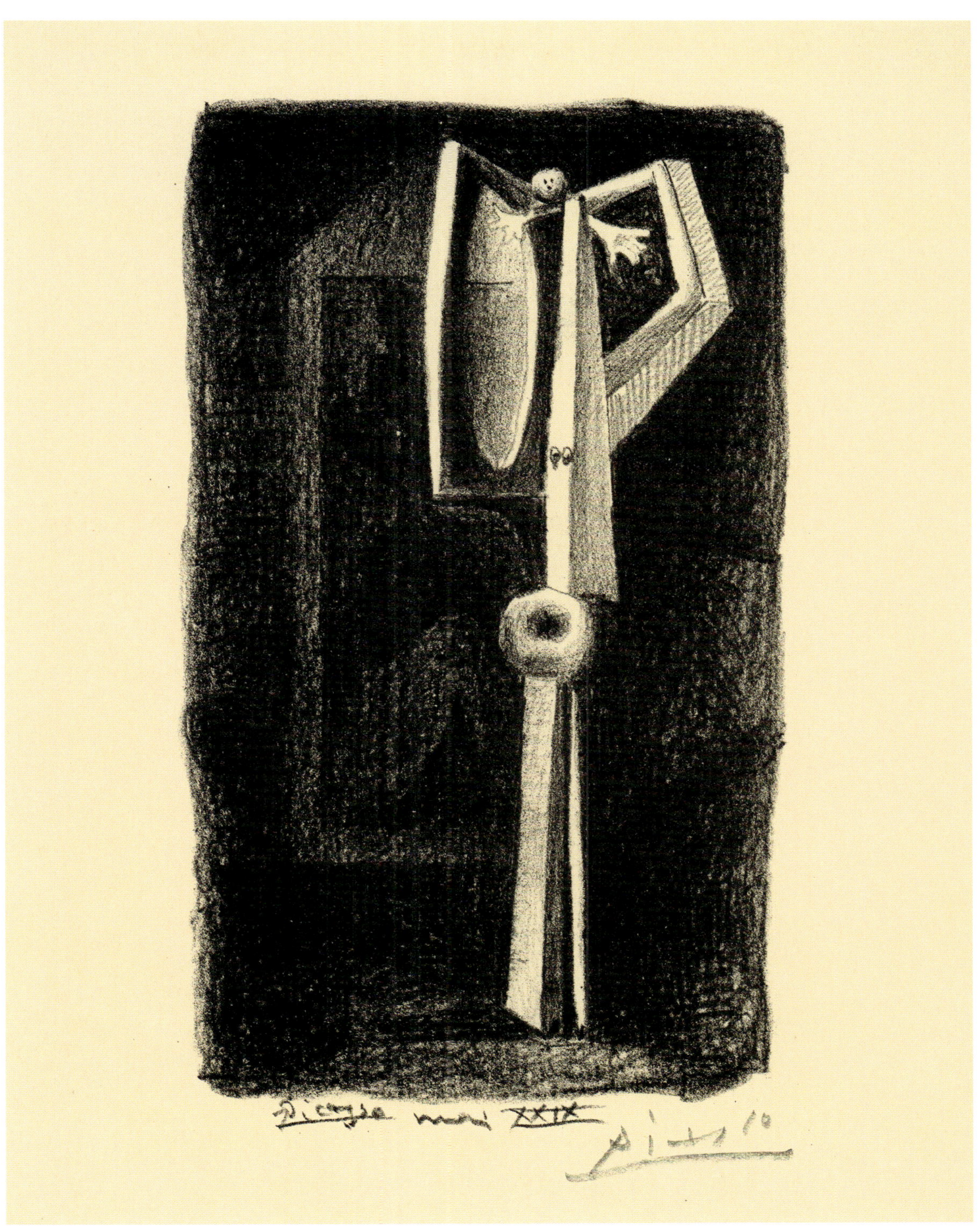

Painter and the model knitting, 1927
Illustration for Honoré de Balzac's *Le chef-d'œuvre
inconnu* (*The Unknown Masterpiece*)
(Paris: Vollard, 1931)
Etching

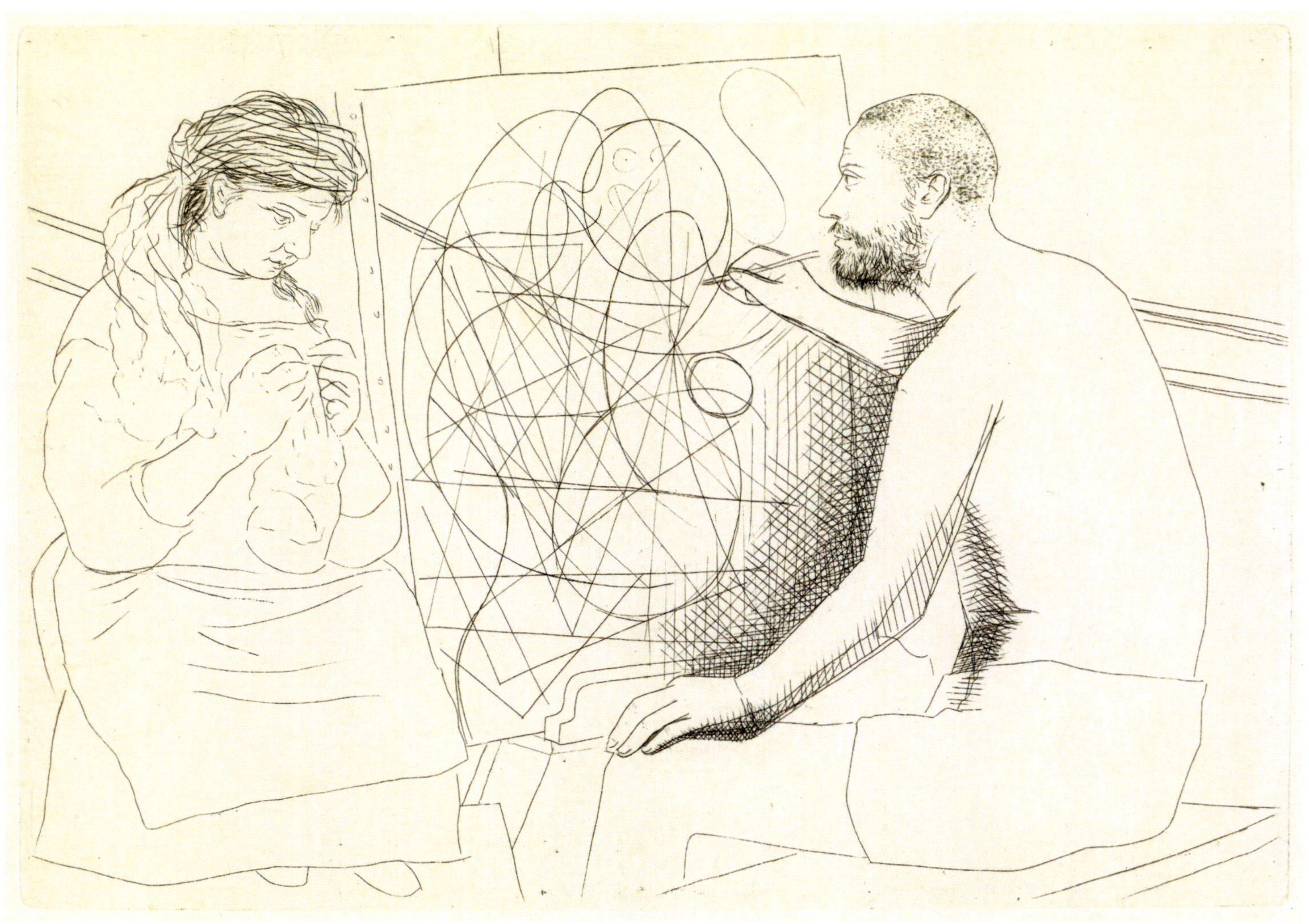

Three standing nudes, 1927
Illustration for Honoré de Balzac's *Le chef-d'œuvre inconnu* (Paris: Vollard, 1931)
Etching

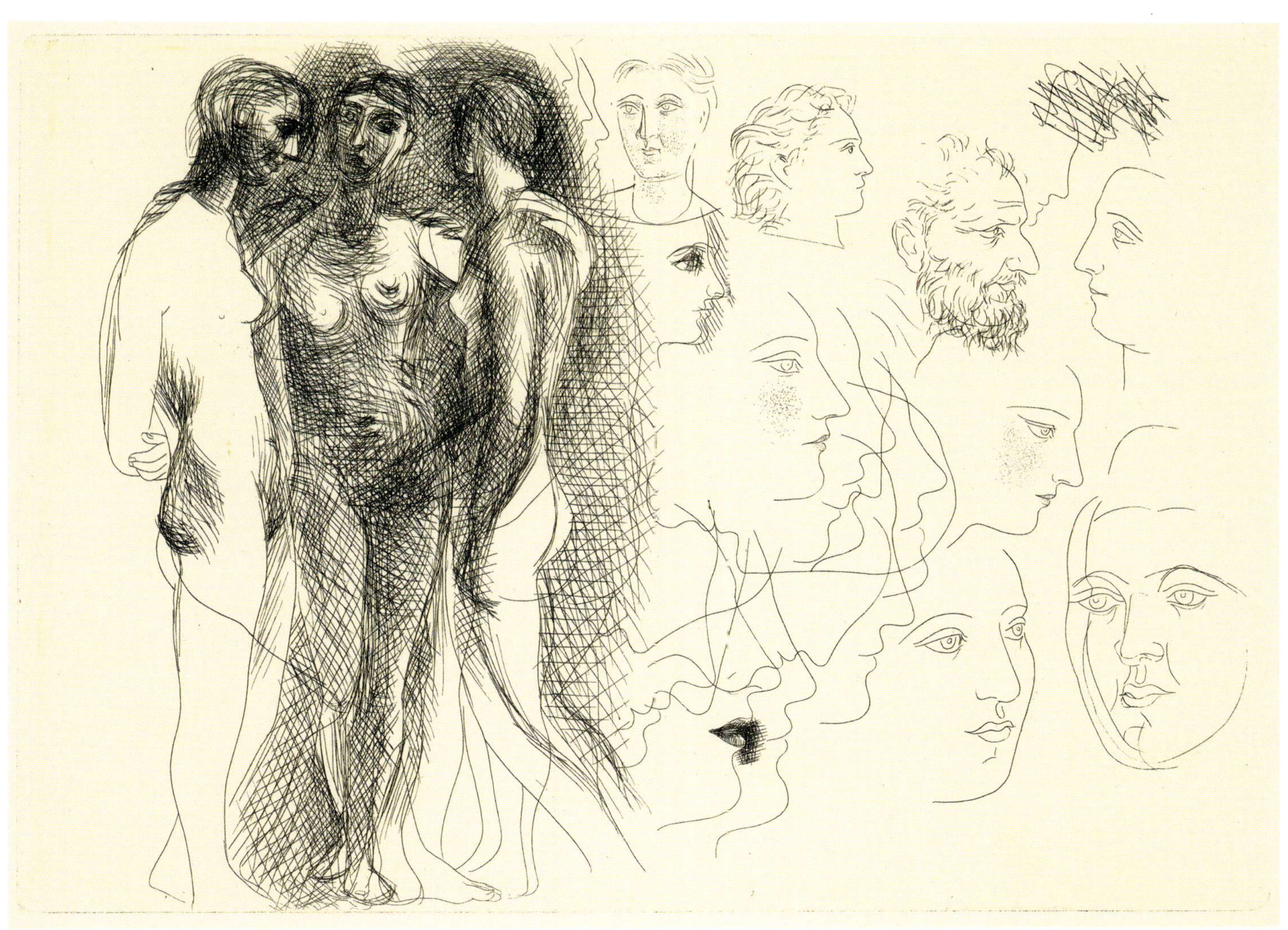

Nude woman crowned with flowers from the
Vollard Suite, 16 September 1930
Etching

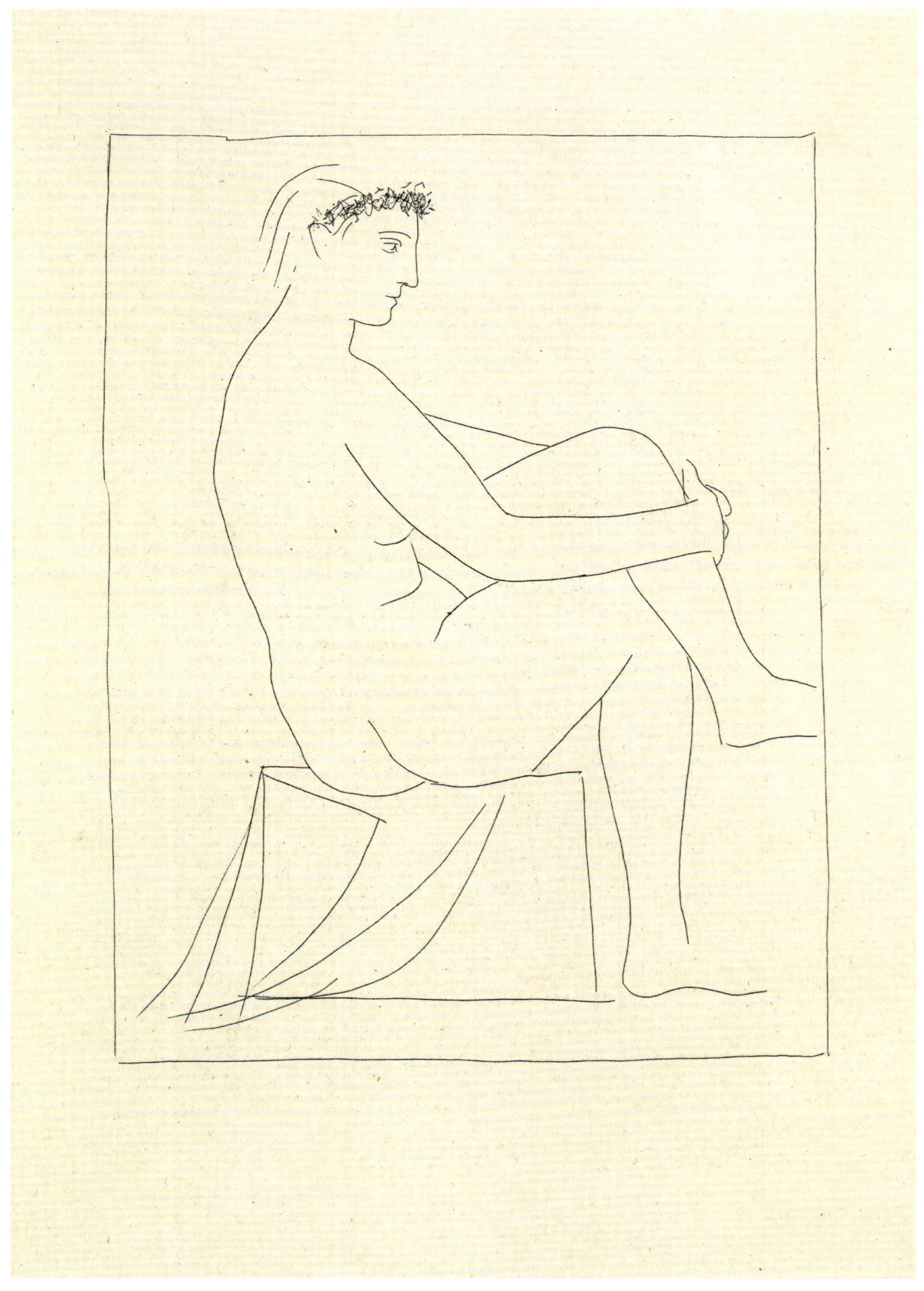

Sculptor, model and sculpted bust from the
Vollard Suite, 17 March 1933
Etching

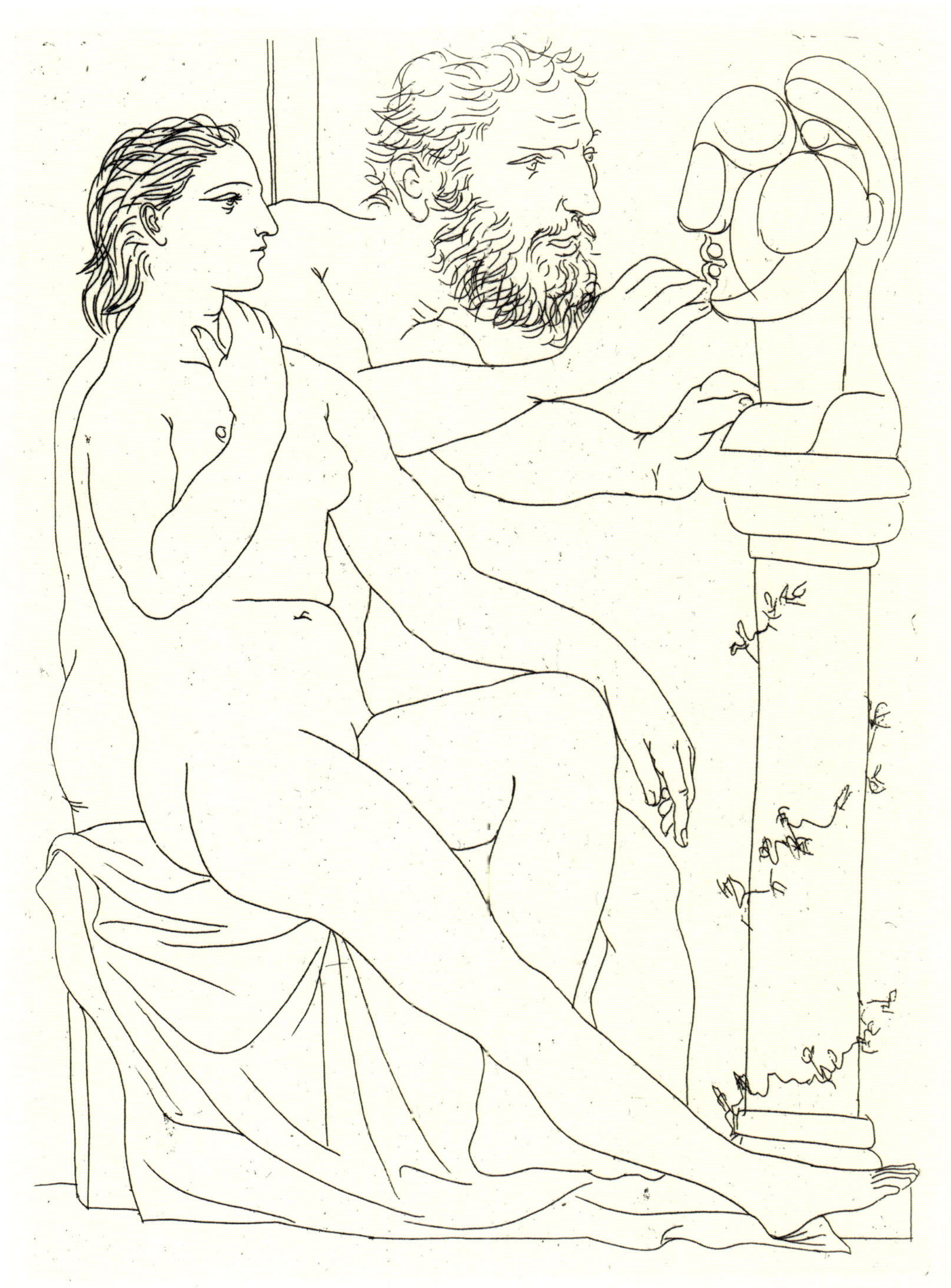

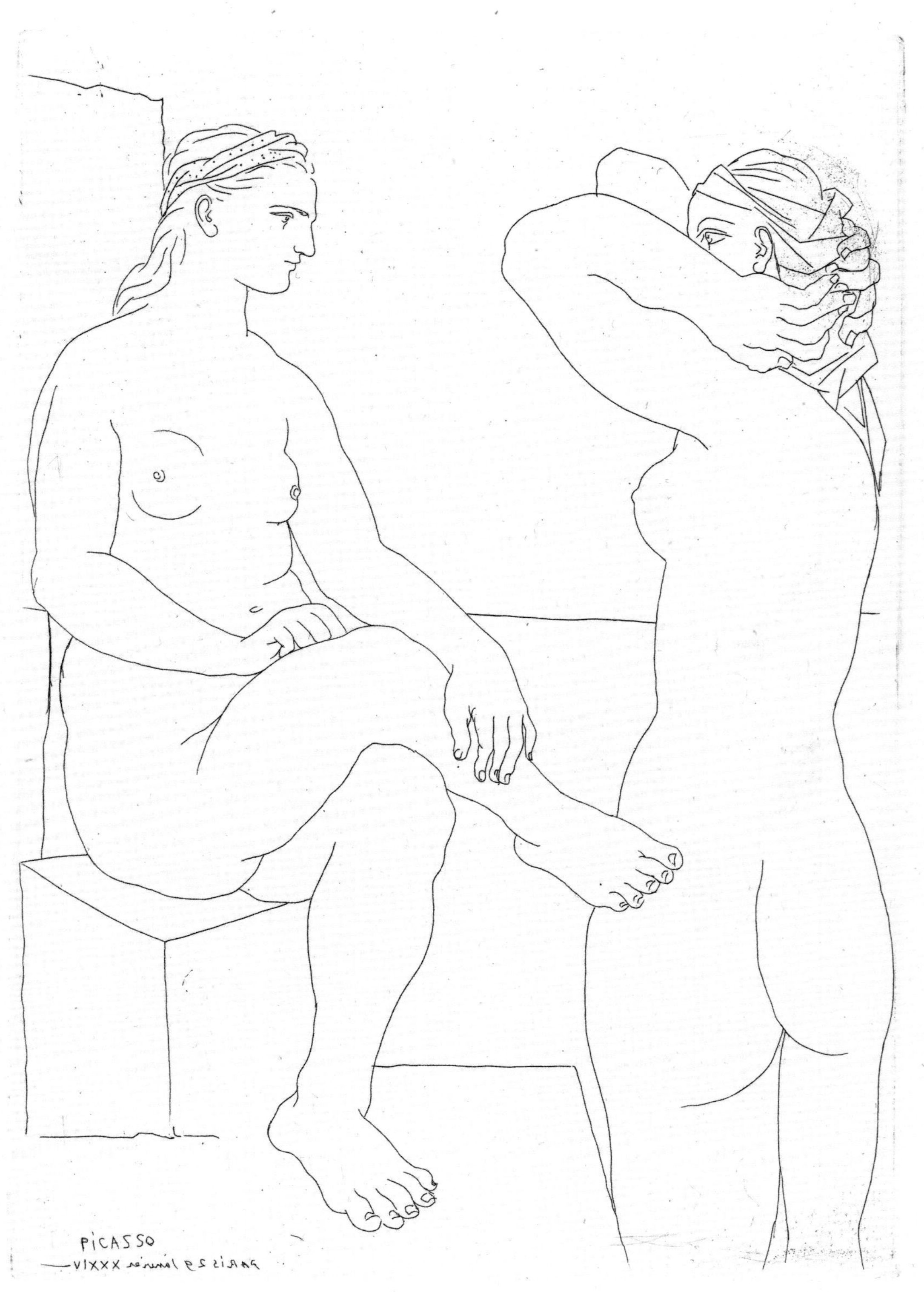

Two models looking at each other from the
Vollard Suite, 29 January 1934
Etching

Sculptor and sculpted group of three dancers
from the *Vollard Suite*, 2 March 1934
Etching

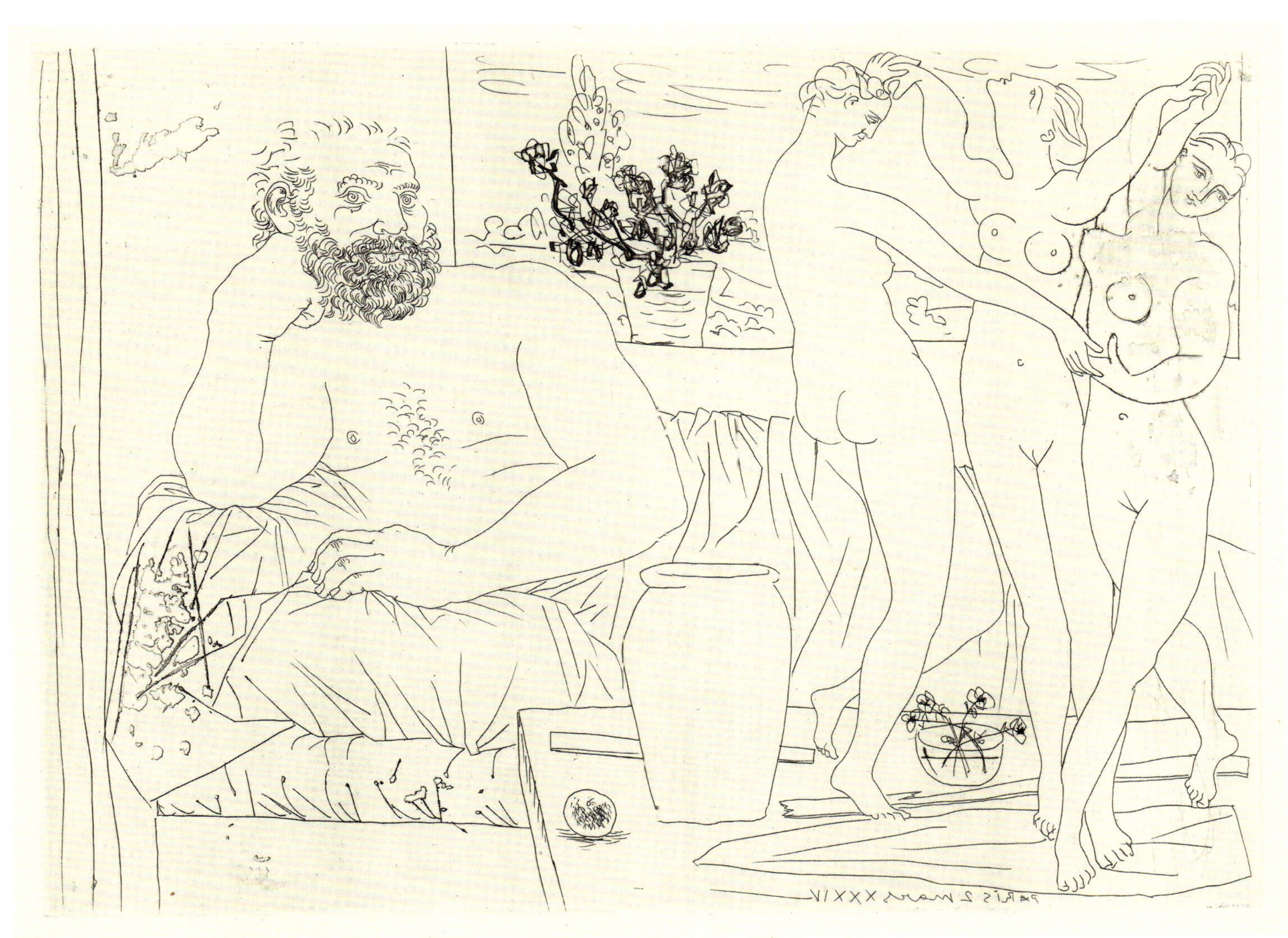

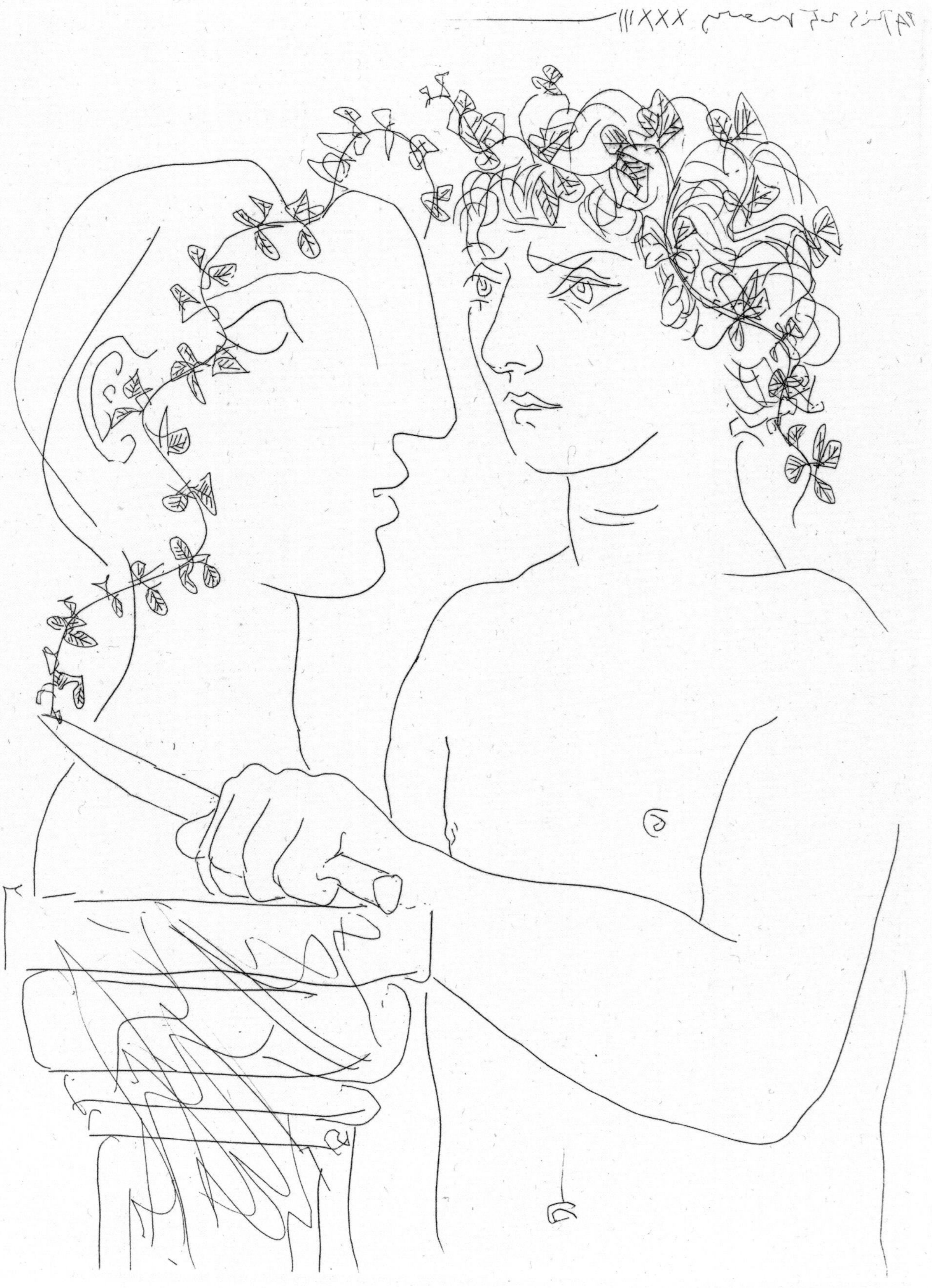

Young sculptor at work from the *Vollard Suite*,
23 March 1933
Etching

Sculptor and his model before a window
from the *Vollard Suite*, 31 March 1933
Etching

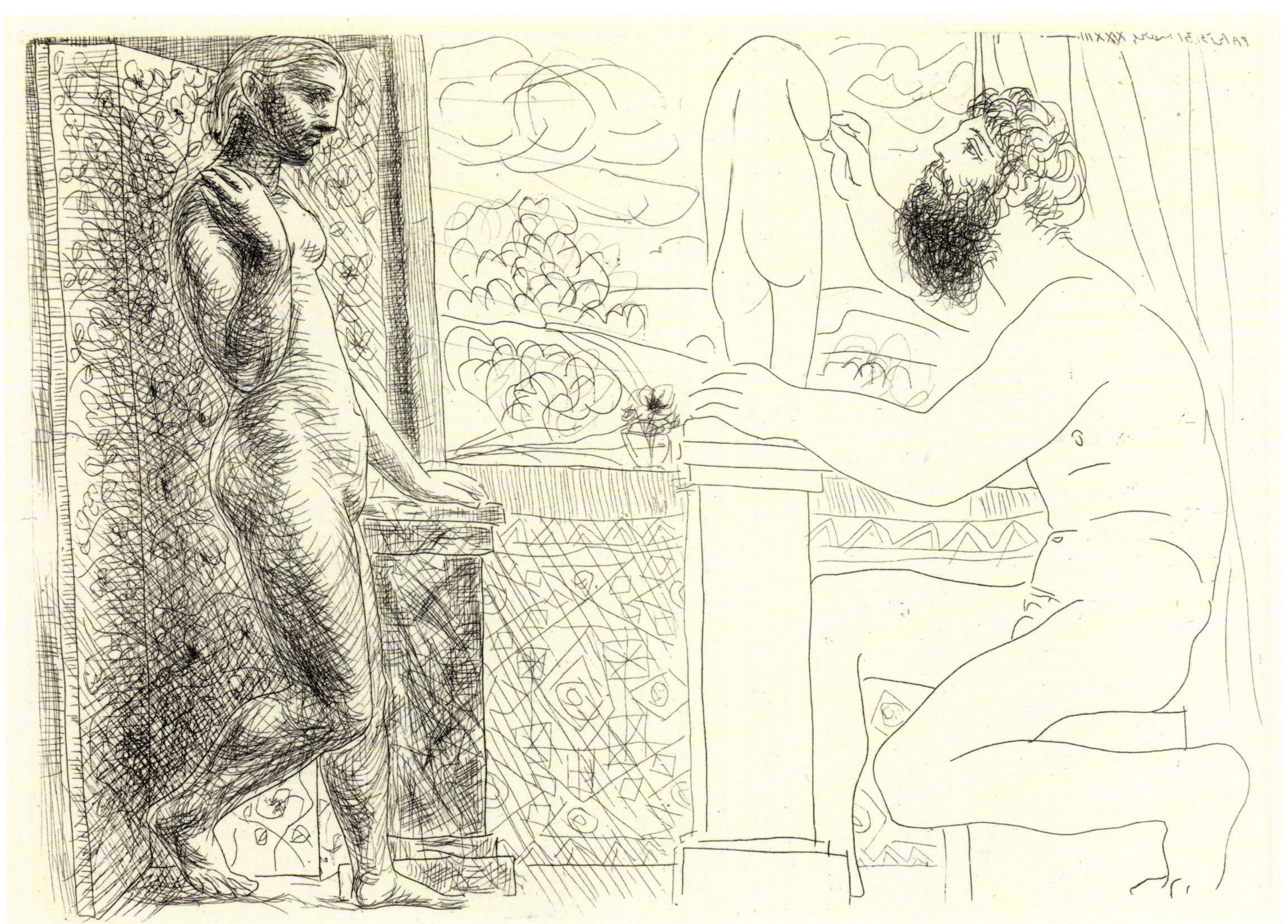

Young sculptor at work from the *Vollard Suite*,
23 March 1933
Etching

Sculptor and his model before a window
from the *Vollard Suite*, 31 March 1933
Etching

Sculptor and kneeling model
from the *Vollard Suite*, 8 April 1933
Etching

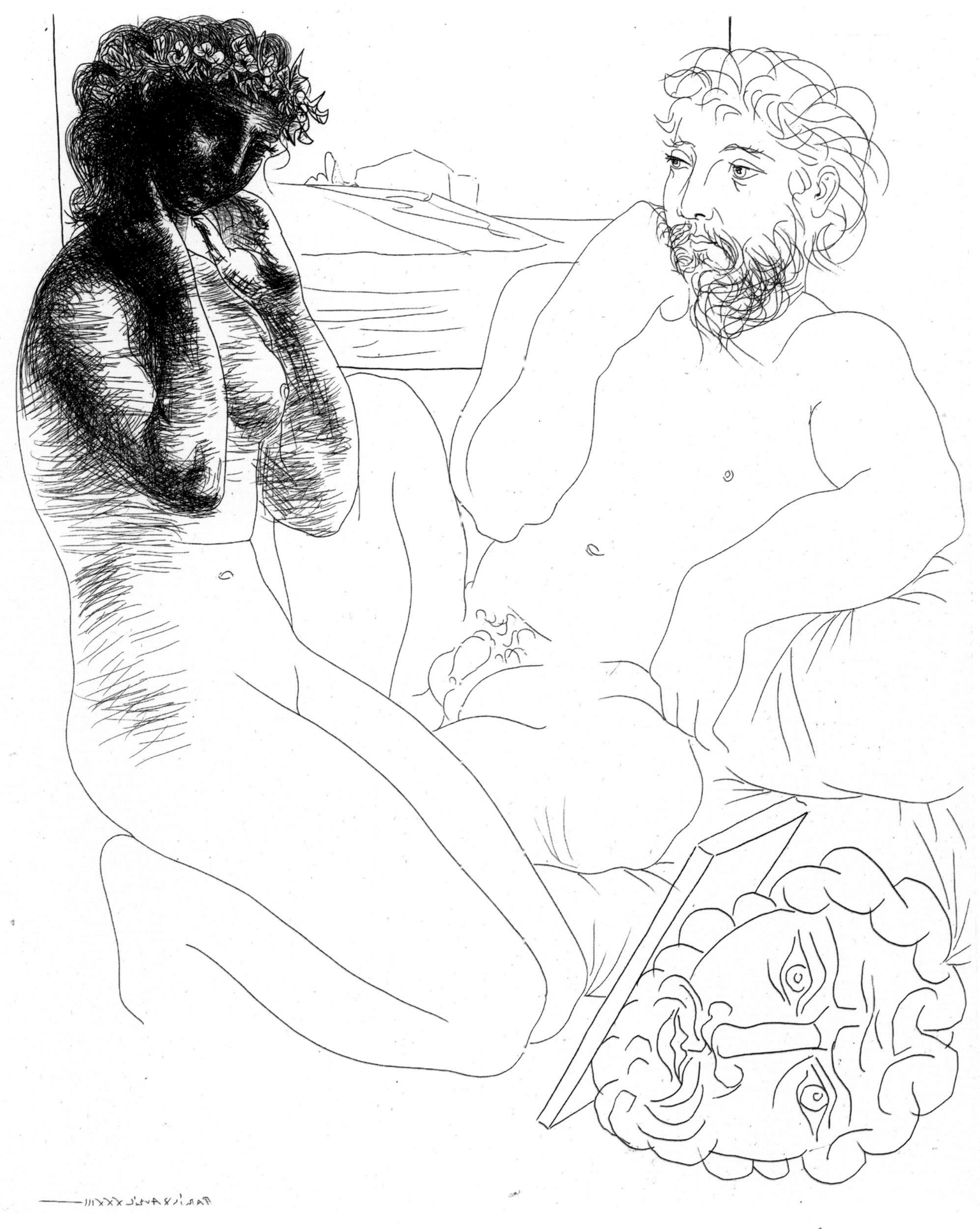

Faun uncovering a woman from the *Vollard Suite*,
12 June 1936
Sugar aquatint, scraper and engraving

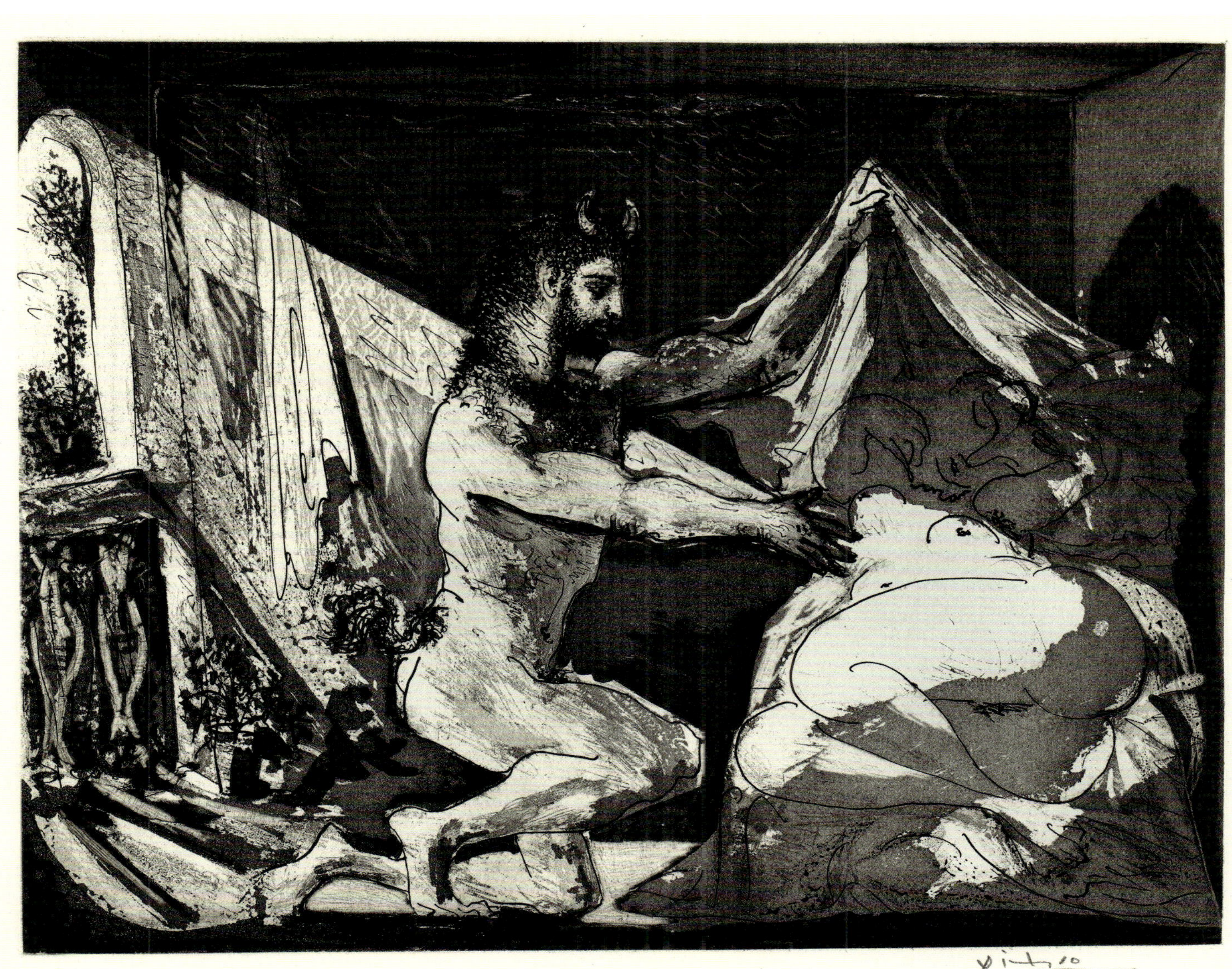

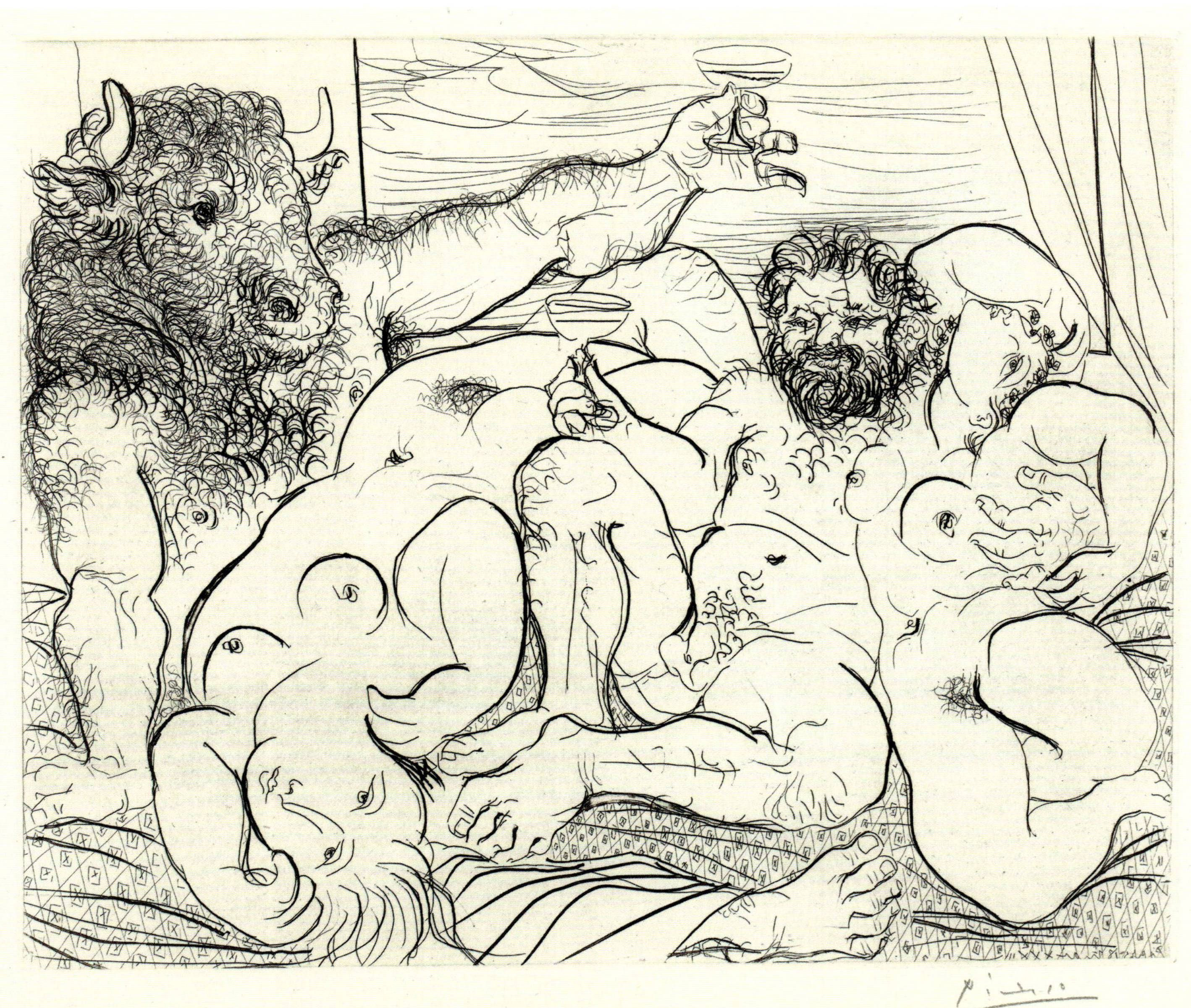

Bacchic scene with Minotaur from the
Vollard Suite, 18 May 1933
Etching

Woman gazing at a sleeping Minotaur from the
Vollard Suite, 18 May 1933
Etching

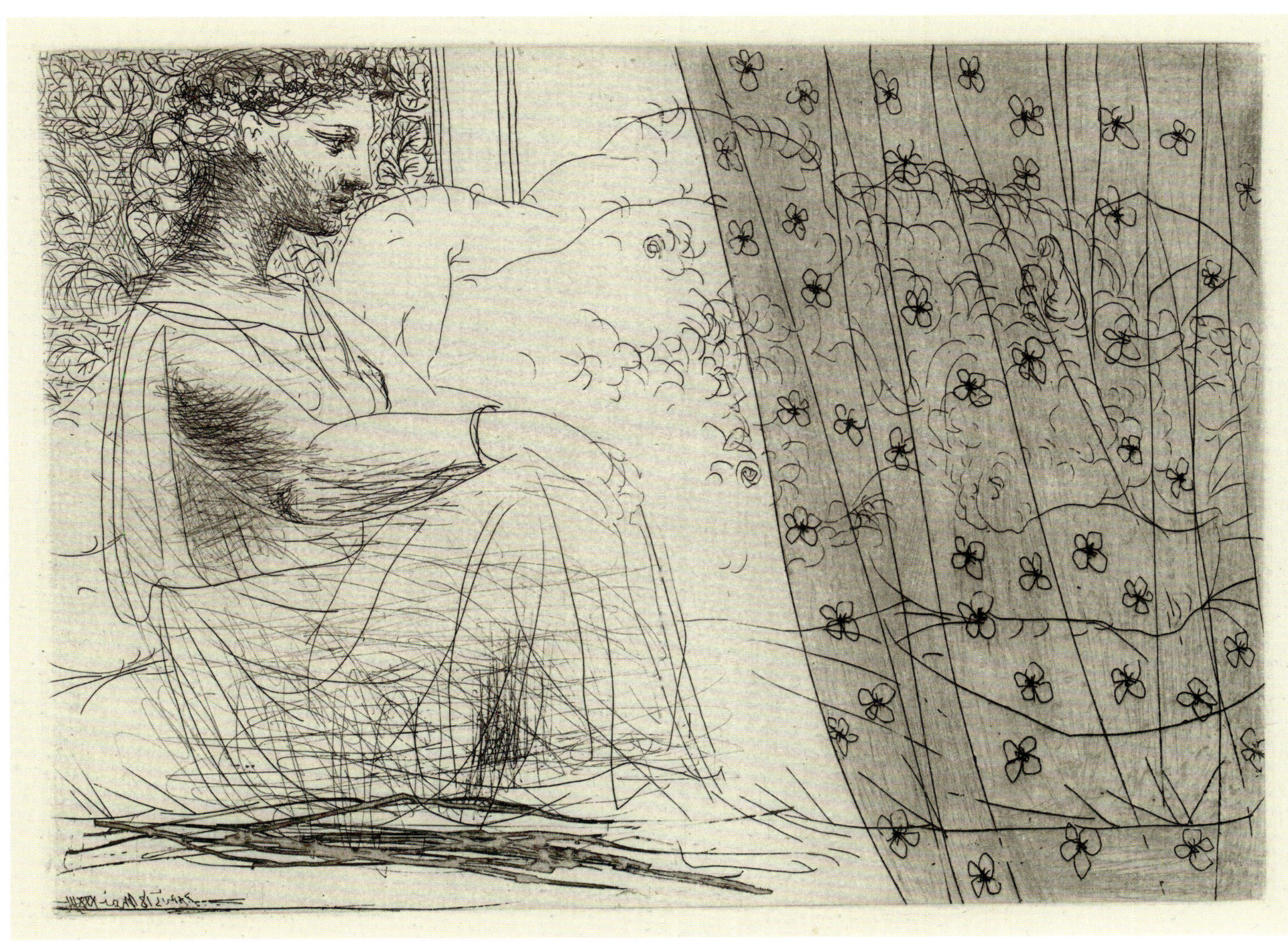

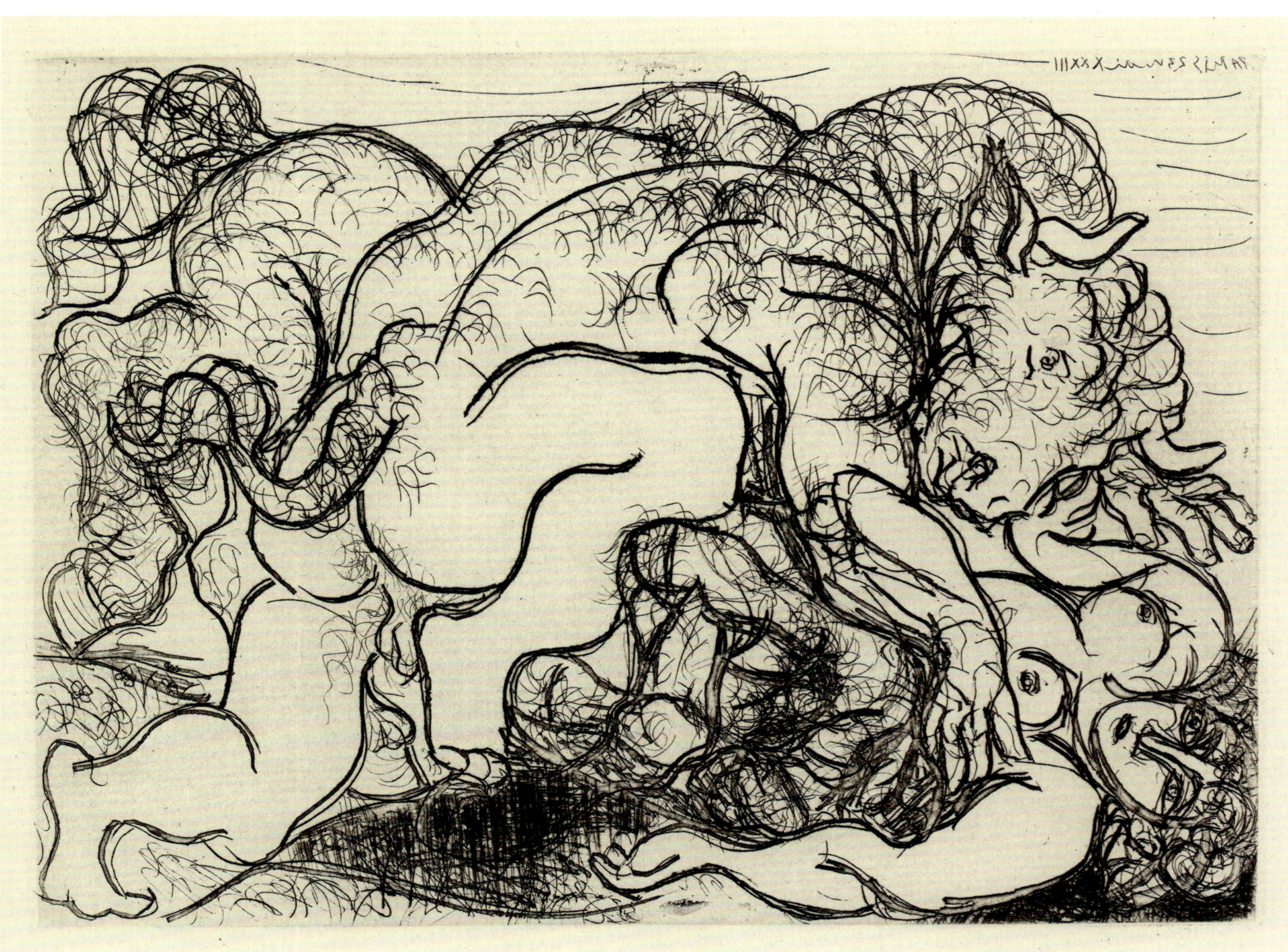

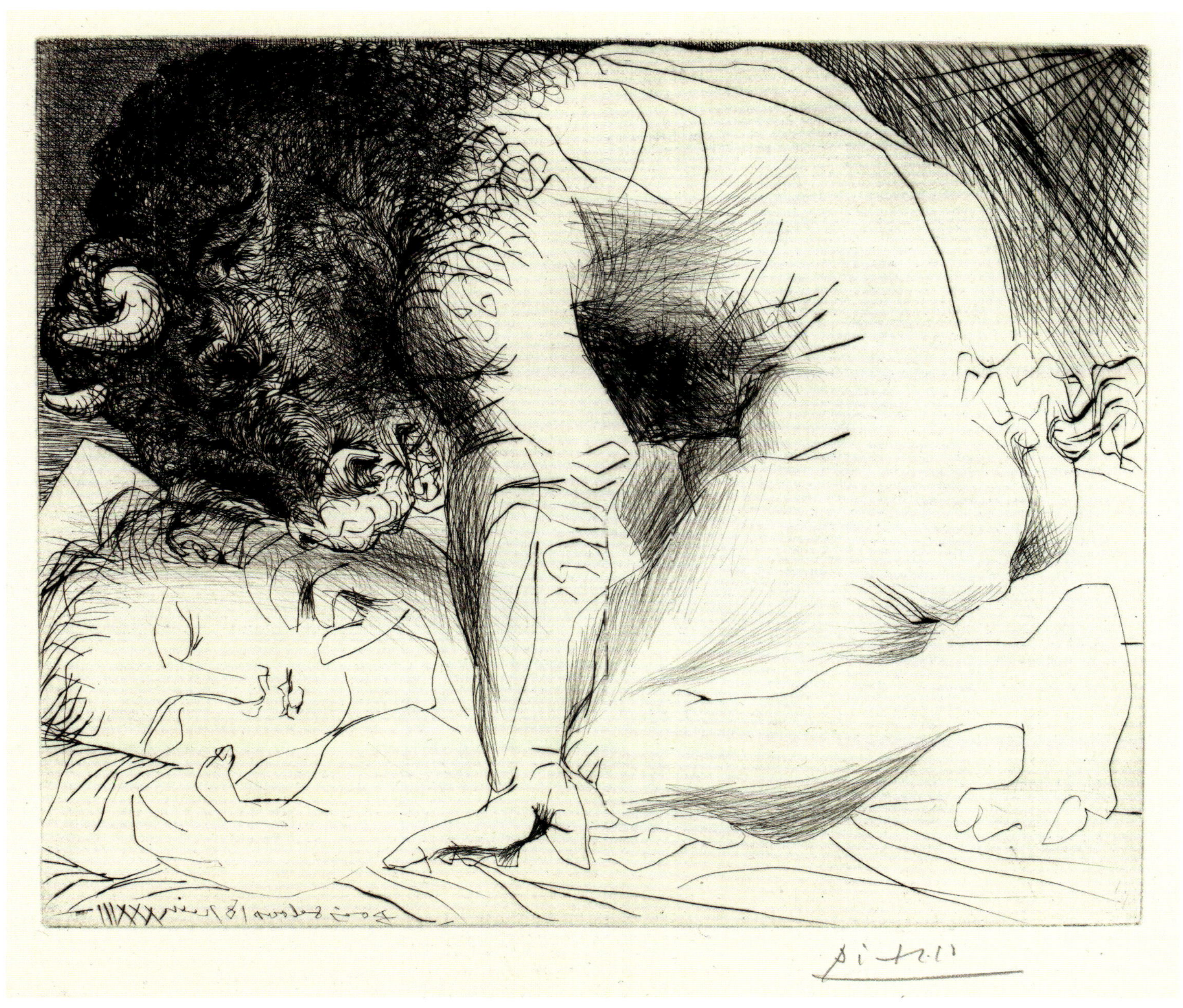

Amorous Minotaur with a female centaur from the
Vollard Suite, 23 May 1933
Etching

Minotaur caressing a sleeping woman from the
Vollard Suite, 18 June 1933, plate reworked
probably at end of 1934
Drypoint

Female bullfighter II from the *Vollard Suite*,
20 June 1934
Etching

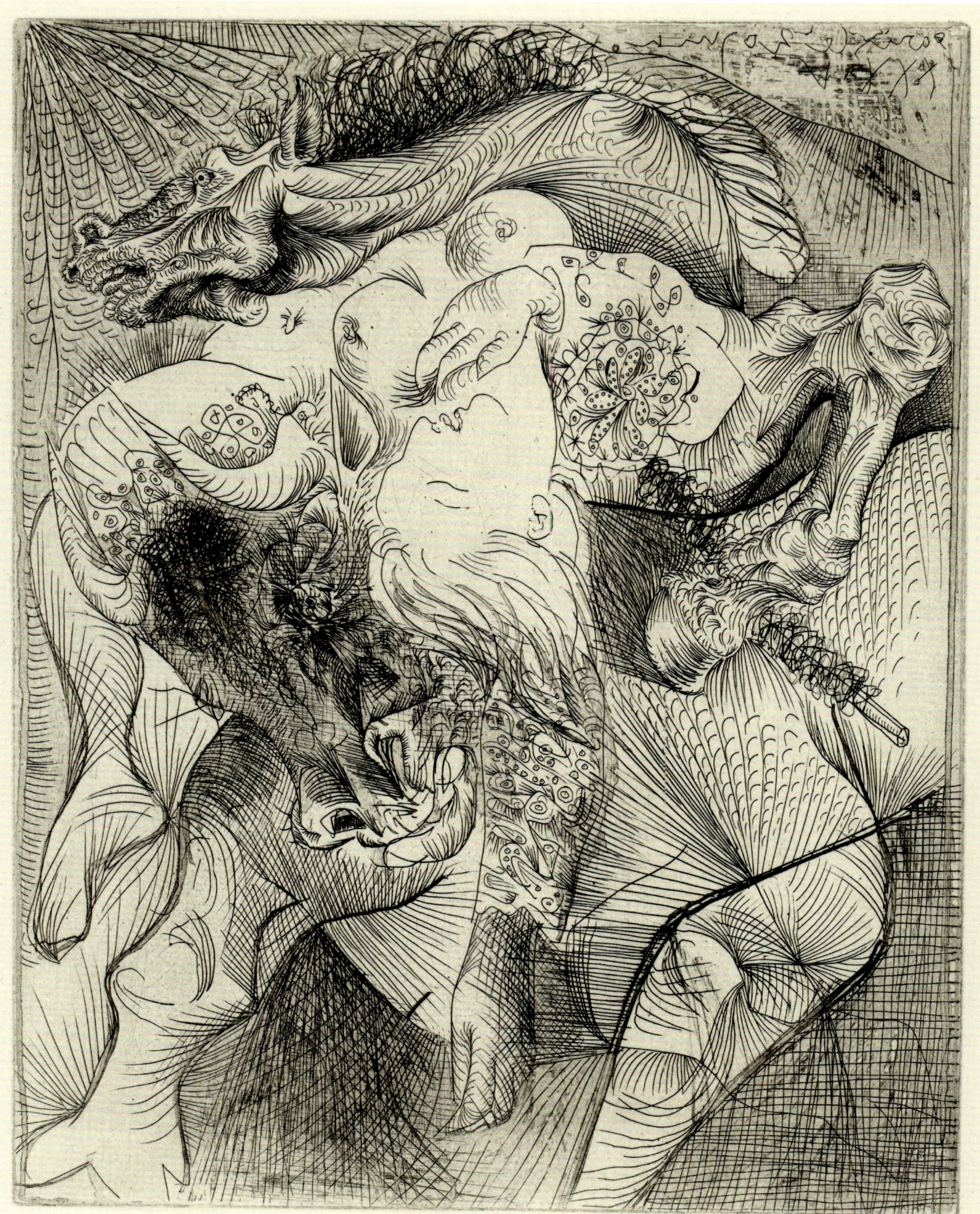

Vanquished Minotaur from the *Vollard Suite*,
29 May 1933
Etching

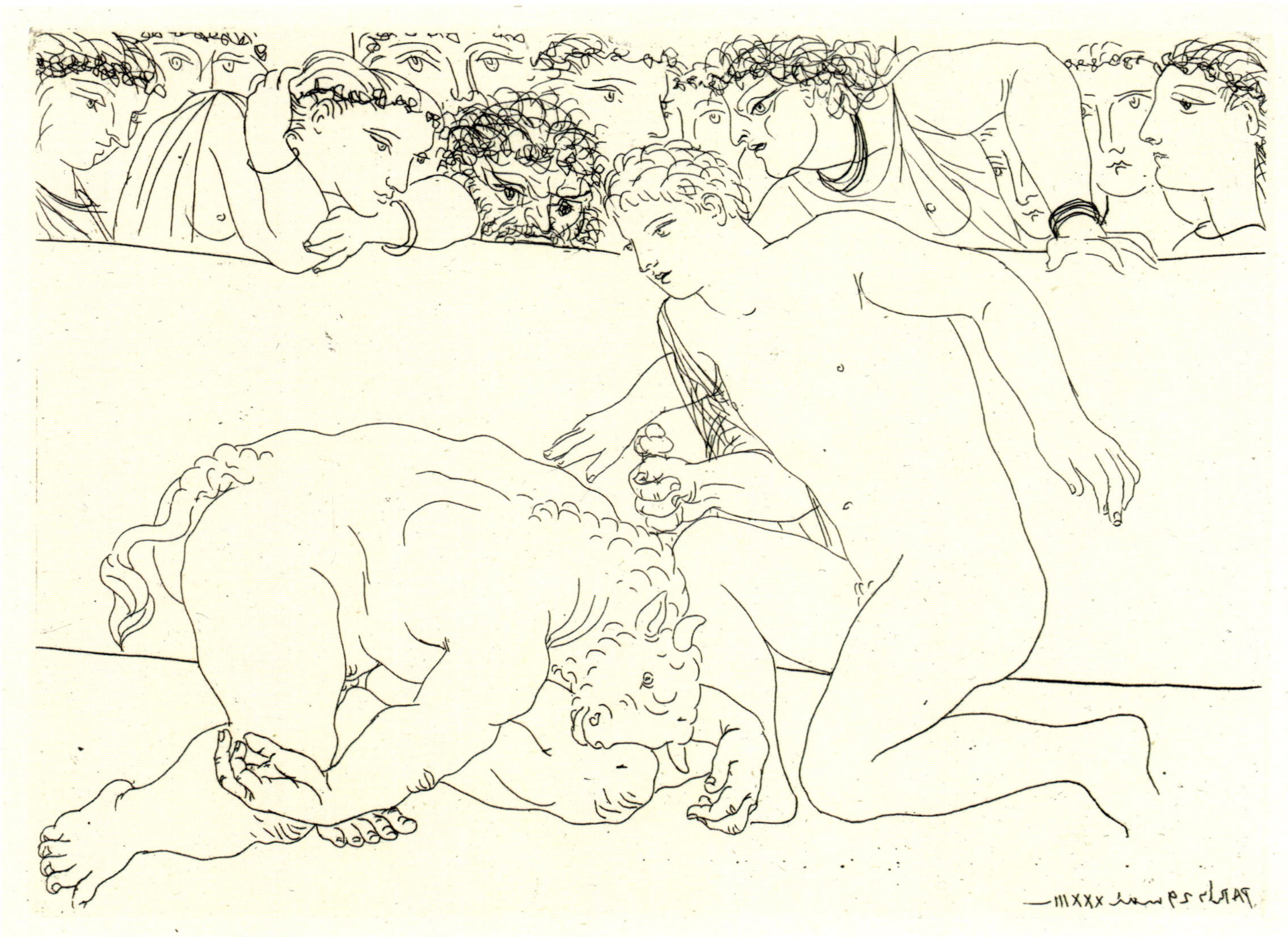

Dying Minotaur from the *Vollard Suite*,
30 May 1933
Etching

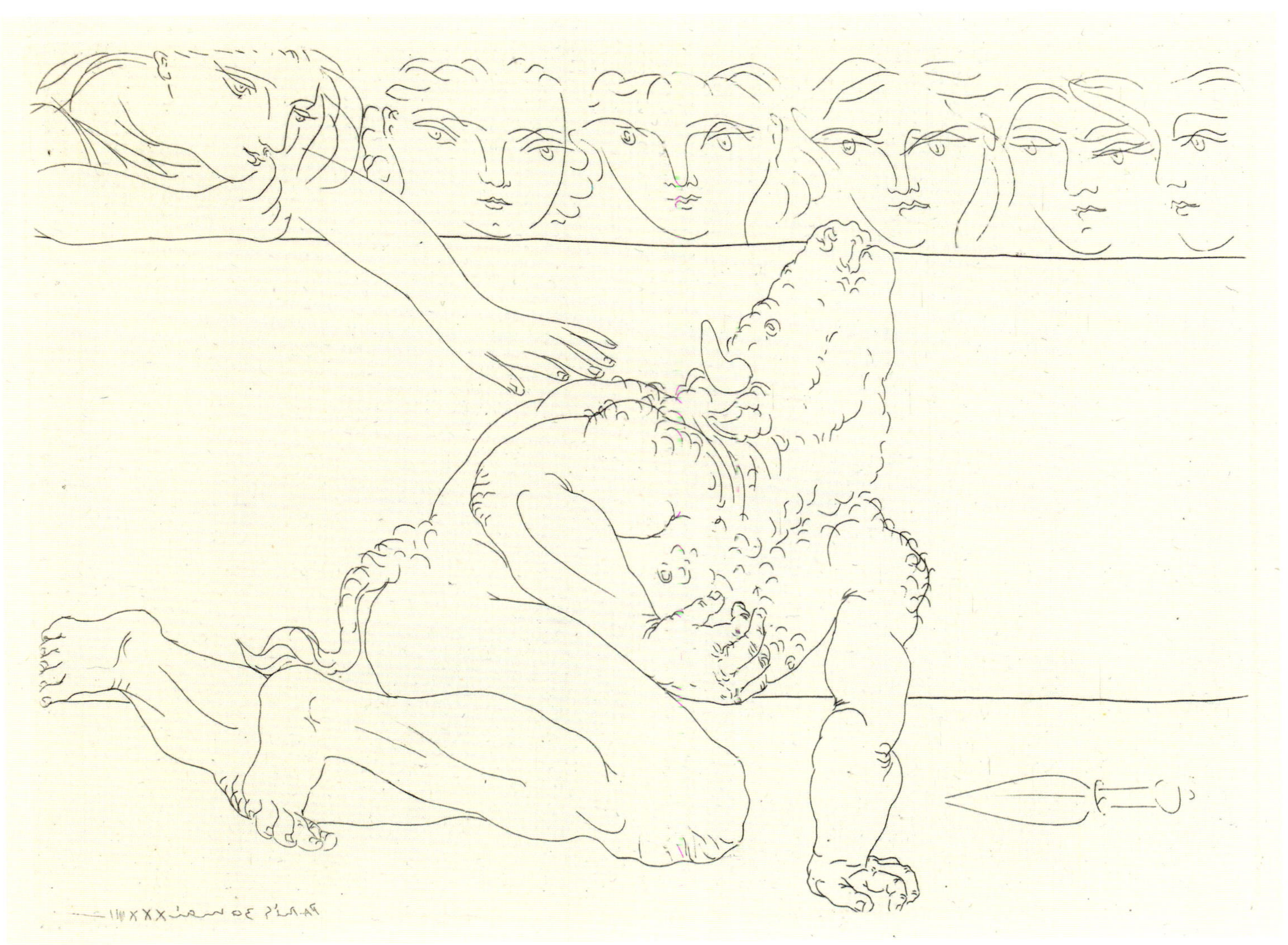

Blind Minotaur led by a little girl in the night from
the *Vollard Suite*, 3–7, 31 December 1934
Aquatint worked with scraper to resemble
mezzotint, drypoint and engraving

Portrait of Vollard I from the *Vollard Suite*,
4 March 1937
Sugar aquatint

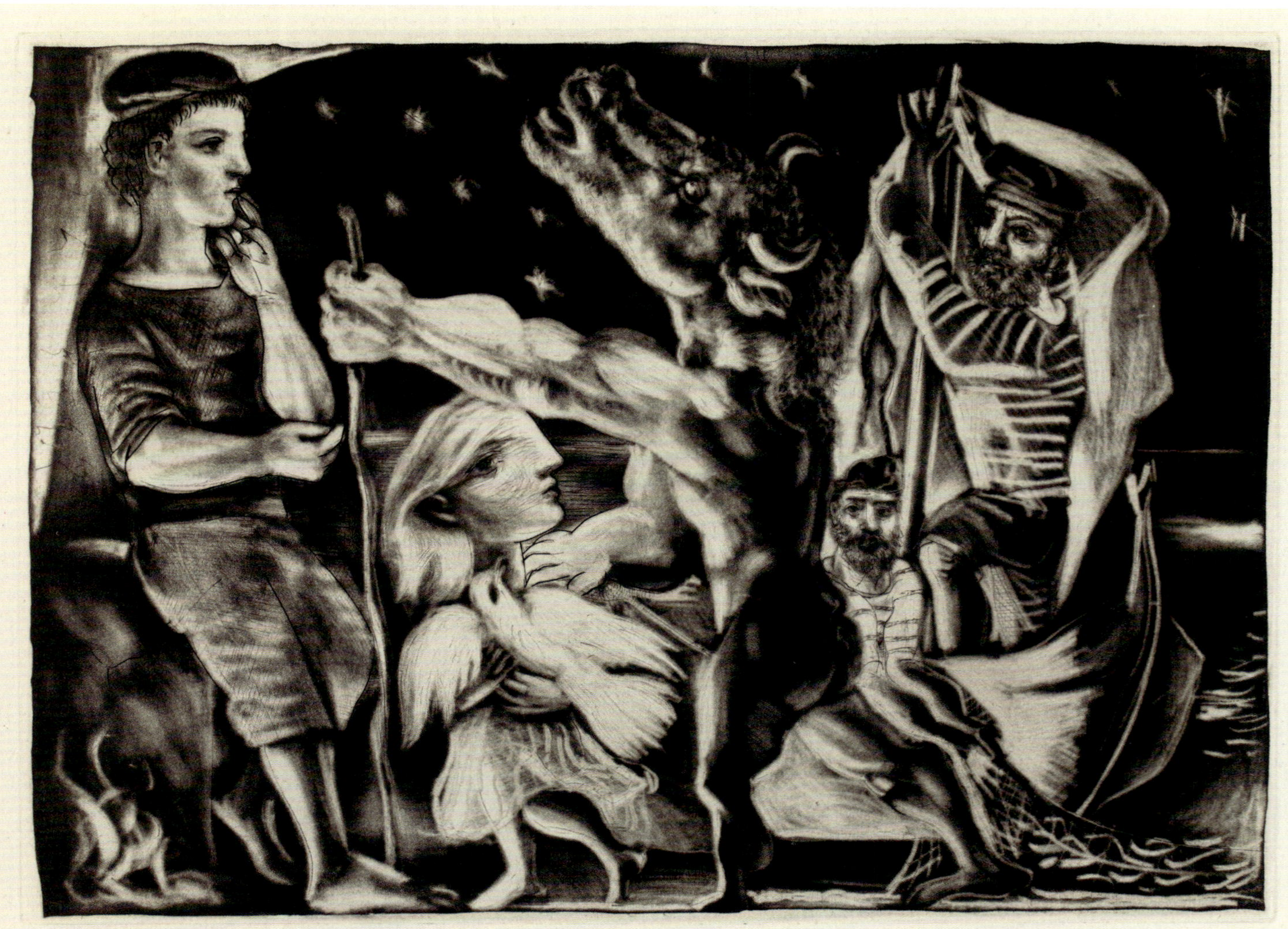

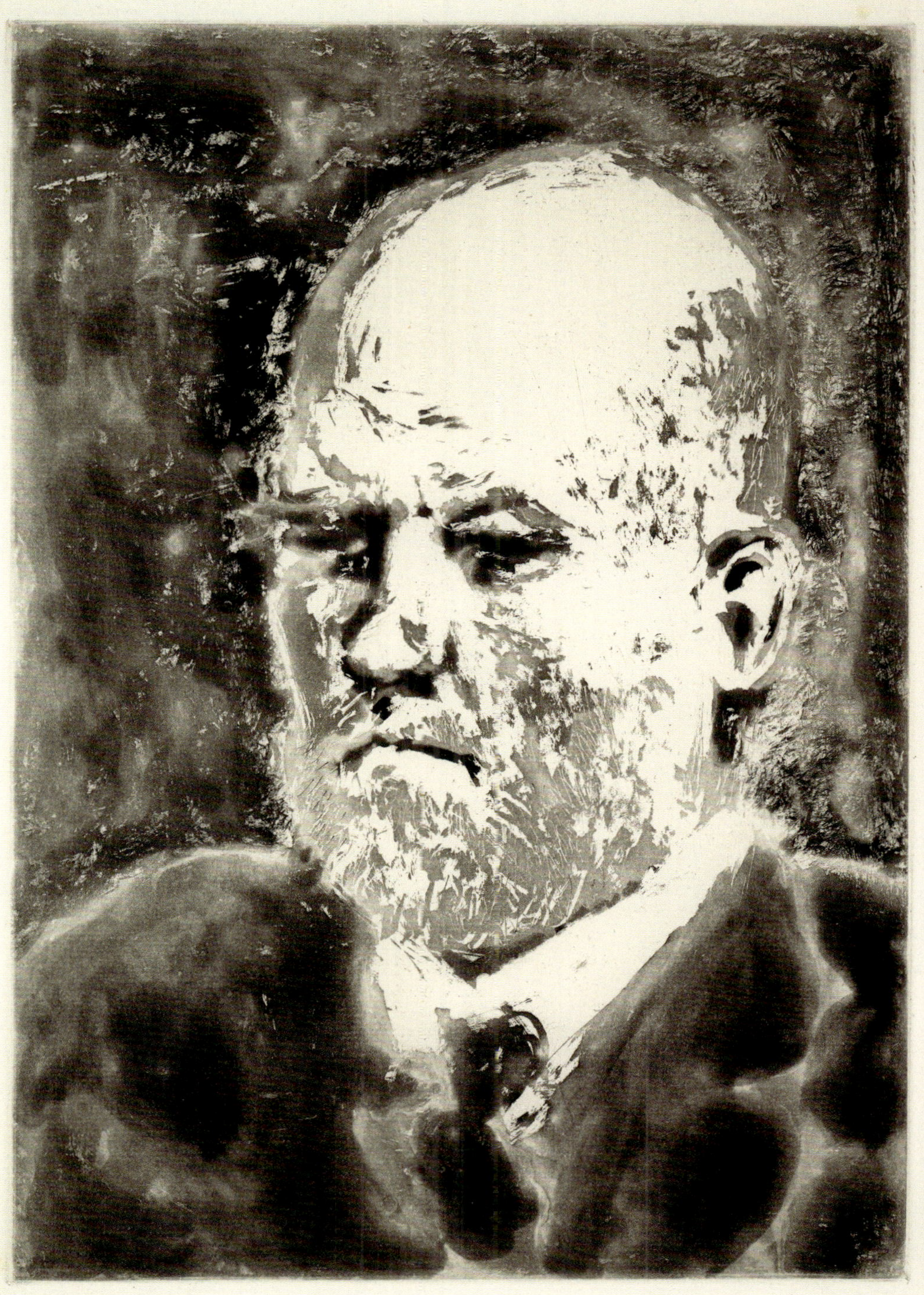

Monkey, 1936
Illustration for *Picasso. Eaux-fortes originales pour
les textes de Buffon* (*Picasso. Original etchings
for texts by Buffon*) (Paris: Martin Fabiani, 1942)
Sugar aquatint, scraper and drypoint

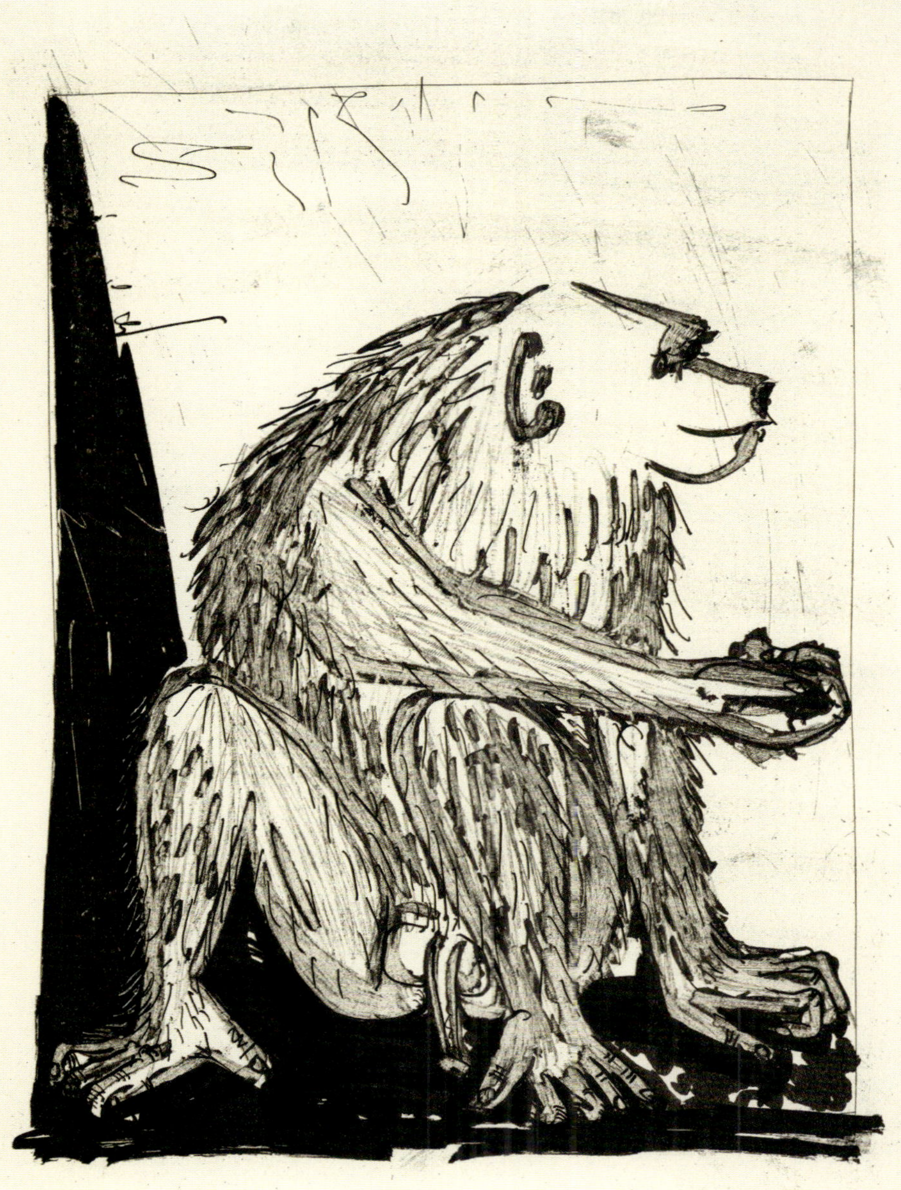

Le Singe

Frogs, 1936
Illustration for *Picasso. Eaux-fortes originales pour les textes de Buffon* (Paris: Martin Fabiani, 1942)
Sugar aquatint, burnisher and drypoint

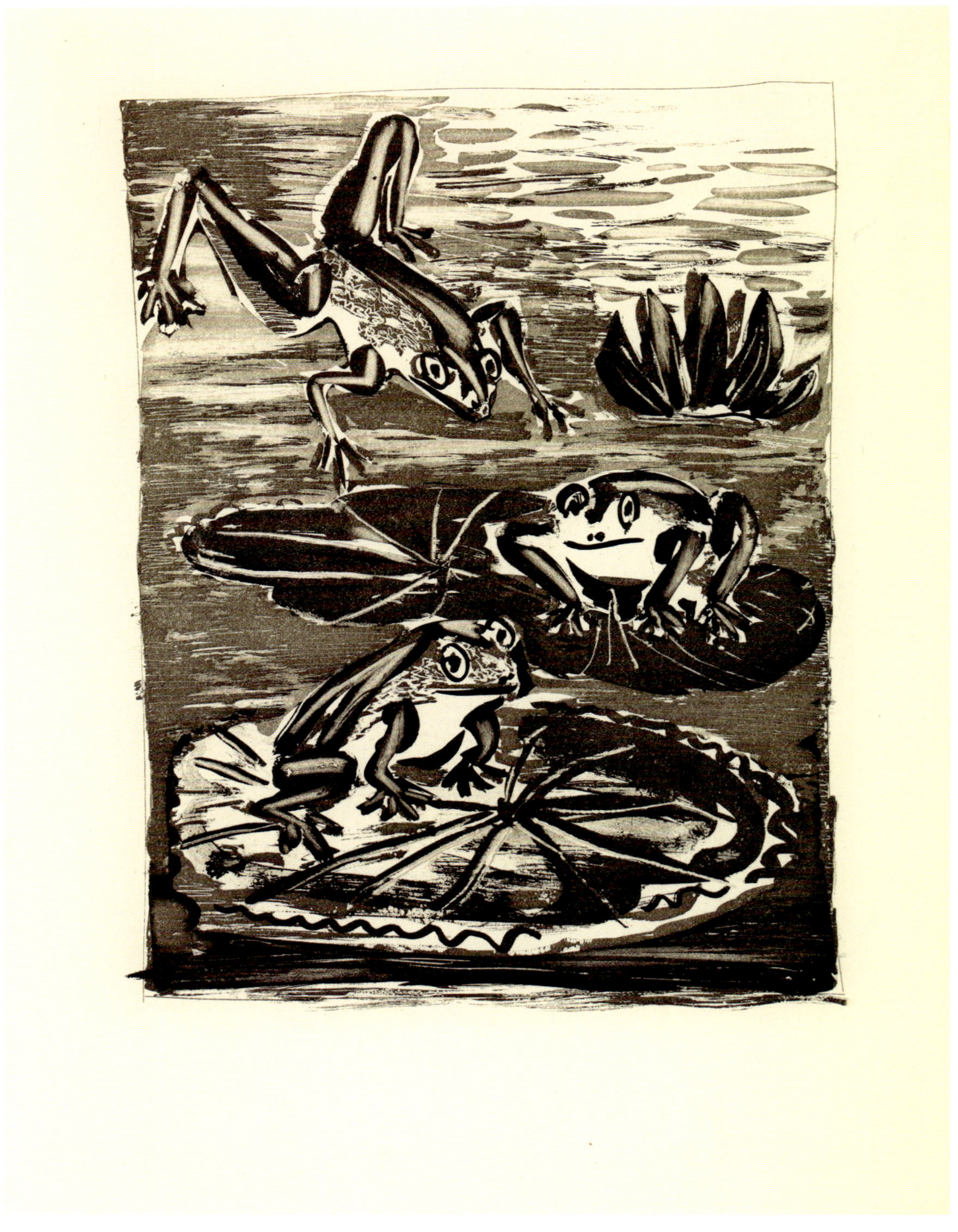

Lizard, 1936
Illustration for *Picasso. Eaux-fortes originales pour les textes de Buffon* (Paris: Martin Fabiani, 1942)
Sugar aquatint and drypoint

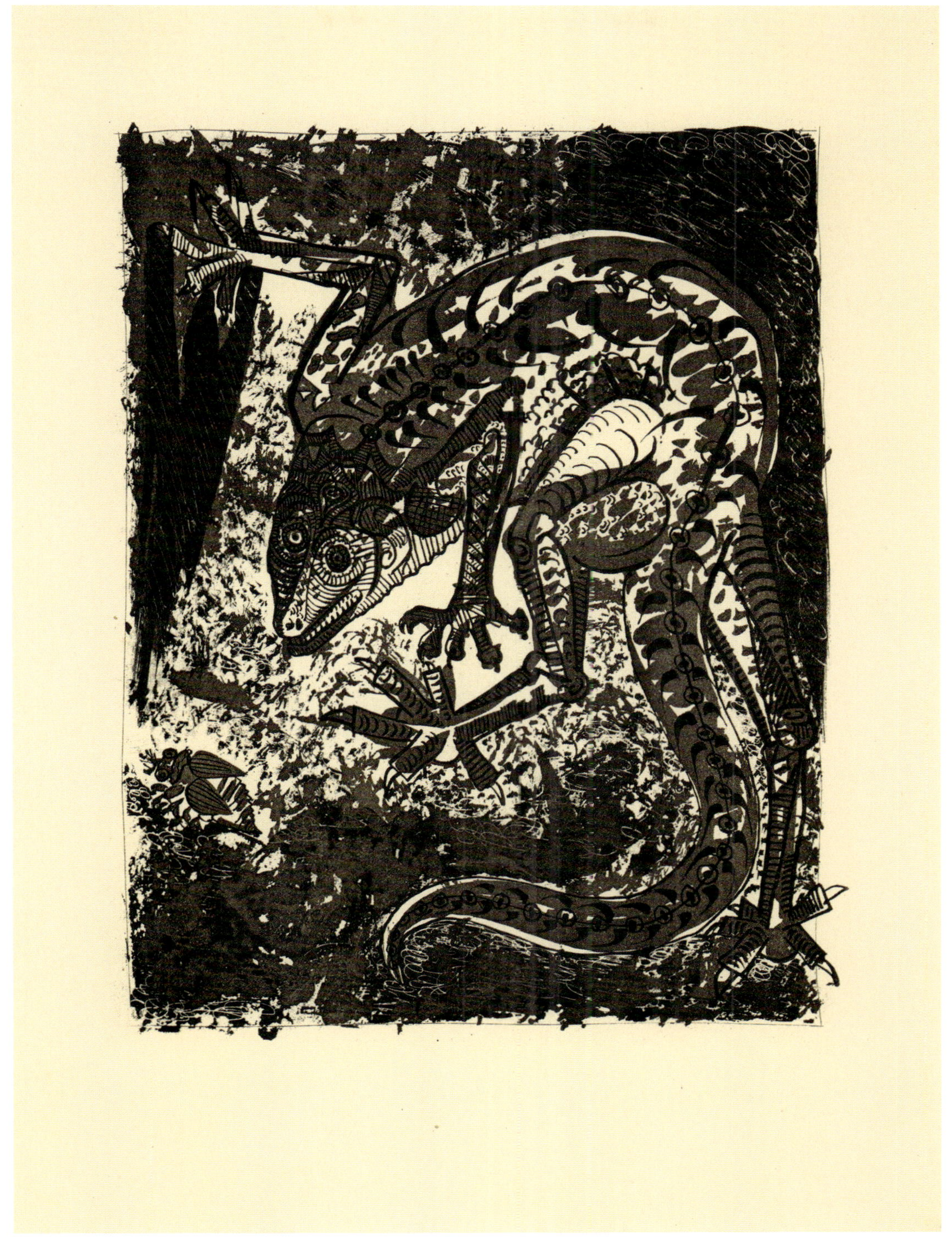

The dream and lie of Franco (plate I),
8 January 1937
Etching and sugar aquatint

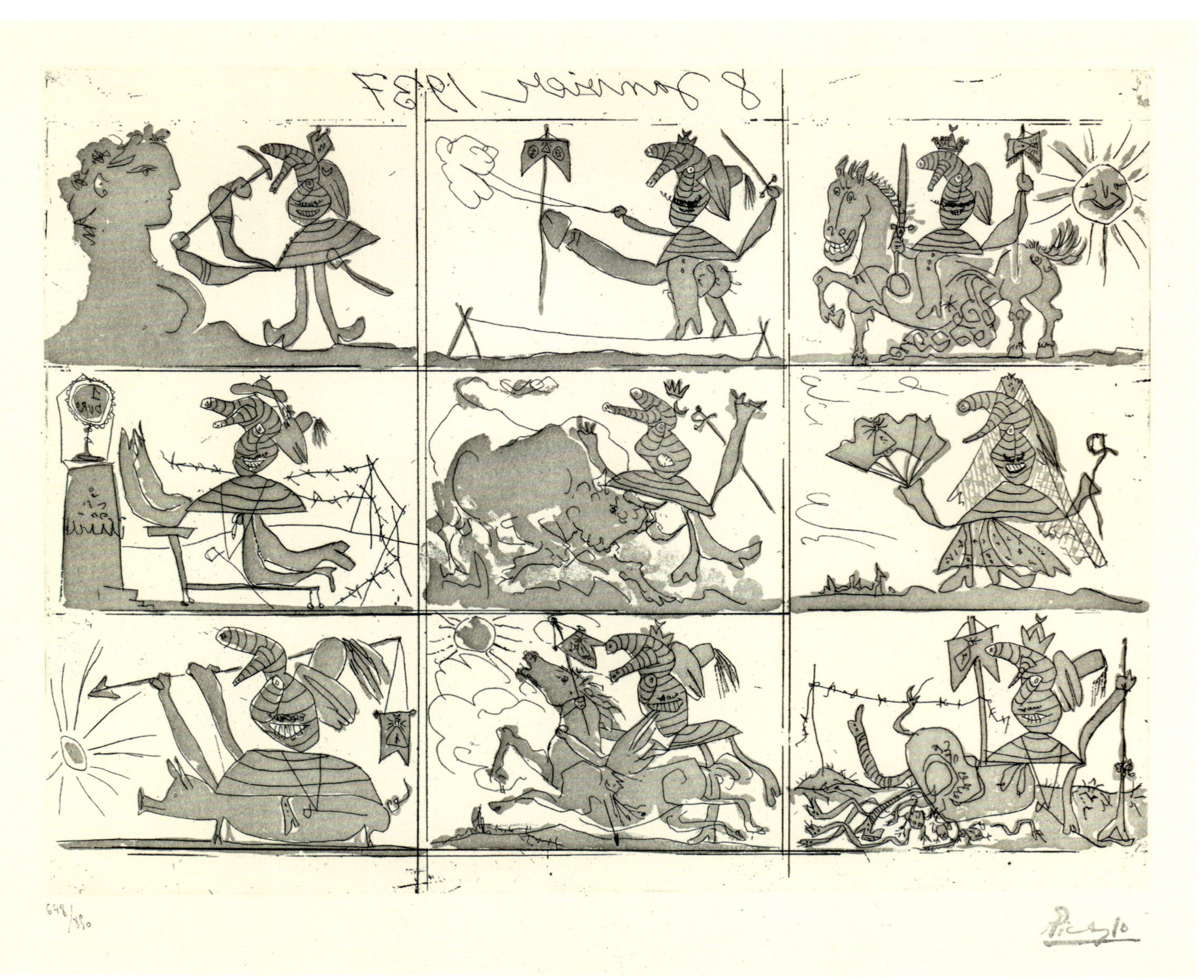

The dream and lie of Franco (plate II),
8, 9 January, 7 June 1937
Etching, sugar aquatint and scraper

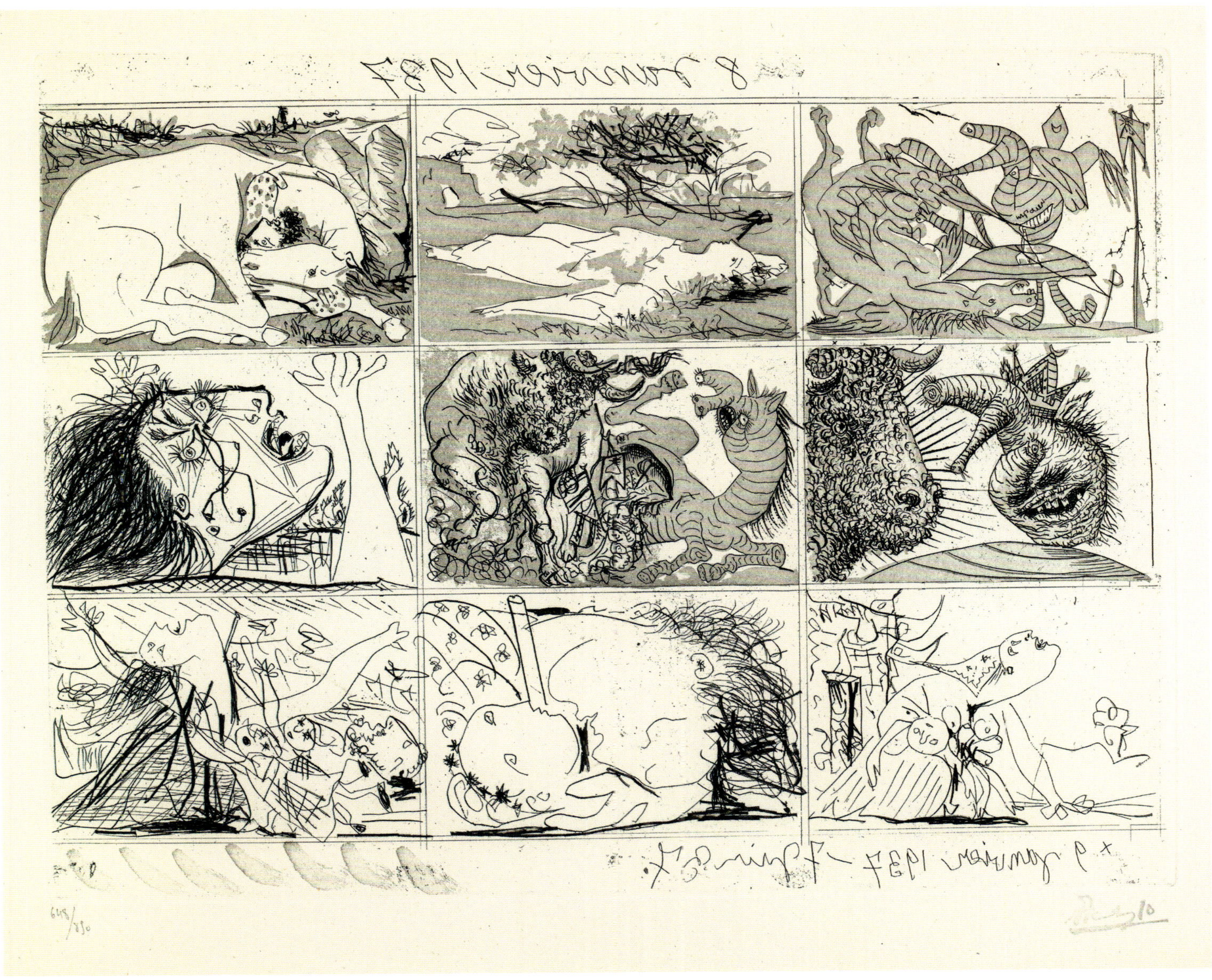

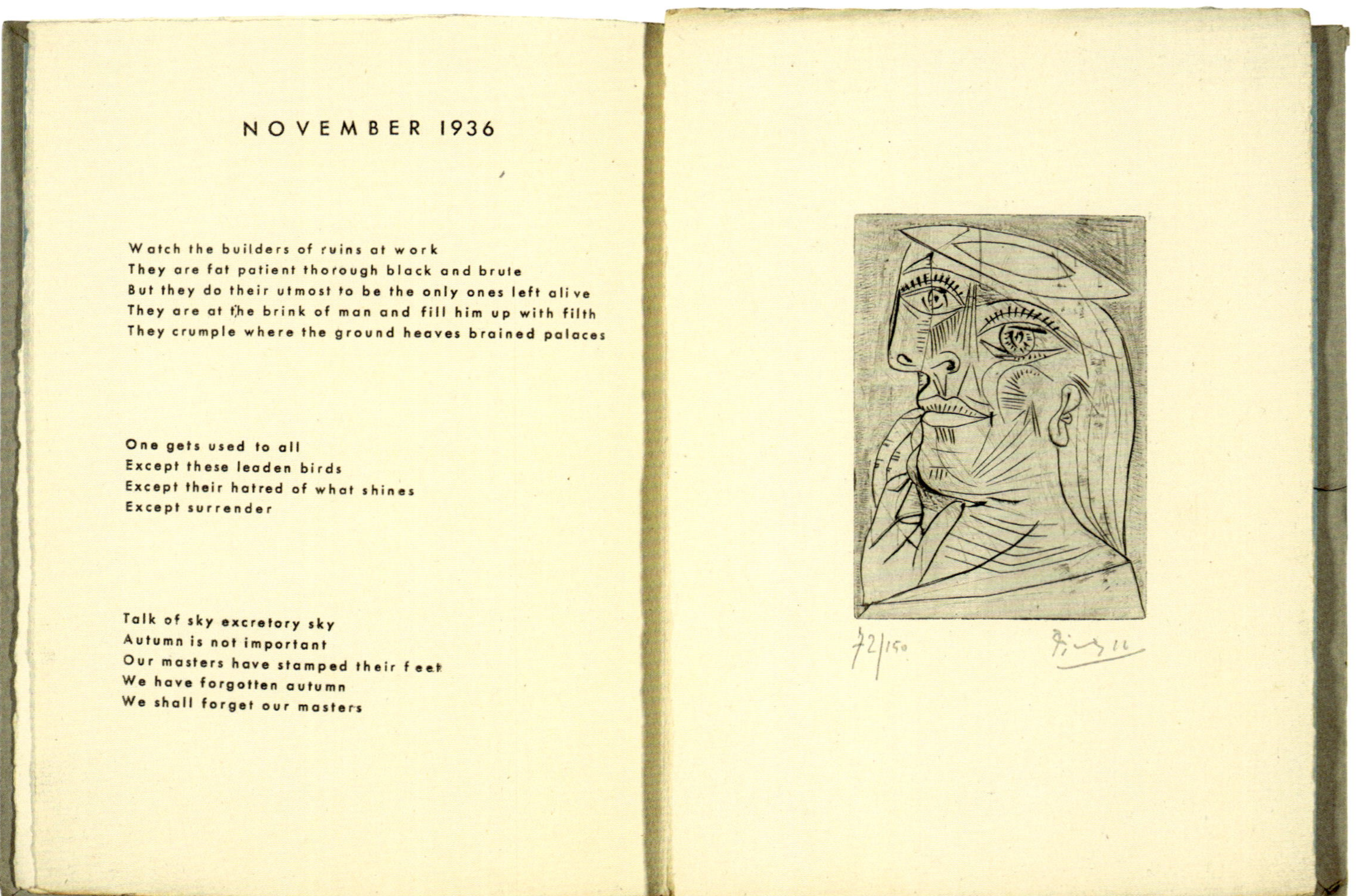

NOVEMBER 1936

Watch the builders of ruins at work
They are fat patient thorough black and brute
But they do their utmost to be the only ones left alive
They are at the brink of man and fill him up with filth
They crumple where the ground heaves brained palaces

One gets used to all
Except these leaden birds
Except their hatred of what shines
Except surrender

Talk of sky excretory sky
Autumn is not important
Our masters have stamped their feet
We have forgotten autumn
We shall forget our masters

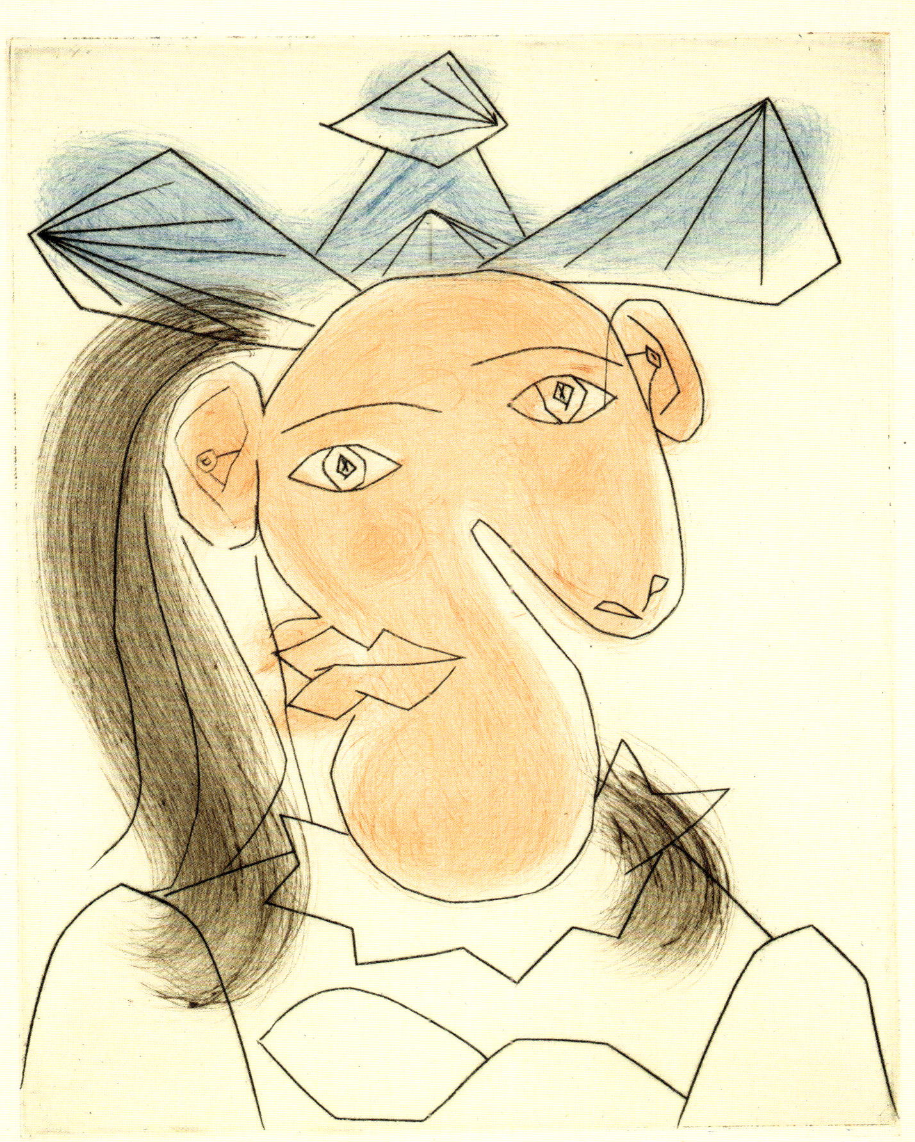

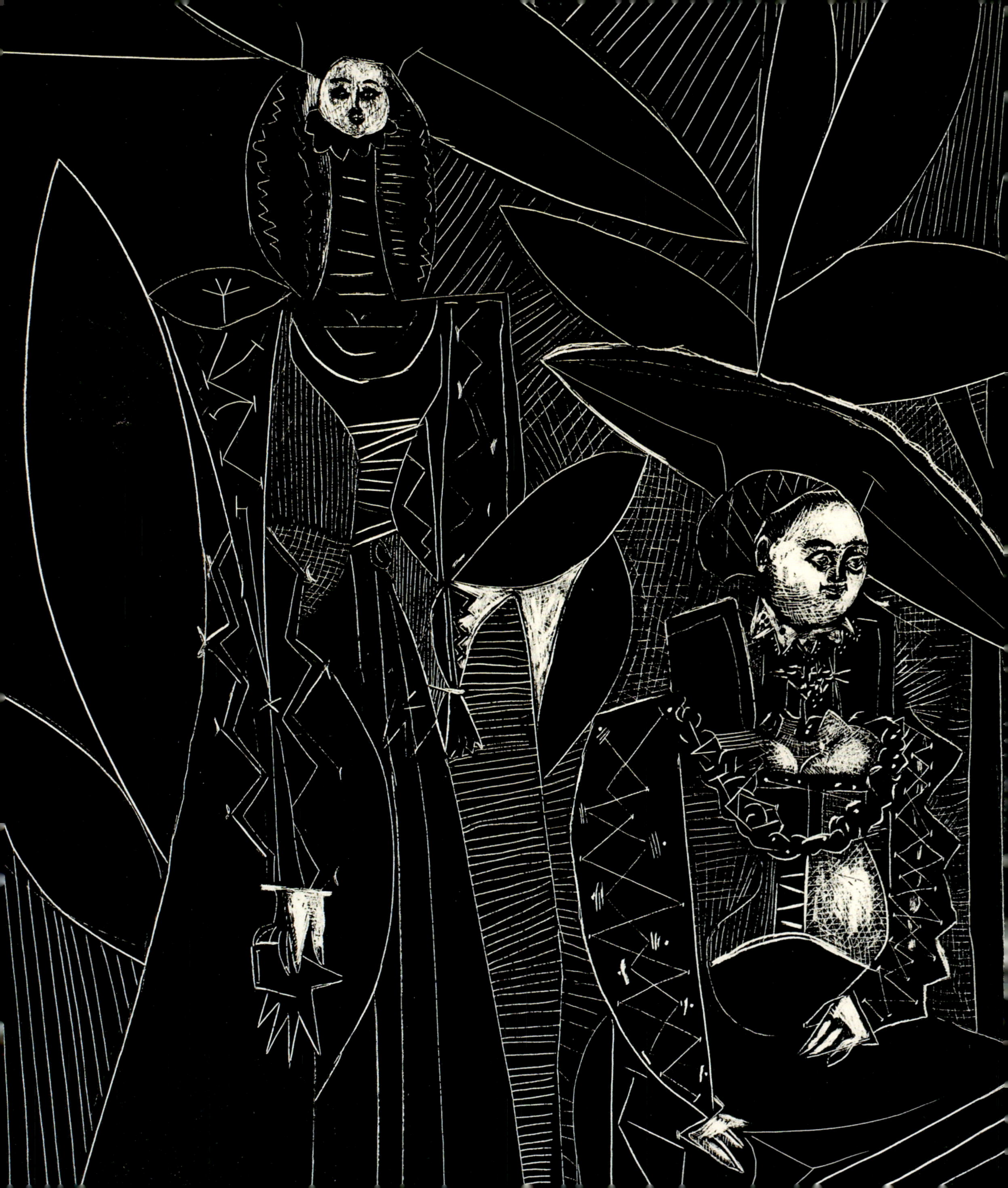

LITHOGRAPHS

*The movement of my thought interests me more
than the thought itself.*

Following the Second World War, Picasso began
to work with the lithographer Fernand Mourlot.
From autumn 1945 to early 1946, he spent most
days in Mourlot's Paris studio, exploring the
possibilities of the medium. This section focuses
on Picasso's post-war lithographs, beginning with
some examples from those intensive first months.
Lithography, a technique that involves drawing
or painting onto a stone or plate, allowed Picasso
to work rapidly and to make significant changes
to an image, which he could print progressively
in 'states' as the composition developed. The three
states of *David and Bathsheba* (1947–9, see
pp. 80–1, 83), a lithograph based on a work by
the German painter Lucas Cranach the Elder
(1472–1553), show how radically different the
states could appear.

After Picasso left Paris for the South of France
in 1948, he continued to work with Mourlot by
visiting the studio on trips to the city or sending
plates back to be printed. His later lithographs
in this section reflect his new life in the heat
and light of the south. *Composition* and *Figure*

(both 1948, pp. 84–5) are representations of
Picasso's new partner, the artist Françoise Gilot,
while *Gardens at Vallauris* (1953, p. 87) depicts
the elaborate gardens around their home on
the French Riviera. *The artist and child* (1949,
p. 88) shows Françoise painting at an easel with
their son, Claude, playing at her feet. A poignant
echo comes in 1954 with the colour lithograph
The little artist (p. 89), an image of Françoise
and their two children on a visit to see Picasso
after the relationship had broken down. Picasso
also continued to make etchings and aquatints
including *The picador* (1952, p. 92), which reflects
his continuing interest in bullfights. When he visited
England in 1950 and was invited to contribute
a drawing to the visitor book of the Institute of
Contemporary Arts, it was leaping bulls that he
chose to depict (p. 93).

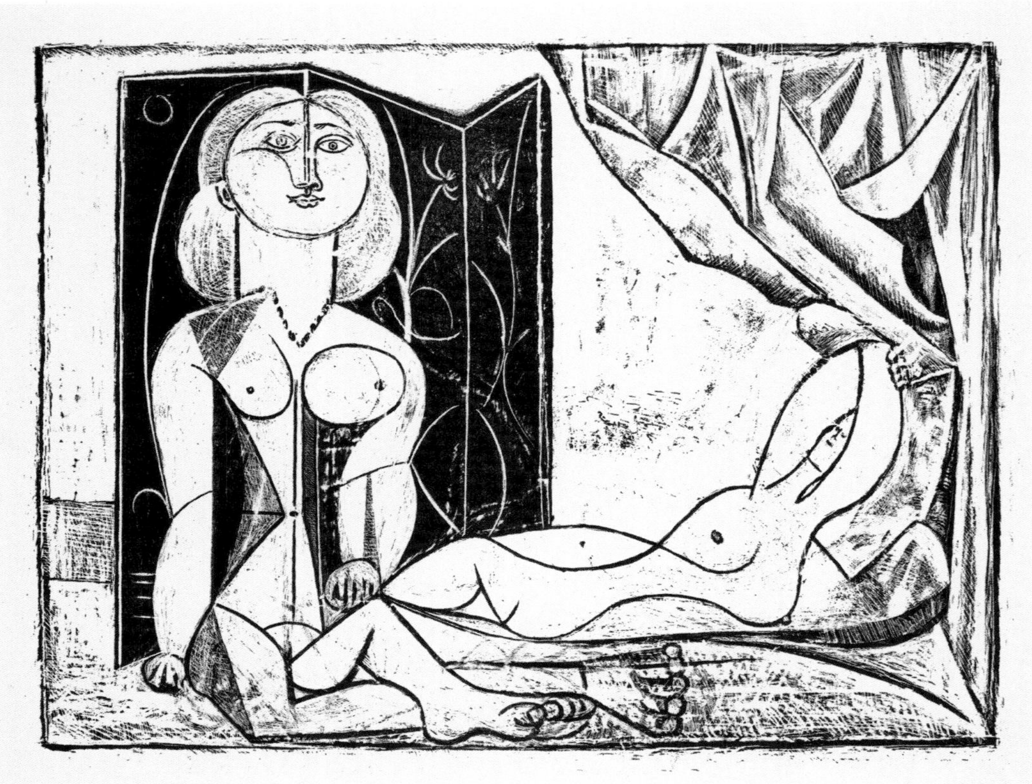

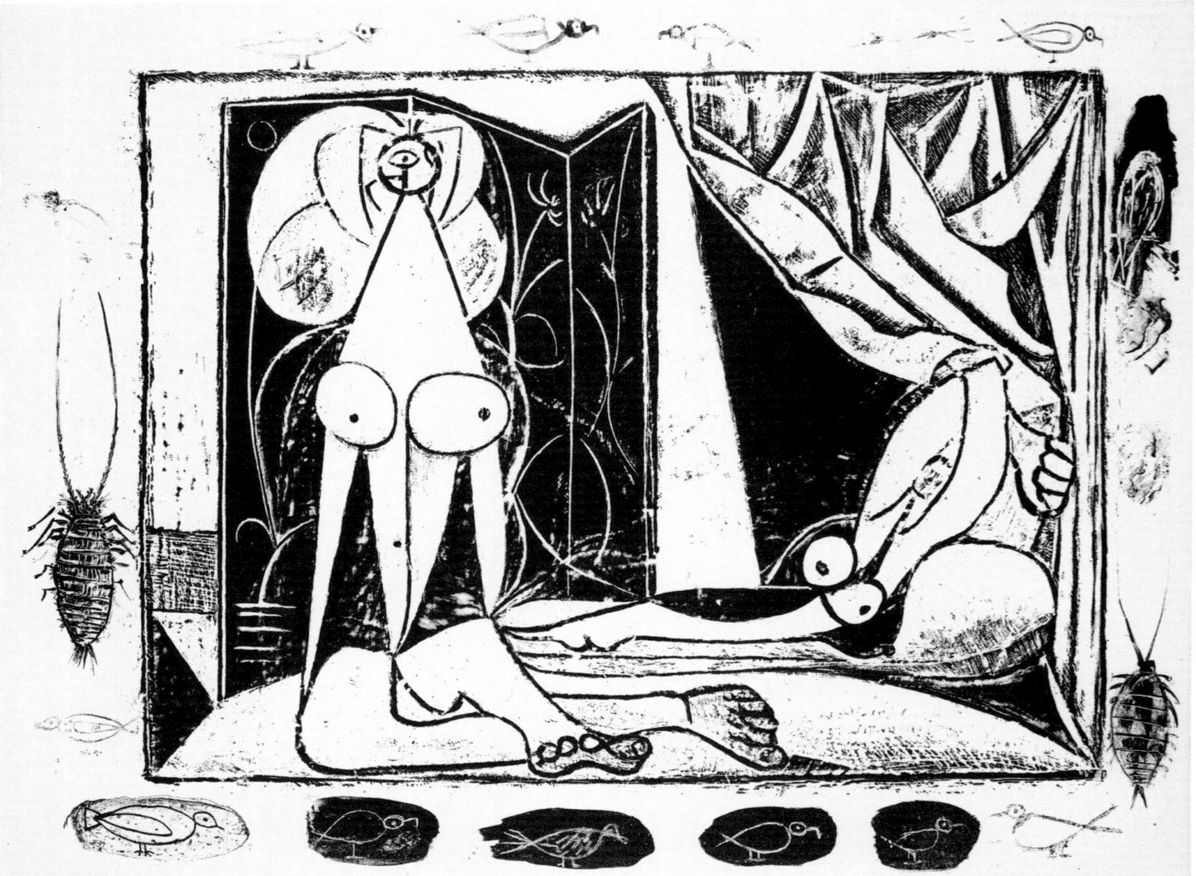

Two nude women, 13th state, 25 January 1946
Lithograph

Two nude women, 18th state, 12 February 1946
Lithograph

Eight silhouettes, 13 January 1946
Lithograph

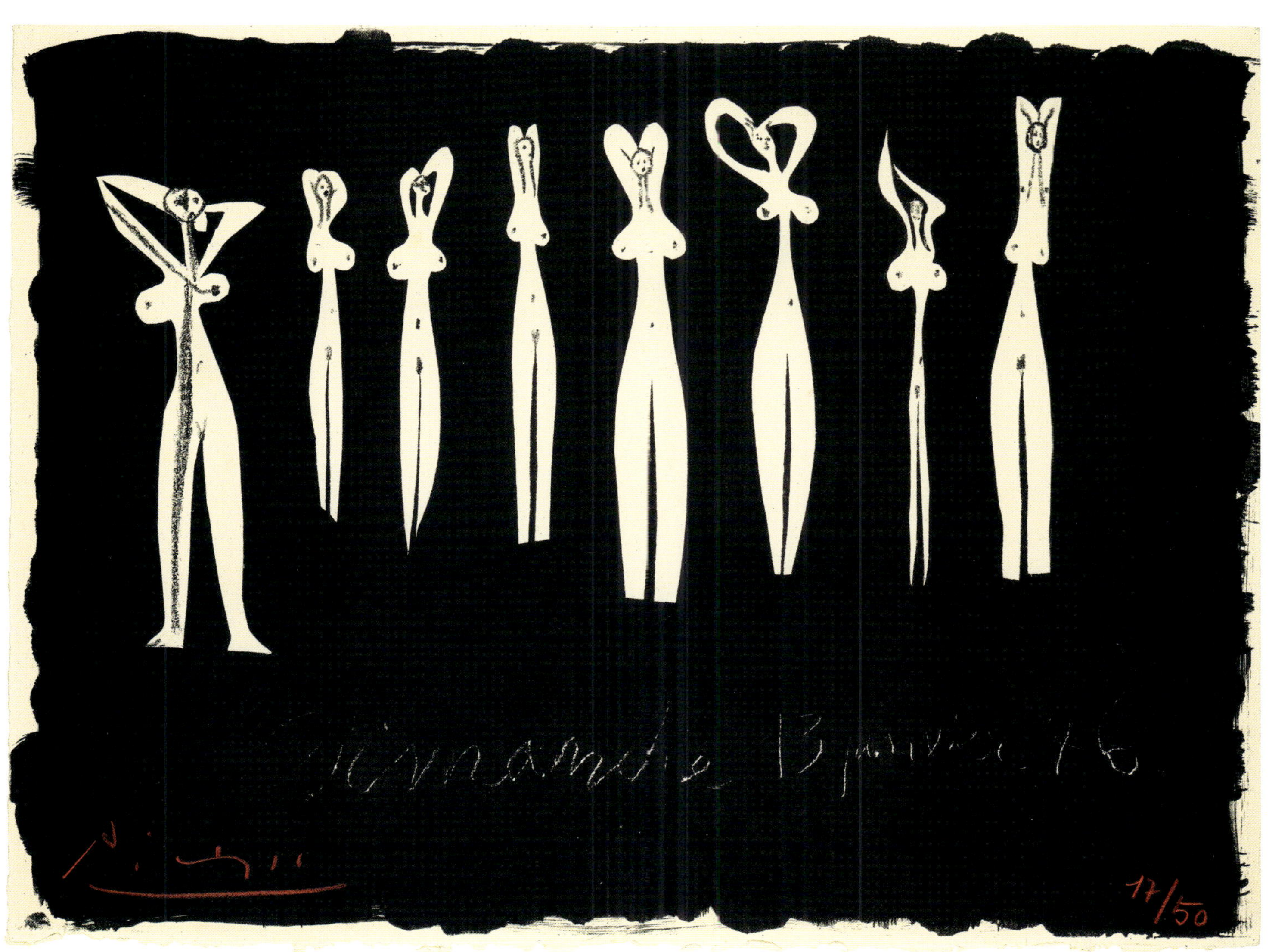

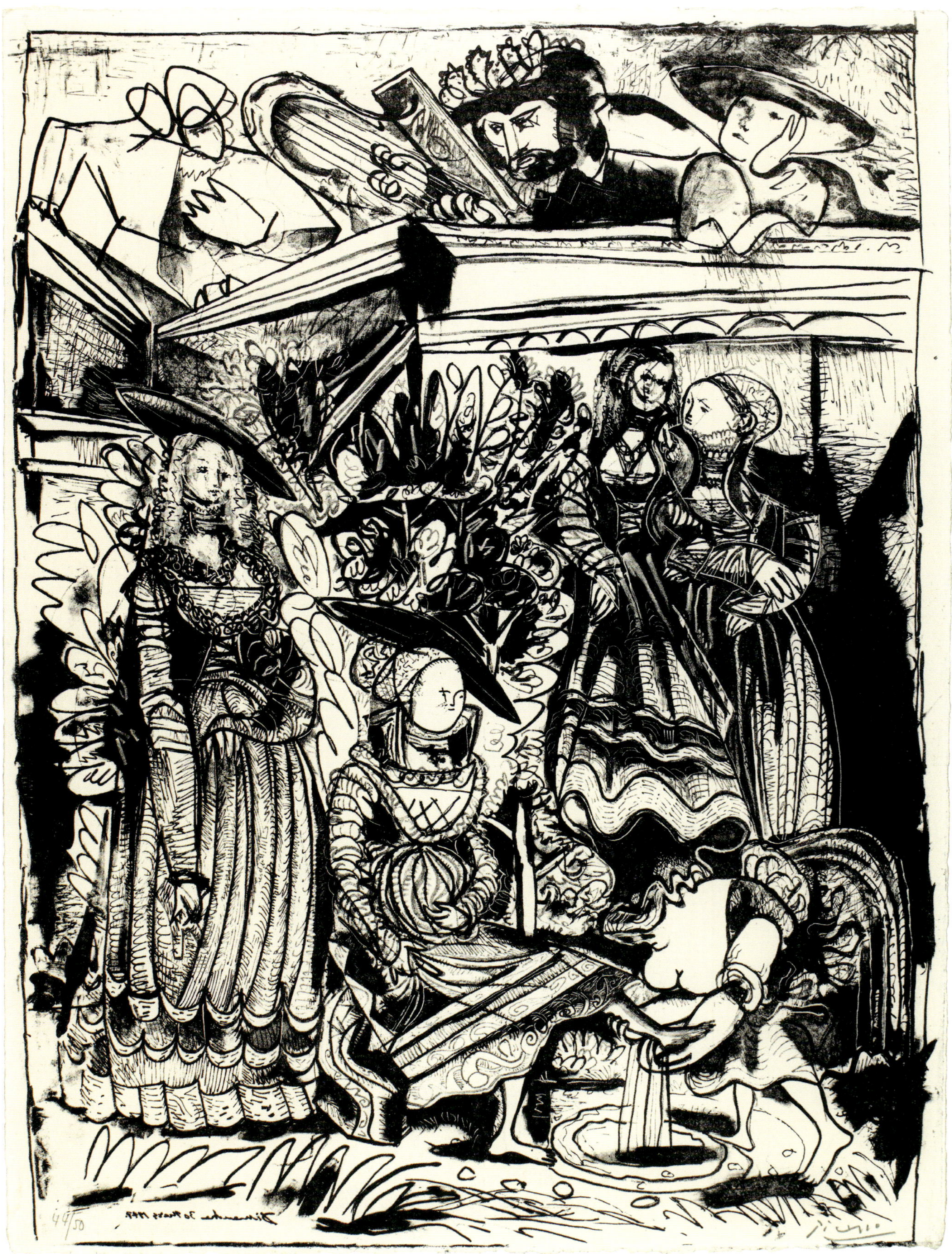

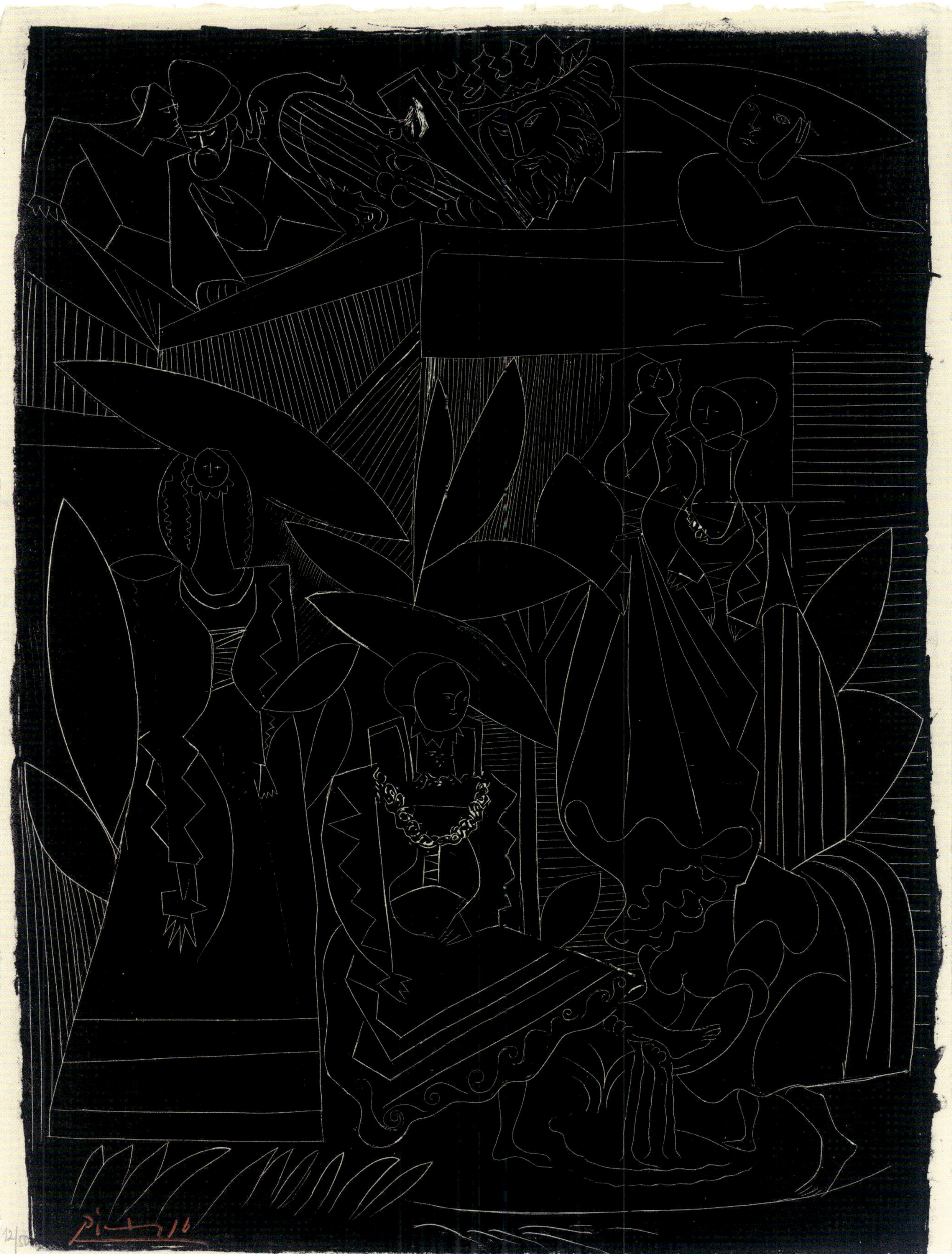
12/50
Picasso

Page 80:
David and Bathsheba, 2nd state, 30 March 1947
Lithograph

Page 81:
David and Bathsheba, 4th state, 30 March 1947
Lithograph

David and Bathsheba, 8th state, 10 April 1949
Lithograph

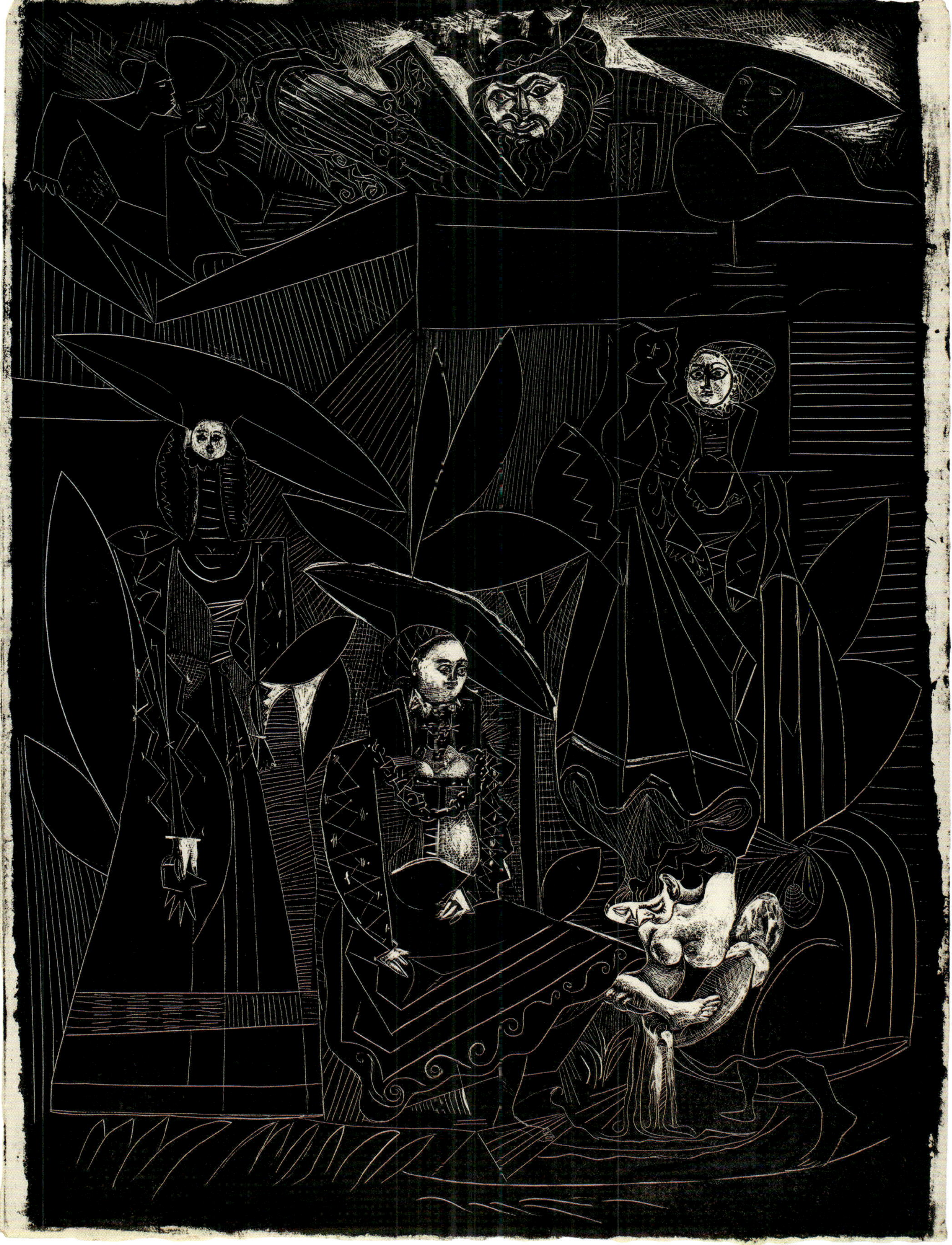

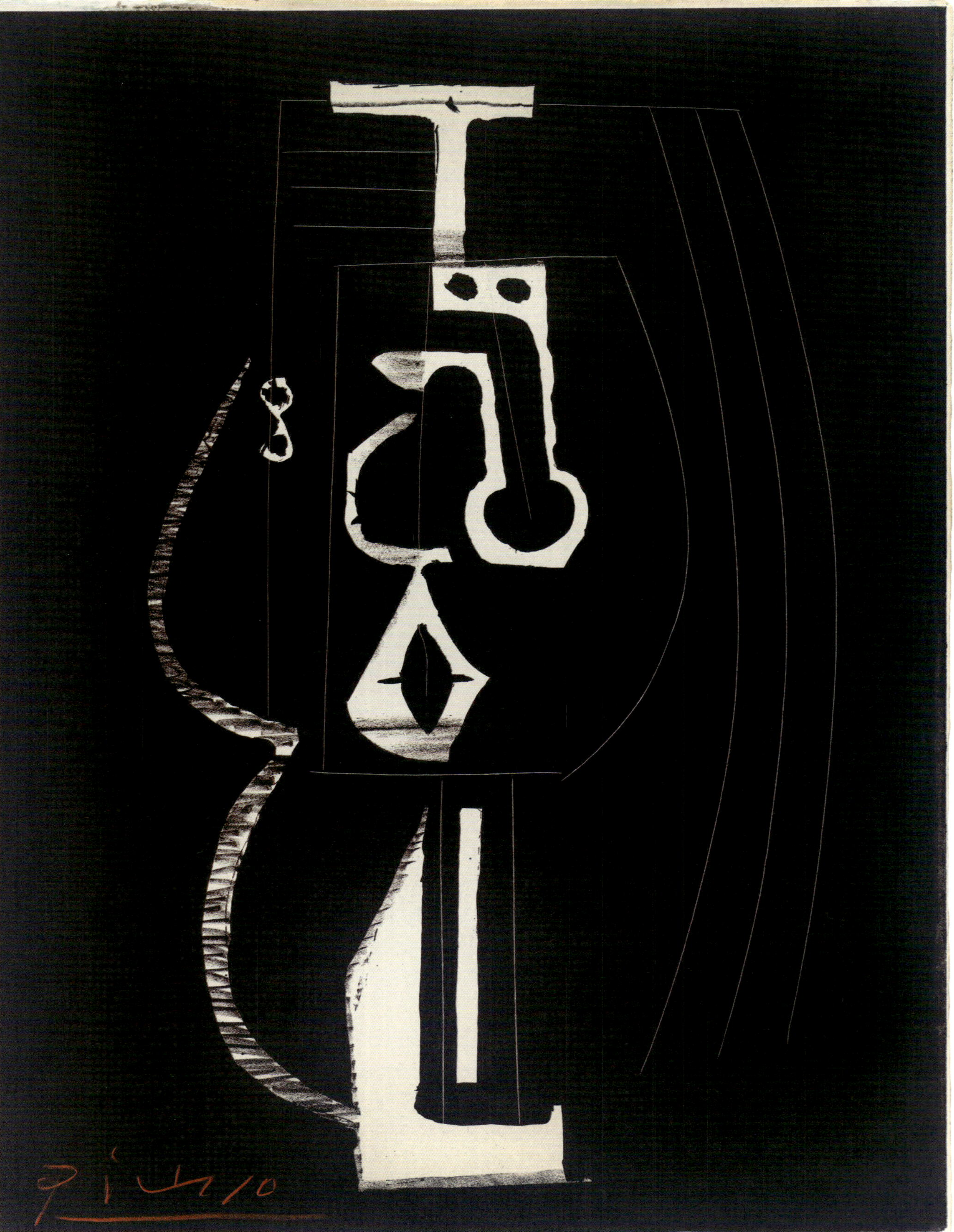

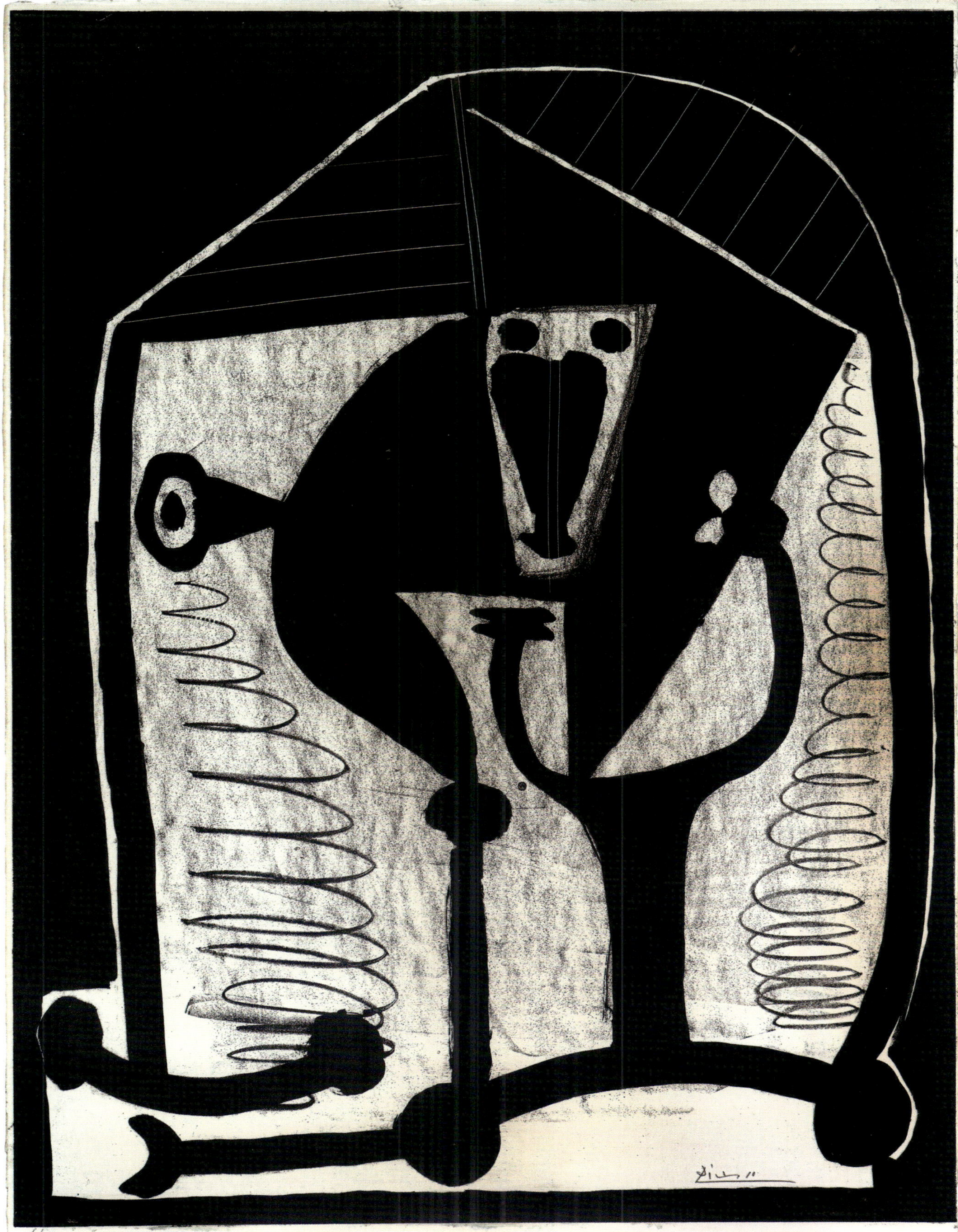
6/50

Women on the beach, 11 May 1947
Transfer lithograph

Gardens at Vallauris, 15 January 1953
Crayon lithograph

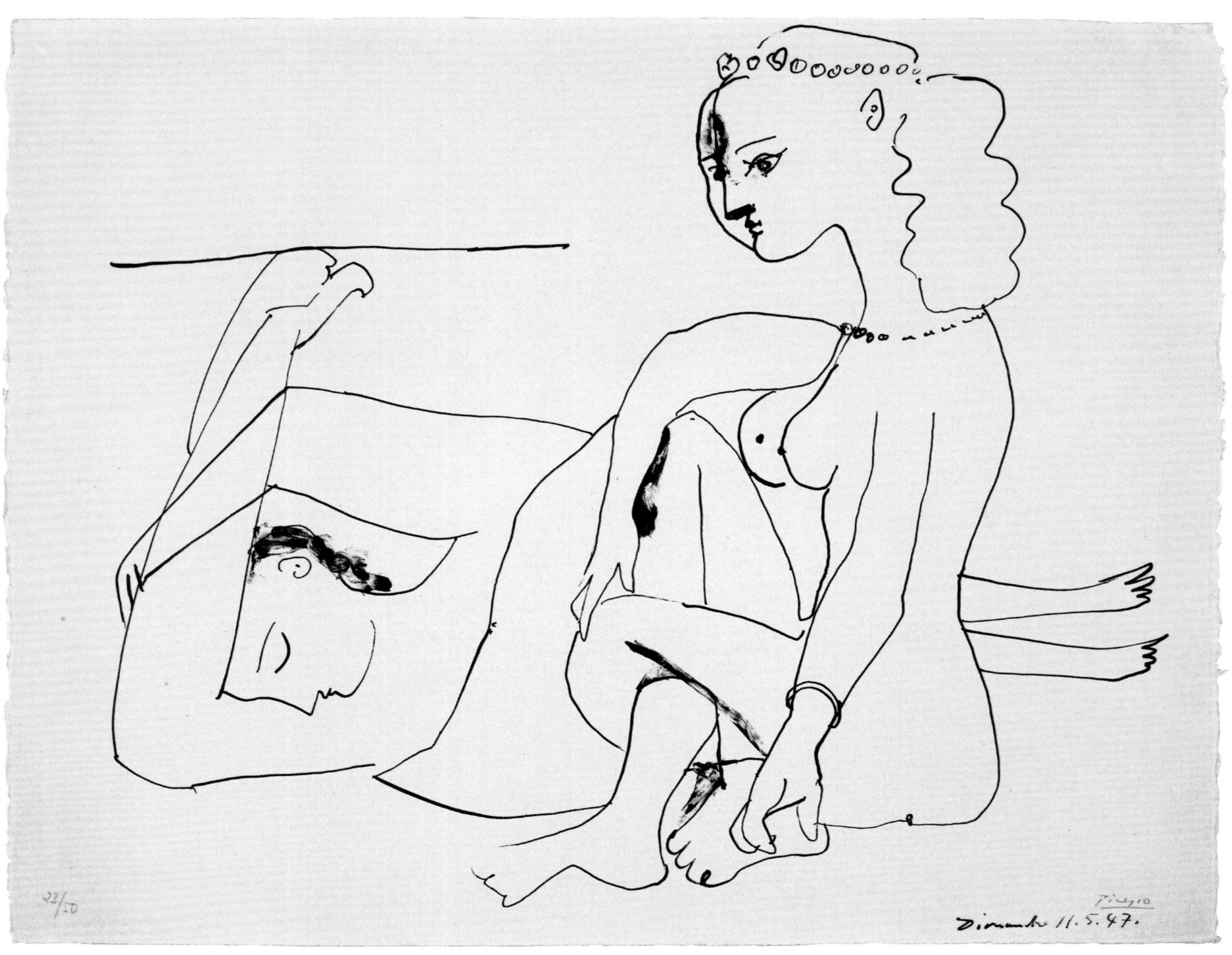

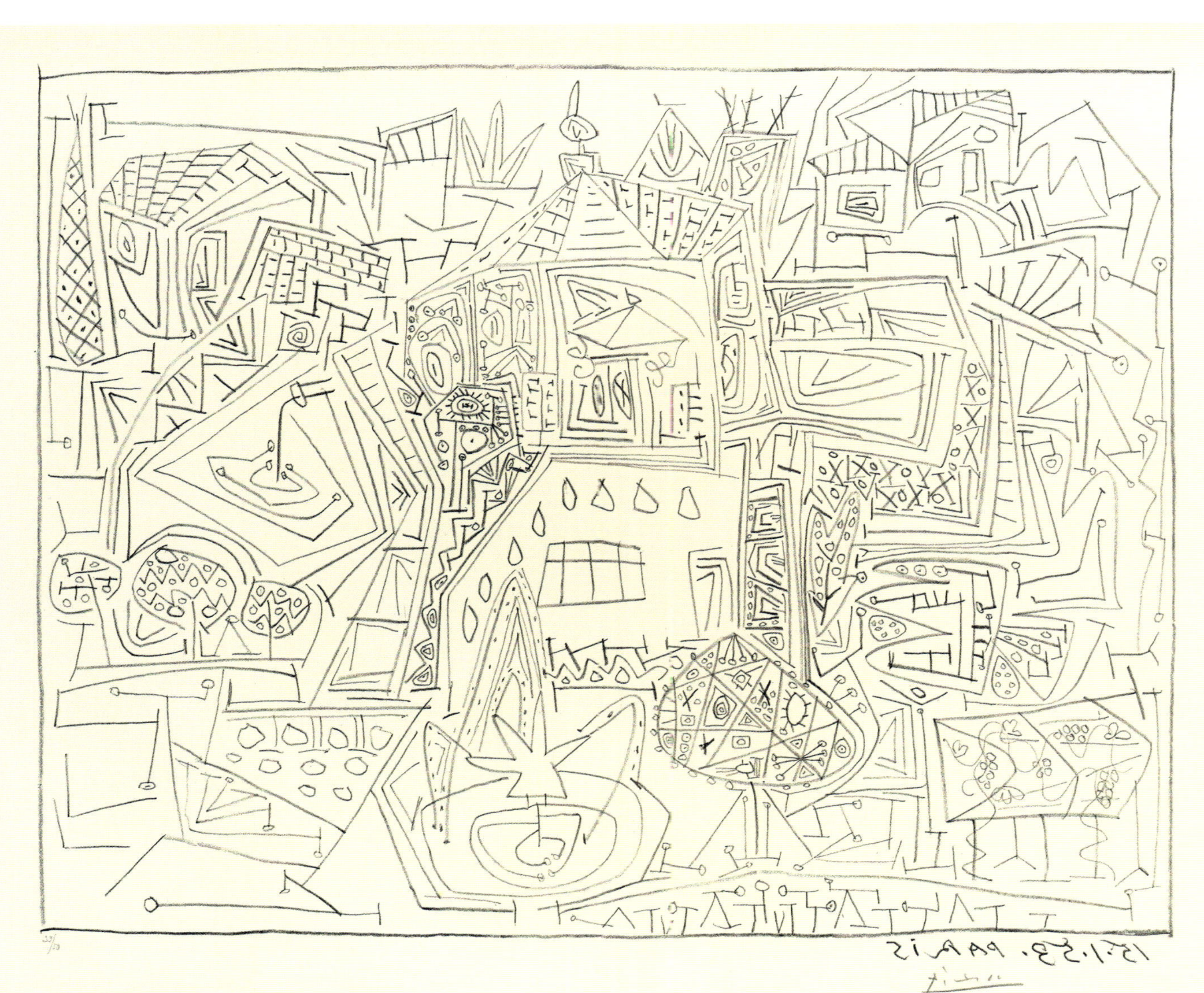

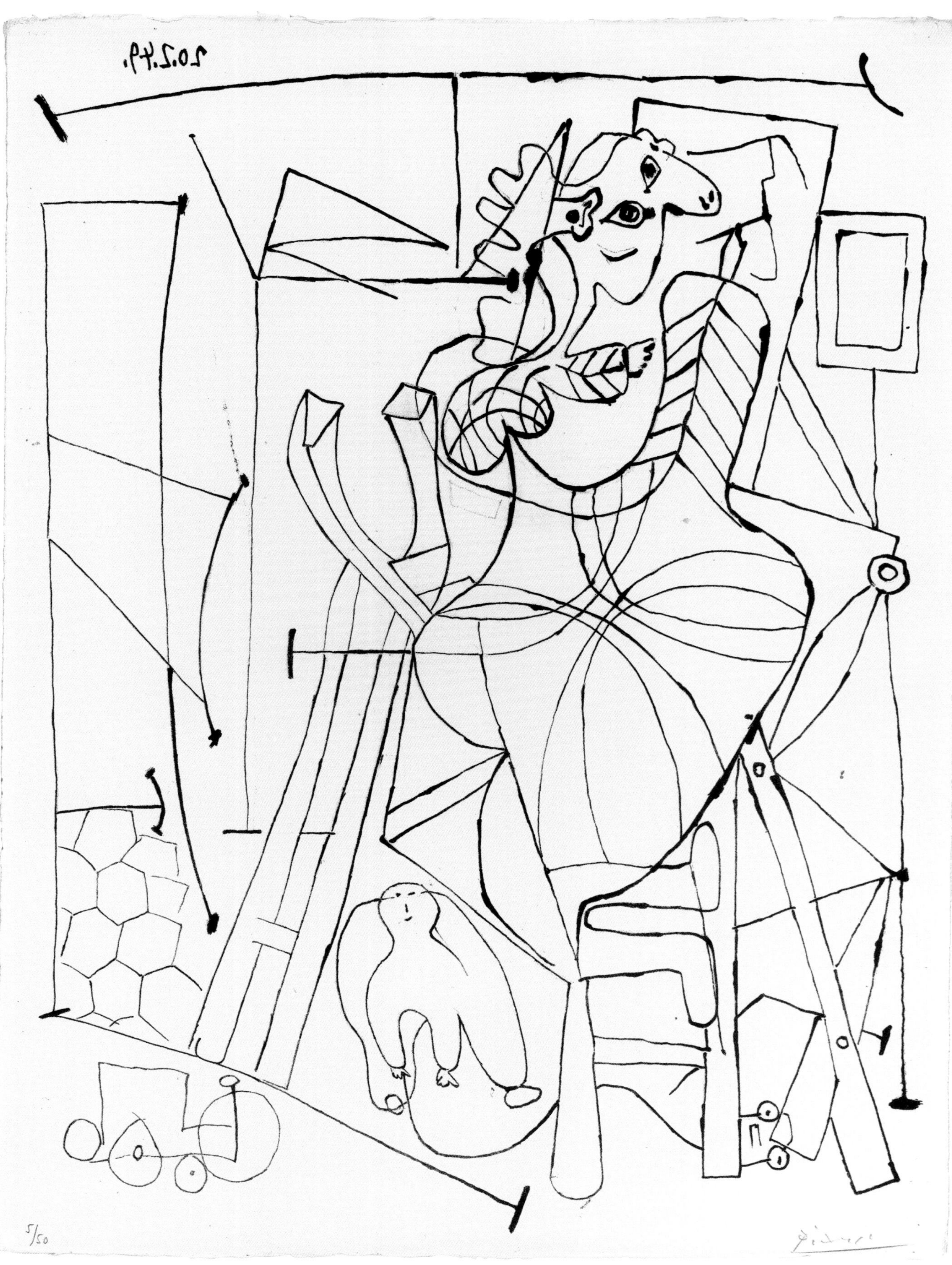

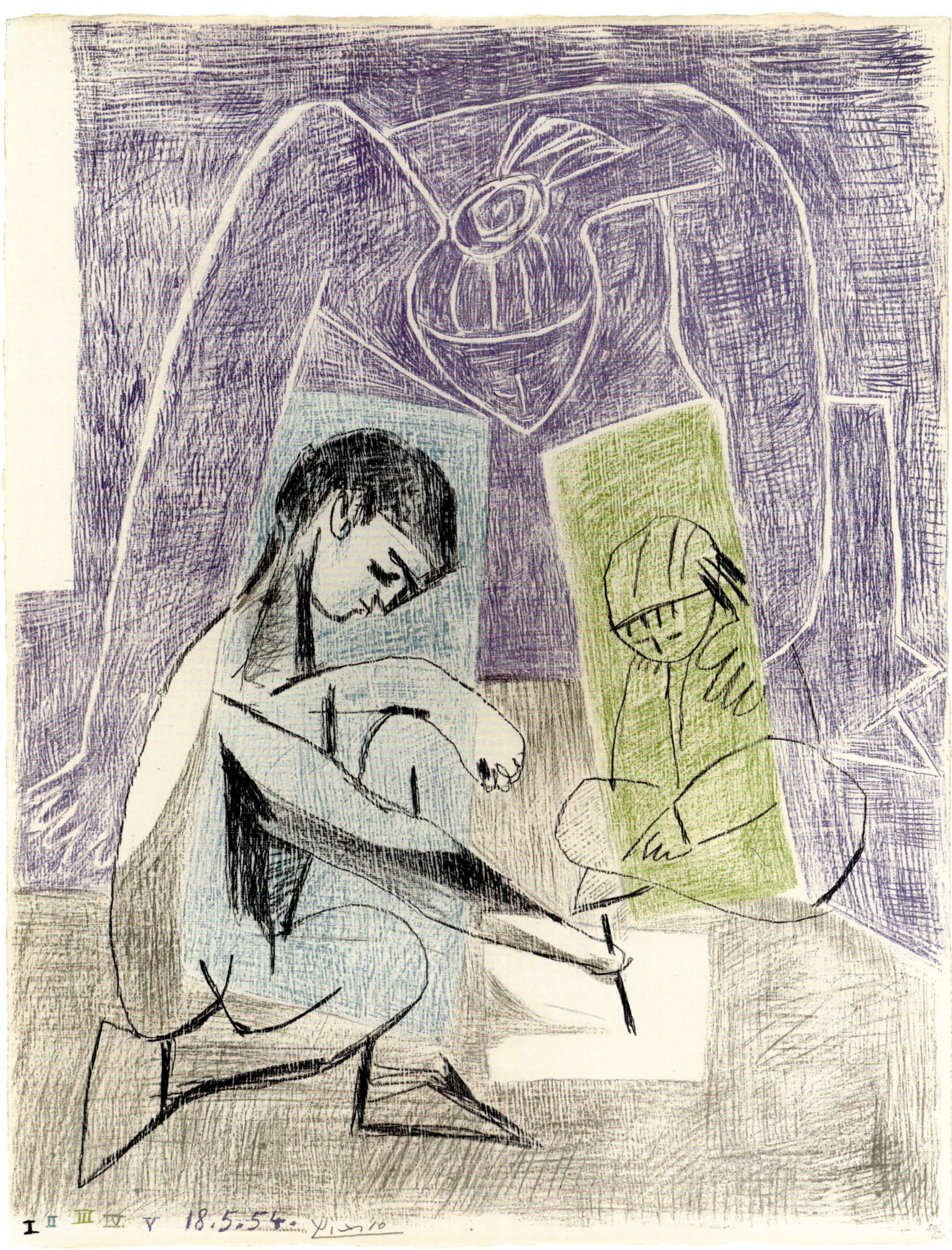
I II III IV V 18.5.54. Picasso

Page 88:
The artist and child, 20 February 1949
Pen lithograph

Page 89:
The little artist, 18 May 1954
Colour crayon transfer lithograph

Bust of a woman with pony-tail: Jacqueline,
19 March 1955
Sugar aquatint with spit-bite

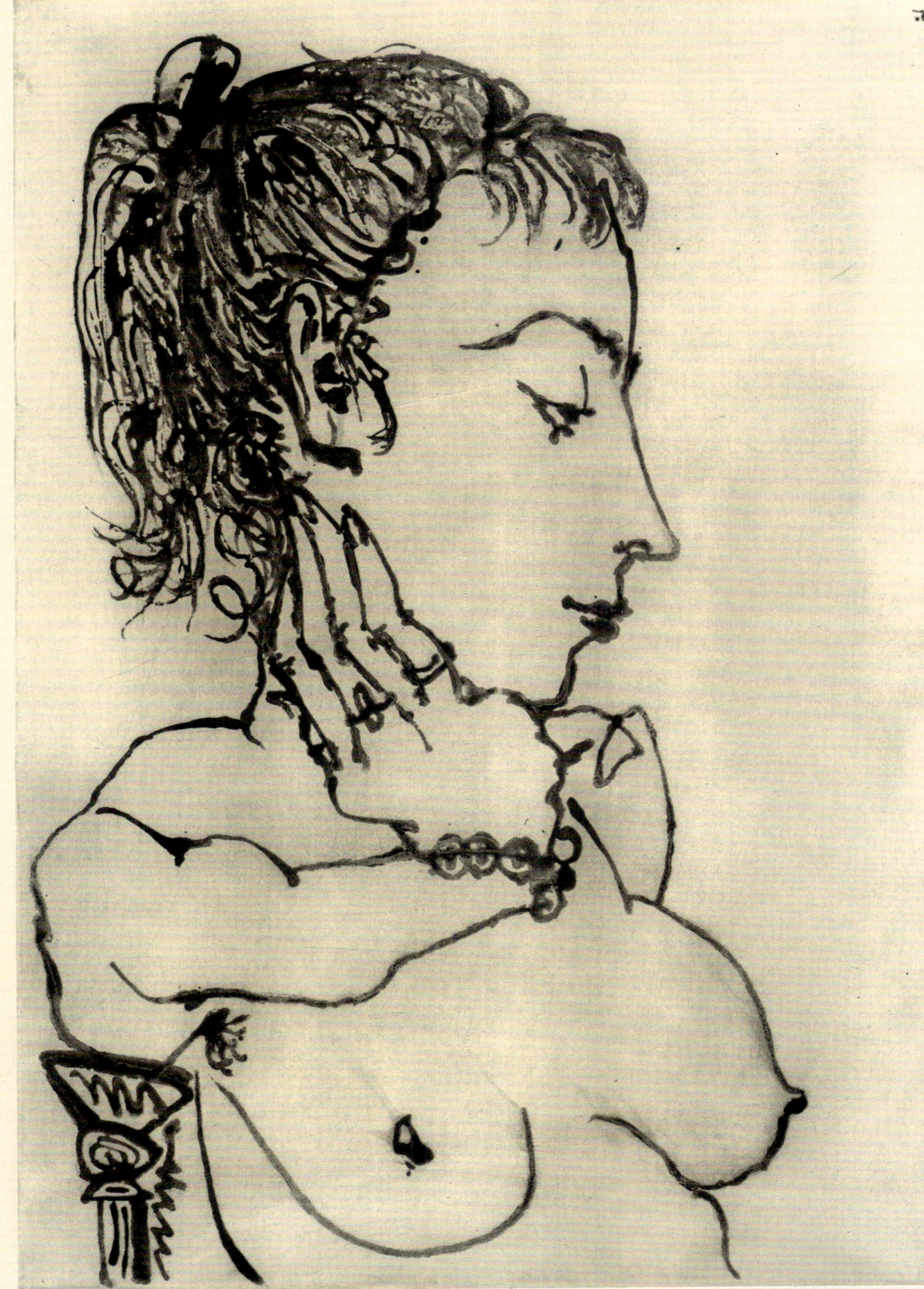

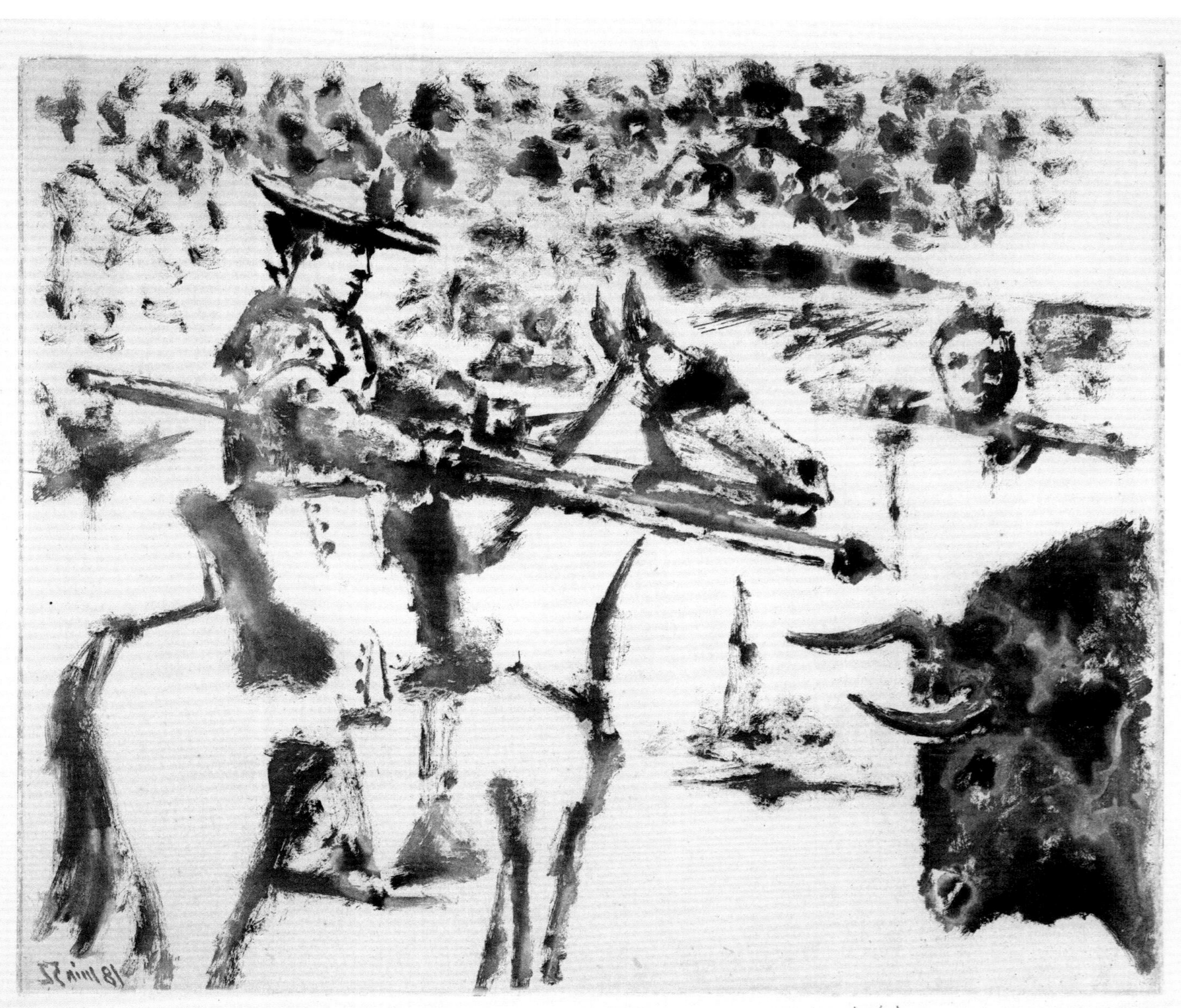
18 juin 52
Bon à tirer Picasso

The picador, 18 June 1952
Sugar aquatint and etching

Leaping bulls from the Institute of Contemporary
Art Visitors' Book, 1950
Watercolour and coloured inks

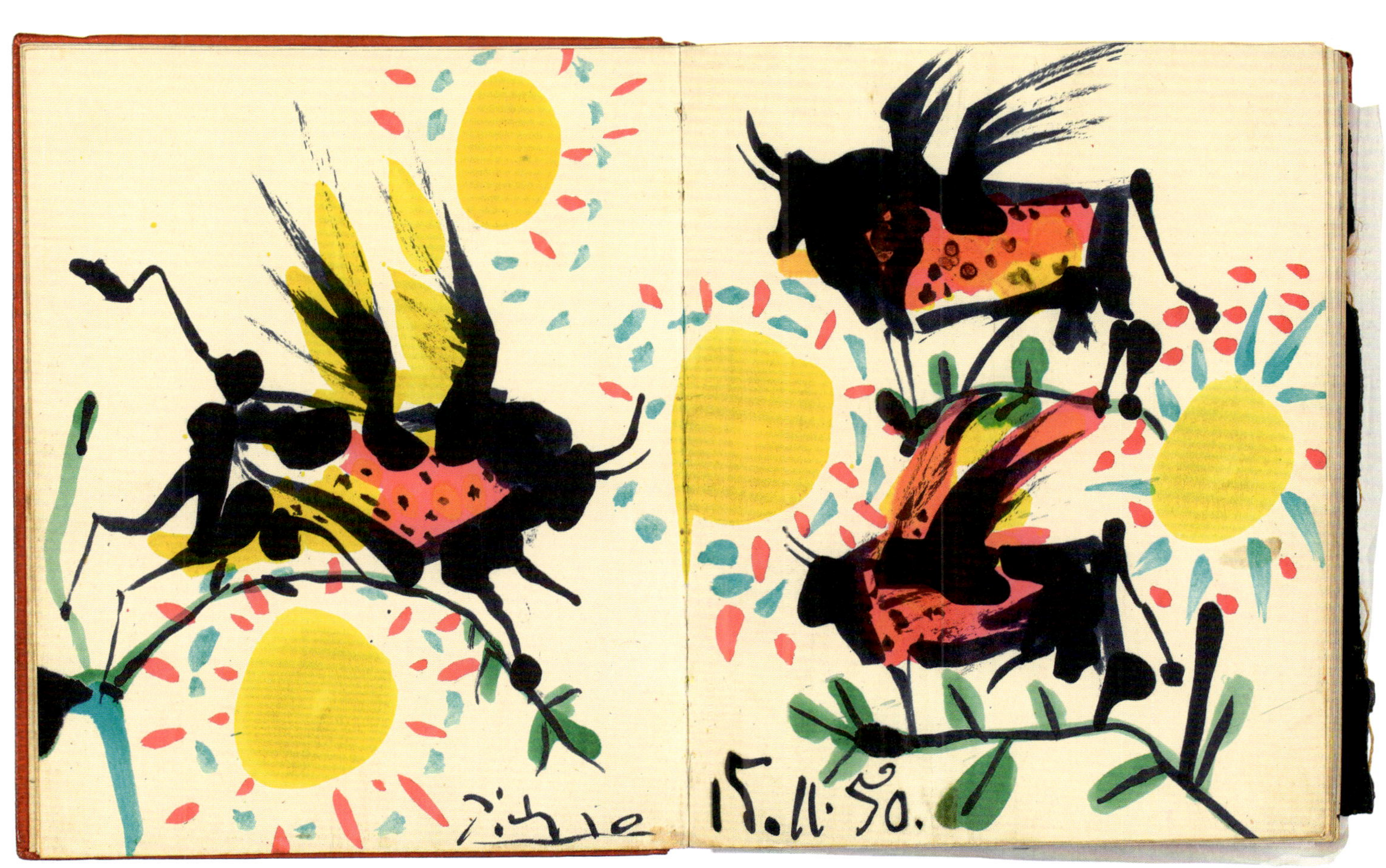

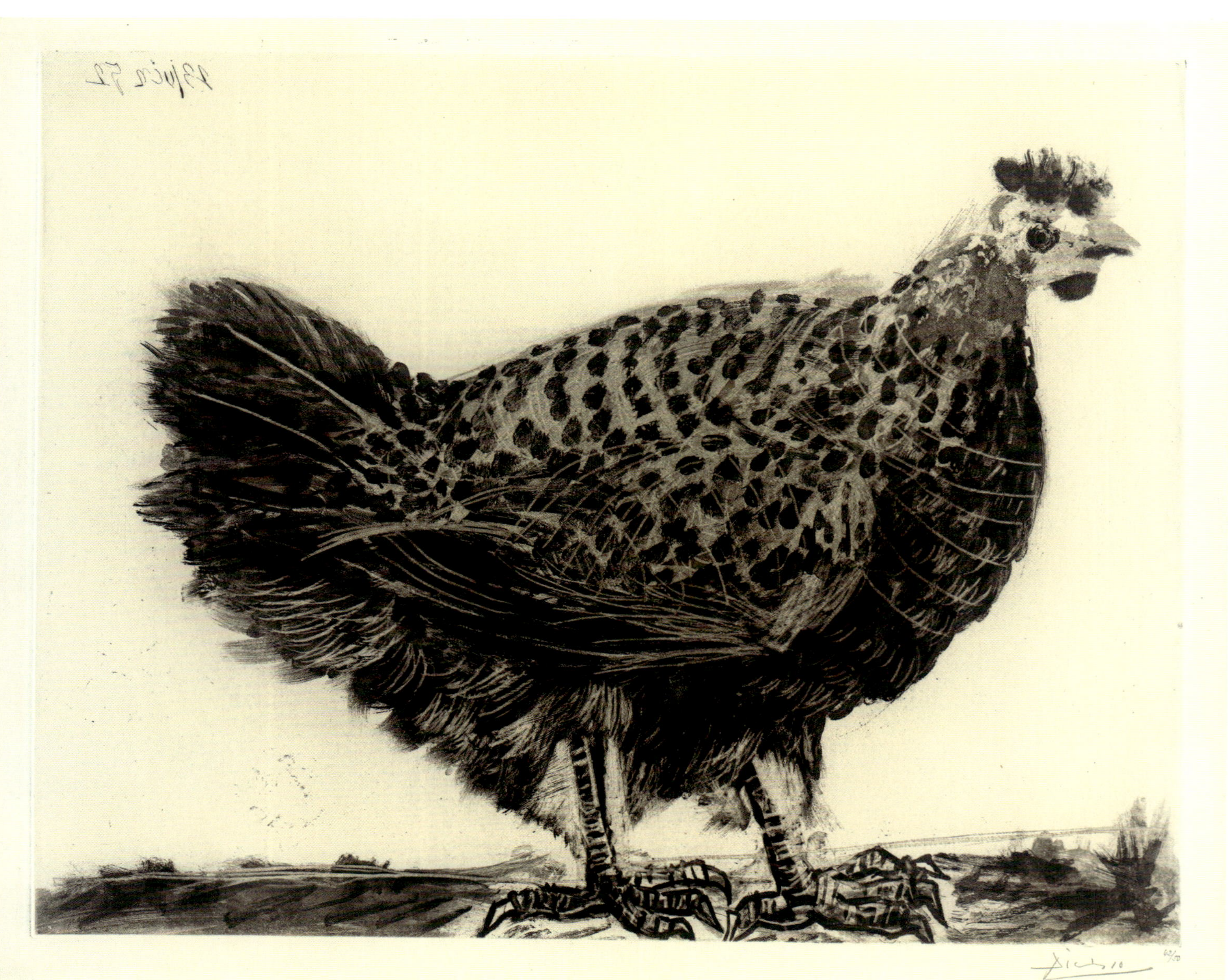

The hen, 23, 25 June 1952
Sugar aquatint and scraper

White pigeon on black background,
4 February 1947
Transfer lithograph

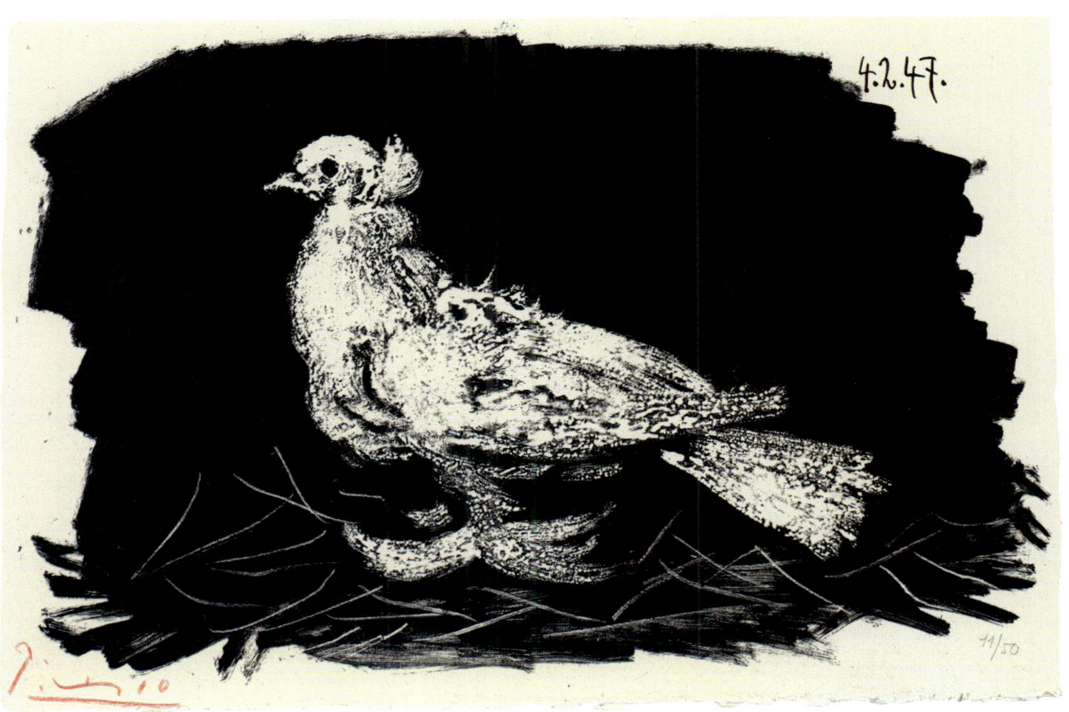

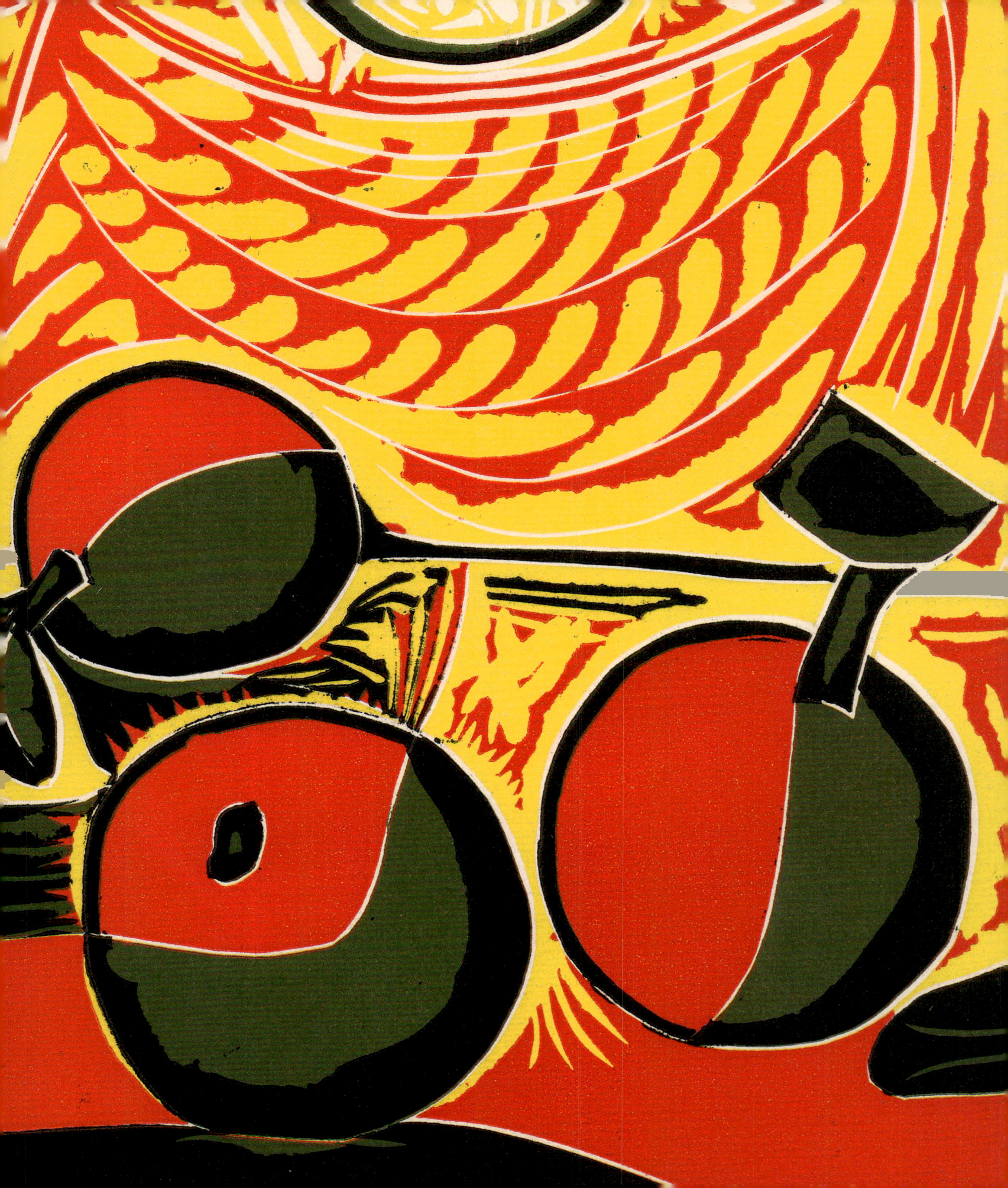

LINOCUTS

If the subjects I have wanted to express have suggested different ways of expression I have never hesitated to adopt them …

In the mid-1950s Picasso began to explore linocut printmaking, working with the local printer Hidalgo Arnéra. Picasso initially worked with Arnéra on posters for annual ceramics exhibitions in the town of Vallauris, home of the Madoura pottery, where Picasso began to make ceramics of his own in 1947. The majority of the linocuts in this section are from the years 1959 to 1962 when he concentrated most intensely on the technique. Many of Picasso's linocuts are printed in monochrome or earthy colours and explore themes from his personal repertoire, including bullfighting, female nudes and mythological scenes. *Bacchanal with owl* (1959, p. 98), for example, depicts a group of naked figures cavorting, playing musical instruments and drinking in celebration of Bacchus, the ancient god of wine and fertility. The revellers are watched from above by an owl, a recurrent creature in Picasso's art. *Pike [Pike II]* (1959, p. 99) presents a picador on a horse spearing a bull with a pike.

Linocut printmaking requires the artist to cut away the negative space around an image, leaving the areas to be printed standing in relief. Traditionally, a linocut composed of more than one colour or layer is printed from multiple blocks. Picasso, however, preferred to use a method called 'reduction linocut printing', which involved printing all colours or layers from a single block as he progressively cut the image. The multicoloured linocut *Still life under the lamp* (1962, pp. 104–7) was produced in this way, using yellow, red, green and black. Picasso initially experimented with a cream background and a brown layer but discounted these colours from the final image. This section includes the progressive proofs of this print, as well as the spectacular final result. Picasso's portrait of his second wife Jacqueline Roque, *Woman with necklace* [*Portrait of Jacqueline with necklace, resting on her elbow*] (1959, p. 102), was also printed using this method.

Bacchanal with owl, 2 December 1959
Linocut in caramel on black

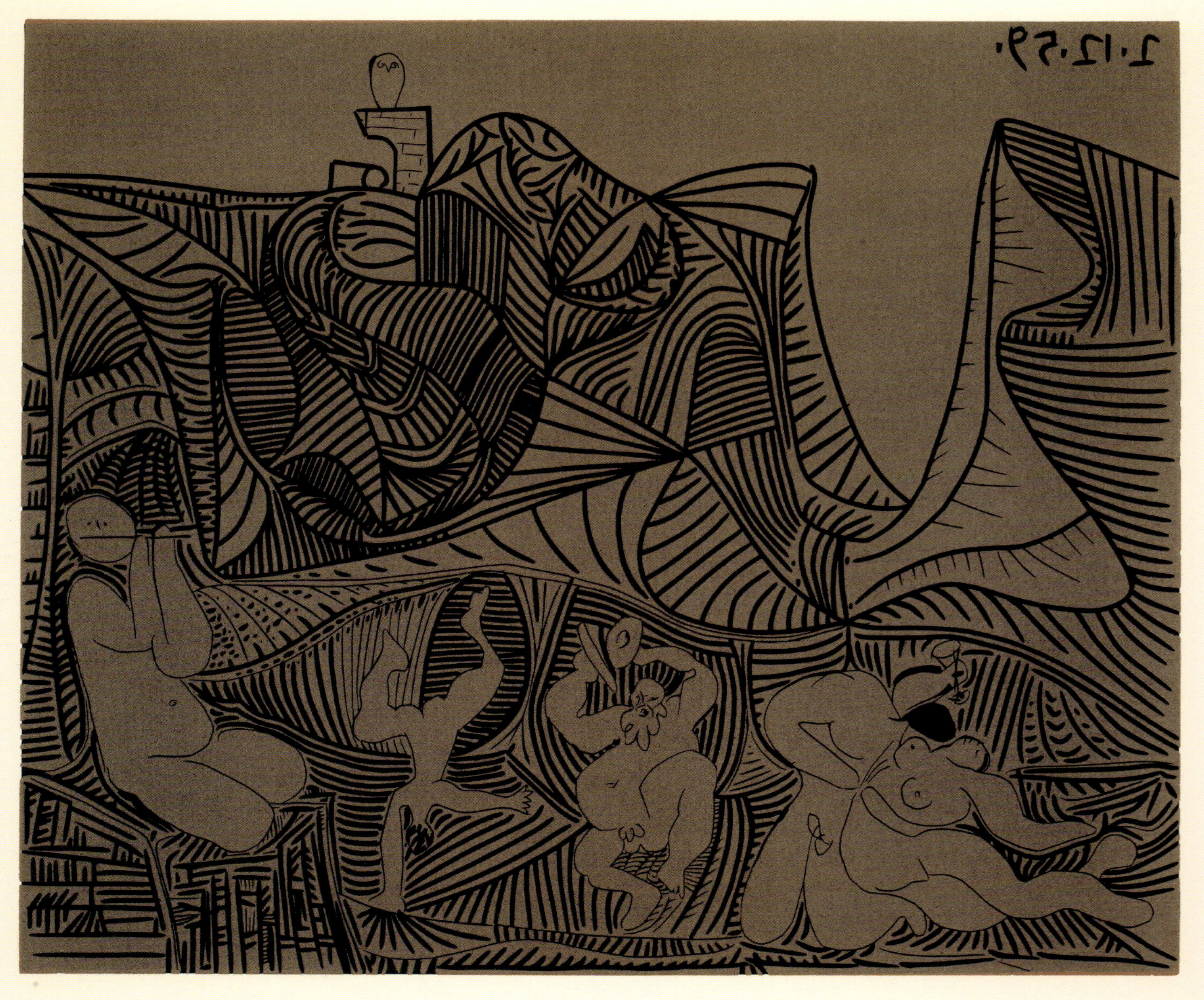

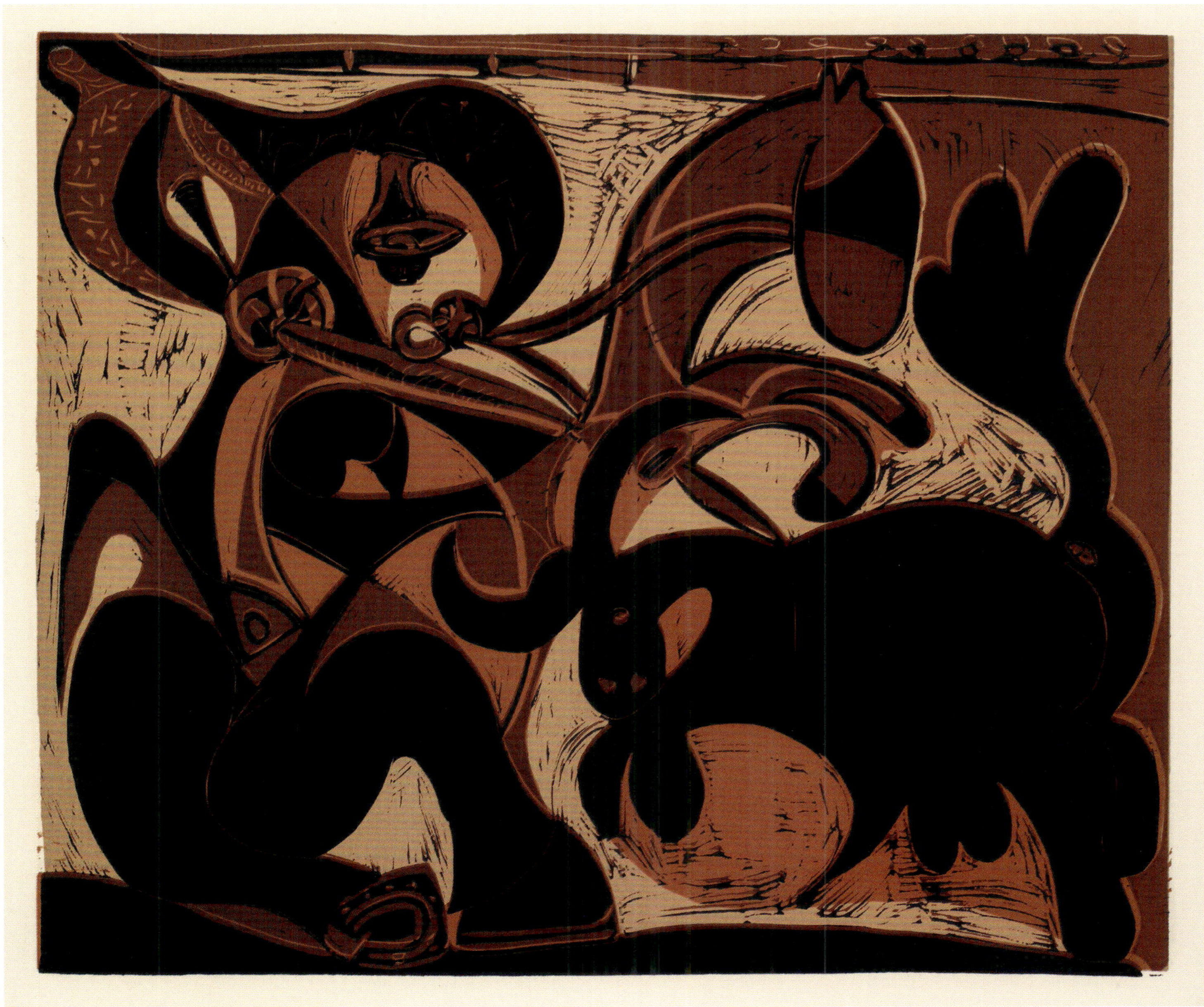

Pike II, 31 August–31 October 1959
Colour linocut

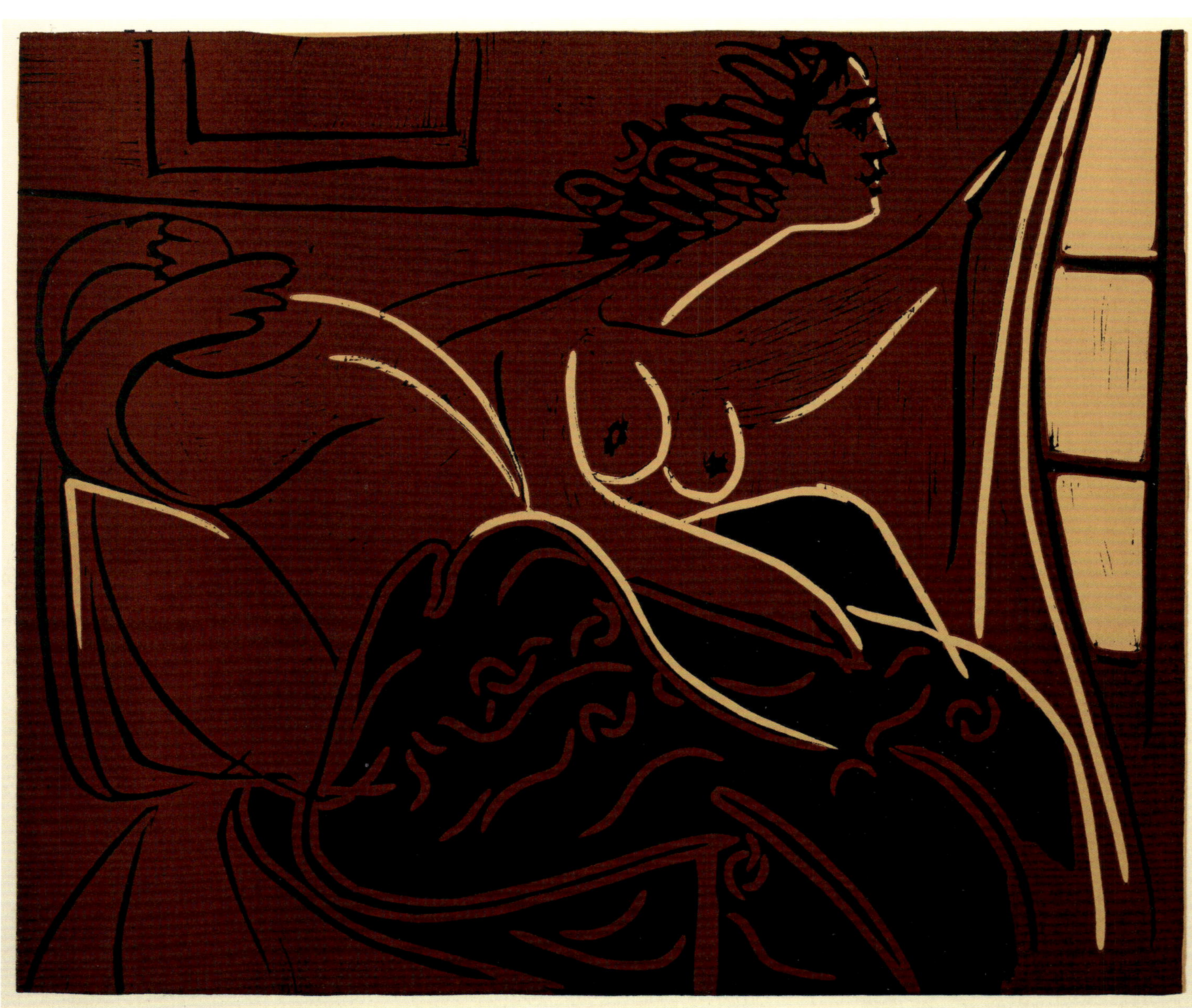

Two women waking up, 8 November 1959,
printed 1960
Linocut in light caramel, dark brown and black

Two women waking up, printed 3 January 1964
Linocut in white ink, brushed over with Indian ink
wash and rinsed

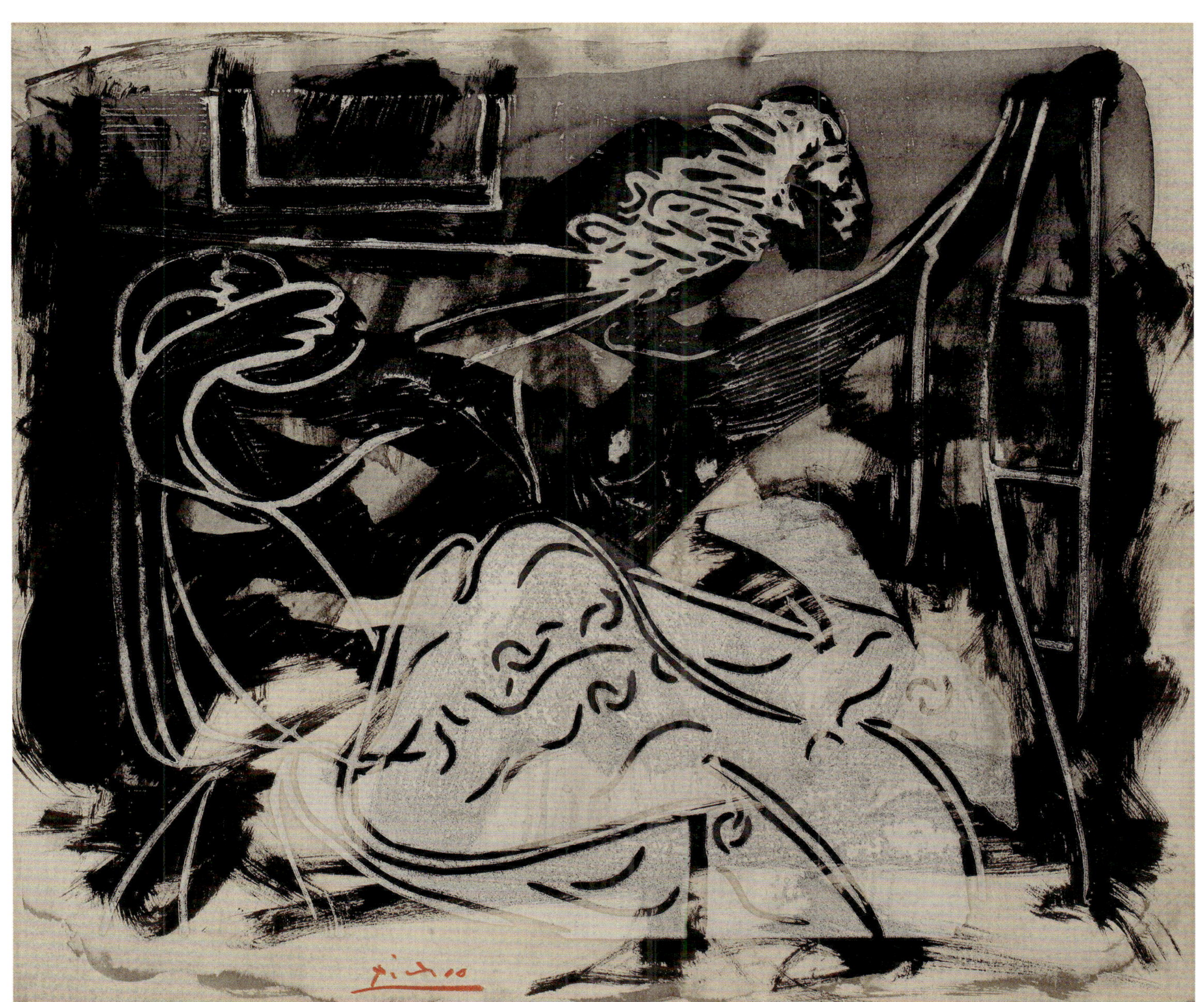

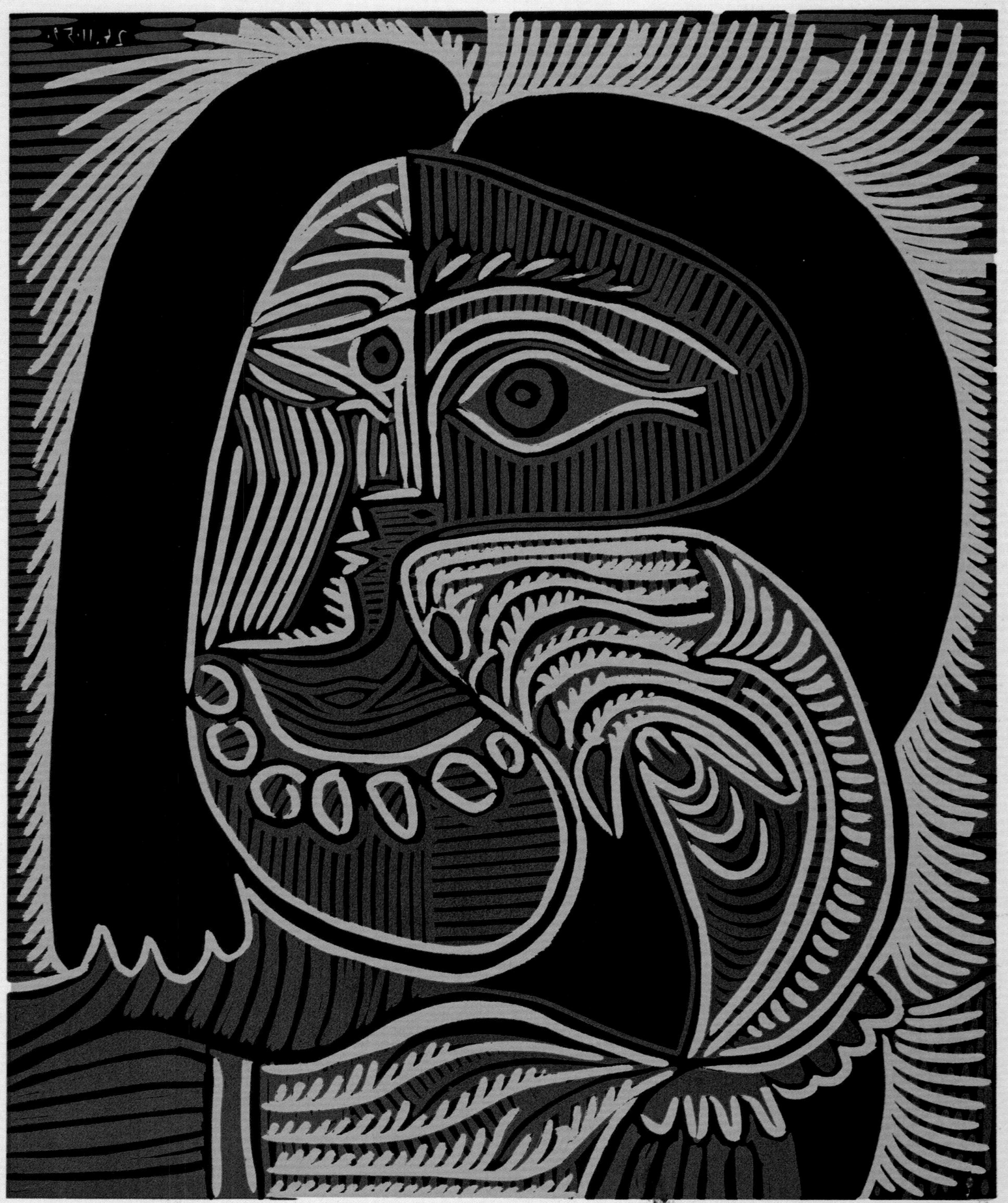

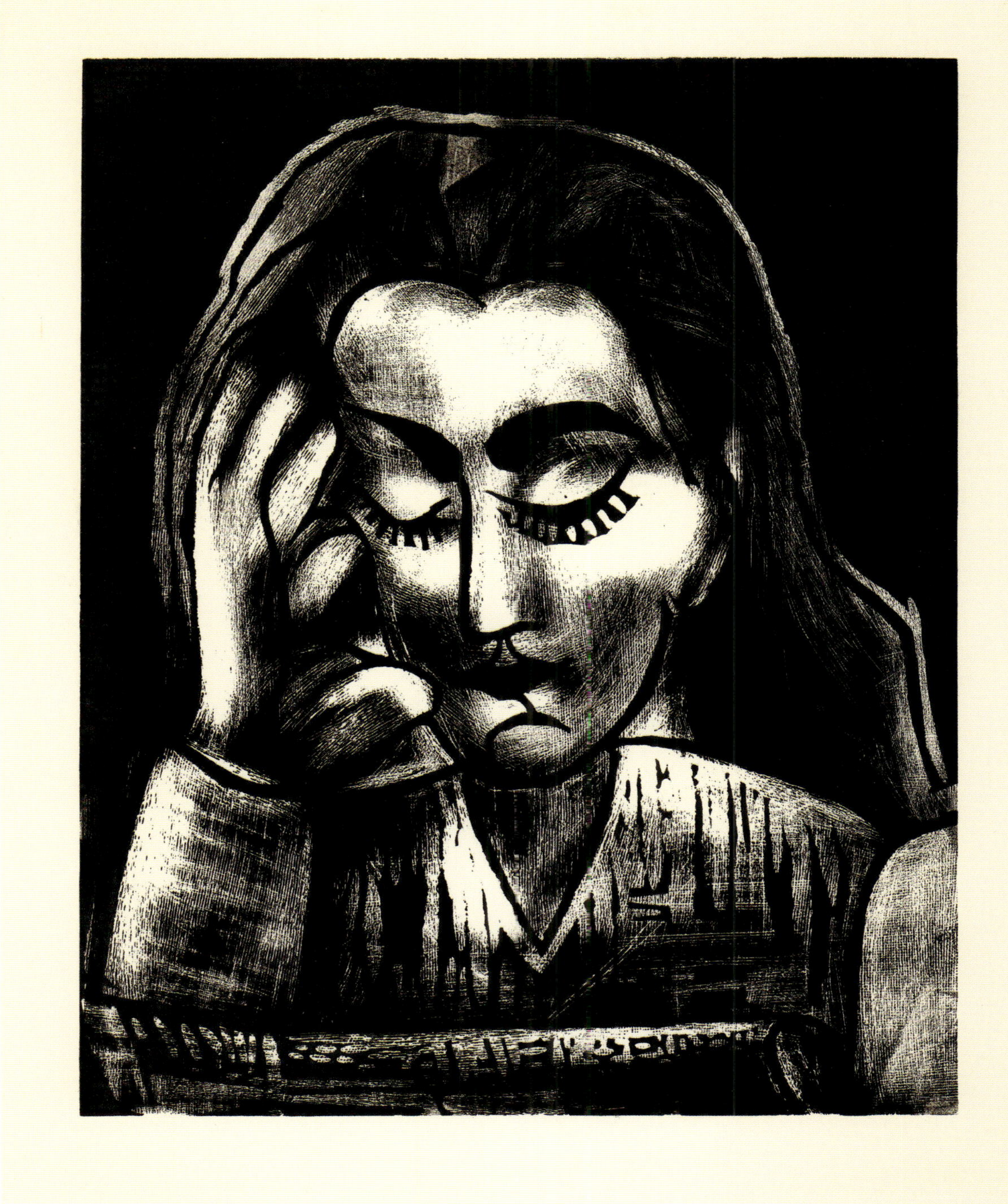

Woman with necklace, 24 November 1959
Colour linocut

Jacqueline reading, trial proof of the final version,
1962
Linocut in black

103

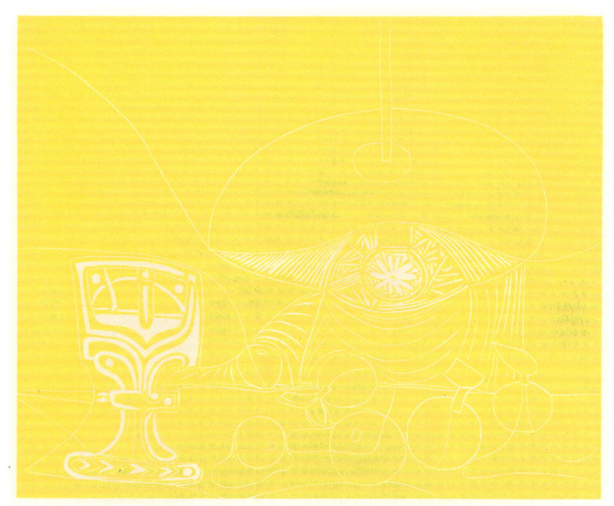
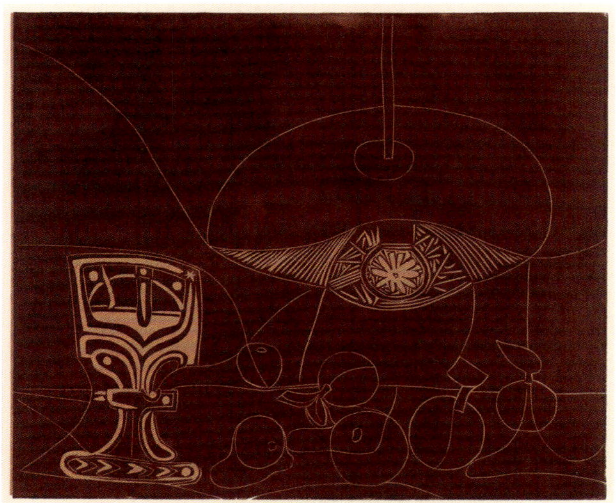
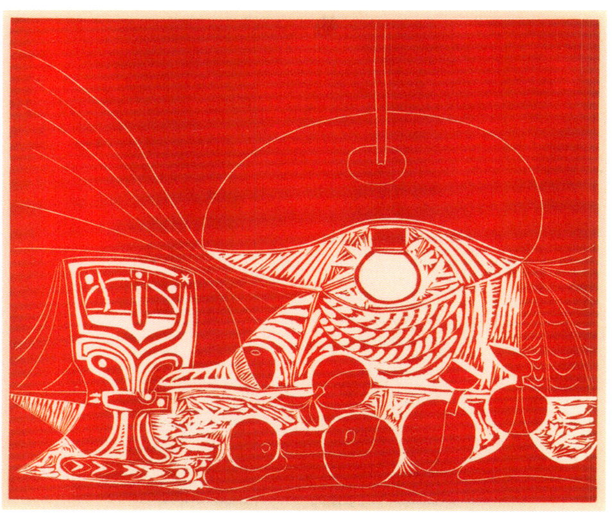
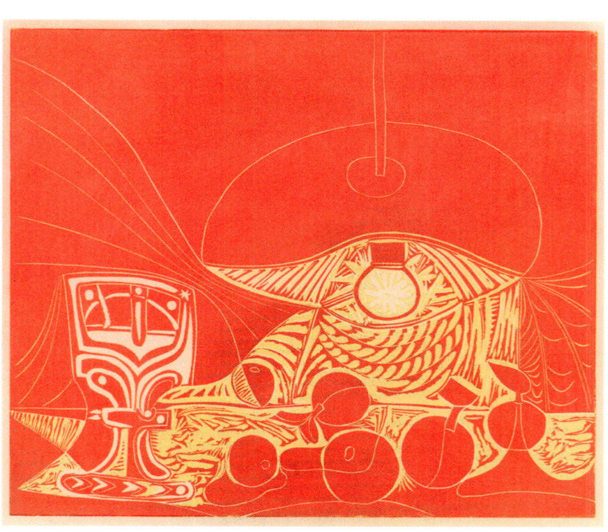

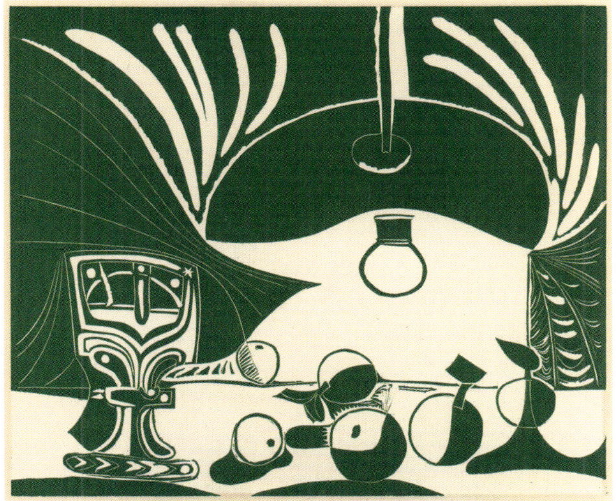

Still life under the lamp, progressive proofs and
final version, 1962
Colour linocut

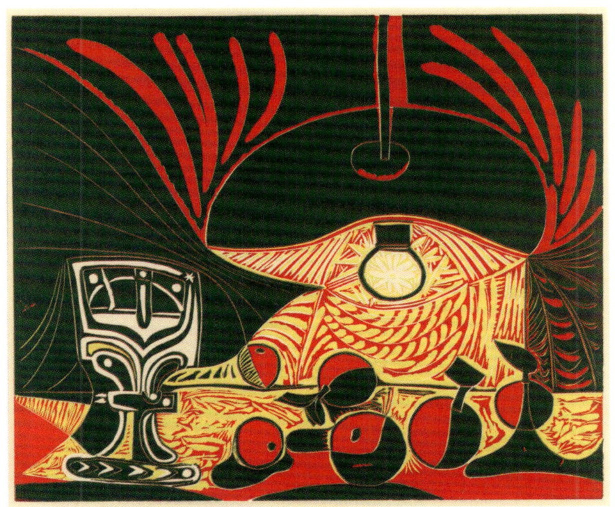

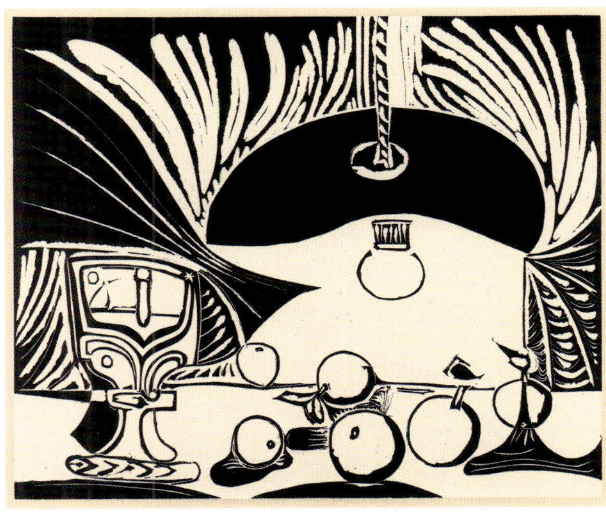

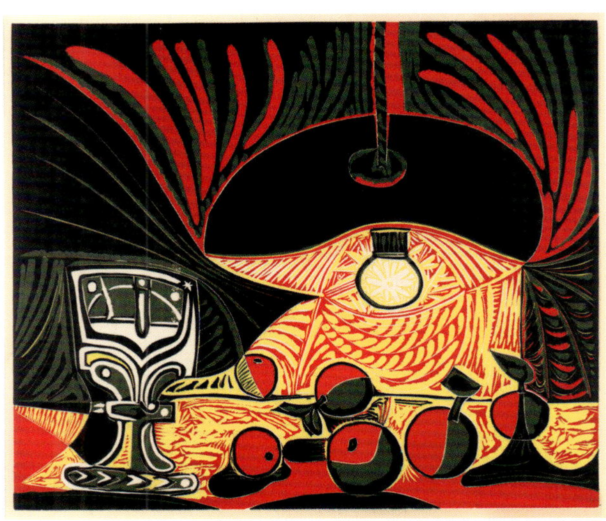

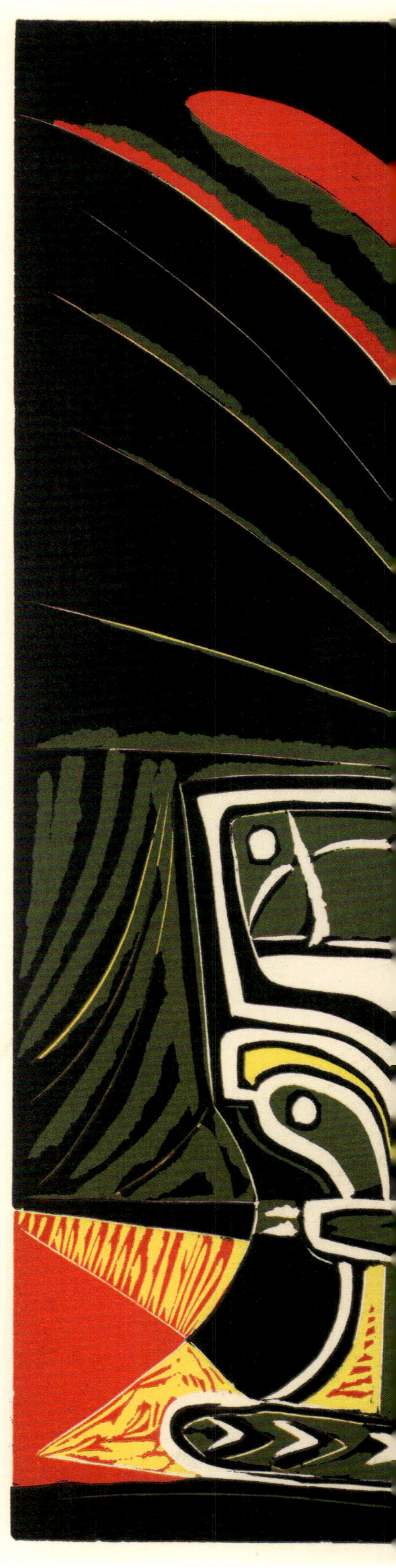

Still life under the lamp, 5th state and definitive
form, 1962
Linocut in black over green, red and yellow

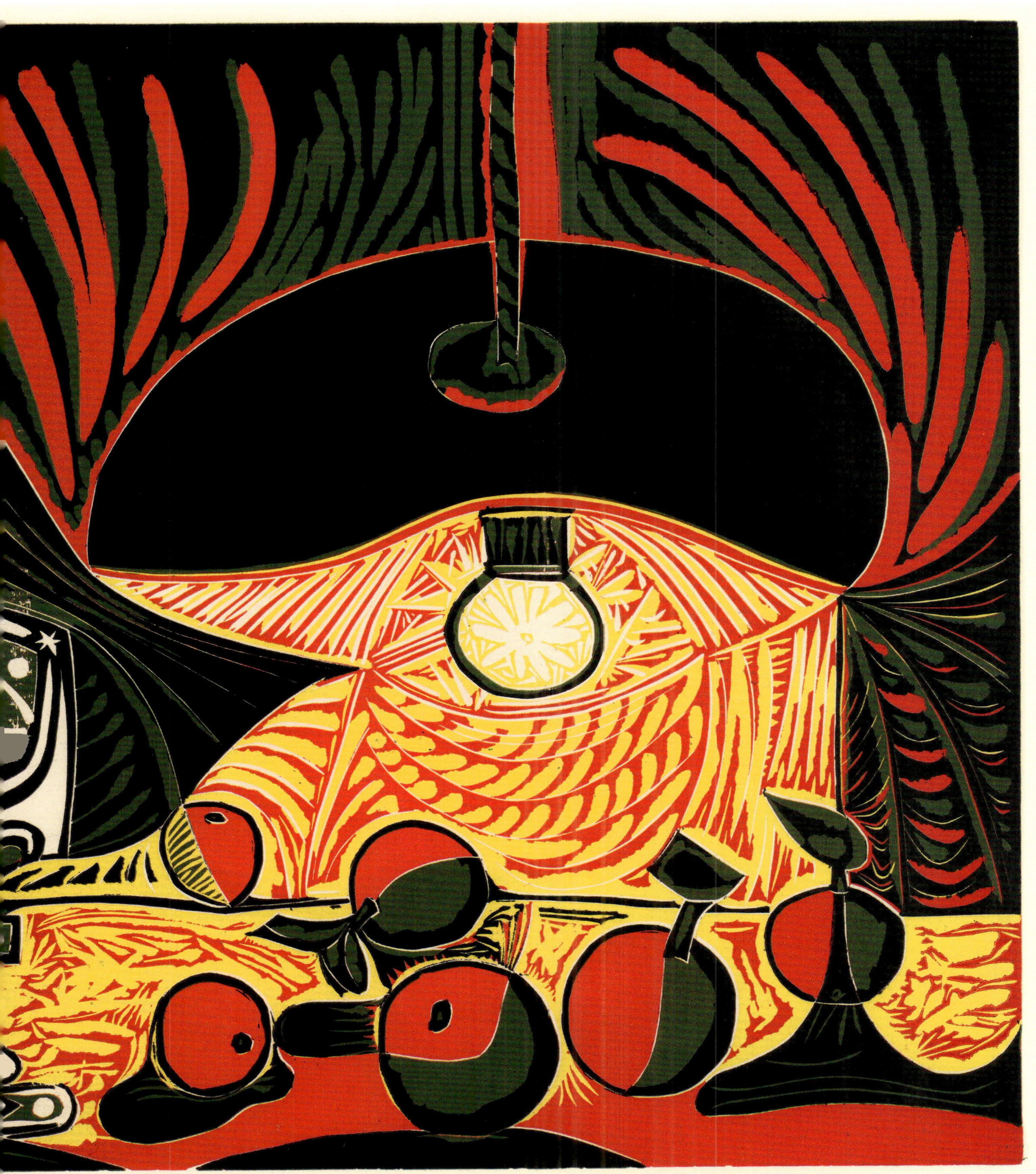

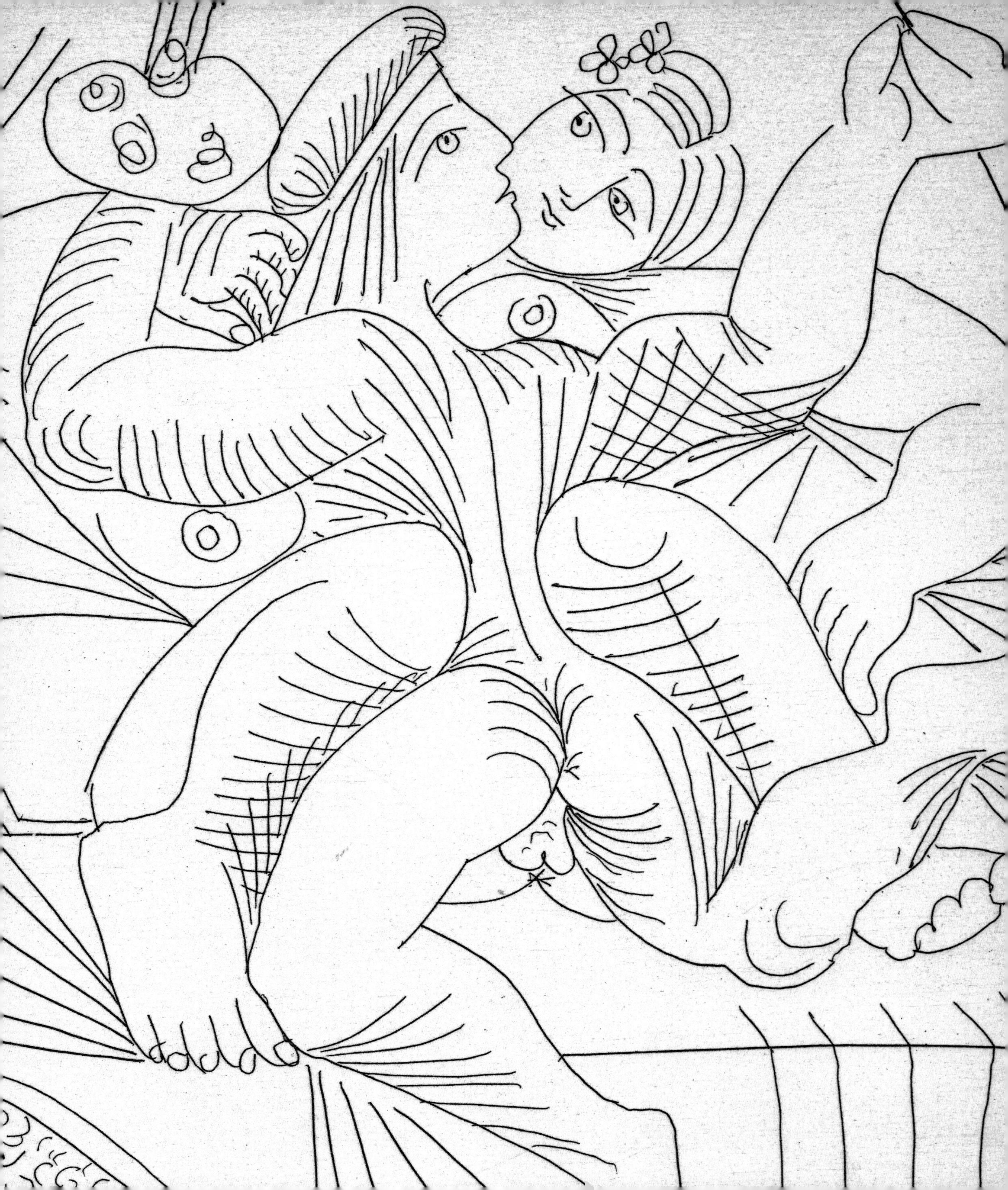

THE FINAL YEARS

… as soon as the drawing gets underway, a story or an idea is born. And that's it. Then the story grows, like theatre or life …

Throughout his life, Picasso focused on printmaking in concentrated bursts of creativity, producing over 2,400 prints in total. In 1968, at the age of 86, he produced 347 of those prints in under seven months. This section presents a selection of the etchings, drypoints and aquatints that make up the *347 Suite*. Sitting at his table at home, Picasso spent day after day drawing on the etching plates prepared for him by the printers Aldo and Piero Crommelynck, who had set up a studio near his home in Mougins in the South of France, sometimes producing six or seven prints in a 24-hour period. His own portrait appears in several of the images, including the first plate, in which he is shown as an old man standing in the wings as a circus scene unfolds in the background (pp. 110–11). Real-life figures appear in the prints, including Jacqueline Roque, whom he had married in 1961, Piero Crommelynck, and great artists of the past to whom he owed a debt, including El Greco, Rembrandt and Manet. Fictional characters also appear, most notably Celestina, an aged procuress and sorceress from Spanish literature, whom Picasso had portrayed in a painting of 1904.

The suite also includes a group of erotic prints on the subject of Raphael and La Fornarina, a story about the excessive lovemaking between the Renaissance artist Raphael and his model, La Fornarina (the baker's daughter), also explored in paint by Ingres in the nineteenth century. Picasso continued to make prints until his final years. In 1971, for example, he produced a suite of 156 intaglio prints, which included *Brothel. Chatter, with parrot, Celestina and the portrait of Degas*, the final print in this section (pp. 134–5).

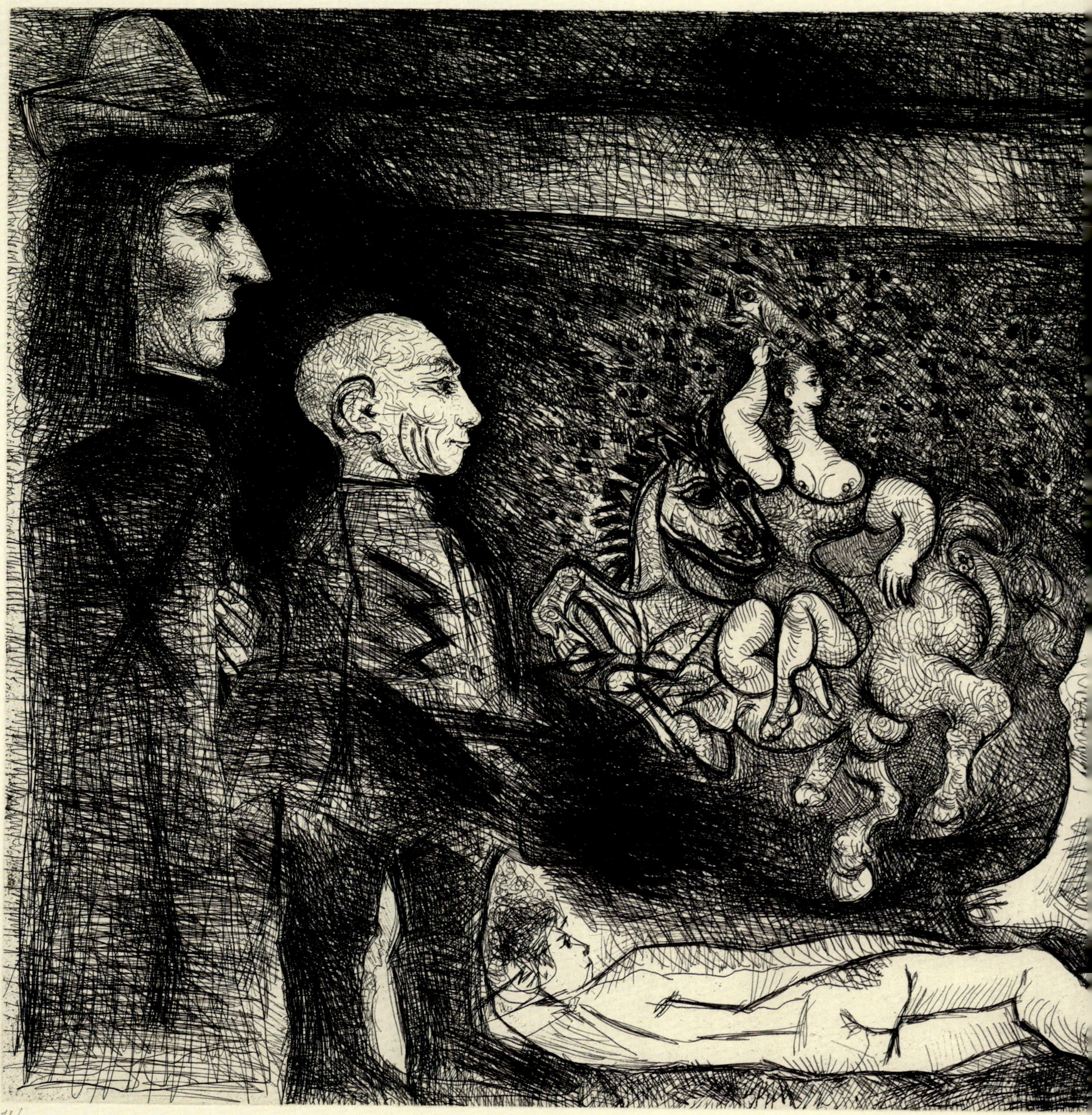

13/50

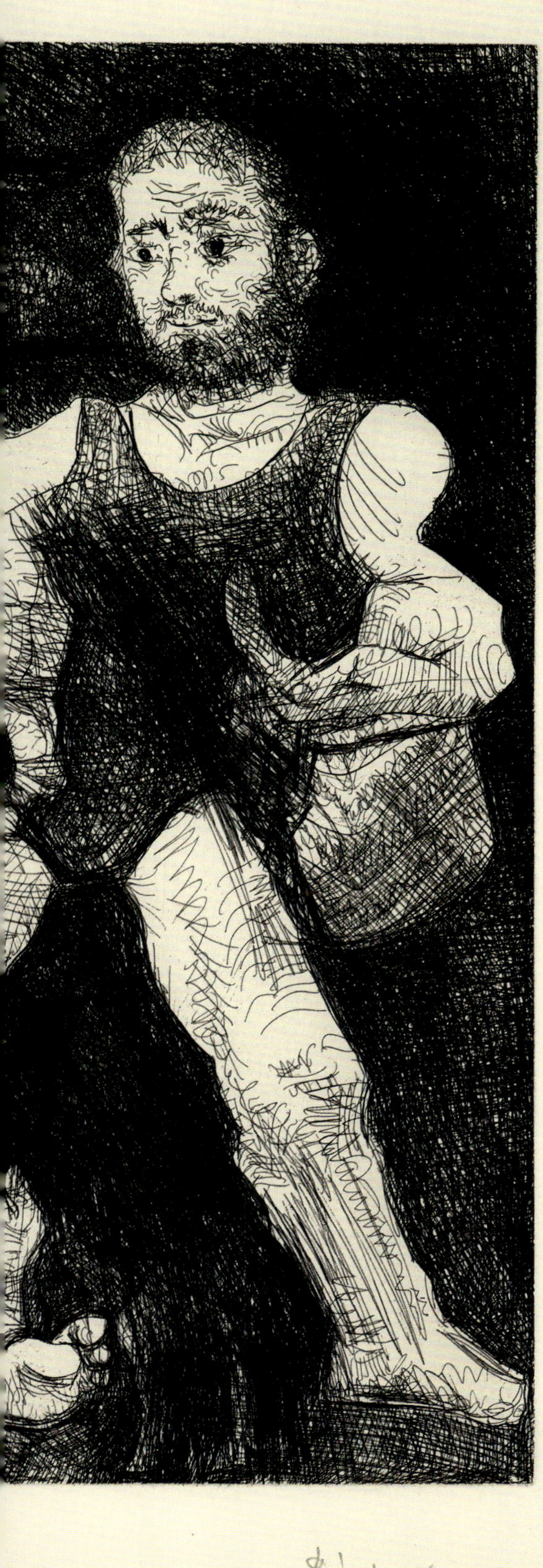

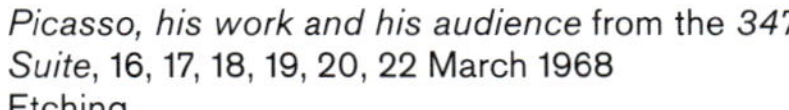

Picasso, his work and his audience from the *347 Suite*, 16, 17, 18, 19, 20, 22 March 1968
Etching

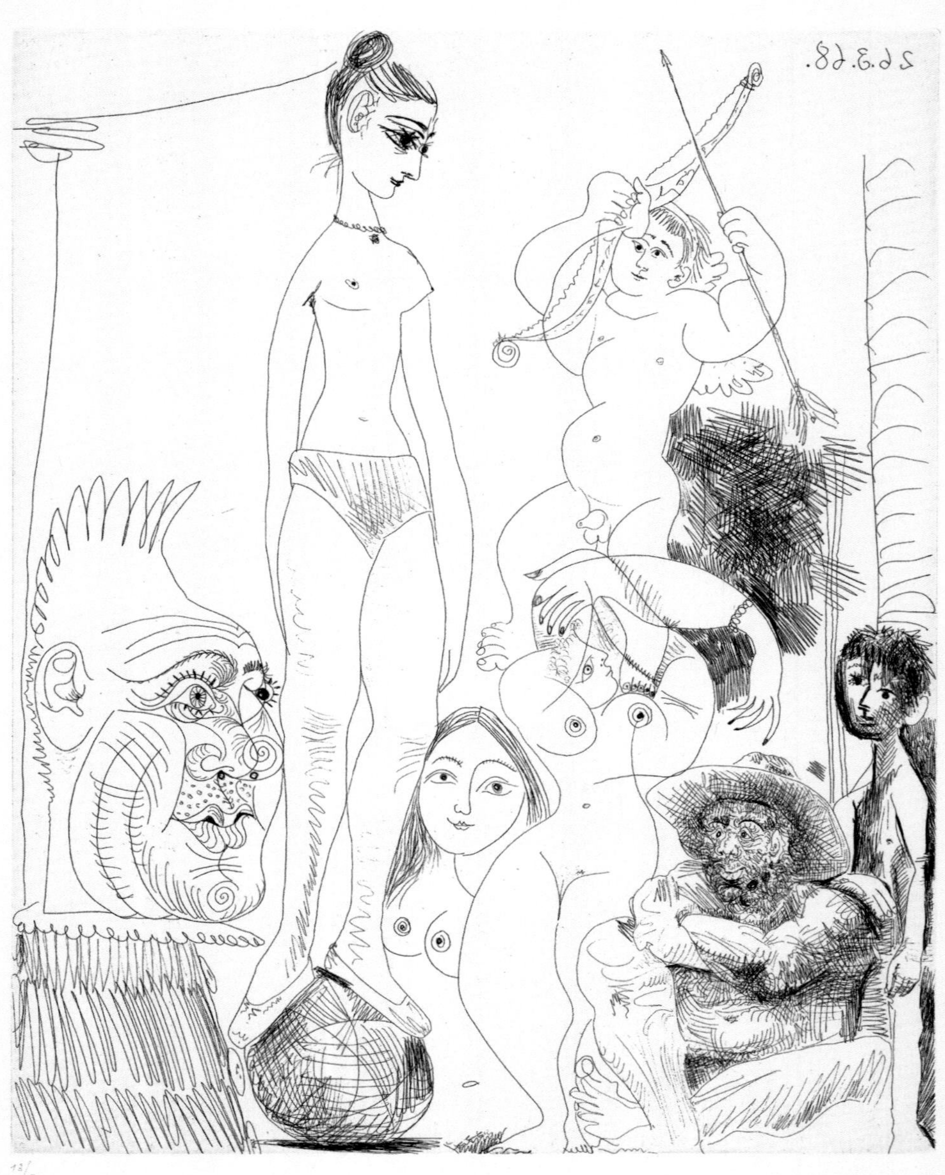

Self-portrait transposed and dreaming of the circus, with Jacqueline as a ball acrobat, from the *347 Suite*, 26 March 1968
Etching

Circus and wrestling, from the *347 Suite*, 11 April 1963 II
Etching

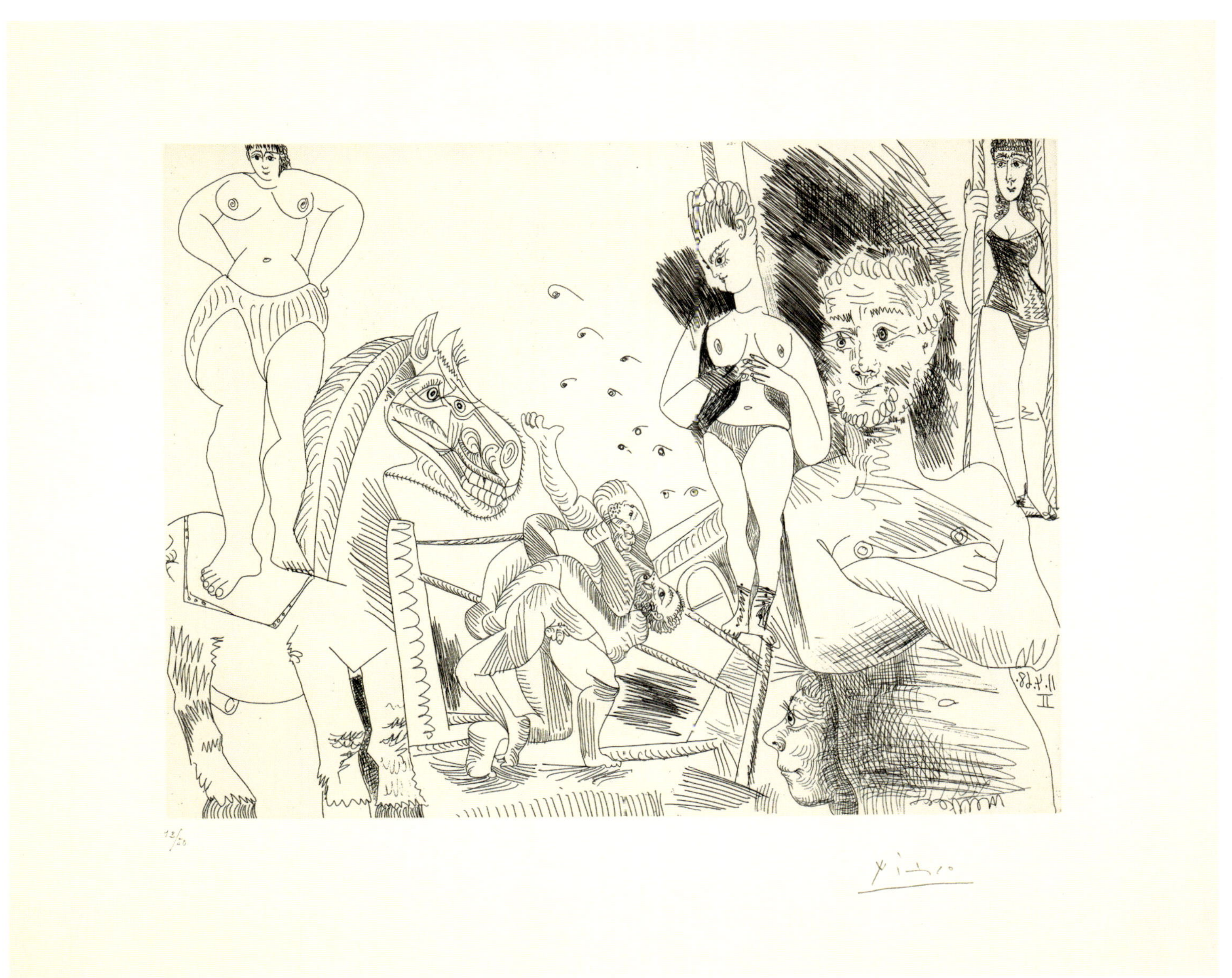

At the circus: rider, clown and Pierrot,
from the *347 Suite*, 19 April 1968
Aquatint and drypoint with stop-out varnish
in reserve

*Caricature of General de
Gaulle, and two women* from
the *347 Suite*, 21 April 1968 I, 22 April 1968
Aquatint, drypoint and scraper

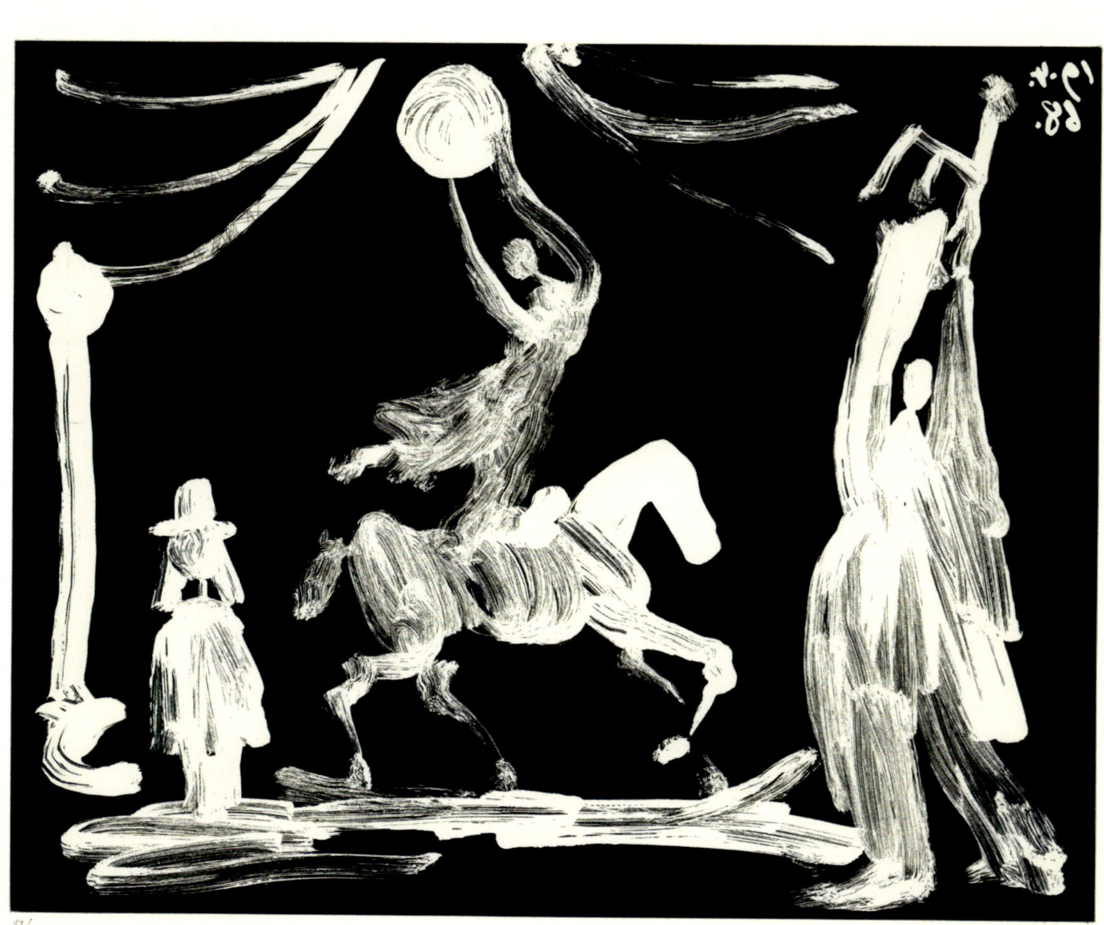

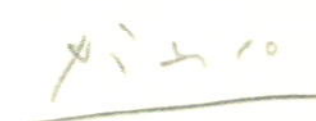

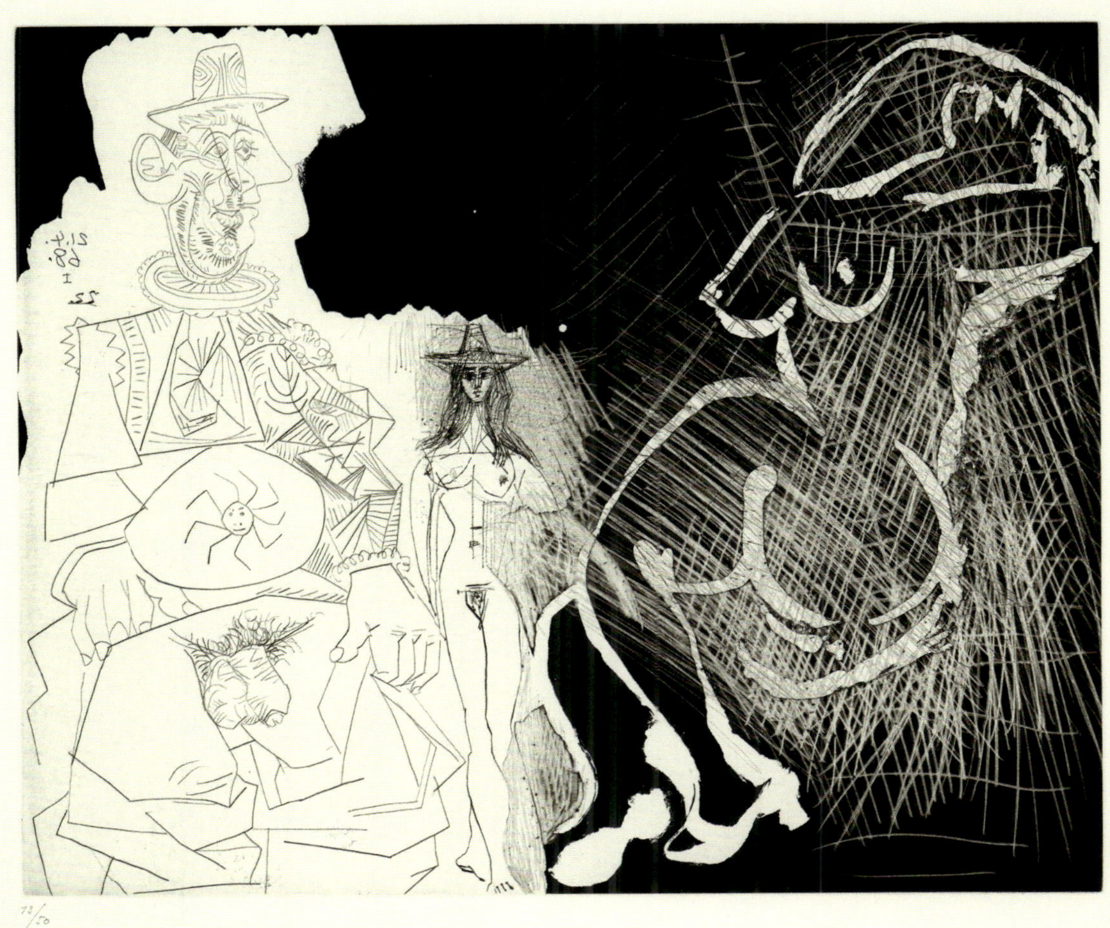

Around El Greco and Rembrandt portraits from
the *347 Suite*, 15 April 1968 II, 17, 18, 19 April 1968
Aquatint, drypoint and scraper

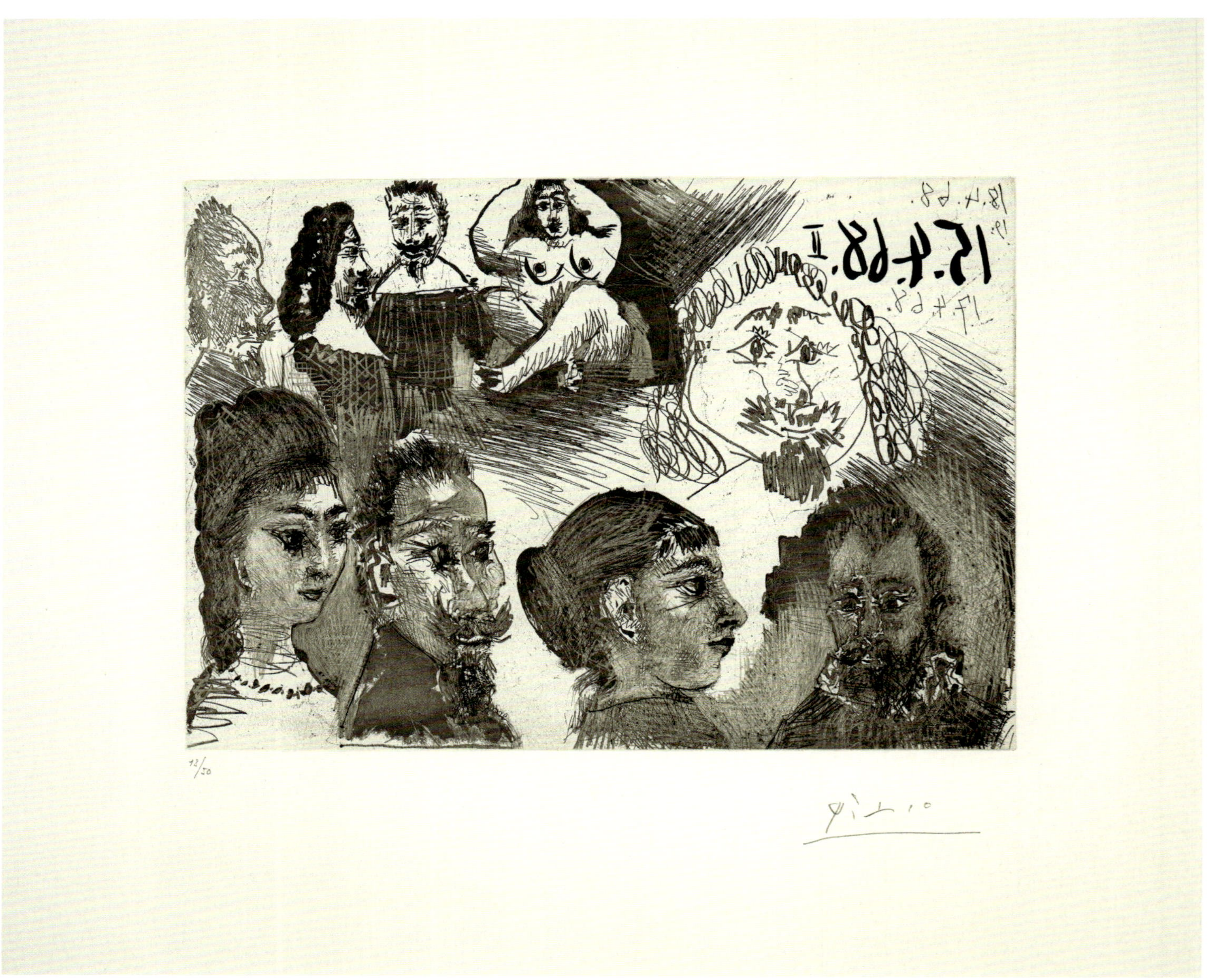

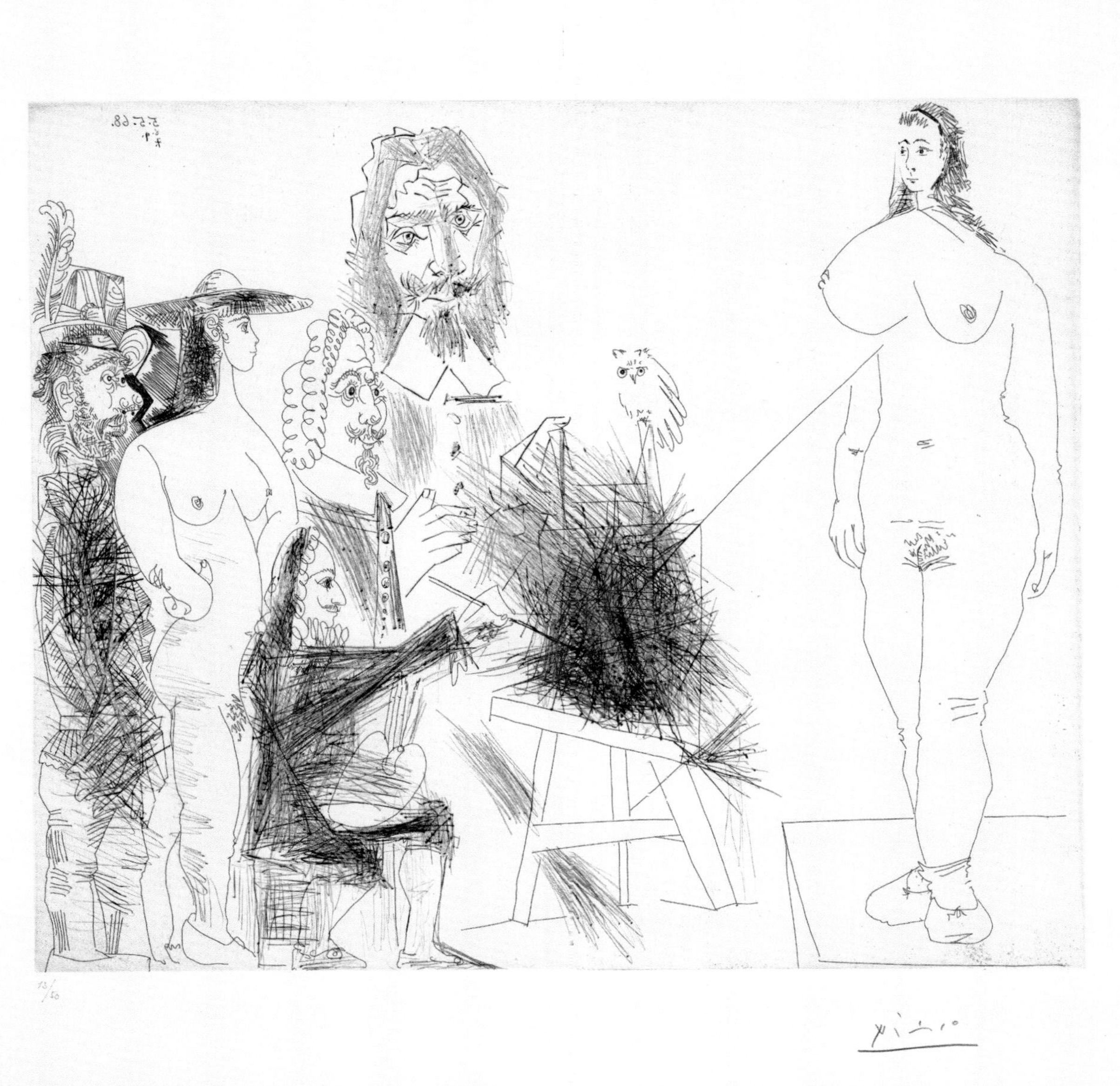

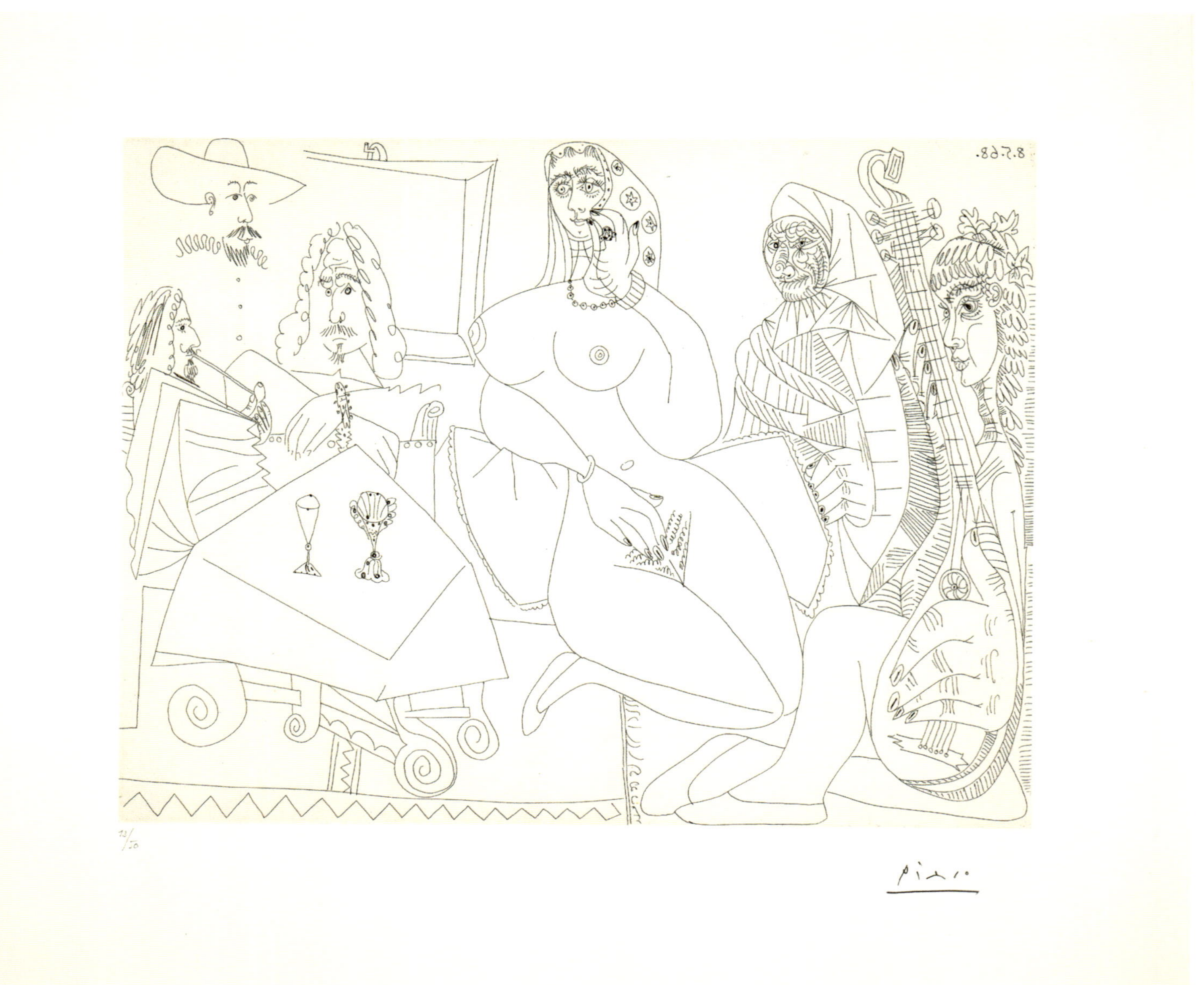

Musical snack at Celestina's from the *347 Suite*,
8 May 1968
Etching

*Celestina, maja or Olympia naked, with Manet and
Marcellin Desboutin: couple of spectators in the
background* from the *347 Suite*, 1 October 1968 l
Sugar aquatint with scraper on greased plate

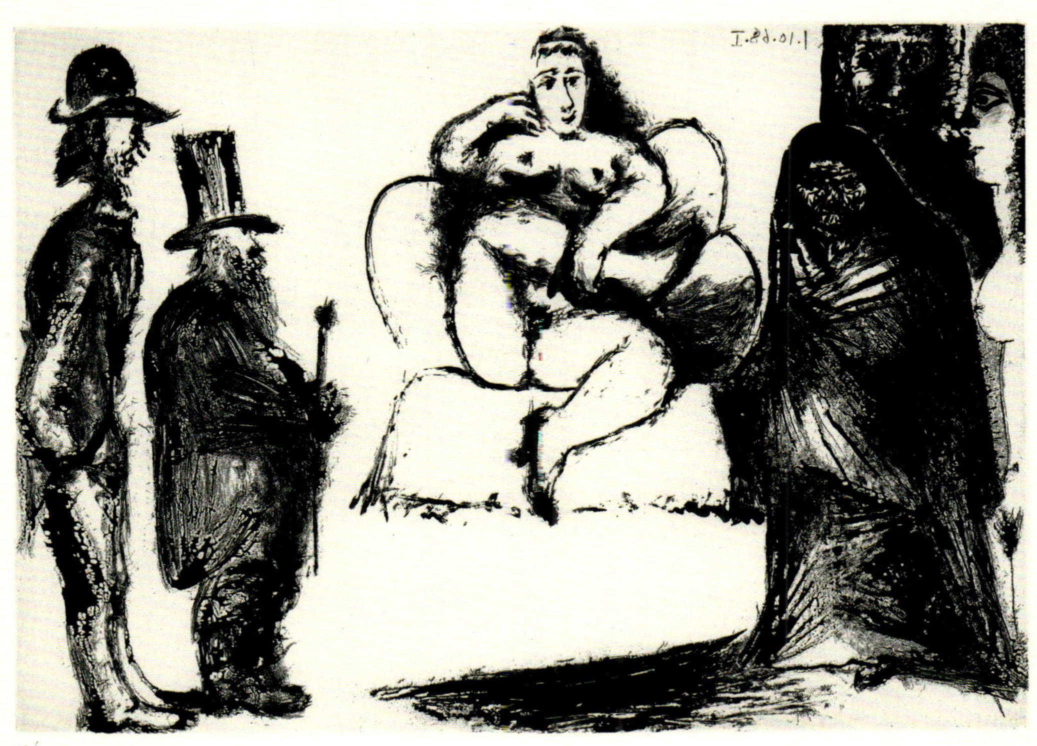

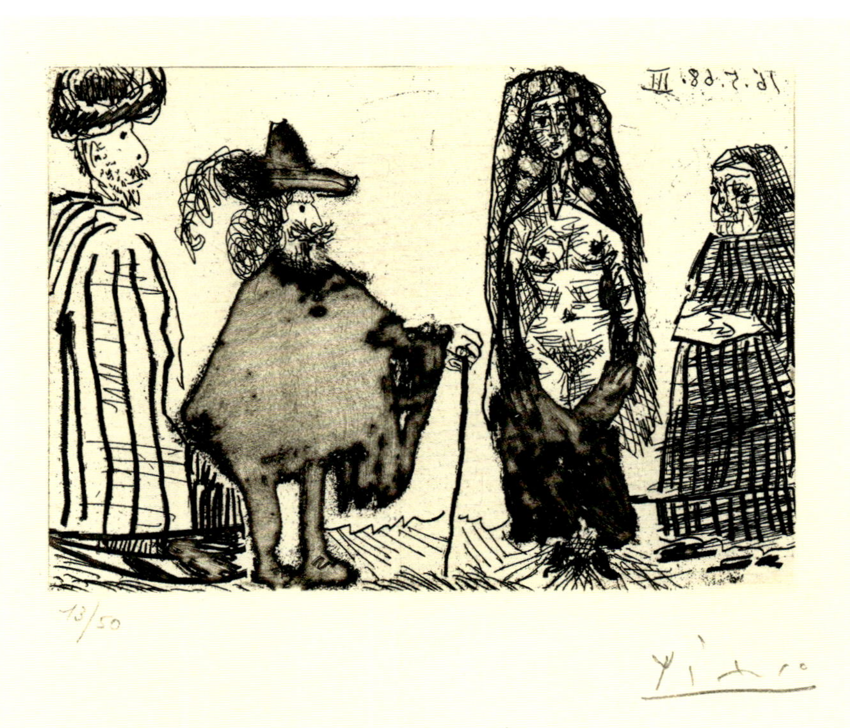

13/50

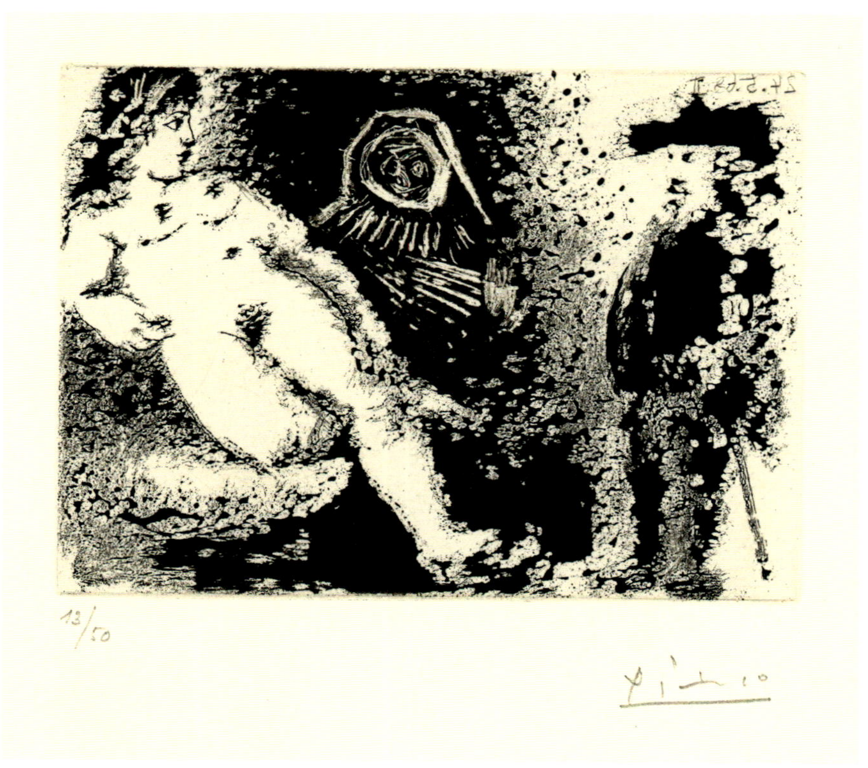

13/50

'A Thousand and One Nights' and 'Célestine': the young slave from the *347 Suite*, 16 May 1968 III
Etching with light areas achieved with turpentine on cotton swab

Celestina, girl and old client from the *347 Suite*, 24 May 1968 II
Sugar aquatint and greased in different areas of the plate

Kidnapping, on foot, with Celestina
from the *347 Suite*, 9 June 1968 II
Sugar aquatint on partially greased plate

Kidnapping on horseback from the
347 Suite, 9 June 1968 III
Sugar aquatint on partially greased plate

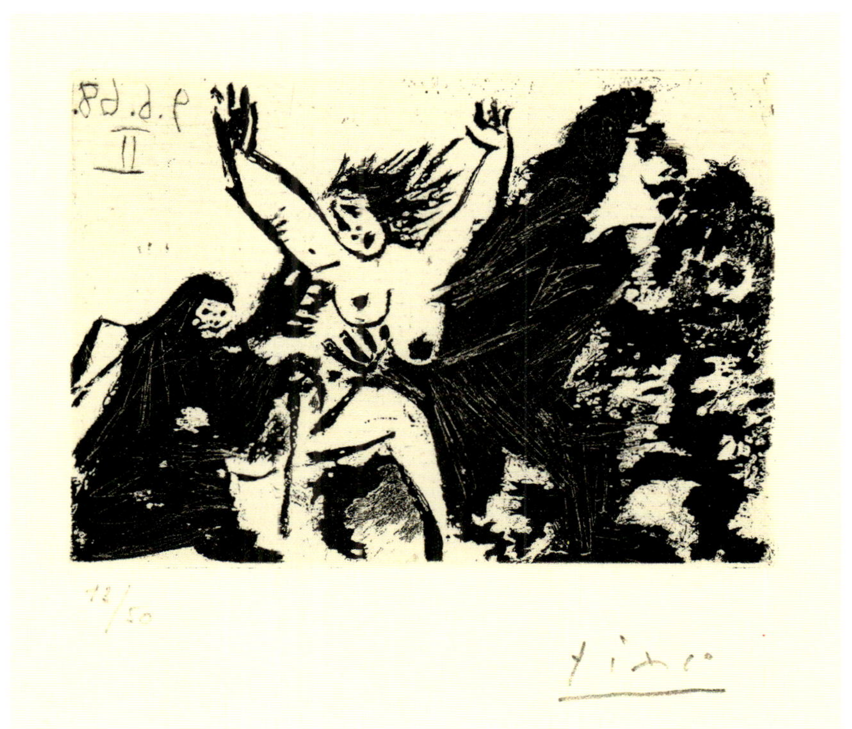

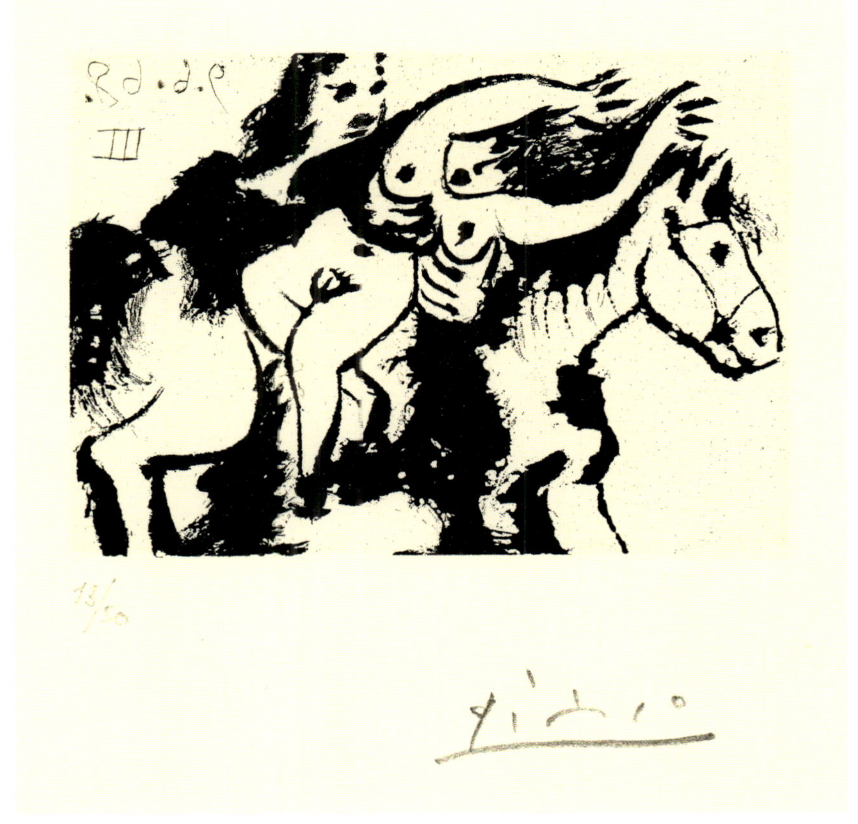

Raphael and La Fornarina, I from the *347 Suite*, 29 August 1968 I
Etching

Raphael and La Fornarina, IX: the Pope arrives from the *347 Suite*, 1 September 1968 IV
Etching

Raphael and La Fornarina, XXII: Michelangelo under the bed; enter Piero Crommelynck from the *347 Suite*, 8 September 1968 II
Etching

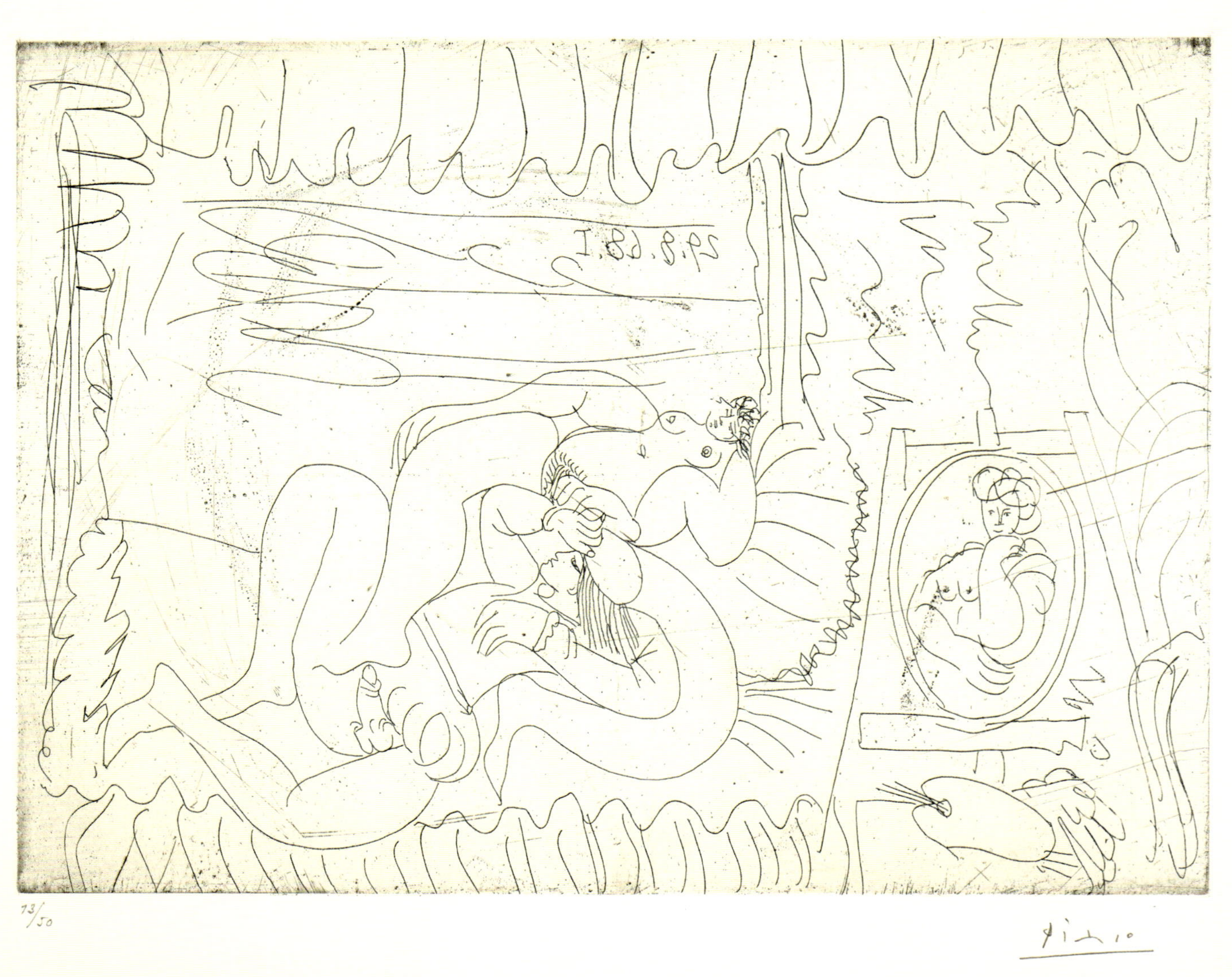

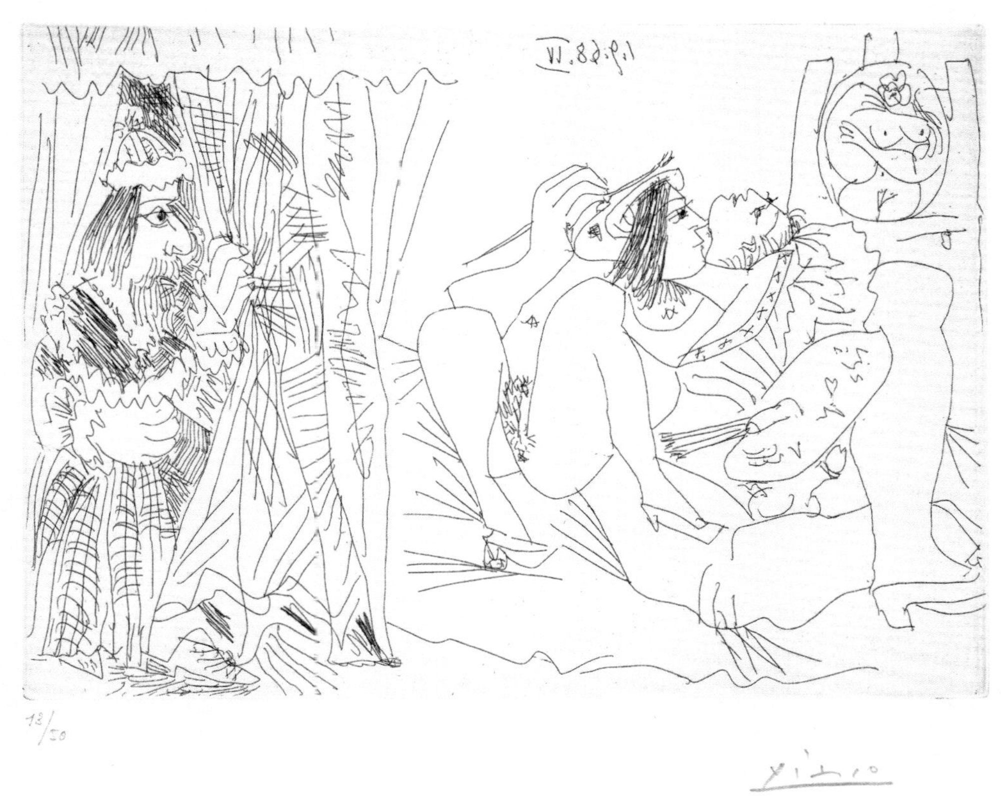

13/50

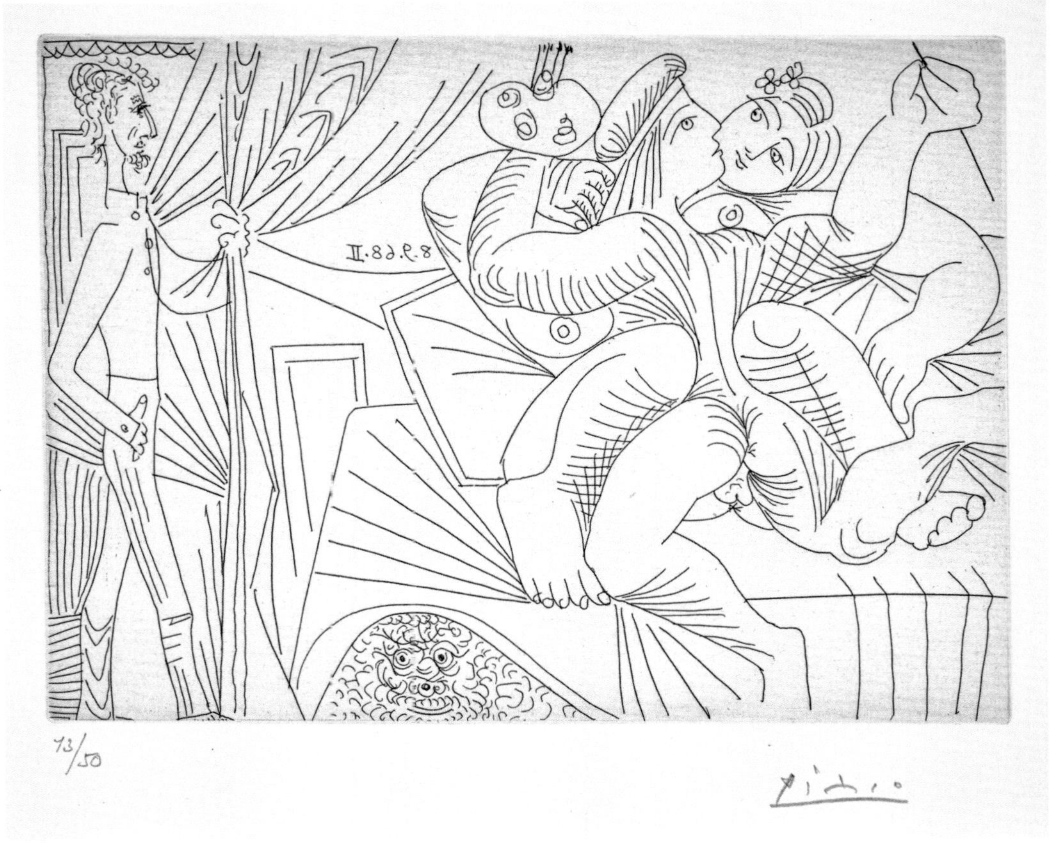

13/50

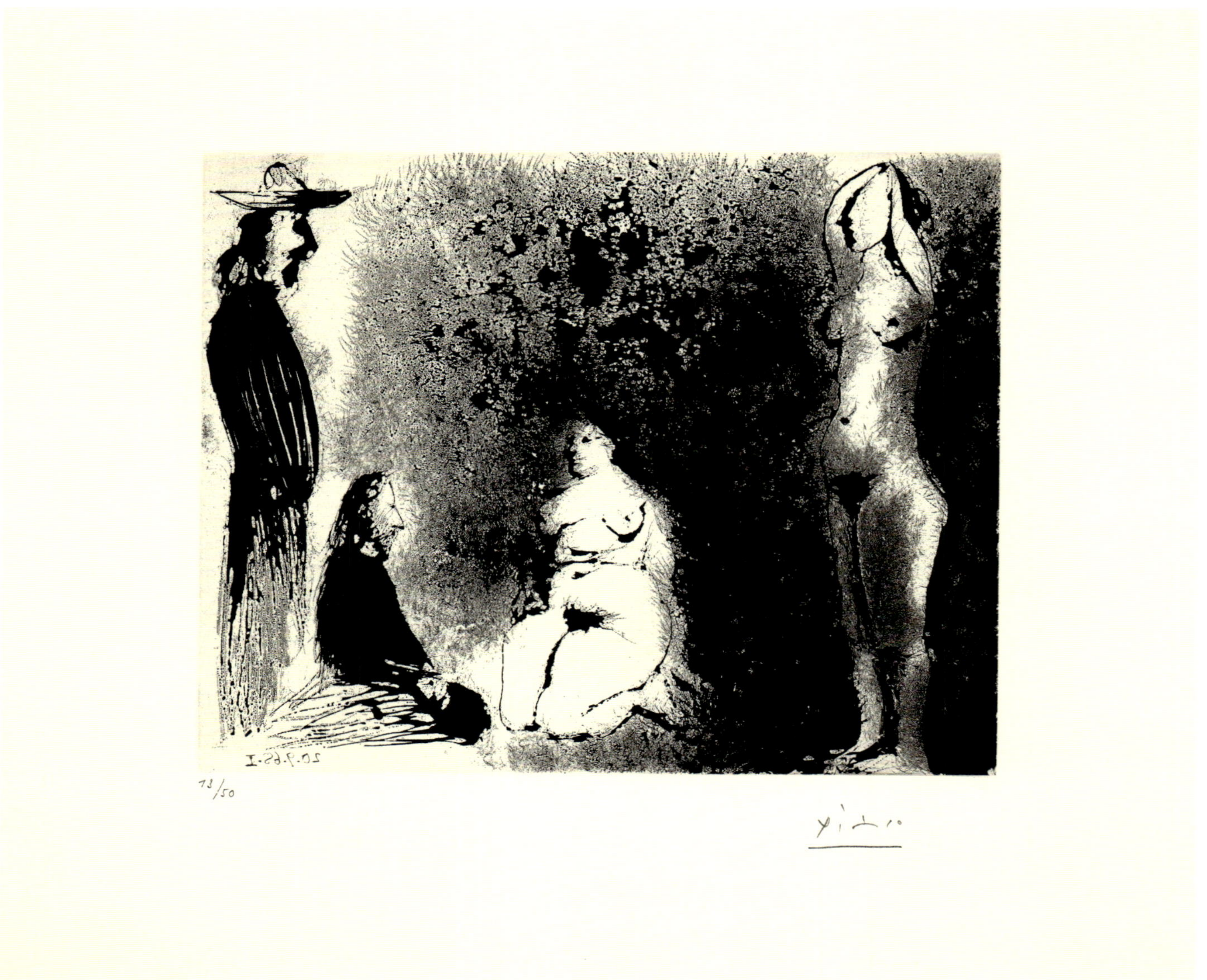

Serenade at sunset in a Monet-style undergrowth
from the *347 Suite*, 5 October 1968 I
Sugar aquatint on greased plate

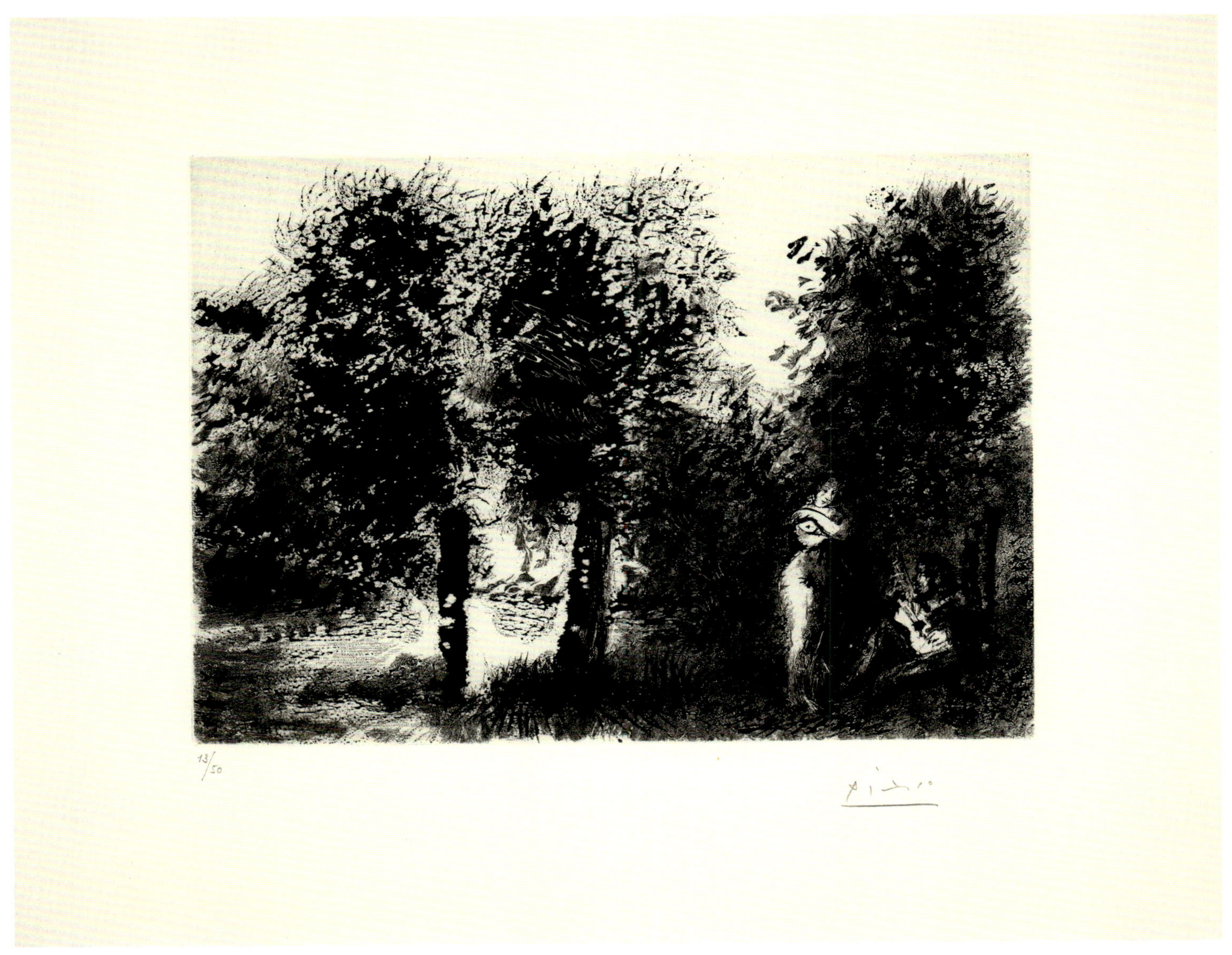

'*The Burial of Count d'Orgaz', after Picasso* from the *347 Suite*, 30 June 1968 I
Sugar aquatint, etching and scraper

Variation on Don Quixote and Dulcinea: travelling actors' stop from the *347 Suite*, 15 June 1968 III
Sugar aquatint on greased plate

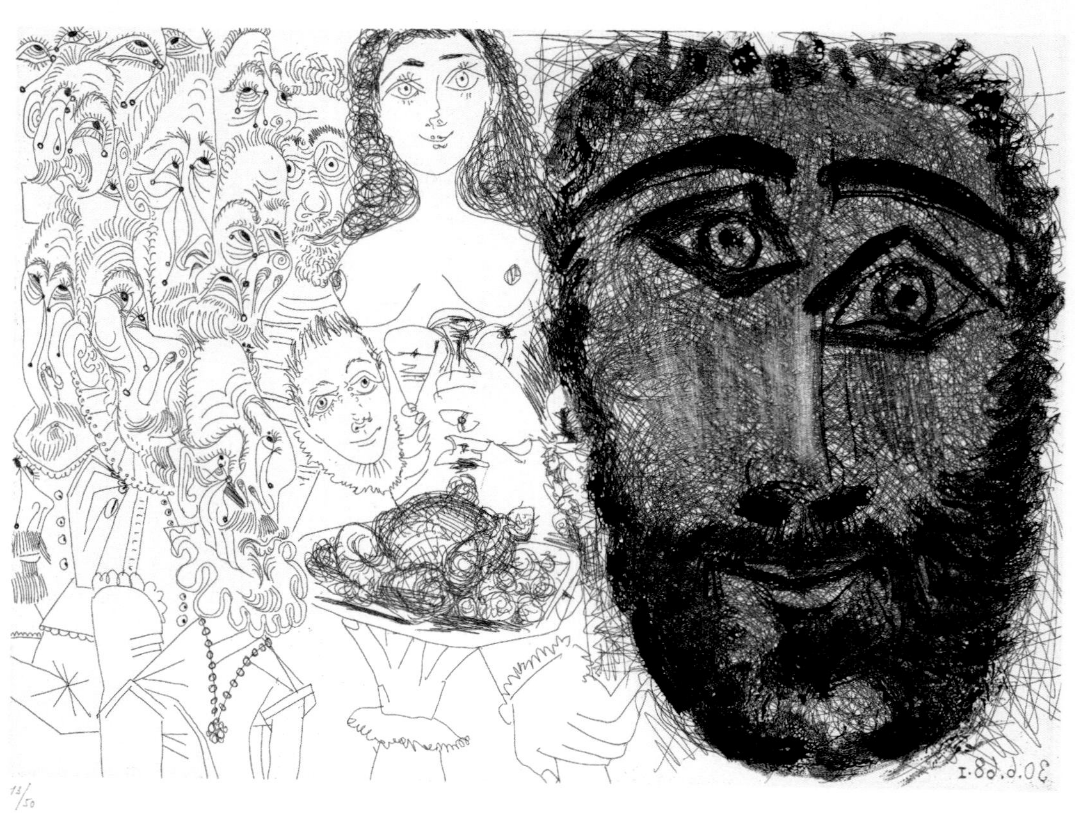

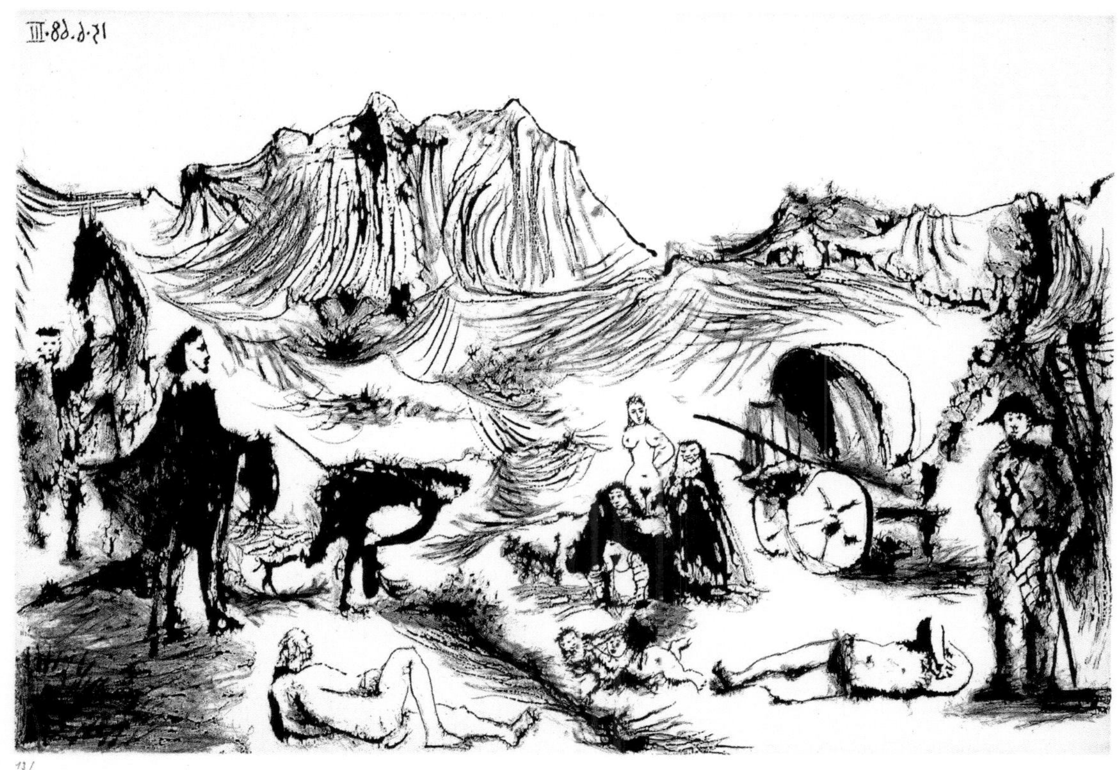
15.6.68. III
13/50

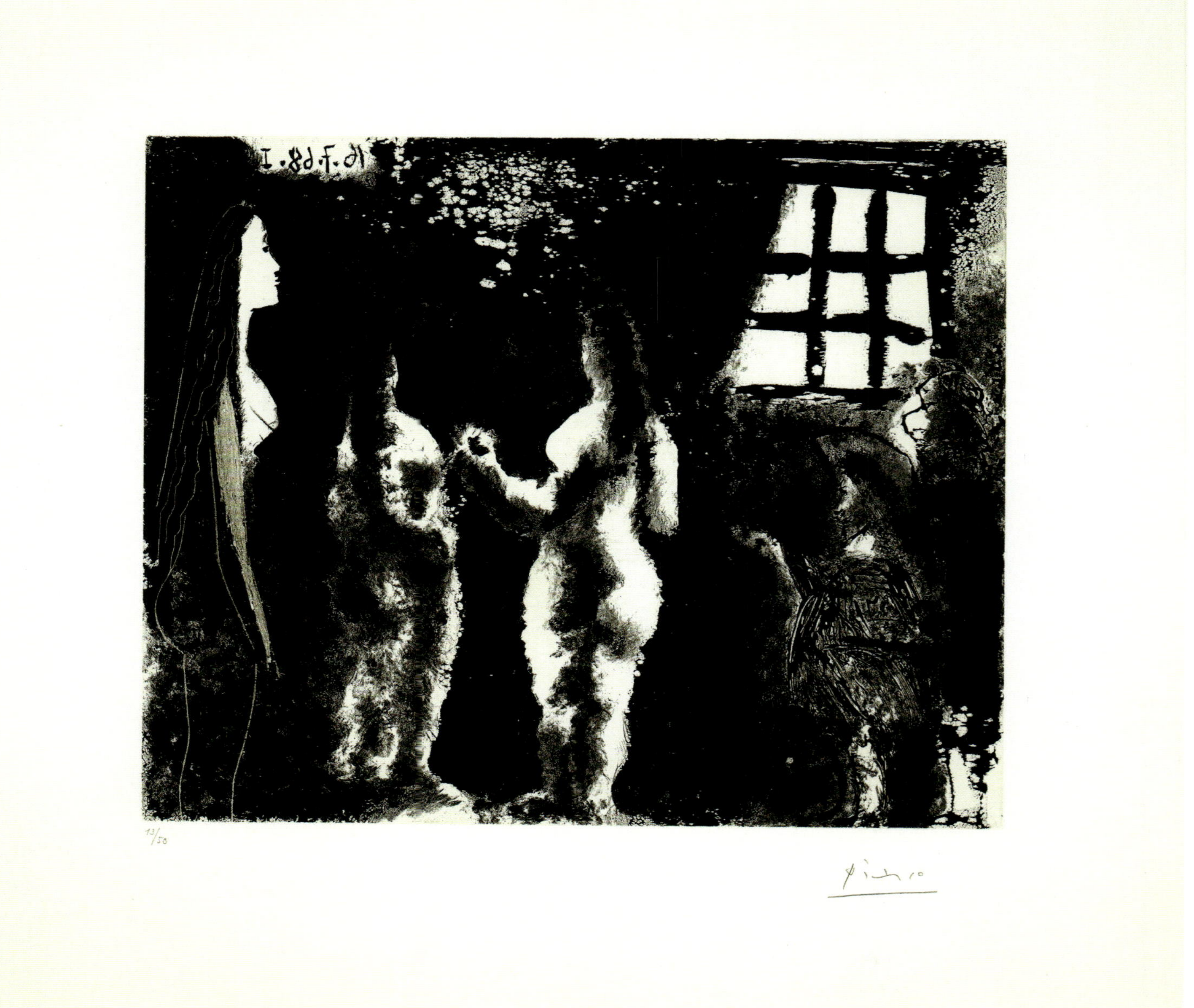

Meninas and gentlemen in the sierra from the *347 Suite*, 1 June 1968 I
Sugar aquatint on greased plate

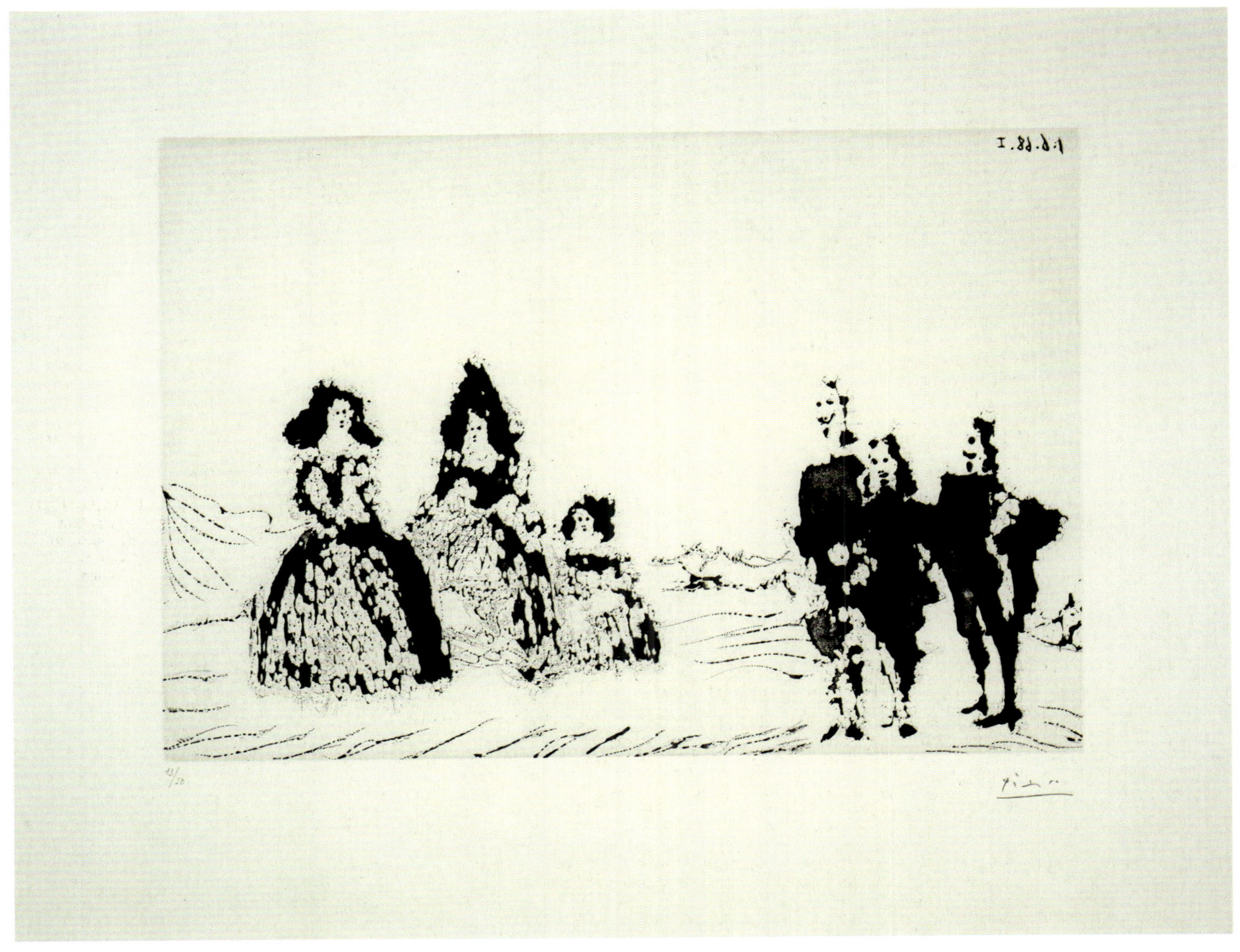

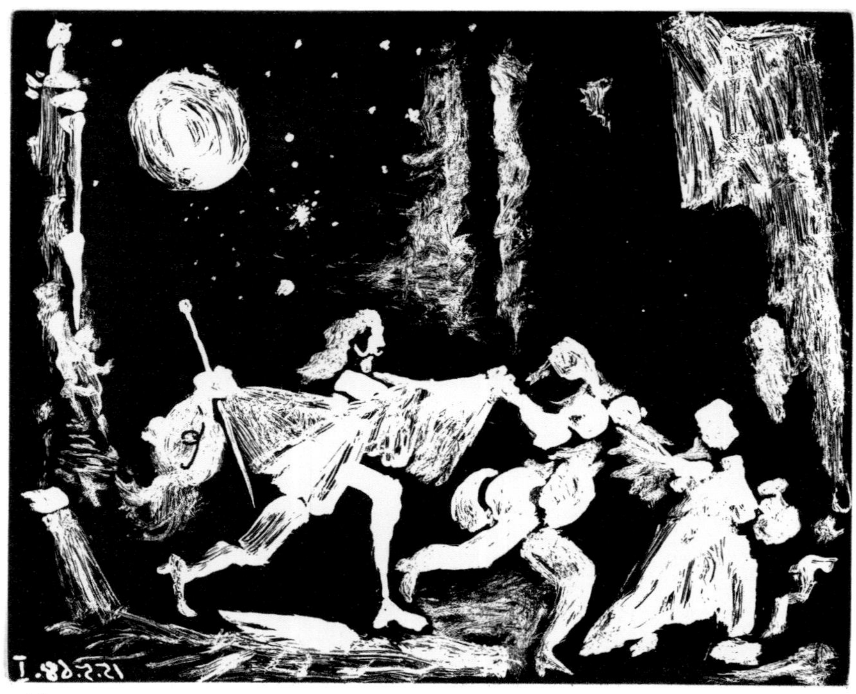

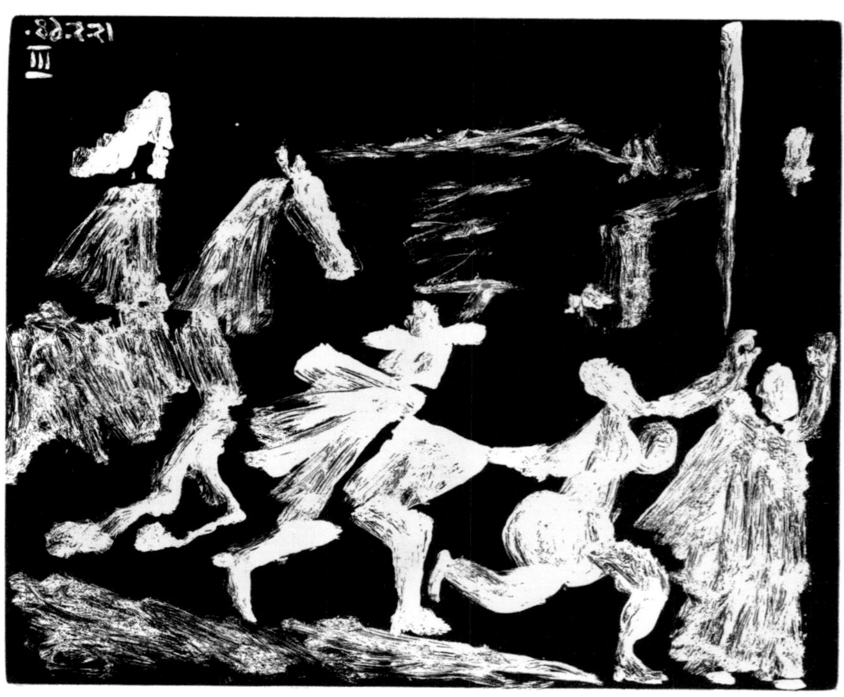

Celestina and her creature lead the gullible and wealthy from the *347 Suite*, 15 May 1968 I
Aquatint and etching with stop-out varnish in reserve

Cloak and sword: pursuit from the *347 Suite*, I, 15 May 1968 III
Aquatint with stop-out varnish in reserve

Cloak and sword: pursuit, II from the *347 Suite*, 15 May 1968 IV
Aquatint with stop-out varnish in reserve

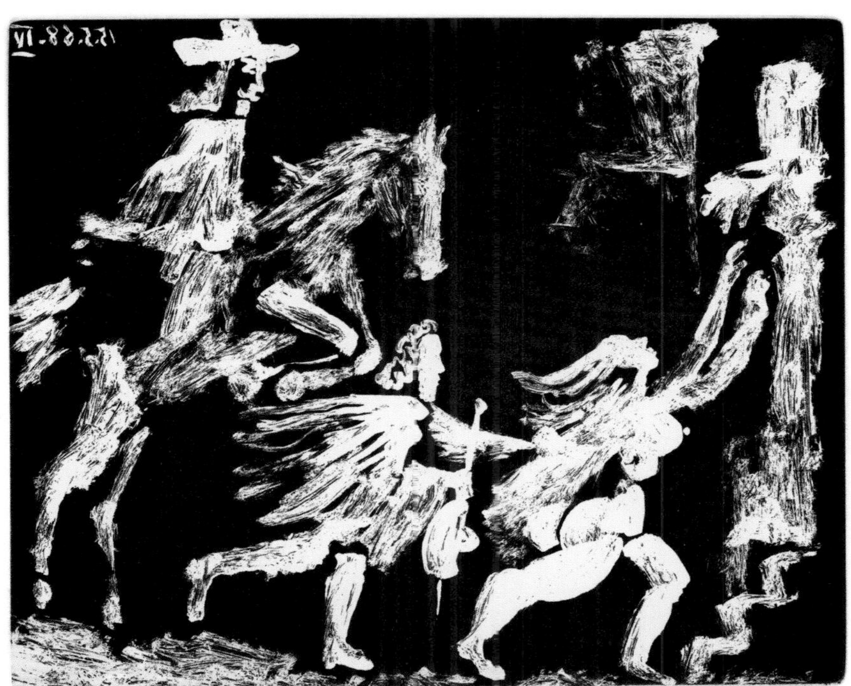

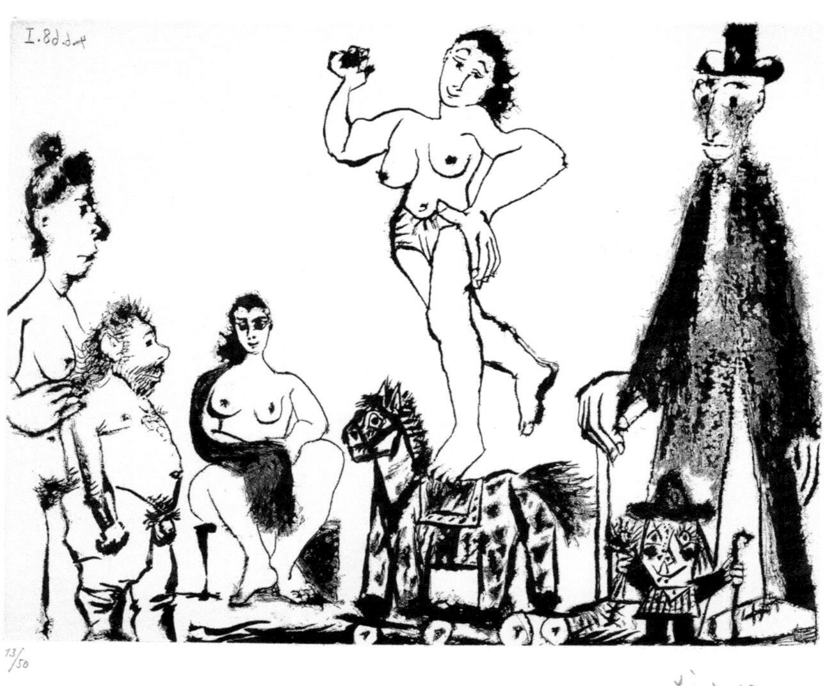

13.9.68.I
13/50

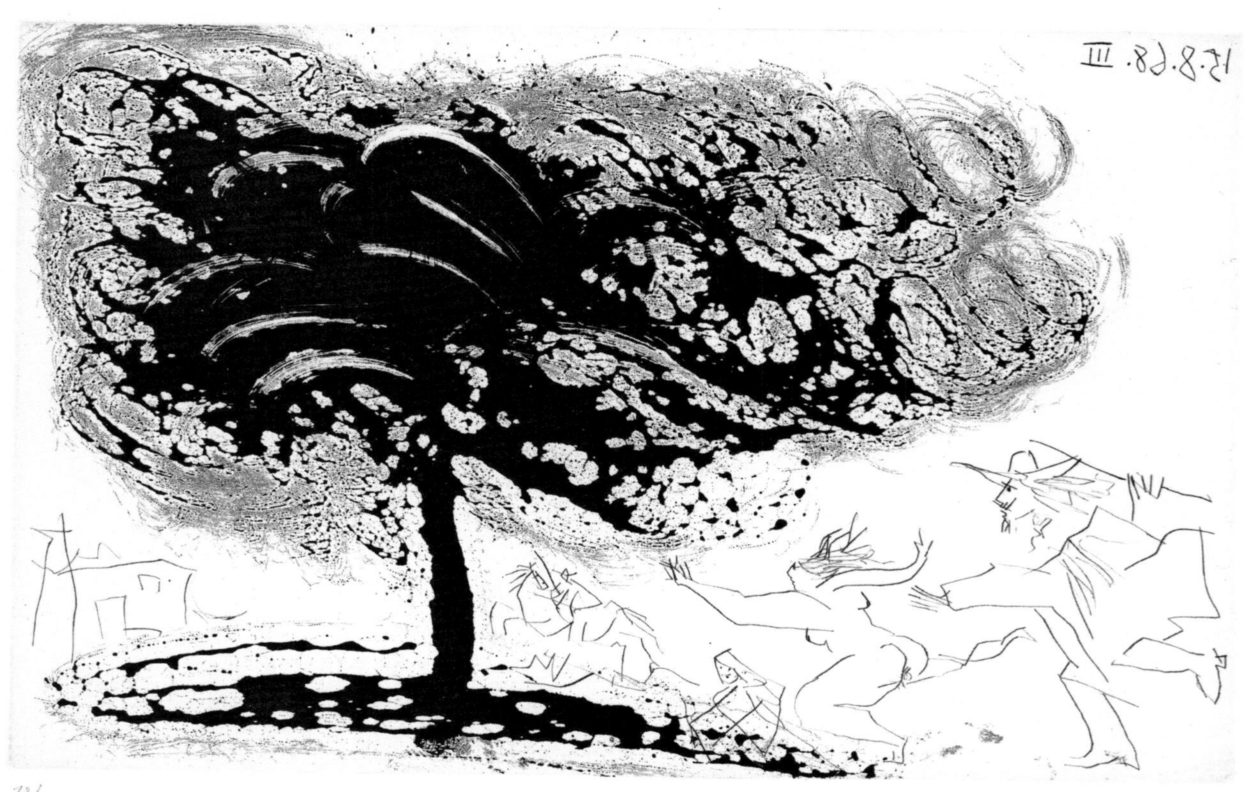

13.8.68.III
13/50

Childhood memories: street party, with 'good guy' and 'El Gigante' from the *347 Suite*, 4 June 1968 I
Sugar aquatint on partially greased plate

Tree in the storm, with flight towards a church from the *347 Suite*, 15 August 1968 III
Sugar aquatint and drypoint on greased plate

Three women from the *347 Suite*, 30 March 1968 II
Etching

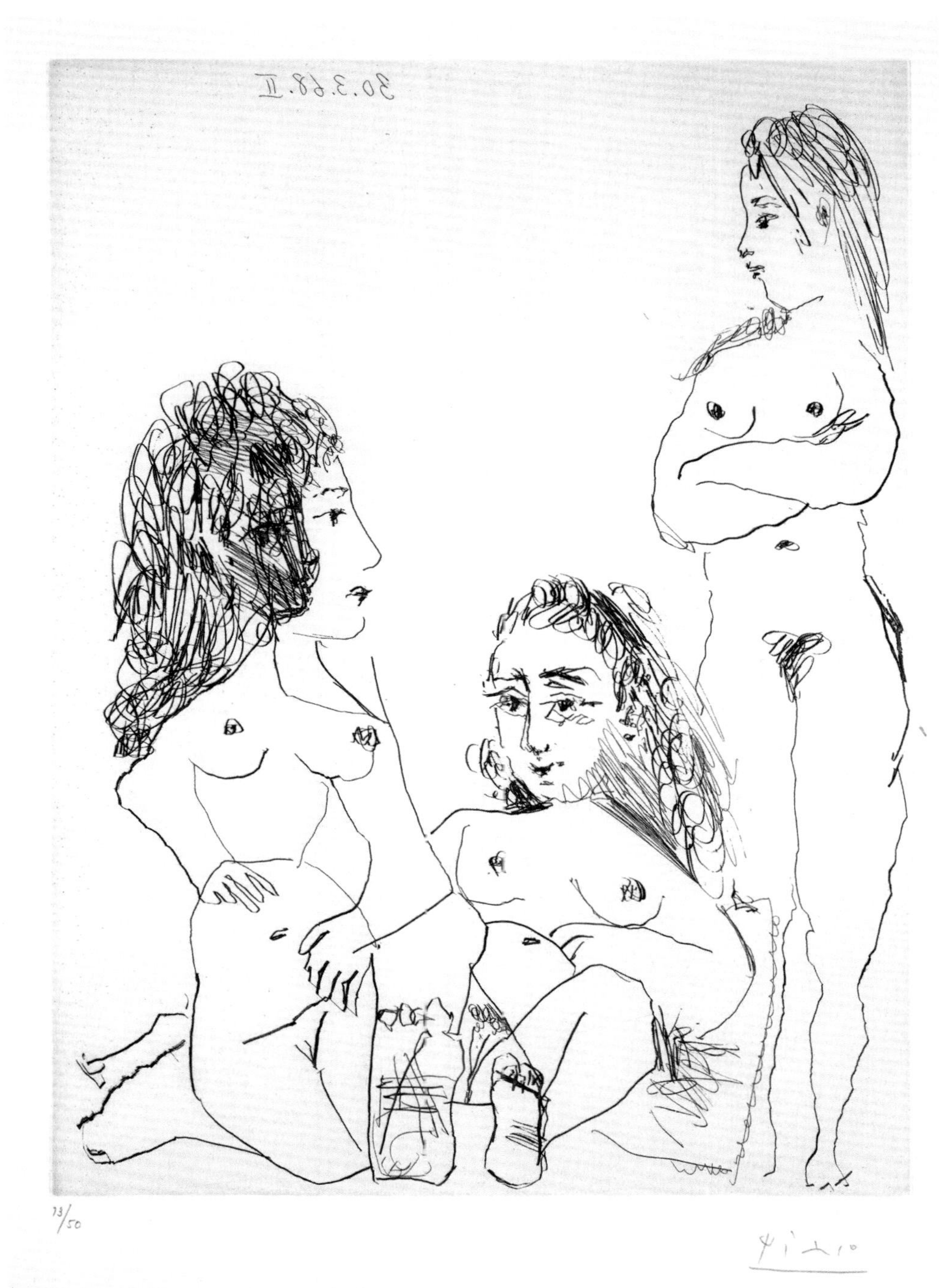

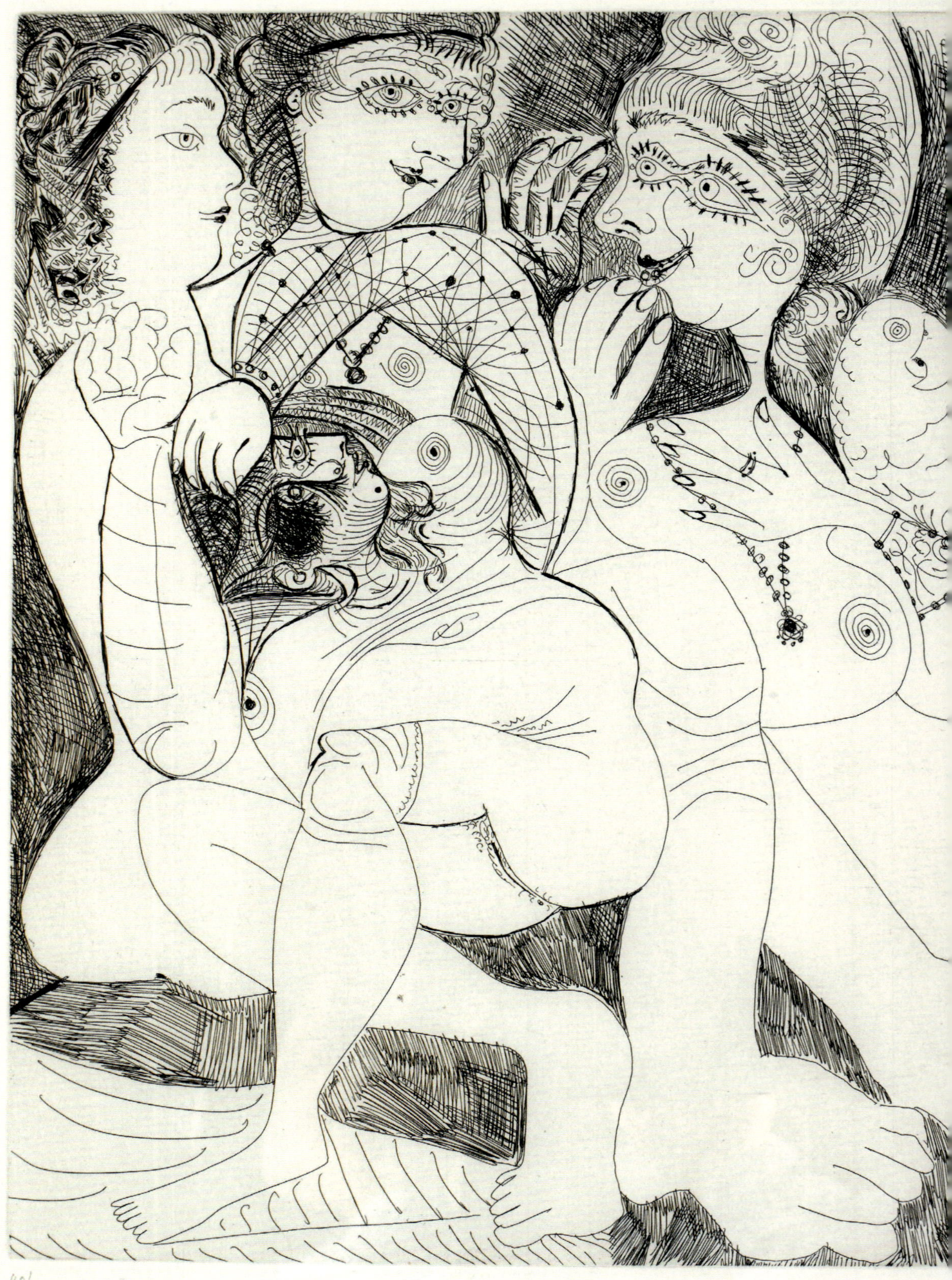

40/50

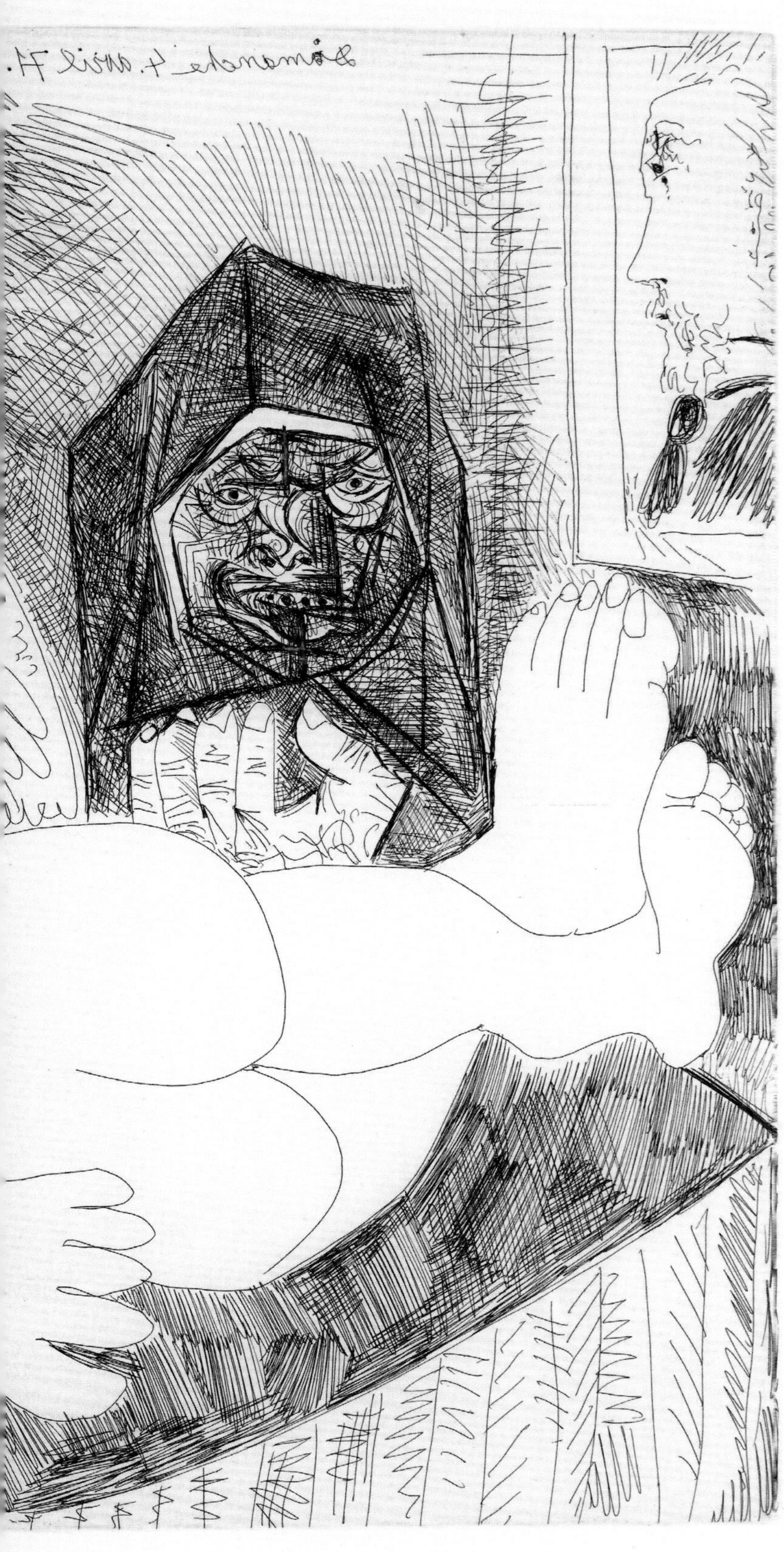

Brothel. Chatter, with parrot, Celestina, and the portrait of Degas from the *156 Suite*, 4 April 1971
Etching

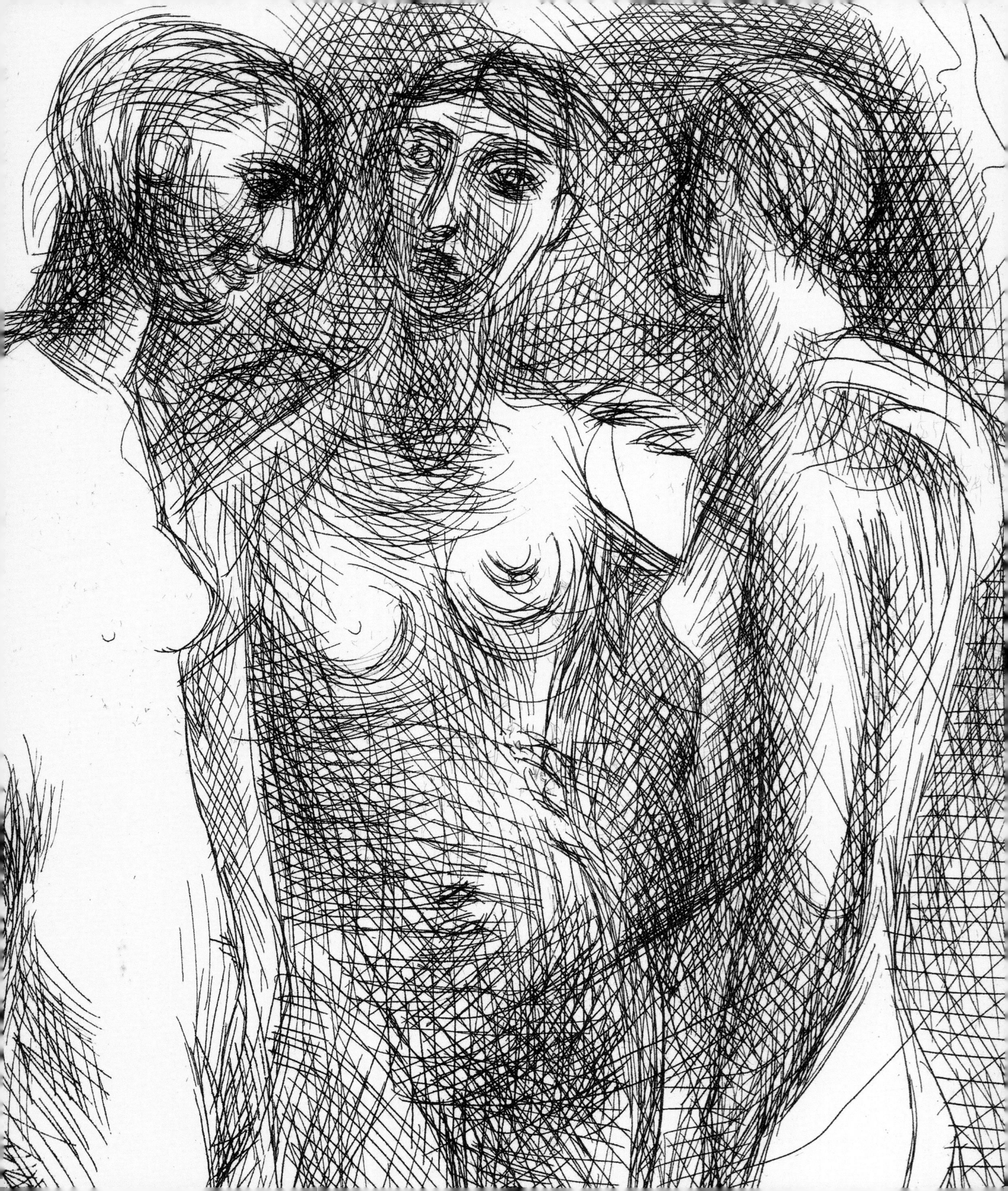

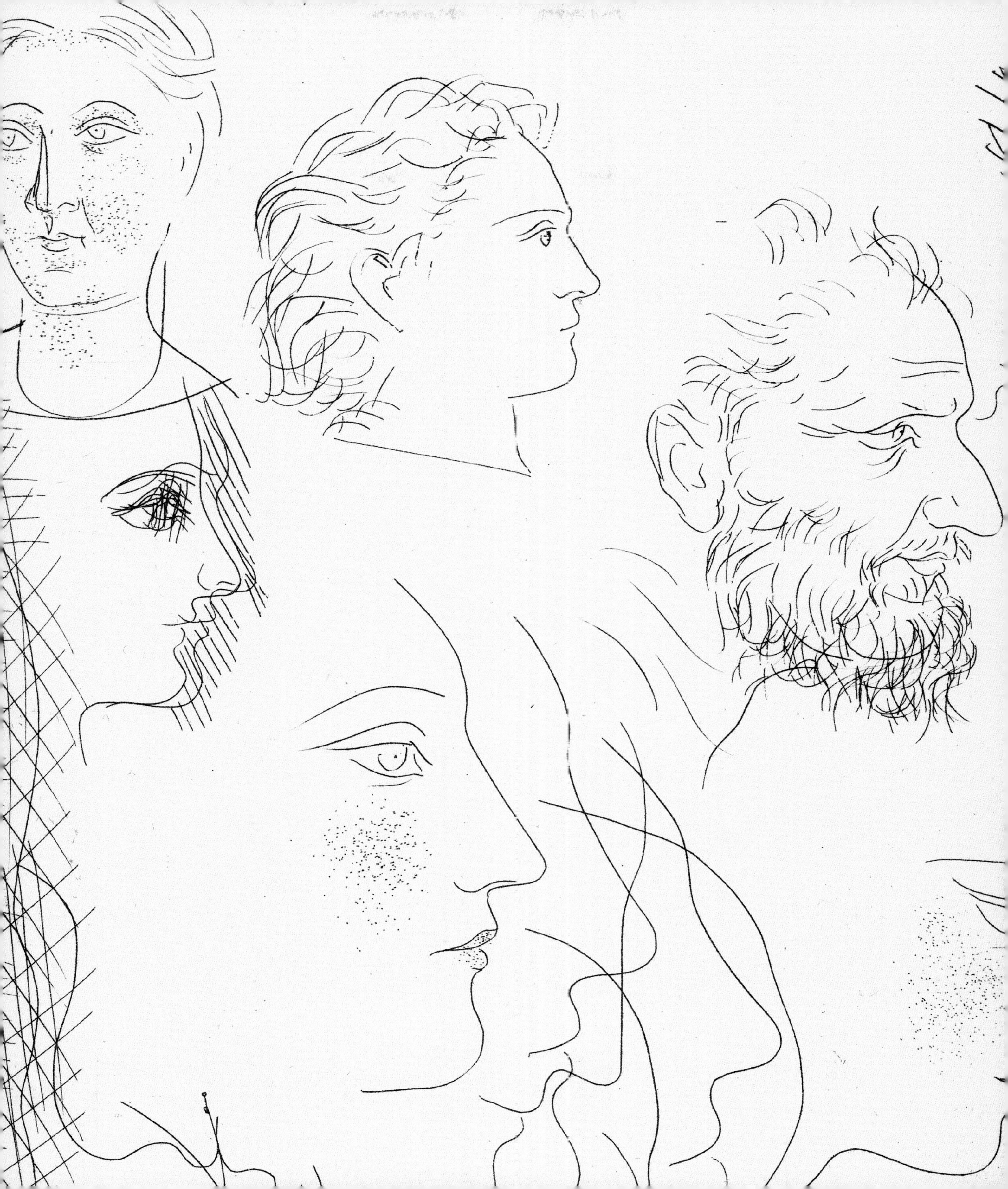

PABLO PICASSO:
THE BRITISH MUSEUM COLLECTION

The British Museum holds the most extensive collection of Pablo Picasso's prints in the UK, comprising 553 individual prints as of 2024. Very few were collected during Picasso's lifetime, however, when the Museum thought it undesirable to spend public money purchasing work by living artists. In 1926, the Museum acquired its first work by Picasso, still one of only five Picasso drawings in the collection, as a donation from the Contemporary Art Society. The Museum's then Keeper (head) of Prints and Drawings, Campbell Dodgson (1867–1948), had been instrumental in founding the Contemporary Art Society's modern graphic fund through private subscriptions and was able to acquire contemporary works for the collection as gifts from the organisation. The first two Picasso prints entered the Museum in this way in 1934 and 1945. Dodgson also had a personal collection and bequeathed over 5,000 works of art to the Museum, including 15 Picasso prints, which were received in 1949.

Little was done to build on this initial group in the years following Dodgson's bequest, and in 1955 the Museum turned down the opportunity to acquire a full set of the *Vollard Suite* for the price of £1,900. But in the mid-1970s, under Director Sir John Pope-Hennessy (1913–1994), the Department of Prints and Drawings received its first curator of the modern collection, Frances Carey, and Antony Griffiths was appointed curator responsible for prints. Together, they set about building up the modern collection, acquiring 28 Picasso prints between 1976 and 1995, most as purchases. The Museum continued to add to the collection into the twenty-first century, receiving funding for purchases from Art Fund (formerly the National Art Collections Fund) and the British Museum Friends, among others, and donations from individuals including the art dealer and Picasso expert Dr Frederick Mulder.

In 2011, the collection more than doubled with the acquisition of a complete set of the *Vollard Suite*, given by the private collector Hamish Parker in memory of his father, Major Horace Parker. The previous year, he had attended the annual Friends of Prints and Drawings event where new acquisitions were displayed, including a print from the *Vollard Suite* presented by the art dealer Karsten Schubert (1961–2019). The print was accompanied by a label written by Stephen Coppel, Frances Carey's successor, expressing the hope that the Museum would, at some point, acquire the whole set. Shortly afterwards, Hamish offered to fund the purchase of a pristine set that came from the heirs of Henri Petiet (1894–1980), the dealer who had acquired Ambroise Vollard's stock of unpublished prints after Vollard's death. In 2014, he completed another remarkable donation, funding the Museum's acquisition of the entire *347 Suite*, which had been purchased by Marlborough Fine Art, Zurich shortly after the prints were published in 1968, and had remained with them ever since.

These two major acquisitions opened up the possibility that the Museum could assemble a comprehensive collection of Picasso's prints that would tell the full story of his printmaking career. To this end, under Keeper Hugo Chapman, Coppel made further important acquisitions including a group of linocuts in 2013 and a group of post-war lithographs and aquatints in 2016. Support for these acquisitions came from Art Fund, the Wolfson Foundation, British Museum Patrons and various individuals, all of whom are named below.

The following checklist comprises all the prints and drawings by Picasso held by the British Museum at the time of publication. As Picasso rarely titled his prints, the titles are taken primarily from Georges Bloch's catalogue raisonné, published in 1968–79, and are translated into English. Brigitte Baer's later catalogue raisonné offered alternative titles for some of the prints, which include assumptions about the iconography that Bloch does not make. Baer's titles are given in addition (also in translation) only when there are important differences in the interpretation or where Bloch's titles are inaccurate or oblique. Only Baer's titles are given for the *347 Suite* because Bloch's titles are restricted to the date on which the print was made and the technique used.

Dimensions given are height followed by width.

REFERENCES

Bloch, Georges, *Pablo Picasso. Catalogue de l'œuvre gravé et lithographié 1904–1972*, vols 1–4, Berne: Éditions Kornfeld & Klipstein, 1968–79

Baer, Brigitte, *Picasso peintre-graveur*, Berne: Editions Kornfeld, vols 1–7 and *Addendum* (revising and extending vols 1–2 by Bernhard Geiser), Berne: Éditions Kornfield, 1986–96

Mourlot, Fernand, *Picasso: Lithographs*, trans. Jean Didry, Paris: André Sauret; Éditions du Livre, 1970

Grauss, Ulrike, ed., *Pablo Picasso: Lithographs*, Münster: Graphikmuseum Pablo Picasso; Ostfildern-Ruit: Hatje Cantz, 2000

The frugal meal, 1904,
Vollard edition 1913
Etching and scraper.
Plate: 464 × 377 mm.
Sheet: 656 × 498 mm
1949,0411.4624. Bequeathed
by Campbell Dodgson
Bloch 1; Baer 2.II.b.2
(illustrated on p. 33)

Head of a woman, 1905,
Vollard edition 1913
Etching. Plate: 115 × 84 mm.
Sheet: 453 × 325 mm
1949,0411.4625. Bequeathed
by Campbell Dodgson
Bloch 2; Baer 3.b.2
(illustrated on p. 35)

The poor, 1905,
Vollard edition 1913
Etching. Plate: 235 × 179 mm.
Sheet: 447 × 322 mm
1949,0411.4626. Bequeathed
by Campbell Dodgson
Bloch 3; Baer 4.II.b.2
(illustrated on p. 34)

Bust of a man, 1905
Drypoint. Plate: 121 × 94 mm.
Sheet: 307 × 220 mm
1949,0411.4627. Bequeathed
by Campbell Dodgson
Bloch 4; Baer 5.a
(illustrated on p. 35)

The watering hole, 1906,
Vollard edition 1913
Drypoint. Plate: 122 × 187 mm.
Sheet: 327 × 510 mm
1949,0411.4628. Bequeathed
by Campbell Dodgson
Bloch 8; Baer 10.b.2

At the circus, 1905–6,
Vollard edition 1913
Drypoint. Plate: 220 × 140 mm.
Sheet: 389 × 297 mm
1949,0411.4629. Bequeathed
by Campbell Dodgson
Bloch 9; Baer 11.b.2
(illustrated on p. 36, detail p. 30)

Salomé, 1905,
Vollard edition 1913
Drypoint. Plate: 400 × 348 mm.
Sheet: 576 × 505 mm
1949,0411.4630. Bequeathed
by Campbell Dodgson
Bloch 14; Baer 17.III.b.2
(illustrated on p. 37)

Still life. Fruit bowl, 1908–9,
Kahnweiler edition 1912
Drypoint and scraper.
Plate: 132 × 110 mm.
Sheet: 613 × 445 mm
1976,0515.12
Bloch 18; Baer 22.III.b

Still life. Fruit bowl, 1908–9,
Kahnweiler edition 1912
Drypoint and scraper.
Plate: 132 × 110 mm.
Sheet: 248 × 218 mm
2004,0602.130. Bequeathed
by Alexander Walker
Bloch 18; Baer 22.III.b
(illustrated on p. 39)

Still life. Bottle [*Still life with
a bottle of marc*], 1911,
Kahnweiler edition 1912
Drypoint. Plate: 498 × 305 mm.
Sheet: 674 × 500 mm
1980,0628.55
Bloch 24; Baer 33.b
(illustrated on p. 40)

Man with dog [*Man with dog
(rue Schœlcher)*], 1915 and
1930, Lucien Vollard-Marcel
Lecomte edition 1947
Etching and scraper.
Plate: 277 × 218 mm.
Sheet: 328 × 248 mm
1982,0724.15
Bloch 28; Baer 39.III.B.b
(illustrated on p. 41)

Group of three women
[*Two women looking at a
nude model*], 1923, Marcel
Guiot edition 1929
Drypoint, scraper and etching.
Plate: 175 × 127 mm.
Sheet: 402 × 299 mm
1934,1208.127. Presented by
the Contemporary Art Society
Bloch 57; Baer 102.VI.a
(illustrated on p. 44)

Woman beside the sea,
1923–4, Galerie Simon
(Kahnweiler) edition 1924
Crayon lithograph.
Image: 200 × 310 mm.
Sheet: 284 × 376 mm
1949,0411.4640. Bequeathed
by Campbell Dodgson
Bloch 67; Baer 237.b; Mourlot
XVII; Gauss 17
(illustrated on p. 16)

Seated woman, 1923, Galerie
Simon (Kahnweiler) edition 1924
Crayon lithograph and scraper.
Image: 295 × 210 mm.
Sheet: 380 × 268 mm
1949,0411.4639. Bequeathed
by Campbell Dodgson
Bloch 69; Baer 239.b; Mourlot
XIX; Gauss 19

Reading, 1925–6, Galerie Simon
(Kahnweiler) edition 1926
Lithograph and scraper.
Image: 326 × 245 mm.
Sheet: 660 × 478 mm
1945,1208.317. Presented by
the Contemporary Art Society
Bloch 75; Baer 242.b; Mourlot
XXII; Gauss 22

Nude model, 1927, printed after
1932, published by the Société
des Amateurs d'Art et des
Collectionneurs, Paris
Etching. Plate: 280 × 192 mm.
Sheet: 374 × 288 mm
1949,0411.4635. Bequeathed
by Campbell Dodgson
Bloch 78; Baer 119.II.c

Painter and the model knitting,
1927
Illustration for Honoré de
Balzac's *Le chef-d'œuvre
inconnu* (*The Unknown
Masterpiece*) (Paris: Vollard, 1931)
Etching. Plate: 195 × 280 mm.
Sheet: 254 × 328 mm (irregular)
1980,0628.15
Bloch 85; Baer 126.b.1
(illustrated on p. 46)

Three standing nudes, 1927
Illustration for Honoré de
Balzac's *Le chef-d'œuvre
inconnu* (Paris: Vollard, 1931)
Etching. Plate: 195 × 277 mm.
Sheet: 245 × 327 mm (irregular)
1970,1031.2
Bloch 90; Baer 131.b.1
(illustrated on p. 47)

Figure [*Figure. Bather
in the cabin*], 1929
Reserved for subscribers
of *Le Manuscrit Autographe*,
no. 21 (May–June 1929),
published by Auguste Blaizot
et fils, Paris
Lithograph.
Image: 240 × 140 mm.
Sheet: 280 × 225 mm
2020,7026.1. Funded by the
Friends of Prints and Drawings
Bloch 96; Baer 246b; Mourlot
XXVI; Gauss 30
(illustrated on p. 45)

Two nude women in a tree [*Two
nude women, one in
a tree*], 1931, probably printed
in 1934
Etching. Plate: 378 × 298 mm.
Sheet: 510 × 393 mm
1949,0411.4631. Bequeathed
by Campbell Dodgson
Bloch 234; Baer 204.B.b

The full suite numbered
2011,7096.1–100 was presented
by Hamish Parker in memory of
Major Horace Parker.

Plate 1: *Nude woman
crowned with flowers*,
16 September 1930
Etching. Plate: 314 × 224 mm.
Sheet: 447 × 340 mm
2011,7096.1
Bloch 134; Baer 192.B.d
(illustrated on p. 48)

Plate 2: *Nude woman
crowning herself with flowers*,
16 September 1930
Etching. Plate: 314 × 223 mm.
Sheet: 447 × 340 mm
2011,7096.2
Bloch 135; Baer 195.B.d

Plate 3: *At the bath*,
1 October 1930
Etching. Plate: 313 × 224 mm.
Sheet: 447 × 340 mm
2011,7096.3
Bloch 136; Baer 201.B.d

Plate 4: *Nude woman seated in
front of a curtain*, 3 April 1931
Etching. Plate: 312 × 224 mm.
Sheet: 447 × 340 mm
2011,7096.4
Bloch 137; Baer 202.B.d

Plate 5: *Man uncovering
a woman*, 20 June 1931
Drypoint. Plate: 367 × 295 mm.
Sheet: 447 × 340 mm
2011,7096.5
Bloch 138; Baer 203.II.B.d

Plate 6: *Nude woman in front
of a statue*, 4 July 1931
Etching. Plate: 312 × 223 mm.
Sheet: 447 × 340 mm
2011,7096.6
Bloch 139; Baer 205.B.d

Plate 7: *Two sculptors in front of
a statue*, 9 July 1931
Etching. Plate: 222 × 313 mm.
Sheet: 340 × 447 mm
2011,7096.7
Bloch 140; Baer 207.B.d

Plate 8: *Nude woman with
bent leg*, 9 July 1931
Etching. Plate: 312 × 222 mm.
Sheet: 447 × 340 mm
2011,7096.8
Bloch 141; Baer 208.B.d

Plate 9: *Rape*, 9 July 1931
Etching. Plate: 222 × 310 mm.
Sheet: 340 × 447 mm
2011,7096.9
Bloch 142; Baer 209.B.d

Plate 10: *Resting women*,
29 September 1931
Drypoint. Plate: 296 × 365 mm.
Sheet: 340 × 447 mm
2011,7096.10
Bloch 143; Baer 210.B.d

Plate 11: *Flautist and three
nude women*, 21 July 1932
Drypoint and scraper.
Plate: 295 × 365 mm.
Sheet: 340 × 447 mm
2011,7096.11
Bloch 144; Baer 258.B.d

Plate 12: *Two Catalan drinkers*,
29 November 1934
Etching. Plate: 237 × 297 mm.
Sheet: 340 × 447 mm
2011,7096.12
Bloch 228; Baer 442.B.d

Plate 13: *Winged bull
watched by four children*,
December 1934
Etching. Plate: 237 × 297 mm.
Sheet: 340 × 447 mm
2011,7096.13
Bloch 229; Baer 444.B.d

Plate 14: *Startled bathers*,
22 May 1933
Etching and drypoint.
Plate: 194 × 265 mm.
Sheet: 340 × 447 mm
2011,7096.14
Bloch 194; Baer 355.II.B.d

Plate 15: *Bull and horses
in the arena*, 7 November 1933
Etching with plate tone.
Plate: 194 × 270 mm.
Sheet: 340 × 447 mm
2011,7096.15
Bloch 203; Baer 380.B.d

Plate 16: *Death in the sun IV
[Bullfight. Wounded female
bullfighter III]*, 8 November 1933
Drypoint, scraper and etching
with plate tone.
Plate: 197 × 275 mm.
Sheet: 340 × 447 mm
2011,7096.16
Bloch 204; Baer 384.IV.B.d

Plate 17: *The circus*,
11 November 1933
Drypoint and scraper.
Plate: 200 × 280 mm.
Sheet: 340 × 447 mm
2011,7096.17
Bloch 205; Baer 385.VI.B.d

Plate 18: *Heads and figures
entangled*, 30 January 1934
Etching. Plate: 275 × 195 mm.
Sheet: 447 × 340 mm
2011,7096.18
Bloch 211; Baer 410.B.d

Plate 19: *Young couple
crouching, the man with
a tambourine*, 30 January 1934
Etching. Plate: 276 × 198 mm.
Sheet: 447 × 340 mm
2011,7096.19
Bloch 212; Baer 411.B.d

Plate 20: *Flautist and young
girl with a tambourine*,
30 January 1934
Etching. Plate: 275 × 195 mm.
Sheet: 447 × 340 mm
2011,7096.20
Bloch 213; Baer 412.B.d

Plate 21: *Seated nude woman
with her head resting on her
hand*, 9 March 1934
Etching with plate tone.
Plate: 280 × 197 mm.
Sheet: 447 × 340 mm
2011,7096.21
Bloch 218; Baer 423.B.d

Plate 22: *Female bullfighter I*,
20 June 1934
Etching. Plate: 297 × 236 mm.
Sheet: 502 × 386 mm
1979,0721.64
Bloch 220; Baer 426.B.c

Plate 22: *Female bullfighter I*,
20 June 1934
Etching. Plate: 297 × 236 mm.
Sheet: 447 × 340 mm
2011,7096.22
Bloch 220; Baer 426.B.d
(illustrated on p. 63)

Plate 23: *Female bullfighter II*,
22 June 1934
Etching. Plate: 235 × 300 mm.
Sheet: 340 × 447 mm
2011,7096.23
Bloch 221; Baer 427.B.d

Plate 24: *Masked figures and
bird-woman*, 19 November 1934
Aquatint and etching.
Plate: 247 × 345 mm.
Sheet: 340 × 447 mm
2011,7096.24
Bloch 227; Baer 441.B.d

Plate 25: *Nude seated woman
and three bearded heads*,
19 November–7 December 1934
Sugar aquatint, scraper,
engraving and etching.
Plate: 130 × 180 mm.
Sheet: 340 × 447 mm
2011,7096.25
Bloch 216; Baer 416.VI.B.d

Plate 26: *Boy and sleeping
woman by candlelight*,
18 November 1934
Etching, scraper, engraving and
aquatint. Plate: 235 × 297 mm.
Sheet: 340 × 447 mm
2011,7096.26
Bloch 226; Baer 440.III.B.d

Plate 27: *Faun uncovering
a woman*, 12 June 1936
Sugar aquatint, scraper and
engraving. Plate: 315 × 415 mm.
Sheet: 340 × 447 mm
2011,7096.27
Bloch 230; Baer 609.VI.B.d
(Illustrated on p. 57)

Plate 28: *Rape beneath
the window*, probably begun
in November 1933
Etching, aquatint and drypoint.
Plate: 275 × 196 mm.
Sheet: 447 × 340 mm
2011,7096.28
Bloch 183; Baer 342.XIV.B.d

Plate 29: *Rape IV [Coupling I]*,
2 November 1933
Etching, aquatint and drypoint.
Plate: 195 × 275 mm.
Sheet: 340 × 448 mm
2010,7079.7. Presented by
Karsten Schubert in honour
of Frances Carey
Bloch 181; Baer 340.II.B.d

Plate 29: *Rape IV [Coupling I]*,
2 November 1933
Etching, aquatint and drypoint.
Plate: 195 × 275 mm.
Sheet: 340 × 447 mm
2011,7096.29
Bloch 181; Baer 340.II.B.d

Plate 30: *Rape II
[The Embrace I]*, 22 April 1933
Drypoint. Plate: 297 × 366 mm.
Sheet: 340 × 447 mm
2011,7096.30
Bloch 180; Baer 338.B.d

Plate 31: *Rape V
[The Embrace III]*, 23 April 1933
Drypoint. Plate: 297 × 363 mm.
Sheet: 340 × 447 mm
2011,7096.31
Bloch 182; Baer 341.B.d

Plate 32: *Rape VII [Couple
making love]*, 2 November 1933
Etching, aquatint, scraper and
drypoint. Plate: 195 × 275 mm.
Sheet: 340 × 447 mm
2011,7096.32
Bloch 202; Baer 378.IX.B.d

Plate 33: *Rembrandt and female
heads*, 27 January 1934
Etching. Plate: 135 × 210 mm.
Sheet: 340 × 447 mm
2011,7096.33
Bloch 207; Baer 405.B.d

Plate 34: *Rembrandt with
palette*, 27 January 1934
Etching. Plate: 275 × 198 mm.
Sheet: 447 × 340 mm
2011,7096.34
Bloch 208; Baer 406.III.B.d

Plate 35: *Rembrandt and two
women*, 31 January 1934
Etching and scraper with plate
tone. Plate: 275 × 198 mm.
Sheet: 447 × 340 mm
2011,7096.35
Bloch 215; Baer 414.B.d

Plate 36: *Rembrandt and
woman with a veil*,
31 January 1934
Etching. Plate: 275 × 198 mm.
Sheet: 447 × 340 mm
2011,7096.36
Bloch 214; Baer 413.B.d

Plate 37: *Sculptor, reclining
model and sculpture*,
17 March 1933
Etching. Plate: 265 × 194 mm.
Sheet: 447 × 340 mm
2011,7096.37
Bloch 147; Baer 298.B.d

Plate 38: *Sculptor, model and
sculpted bust*, 17 March 1933
Etching. Plate: 265 × 194 mm.
Sheet: 447 × 340 mm
2011,7096.38
Bloch 148; Baer 300.B.d
(illustrated on p. 49)

Plate 39: *Sculptor, crouching
model and sculpted head*,
23 March 1933
Etching. Plate: 265 × 194 mm.
Sheet: 447 × 340 mm
2011,7096.39
Bloch 155; Baer 308.II.B.d

Plate 40: *Sculptor, model and
sculpture of a seated figure*,
15 March 1933
Drypoint and scraper.
Plate: 320 × 185 mm.
Sheet: 447 × 340 mm
2011,7096.40
Bloch 146; Baer 297.VI.B.d

Plate 41: *Sculptors, models
and sculpture*, 20 March 1933
Etching. Plate: 194 × 265 mm.
Sheet: 340 × 447 mm
2011,7096.41
Bloch 149; Baer 301.B.d

Plate 42: *Two clothed models*,
21 March 1933
Etching. Plate: 265 × 194 mm.
Sheet: 447 × 340 mm
2011,7096.42
Bloch 150; Baer 302.B.d

Plate 43: *Model leaning on
a painting*, 21 March 1933
Etching. Plate: 265 × 194 mm.
Sheet: 447 × 340 mm
2011,7096.43
Bloch 151; Baer 303.B.d

Plate 44: *Sculptor with goblet and crouching model*,
21 March 1933
Etching. Plate: 265 × 194 mm.
Sheet: 447 × 340 mm
2011,7096.44
Bloch 152; Baer 304.II.B.d

Plate 45: *Sculptor and model admiring a sculpted head*,
23 March 1933
Etching. Plate: 265 × 194 mm.
Sheet: 447 × 340 mm
2011,7096.45
Bloch 154; Baer 307.B.d

Plate 46: *Young sculptor at work*, 23 March 1933
Etching. Plate: 265 × 194 mm.
Sheet: 447 × 340 mm
2011,7096.46
Bloch 156; Baer 309.B.d
(illustrated on p. 52)

Plate 47: *Old sculptor at work*,
25 March 1933
Etching with plate tone.
Plate: 265 × 190 mm.
Sheet: 447 × 340 mm
2011,7096.47
Bloch 153; Baer 305.B.d

Plate 48: *Sculptor and two sculpted heads*, 26 March 1933
Etching. Plate: 268 × 194 mm.
Sheet: 447 × 340 mm
2011,7096.48
Bloch 157; Baer 310.B.d

Plate 49: *Sculptor, half-length, at work*, 26 March 1933
Etching. Plate: 268 × 194 mm.
Sheet: 447 × 340 mm
2011,7096.49
Bloch 158; Baer 311.B.d

Plate 50: *Reclining sculptor and model with mask*,
27 March 1933
Etching. Plate: 268 × 194 mm.
Sheet: 447 × 340 mm
2011,7096.50
Bloch 159; Baer 312.B.d

Plate 51: *Reclining sculptor in front of draped nude*,
27 March 1933
Etching. Plate: 268 × 194 mm.
Sheet: 340 × 447 mm
2011,7096.51
Bloch 160; Baer 313.B.d

Plate 52: *Two male sculptures*,
27 March 1933
Etching. Plate: 268 × 194 mm.
Sheet: 447 × 340 mm
2011,7096.52
Bloch 161; Baer 314.B.d

Plate 53: *Reclining sculptor before the small torso*,
30 March 1933
Etching. Plate: 194 × 268 mm.
Sheet: 340 × 447 mm
2011,7096.53
Bloch 162; Baer 315.B.d

Plate 53: *Reclining sculptor before the small torso*,
30 March 1933
Etching on vellum.
Plate: 194 × 268 mm.
Sheet: 407 × 528 mm
2020,7016.88. Accepted under the Cultural Gifts Scheme by HM Government from Hamish Parker and allocated to the British Museum, 2020
Bloch 162; Baer 315.B.b

Plate 54: *Family of acrobats*,
30 March 1933
Etching. Plate: 194 × 268 mm.
Sheet: 340 × 447 mm.
2011,7096.54
Bloch 163; Baer 316.B.d

Plate 55: *Reclining sculptor in front of the young horseman*,
30 March 1933
Etching. Plate: 194 × 268 mm.
Sheet: 340 × 447 mm
2011,7096.55
Bloch 164; Baer 317.B.d

Plate 56: *Reclining sculptor in front of bacchanal with bull*,
30 March 1933
Etching. Plate: 194 × 268 mm.
Sheet: 340 × 447 mm
2011,7096.56
Bloch 165; Baer 318.B.d

Plate 57: *Reclining sculptor in front of horses and bull*,
31 March 1933
Etching. Plate: 194 × 268 mm.
Sheet: 340 × 447 mm
2011,7096.57
Bloch 166; Baer 319.B.d

Plate 58: *Reclining sculptor in front of a centaur and a woman*,
31 March 1933
Etching. Plate: 194 × 268 mm.
Sheet: 340 × 447 mm
2011,7096.58
Bloch 167; Baer 320.B.d

Plate 59: *Sculptor and his model before a window*,
31 March 1933
Etching. Plate: 197 × 268 mm.
Sheet: 340 × 447 mm
2011,7096.59
Bloch 168; Baer 321.II.B.d
(illustrated on p. 53)

Plate 60: *Reclining sculptor and surrealist sculpture*,
31 March 1933
Etching. Plate: 194 × 268 mm.
Sheet: 340 × 447 mm
2011,7096.60
Bloch 169; Baer 322.B.d

Plate 61: *Model and large sculpted head*, 1 April 1933
Etching. Plate: 268 × 194 mm.
Sheet: 447 × 340 mm
2011,7096.61
Bloch 170; Baer 323.B.d

Plate 62: *Reclining sculptor I*,
2 April 1933
Etching. Plate: 194 × 268 mm.
Sheet: 387 × 505 mm
1979,0721.65
Bloch 171; Baer 324.B.c

Plate 62: *Reclining sculptor I*,
2 April 1933
Etching. Plate: 194 × 268 mm.
Sheet: 340 × 447 mm
2011,7096.62
Bloch 171; Baer 324.B.d

Plate 63: *Reclining sculptor II*, 3 April 1933
Etching. Plate: 194 × 268 mm.
Sheet: 340 × 447 mm
2011,7096.63
Bloch 172; Baer 325.B.d

Plate 64: *Reclining sculptor III*,
3 April 1933
Etching. Plate: 194 × 268 mm.
Sheet: 340 × 447 mm
2011,7096.64
Bloch 173; Baer 326.B.d

Plate 65: *Reclining sculptor IV*,
4 April 1933
Etching. Plate: 194 × 268 mm.
Sheet: 340 × 447 mm
2011,7096.65
Bloch 174; Baer 327.B.d

Plate 66: *Model contemplating a sculpted group*, 5 April 1933
Etching. Plate: 300 × 365 mm.
Sheet: 340 × 447 mm
2011,7096.66
Bloch 175; Baer 328.B.d

Plate 67: *Three nude women near a window*, 6 April 1933
Etching. Plate: 365 × 300 mm.
Sheet: 447 × 340 mm
2011,7096.67
Bloch 176; Baer 329.B.d

Plate 68: *Sculptor and standing model*, 7 April 1933
Etching. Plate: 367 × 297 mm.
Sheet: 447 × 340 mm
2011,7096.68
Bloch 177; Baer 330.B.d

Plate 69: *Sculptor and kneeling model*, 8 April 1933
Etching. Plate: 365 × 295 mm.
Sheet: 500 × 385 mm
1979,0721.66
Bloch 178; Baer 331.B.c

Plate 69: *Sculptor and kneeling model*, 8 April 1933
Etching. Plate: 365 × 295 mm.
Sheet: 447 × 340 mm
2011,7096.69
Bloch 178; Baer 331.B.d
(illustrated on p. 55)

Plate 70: *Sculptor of a young man with a goblet*, 11 April 1933
Etching. Plate: 268 × 194 mm.
Sheet: 447 × 340 mm
2011,7096.70
Bloch 179; Baer 332.B.d

Plate 71: *Woman leaning on her elbow, sculpture from rear and bearded head*,
3 May 1933
Etching. Plate: 378 × 295 mm.
Sheet: 447 × 340 mm
2011,7096.71
Bloch 184; Baer 343.B.d

Plate 72: *Nude model and sculptures*, 3 May 1933
Etching. Plate: 378 × 300 mm.
Sheet: 447 × 340 mm
2011,7096.72
Bloch 185; Baer 344.B.d

Plate 73: *Model and large sculpture viewed from behind*,
4 May 1933
Etching. Plate: 268 × 194 mm.
Sheet: 447 × 340 mm
2011,7096.73
Bloch 186; Baer 345.IV.B.d

Plate 74: *Model and surrealist sculpture*, 4 May 1933
Etching. Plate: 268 × 194 mm.
Sheet: 447 × 340 mm
2011,7096.74
Bloch 187; Baer 346.B.d

Plate 75: *Crouching model, sculpture viewed from behind and bearded head*, 5 May 1933
Etching. Plate: 268 × 194 mm.
Sheet: 447 × 340 mm
2011,7096.75
Bloch 188; Baer 347.B.d

Plate 76: *Sculptures and vase of flowers*, 5 May 1933
Etching. Plate: 265 × 190 mm.
Sheet: 447 × 335 mm
2011,7096.76
Bloch 189; Baer 348.III.B.d

Plate 77: *Three actors*,
14 March 1933
Etching. Plate: 280 × 180 mm.
Sheet: 447 × 340 mm
2011,7096.77
Bloch 145; Baer 296.II.B.d

Plate 78: *Seated woman and woman viewed from behind*,
27 January 1934
Etching. Plate: 280 × 195 mm.
Sheet: 447 × 340 mm
2011,7096.78
Bloch 206; Baer 404.B.d

Plate 79: *Seated woman with a hat and draped standing woman*, 29 January 1934
Etching. Plate: 280 × 195 mm.
Sheet: 447 × 340 mm
2011,7096.79
Bloch 210; Baer 408.B.d

Plate 80: *Two models looking at each other*, 29 January 1934
Etching. Plate: 280 × 195 mm.
Sheet: 447 × 340 mm
2011,7096.80
Bloch 209; Baer 407.B.d
(illustrated on p. 50)

Plate 81: *Sculptor and sculpted group of three dancers*,
2 March 1934
Etching. Plate: 220 × 313 mm.
Sheet: 340 × 447 mm
2011,7096.81
Bloch 217; Baer 421.B.d
(illustrated on p. 51, detail p.42)

Plate 82: *Four nude women and a sculpted head*,
10 March 1934
Etching, scraper and engraving.
Plate: 220 × 313 mm.
Sheet: 340 × 447 mm
2011,7096.82
Bloch 219; Baer 424.V.B.d

Plate 83: *Minotaur with a goblet in his hand and a young woman*, 17 May 1933
Etching. Plate: 194 × 267 mm.
Sheet: 340 × 447 mm
2011,7096.83
Bloch 190; Baer 349.B.d

Plate 84: *Minotaur caressing a woman*, 18 May 1933
Etching. Plate: 299 × 367 mm.
Sheet: 340 × 447 mm
2011,7096.84
Bloch 191; Baer 350.B.d

Plate 85: *Bacchic scene with Minotaur*, 18 May 1933
Etching. Plate: 295 × 365 mm.
Sheet: 385 × 503 mm
1979,0623.57
Bloch 192; Baer 351.III.B.c

Plate 85: *Bacchic scene with Minotaur*, 18 May 1933
Etching. Plate: 295 × 365 mm.
Sheet: 340 × 447 mm
2011,7096.85
Bloch 192; Baer 351.III.B.d
(illustrated on p. 58)

Plate 86: *Woman gazing at a sleeping Minotaur*, 18 May 1933
Etching. Plate: 190 × 265 mm.
Sheet: 340 × 447 mm
2011,7096.86
Bloch 193; Baer 352.III.B.d
(illustrated on p. 59)

Plate 87: *Minotaur attacking an Amazon* [*Amorous Minotaur with a female centaur*], 23 May 1933
Etching. Plate: 190 × 265 mm.
Sheet: 340 × 447 mm
2011,7096.87
Bloch 195; Baer 356.III.B.d
(illustrated on p. 60)

Plate 88: *Wounded Minotaur VI*,
26 May 1933
Etching. Plate: 190 × 265 mm.
Sheet: 340 × 447 mm
2011,7096.88
Bloch 196; Baer 363.B.d

Plate 89: *Vanquished Minotaur*,
29 May 1933
Etching. Plate: 190 × 265 mm.
Sheet: 340 × 447 mm
2011,7096.89
Bloch 197; Baer 365.B.d
(illustrated on p. 64)

Plate 90: *Dying Minotaur*,
30 May 1933
Etching. Plate: 194 × 268 mm.
Sheet: 340 × 447 mm
2011,7096.90
Bloch 198; Baer 366.B.d
(illustrated on p. 65)

Plate 91: *Minotaur and woman behind a curtain*, 16 June 1933
Etching. Plate: 190 × 265 mm.
Sheet: 340 × 447 mm
2011,7096.91
Bloch 199; Baer 367.B.d

Plate 92: *Minotaur, drinker and women*, 18 June 1933
Drypoint, etching, scraper and engraving. Plate: 295 × 365 mm.
Sheet: 340 × 447 mm
2011,7096.92
Bloch 200; Baer 368.IV.B.d

Plate 93: *Minotaur caressing a sleeping woman*,
18 June 1933, plate reworked probably at end of 1934
Drypoint. Plate: 299 × 365 mm.
Sheet: 390 × 502 mm
1979,0721.67
Bloch 201; Baer 369.II.B.c

Plate 93: *Minotaur caressing a sleeping woman*,
18 June 1933, plate reworked probably at end of 1934
Drypoint. Plate: 299 × 365 mm.
Sheet: 340 × 447 mm
2011,7096.93
Bloch 201; Baer 369.II.B.d
(illustrated on p. 61)

Plate 94: *Blind Minotaur led by a little girl I*, 22 September 1934
Drypoint, scraper and engraving.
Plate: 250 × 345 mm.
Sheet: 340 × 447 mm
2011,7096.94
Bloch 222; Baer 434.XII.B.d

Plate 95: *Blind Minotaur led by a little girl III*, 4 November 1934
Etching, engraving and scraper.
Plate: 225 × 310 mm.
Sheet: 340 × 447 mm
2011,7096.95
Bloch 224; Baer 436.IV.B.d

Plate 96: *Blind Minotaur led by a little girl II*, 23 Oct 1934
Etching. Plate: 240 × 298 mm.
Sheet: 340 × 447 mm
2011,7096.96
Bloch 223; Baer 435.B.d

Plate 97: *Blind Minotaur led by a little girl in the night*, 3–7, 31 December 1934
Aquatint worked with scraper to resemble mezzotint, drypoint and engraving.
Plate: 247 × 345 mm.
Sheet: 340 × 447 mm
2011,7096.97
Bloch 225; Baer 437.IV.B.d
(illustrated on p. 66)

Plate 98: *Portrait of Vollard II*,
4 March 1937
Sugar aquatint.
Plate: 345 × 245 mm.
Sheet: 452 × 338 mm
1981,0620.18
Bloch 231; Baer 618.B.d

Plate 98: *Portrait of Vollard II*,
4 March 1937
Sugar aquatint.
Plate: 345 × 245 mm.
Sheet: 447 × 340 mm
2011,7096.98
Bloch 231; Baer 618.Bd

Plate 99: *Portrait of Vollard III* [*Portrait of Vollard I*],
4 March 1937
Sugar aquatint.
Plate: 345 × 245 mm.
Sheet: 447 × 340 mm
2011,7096.99
Bloch 232; Baer 617.B.d
(illustrated on p. 67)

Plate 100: *Portrait of Vollard IV* [*Portrait of Vollard III*],
4 March 1937
Etching. Plate: 345 × 245 mm.
Sheet: 447 × 340 mm
2011,7096.100
Bloch 233; Baer 619.B.d

Woman bullfighter I,
12 June 1934, printed in 1939
Etching. Plate: 497 × 694 mm.
Sheet: 570 × 775 mm
1980,1108.8
Bloch 1329; Baer 425.C

Bullfight [*The large bullfight, with woman bullfighter*],
8 September 1934, printed in 1939
Etching. Plate: 495 × 692 mm.
Sheet: 570 × 770 mm
1980,1108.9
Bloch 1330; Baer 433.C

Monkey, 1936
Illustration for *Picasso. Eaux-fortes originales pour les textes de Buffon* (*Picasso. Original etchings for texts by Buffon*)
(Paris: Martin Fabiani, 1942)
Sugar aquatint, scraper and drypoint. Plate: 275 × 207 mm.
Sheet: 370 × 277 mm
2012,7014.3. Funded by John and Caryl Hubbard
Bloch 339; Baer 586.II.B.b
(illustrated on p. 69)

Goldfinch, 1936
Illustration for *Picasso. Eaux-fortes originales pour les textes de Buffon* (Paris: Martin Fabiani, 1942)
Sugar aquatint, scraper and drypoint. Plate: 265 × 280 mm.
Sheet: 367 × 282 mm
1949,0411.4634. Bequeathed by Campbell Dodgson
Bloch 348; Baer 595.III.A

Lizard, 1936
Illustration for *Picasso. Eaux-fortes originales pour les textes de Buffon* (Paris: Martin Fabiani, 1942)
Sugar aquatint and drypoint.
Plate: 268 × 215 mm.
Sheet: 369 × 282 mm
1949,0411.4633. Bequeathed by Campbell Dodgson
Bloch 355; Baer 602.II.B
(illustrated on p. 71, detail p. 8)

Frogs, 1936
Illustration for *Picasso. Eaux-fortes originales pour les textes de Buffon* (Paris: Martin Fabiani, 1942)
Sugar aquatint, burnisher and drypoint. Plate: 267 × 204 mm.
Sheet: 370 × 280 mm
1949,0411.4632. Bequeathed by Campbell Dodgson
Bloch 357; Baer 604.II.B
(illustrated on p. 70)

The dream and lie of Franco
(plate I), 8 January 1937
Etching and sugar aquatint.
Plate: 318 × 422 mm.
Sheet: 385 × 570 mm
1980,1108.10.1
Bloch 297; Baer 615.II.B.e
(illustrated on p. 72)

The dream and lie of Franco
(plate II), 8, 9 January,
7 June 1937
Etching, sugar aquatint and
scraper. Plate: 318 × 422 mm.
Sheet: 388 × 567 mm
1980,1108.10.2
Bloch 298; Baer 616.V.B.e
(illustrated on p. 73)

Head of a woman, 1938
Illustration for Paul Éluard,
Solidarité (*Solidarity*), translated
by Brian Coffey (Paris: GLM,
1938)
Etching and engraving.
Plate: 104 × 75 mm.
Sheet: 230 × 164 mm
1949,0411.5094.1. Bequeathed
by Campbell Dodgson
Bloch 317; Baer 635.c
(illustrated on p. 74)

Head of a woman [*Head of a
woman no. 7. Portrait of Dora
Maar*], 1939
Drypoint in pink, blue, brown
and black. Plate: 297 × 237 mm.
Sheet: 445 × 337 mm (irregular)
1994,1002.7
Bloch 1336; Baer 655.B.a
(illustrated on p. 75)

Eight silhouettes,
13 January 1946
Lithograph.
Image: 320 × 435 mm.
Sheet: 330 × 443 mm (irregular)
1984,1006.23
Bloch 388; Mourlot 29; Gauss
129 (illustrated on p. 79)

Two nude women,
13th state, 25 January 1946
Lithograph.
Image: 265 × 358 mm.
Sheet: 327 × 442 mm
1990,0407.14. Presented by
Dr Frederick Mulder
Bloch 390; Mourlot 16.XIII;
Gauss 89 (illustrated on p. 78)

Two nude women,
18th state, 12 February 1946
Lithograph.
Image: 318 × 430 mm.
Sheet: 328 × 443 mm
1990,0407.15
Bloch 390; Mourlot 16.XVIII;
Gauss 95 (illustrated on p. 78)

David and Bathsheba,
2nd state, 30 March 1947
Lithograph.
Image: 644 × 485 mm.
Sheet: 660 × 498 mm (irregular)
1966,0723.4. Presented
by Nicolete Gray
Bloch 440; Mourlot 109.II;
Gauss 203 (illustrated on p. 80)

David and Bathsheba,
4th state, 30 March 1947
Lithograph.
Image: 645 × 478 mm.
Sheet: 654 × 498 mm
2016,7048.2. Funded by Art
Fund (with a contribution from
Art Partners), the Wolfson
Foundation, the Vollard Group,
Hamish Parker, Clive Gillmore,
Katrin Bellinger, Margaret
Conklin, Anthony Diamond,
Christian Duerckheim, David
Lawson, Dr Frederick Mulder,
David Sabel and Daniel Thierry*
Bloch 441; Mourlot 109.IV;
Gauss 205 (illustrated on p. 81)

David and Bathsheba,
8th state, 10 April 1949
Lithograph.
Image: 655 × 488 mm.
Sheet: 660 × 500 mm
1995,0618.27
Mourlot 109.VIII; Gauss 210
(illustrated on p. 83, detail p. 76)

*White pigeon on black
background*, 4 February 1947
Transfer lithograph.
Image: 270 × 450 mm.
Sheet: 328 × 497 mm
2016,7048.1. *
Bloch 420; Mourlot 65; Gauss
175 (illustrated on p. 95)

Women on the beach,
11 May 1947
Transfer lithograph.
Image: 497 × 650 mm.
Sheet: 500 × 653 mm
2006,0929.18. Presented by
Gordon and Ursula Bowyer
Bloch 452; Mourlot 101; Gauss
233 (illustrated on p. 86)

*Illustration. Woman with a long
neck* [Baer], 26 February 1947
Illustration for *Vingt poëmes
de Góngora* (*Twenty poems
by Góngora*) (Paris: Les Grands
Peintres Modernes et le Livre,
1948)
Sugar aquatint and etching.
Plate: 379 × 280 mm.
Sheet: 385 × 285 mm
2006,0929.17. Presented by
Gordon and Ursula Bowyer
Baer 755

Black figure, 20 November 1948
Lithograph.
Image: 643 × 498 mm.
Sheet: 655 × 500 mm
1996,0929.4
Bloch 577; Mourlot 126;
Gauss 387

Composition, 21 November 1948
Lithograph.
Image: 645 × 497 mm.
Sheet: 655 × 505 mm
2016,7048.3. *
Bloch 578; Mourlot 127; Gauss
388 (illustrated on p. 84)

Figure, 21 November 1948
Lithograph.
Image: 650 × 500 mm.
Sheet: 660 × 504 mm
2016,7048.4. *
Bloch 579; Mourlot 128; Gauss
389 (illustrated on p. 85)

The artist and child,
20 February 1949
Pen lithograph.
Image: 630 × 470 mm.
Sheet: 650 × 498 mm
2016,7048.5. *
Bloch 590; Mourlot 156;
Gauss 463 (illustrated on p. 88)

Figure, 4 March 1949
Lithograph.
Image: 650 × 500 mm.
Sheet: 657 × 502 mm
2016,7048.6. *
Bloch 593; Mourlot 162;
Gauss 471

The picador, 18 June 1952
Sugar aquatint.
Plate: 458 × 553 mm.
Sheet: 503 × 660 mm
1994,1002.8
Bloch 692; Baer 894.B.a
(illustrated on p. 92)

The hen, 23, 25 June 1952
Sugar aquatint and scraper.
Plate: 515 × 667 mm.
Sheet: 570 × 760 mm
2016,7048.17. *
Bloch 694; Baer 896.VI.B.b.1
(illustrated on p. 94, detail pp. 6–7)

Gardens at Vallauris,
15 January 1953
Crayon lithograph.
Image: 510 × 640 mm.
Sheet: 566 × 761 mm
2016,7048.7. *
Bloch 733; Mourlot 236;
Gauss 620 (illustrated on p. 87)

Head on black background,
9 May 1953
Lithograph.
Image: 693 × 543 mm.
Sheet: 760 × 555 mm
2016,7048.8. *
Bloch 742; Mourlot 241;
Gauss 627

The rehearsal,
21–26 February 1954
Crayon transfer lithograph.
Image and sheet: 498 × 653 mm
2016,7048.10. *
Bloch 756; Mourlot 252;
Gauss 644

Figures and dove,
18 February 1954
Crayon transfer lithograph.
Image: 495 × 650 mm.
Sheet: 495 × 655 mm
2016,7048.9. *
Bloch 758; Mourlot 254;
Gauss 643

The little artist, 18 May 1954
Colour crayon transfer
lithograph.
Image: 640 × 495 mm.
Sheet: 660 × 504 mm
2016,7048.11. *
Bloch 768; Mourlot 263;
Gauss 657 (illustrated on p. 89,
detail p. 2)

The little artist, stage proof, 1954
Crayon transfer lithograph.
Image: 660 × 500 mm.
Sheet: 660 × 500 mm
2016,7061.1. Presented by
Dr Frederick Mulder in honour
of Hugo Chapman

Divine visitors to the studio
[*Variation on the theme of
'Las Meninas': Visitors to the
studio*], 18 February 1955
Sugar aquatint and scraper.
Plate: 495 × 647 mm.
Sheet: 571 × 764 mm
2016,7048.18. *
Bloch 770; Baer 920.III.B.a

Brothel: chocolate I [Baer],
9 March 1955
Sugar aquatint, etching,
engraving and scraper.
Plate: 493 × 645 mm.
Sheet: 568 × 763 mm
2006,1030.8
Purchased with a contribution
from the Martineau Family Charity
Baer 921.I

Bust of a woman [*Bust of
a woman with pony-tail:
Jacqueline*], 19 March 1955
Sugar aquatint with spit-bite.
Plate: 645 × 495 mm.
Sheet: 761 × 569 mm
2016,7048.19. *
Bloch 771; Baer 927.B.a
(illustrated on p. 91)

Exhibition (19)55 Vallauris, 1955
Linocut in brown.
Block: 661 × 530 mm.
Sheet: 897 × 594 mm
2010,7007.2. Presented by
Dr Frederick Mulder in honour
of Yvonne Ashcroft
Bloch 1268; Baer 1032.B
(illustrated on p. 25)

Bacchanal, 24 May 1957
Crayon lithograph.
Image: 530 × 710 mm.
Sheet: 566 × 762 mm
2016,7048.12. *
Bloch 831; Mourlot 292;
Gauss 700

Portrait of D.H. Kahnweiler I,
3 June 1957
Crayon transfer lithograph.
Image: 645 × 495 mm.
Sheet: 652 × 506 mm
2016,7048.13. *
Bloch 834; Mourlot 295;
Gauss 703

Portrait of D.H. Kahnweiler II,
3 June 1957
Crayon transfer lithograph.
Image: 650 × 495 mm.
Sheet: 655 × 506 mm
2016,7048.14. *
Bloch 835; Mourlot 296; Gauss
705 (illustrated on p. 14)

Portrait of D.H. Kahnweiler III,
3 June 1957
Crayon transfer lithograph.
Image: 640 × 490 mm.
Sheet: 653 × 505 mm
2016,7048.15. *
Bloch 836; Mourlot 297;
Gauss 706

Pike [Pike II], trial proof,
31 August–31 October 1959
Colour linocut.
Block: 530 × 640 mm.
Sheet: 622 × 752 mm
1994,1002.10
Bloch 911; Baer 1228.B.b.1
(illustrated on p. 99)

Pike III, undescribed 1st state
(probably unique),
2 September 1959
Lithograph.
Image: 530 × 640 mm.
Sheet: 505 × 655 mm
1994,1002.9.1. Presented by
Dr Frederick Mulder
Mourlot 326; Gauss 757

Pike III, undescribed 3rd state
(probably unique),
2 September 1959
Lithograph.
Image: 502 × 658 mm.
Sheet: 505 × 655 mm
1994,1002.9.2
Mourlot 326; Gauss 758

*Two women [Two women
with a vase of flowers]*,
27 September 1959
Linocut in cream on black.
Block: 530 × 640 mm.
Sheet: 621 × 752 mm
2000,0930.26. Purchased
with a contribution from
British Museum Friends
Bloch 915; Baer 1239.IV.A

*Woman looking out of the
window [Two women waking
up]*, 8 November 1959, printer's
proof outside of the Galerie
Louise Leiris edition 1960
Linocut in light caramel,
dark brown and black.
Block: 533 × 640 mm.
Sheet: 620 × 754 mm
1996,0427.1
Bloch 925; Baer 1249.II.B.b
(illustrated on p. 100)

*Woman looking out of the
window [Two women waking
up]*, printed 3 January 1964
Linocut in white ink and
brushed over with Indian ink
wash and rinsed.
Block: 533 × 640 mm.
Sheet: 617 × 750 mm
1996,0427.2
Baer 1249.II.C (illustrated on
p. 101)

*Woman with necklace
[Portrait of Jacqueline with
necklace, resting on her elbow]*,
24 November 1959
Colour linocut.
Block: 635 × 528 mm.
Sheet: 750 × 620 mm
1994,1002.11
Bloch 928; Baer 1258.II.A
(illustrated on p. 102)

Bacchanal with owl,
2 December 1959
Linocut in caramel on black.
Block: 532 × 642 mm.
Sheet: 622 × 753 mm
1998,1004.29. Purchased
with a contribution from
British Museum Friends
(as British Museum Society)
Bloch 938; Baer 1265.A.3
(illustrated on p. 98)

Bacchanal I, 6 December 1959
Crayon lithograph.
Image: 455 × 590 mm.
Sheet: 504 × 658 mm
2016,7048.16. *
Bloch 901; Mourlot 328;
Gauss 761

*Large female nude [Large
dancing nude]*, 4 March 1962
Colour linocut.
Block: 640 × 530 mm.
Sheet: 754 × 620 mm
1999,0926.1. Purchased
with a contribution from
British Museum Friends
(as British Museum Society)
Bloch 1085; Baer 1309.VI.A

Nude woman at the spring,
1st state, progressive proof, 1962
Linocut in light chocolate brown.
Block: 528 × 623 mm.
Sheet: 638 × 752 mm
2000,0521.1. Purchased with
assistance from Art Fund (as
the National Art Collections Fund)
Bloch 1093; Baer 1326.I.1

Nude woman at the spring,
1st state, progressive proof, 1962
Linocut in light chocolate brown
over uniform caramel tone.
Block: 528 × 623 mm.
Sheet: 638 × 752 mm
2000,0521.2. Purchased with
the assistance of Art Fund (as
the National Art Collections Fund)
Bloch 1093; Baer 1326.I.2

Nude woman at the spring,
2nd state, progressive proof, 1962
Linocut in dark chocolate brown.
Block: 528 × 623 mm.
Sheet: 638 × 752 mm
2000,0521.3. Purchased with
the assistance of Art Fund (as
the National Art Collections Fund)
Bloch 1093; Baer 1326.II.1

Nude woman at the spring,
2nd state, progressive proof, 1962
Linocut in dark chocolate brown
over light chocolate brown and
the caramel tone of the 1st state.
Block: 528 × 623 mm.
Sheet: 640 × 752 mm
2000,0521.4. Purchased with
the assistance of Art Fund (as
the National Art Collections Fund)
Bloch 1093; Baer 1326.II.2

Nude woman at the spring,
3rd state, progressive proof
(unrecorded), 1962
Linocut in black.
Block: 528 × 623 mm.
Sheet: 638 × 752 mm
2000,0521.5. Purchased with
the assistance of Art Fund (as
the National Art Collections Fund)
Bloch 1093; Baer 1326.III

Nude woman at the spring,
3rd state, progressive proof
in its definitive form, 1962
Linocut in black over the
dark chocolate brown of
the 2nd state and over the
light chocolate brown and
caramel tone of the 1st state.
Block: 528 × 623 mm.
Sheet: 640 × 752 mm
2000,0521.6. Purchased with
the assistance of Art Fund (as
the National Art Collections Fund)
Bloch 1093; Baer 1326.III.A

Nude woman at the spring,
background block, 1962
Linocut in uniform beige.
Block: 526 × 637 mm.
Sheet: 620 × 752 mm
2010,7007.1. Presented by
Dr Frederick Mulder

Still life under the lamp,
progressive proof of
background colour (not used
for final image), 1962
Linocut in cream ink.
Block: 528 × 639 mm.
Sheet: 623 × 752 mm
2013,7075.1. Funded by Art
Fund, Patrons of the British
Museum, James and Béatrice
Lupton, the Vollard Group,
Hamish Parker, and Simon and
Virginia Robertson**
Bloch 1101; Baer 1312 (illustrated
on p. 104)

Still life under the lamp,
progressive proof (not used for
final image), 1962
Linocut in brown over caramel
background.
Block: 528 × 639 mm.
Sheet: 623 × 752 mm
2013,7075.2. **
Bloch 1101; Baer 1312 (illustrated
on p. 104)

Still life under the lamp,
1st state, progressive proof, 1962
Linocut in yellow.
Block: 528 × 639 mm.
Sheet: 623 × 752 mm
2013,7075.3. **
Bloch 1101; Baer 1312.I
(illustrated on p. 104)

Still life under the lamp,
2nd state, progressive proof, 1962
Linocut in red over the 1st state
printed in yellow.
Block: 528 × 639 mm.
Sheet: 623 × 752 mm
2013,7075.4. **
Bloch 1101; Baer 1312.II
(illustrated on p. 104)

Still life under the lamp,
3rd state, progressive proof, 1962
Linocut in red.
Block: 528 × 639 mm.
Sheet: 623 × 752 mm
2013,7075.5. **
Bloch 1101; Baer 1312.III
(illustrated on p. 104)

Still life under the lamp,
4th state, progressive proof, 1962
Linocut in green.
Block: 528 × 639 mm.
Sheet: 623 × 752 mm
2013,7075.6. **
Bloch 1101; Baer 1312.IV
(illustrated on p. 105)

Still life under the lamp,
progressive proof, 1962
Linocut in green over the
2nd state printed in red, over
the 1st state printed in yellow.
Block: 528 × 639 mm.
Sheet: 623 × 752 mm
2013,7075.7. **
Bloch 1101; Baer 1312 (illustrated
on p. 105)

Still life under the lamp,
5th state, progressive proof, 1962
Linocut in black.
Block: 528 × 639 mm.
Sheet: 623 × 752 mm
2013,7075.8. **
Bloch 1101; Baer 1312.V
(illustrated on p. 105)

Still life under the lamp,
5th state and definitive form,
progressive proof, 1962
Linocut in black over green,
red and yellow.
Block: 528 × 639 mm.
Sheet: 623 × 752 mm
2013,7075.9. **
Bloch 1101; Baer 1312.V.B.a
(illustrated on pp. 105, 106–7
and detail p. 96)

*Family scene [Portrait of
Ingresque family IV]*,
2 October 1962
Colour linocut.
Image: 390 × 540 mm.
Sheet: 505 × 660 mm
2011,7064.1. Presented by
Dr Frederick Mulder in honour
of Antony Griffiths
Bloch 1146; Baer 1337.A.b

Jacqueline reading, trial proof
from the first block, 1962
Linocut in black.
Block: 640 × 530 mm.
Sheet: 750 × 620 mm
2013,7075.10. **
Bloch 1181; Baer 1292.I

Jacqueline reading, trial proof
from the first block after further
cutting, 1962
Linocut in black.
Block: 640 × 530 mm.
Sheet: 750 × 620 mm
2013,7075.11. **.
Bloch 1181; Baer 1292.II

Jacqueline reading, trial proof
from the second block, 1964
Linocut in black on light cream
background.
Block: 640 × 530 mm.
Sheet: 750 × 620 mm
2013,7075.12. **
Bloch 1181; Baer 1292

Jacqueline reading, trial proof of
the final version, 1962–4
Linocut in black.
Block: 640 × 530 mm.
Sheet: 750 × 620 mm
2013,7075.13. **
Bloch 1181; Baer 1292.B
(illustrated on p. 103)

Painter at work, 1 November 1963
Soft-ground etching in greenish
bistre on thin tissue.
Plate: 318 × 417 mm.
Sheet: 368 × 544 mm
1995,1210.3. Presented by an
anonymous donor
Bloch 1121; Baer 1115.B

In the studio, 8 November 1963,
Galerie Louise Leiris edition, 1967
Etching and aquatint.
Plate: 315 × 415 mm.
Sheet: 450 × 551 mm
1993,0725.1
Bloch 1123; Baer 1117.III.B.b

The painter and his model, trial
proof, 7 February 1965
Linocut in black.
Block: 528 × 638 mm.
Sheet: 609 × 752 mm
2010,7007.3. Purchased with
funds from the Modern Fund
Bloch 1194; Baer 1357

THE 347 SUITE

The dates given correspond to
Picasso's own inscriptions on
the plates. The Roman numerals
(also from Picasso's inscriptions) record the number of
prints made in a single day and
their sequence.

The full suite numbered
2014,7087.1–347 was presented
by Hamish Parker in honour
of the Department of Prints
and Drawings, with special
thanks to Antony Griffiths and
Frances Carey.

Plate 1: *Picasso, his work and
his audience*, 16, 17, 18, 19, 20,
22 March 1968
Etching. Plate: 395 × 565 mm.
Sheet: 565 × 715 mm
2014,7087.1
Bloch 1481; Baer 1496.B.b.1
(illustrated on pp. 110–1)

Plate 2: *Riders and jugglers*,
16 March 1968 II
Etching. Plate: 395 × 565 mm.
Sheet: 555 × 715 mm
2014,7087.2
Bloch 1482; Baer 1497.B.b.1

Plate 3: *Group including nude
woman with lamb, 'odalisque-
rider' and self-portrait as
mechanic*,
22 March 1968 I
Etching. Plate: 295 × 515 mm.
Sheet: 450 × 630 mm
2014,7087.3
Bloch 1483; Baer 1498.B.b.1

Plate 4: *Group with old man
with torch on a donkey, woman
and harlequin*, 22 March 1968 II
Etching. Plate: 295 × 515 mm.
Sheet: 455 × 630 mm
2014,7087.4
Bloch 1484; Baer 1499.B.b.1

Plate 5: *At the circus: group
with rider and clown*,
24 March 1968 I
Etching. Plate: 425 × 345 mm.
Sheet: 615 × 500 mm
2014,7087.5
Bloch 1485; Baer 1500.B.b.1

Plate 6: *Old man with magician
conjuring three odalisques*,
24 March 1968 II
Etching. Plate: 420 × 345 mm.
Sheet: 615 × 500 mm
2014,7087.6
Bloch 1486; Baer 1501.B.b.1

Plate 7: *Odalisques with two
men dreaming*, 24 March 1968 III
Etching and scraper.
Plate: 415 × 315 mm.
Sheet: 580 × 455 mm
2014,7087.7
Bloch 1487; Baer 1502.B.b.1

Plate 8: *Self-portrait with cane,
with actor in costume and
women*, 25 March 1968
Etching. Plate: 420 × 345 mm.
Sheet: 610 × 500 mm
2014,7087.8
Bloch 1488; Baer 1503.B.b.1

Plate 9: *Self-portrait transposed
and duplicated dreaming of the
circus, with Jacqueline as a ball
acrobat*, 26 March 1968
Etching. Plate: 420 × 345 mm.
Sheet: 610 × 505 mm
2014,7087.9
Bloch 1489; Baer 1504.B.b.1
(illustrated on p. 112)

Plate 10: *Painter in Spanish
costume painting on his model*,
29 March 1968 I
Etching and scraper.
Plate: 415 × 315 mm.
Sheet: 575 × 450 mm
2014,7087.10
Bloch 1490; Baer 1506.B.b.1

Plate 11: *Comic*, 29 March 1968
II, III, IV, V, VI
Etching. Plate: 415 × 315 mm.
Sheet: 580 × 455 mm
2014,7087.11
Bloch 1491; Baer 1507.B.b.1

Plate 12: *Old man thinking about
the old painting of the Virgin and
bird with little St John, character
with fish and young girls*,
29 March 1968 VII
Etching. Plate: 420 × 345 mm.
Sheet: 610 × 500 mm
2014,7087.12
Bloch 1492; Baer 1508.B.b.1

Plate 13: *Four men in
Rembrandtesque costume*,
30 March 1968 I
Etching. Plate: 415 × 315 mm.
Sheet: 580 × 455 mm
2014,7087.13
Bloch 1493; Baer 1509.B.b.1

Plate 14: *Three women*,
30 March 1968 II
Etching. Plate: 415 × 315 mm.
Sheet: 580 × 450 mm
2014,7087.14
Bloch 1494; Baer 1510.B.b.1
(illustrated on p. 133)

Plate 15: *Old man thinking
about his youth: boy on a circus
horse and women*,
1 April 1968
Etching. Plate: 315 × 415 mm.
Sheet: 450 × 565 mm
2014,7087.15
Bloch 1495; Baer 1511.B.b.1

Plate 16: *Old man fantasising:
courtesan with men in
Rembrandtesque costume*,
3 April 1968
Etching. Plate: 315 × 415 mm.
Sheet: 450 × 565 mm
2014,7087.16
Bloch 1496; Baer 1512.B.b.1

Plate 17: *Bearded man
thinking of a scene from
'A Thousand and One Nights',
with disapproving ancestors
behind him*, 6 April 1968
Etching. Plate: 375 × 275 mm.
Sheet: 540 × 425 mm
2014,7087.17
Bloch 1497; Baer 1513.B.b.1

Plate 18: *Man lying down,
with two women, evoking
the relationship between an
old clown and a young girl*,
6 April 1968 II
Etching with stop-out varnish
in reserve and scraper.
Plate: 375 × 275 mm.
Sheet: 550 × 430 mm
2014,7087.18
Bloch 1498; Baer 1514.B.b.1

Plate 19: *Young man presenting
a mirror or portrait to a woman*,
6 April 1968 III
Etching, drypoint and scraper.
Plate: 415 × 315 mm.
Sheet: 580 × 455 mm
2014,7087.19
Bloch 1499; Baer 1515.B.b.1

Plate 20: *Silent conversation*,
8 April 1968
Aquatint with stop-out varnish
in reserve and scraper.
Plate: 315 × 470 mm.
Sheet: 450 × 615 mm
2014,7087.20
Bloch 1500; Baer 1516.B.b.1

Plate 21: *Group with man in
an armchair with balls and
balusters thinking about love*,
8 April 1968 II
Etching. Plate: 315 × 415 mm.
Sheet: 450 × 565 mm
2014,7087.21
Bloch 1501; Baer 1517.B.b.1

Plate 22: *Rembrandtesque
painter with his model*,
8 April 1968 III
Etching. Plate: 315 × 415 mm.
Sheet: 450 × 565 mm
2014,7087.22
Bloch 1502; Baer 1518.B.b.1

Plate 23: *Man in an Afghan
vest thinking about the love
of a 'musketeer' and his
sweetheart*, 8 April 1968 IV
Etching. Plate: 315 × 415 mm.
Sheet: 455 × 565 mm
2014,7087.23
Bloch 1503; Baer 1519.B.b.1

Plate 24: *At the circus: acrobats,
giraffe, swimmers*,
11 April 1968 I
Etching. Plate: 315 × 415 mm.
Sheet: 455 × 565 mm
2014,7087.24
Bloch 1504; Baer 1520.B.b.1

Plate 25: *Circus and wrestling*,
11 April 1968 II
Etching. Plate: 315 × 415 mm.
Sheet: 455 × 565 mm
2014,7087.25
Bloch 1505; Baer 1521.B.b.1
(illustrated on p. 113)

Plate 26: *At the circus:
weightlifter*, 11 April 1968 III
Etching. Plate: 60 × 120 mm.
Sheet: 250 × 330 mm
2014,7087.26
Bloch 1506; Baer 1522.B.b.1

Plate 27: *Woman doing her hair*,
11 April 1968 IV
Etching. Plate: 120 × 60 mm.
Sheet: 325 × 255 mm
2014,7087.27
Bloch 1507; Baer 1523.B.b.1

Plate 28: *Bearded man in
profile*, 11 April 1968 V
Etching. Plate: 85 × 60 mm.
Sheet: 330 × 250 mm
2014,7087.28
Bloch 1508; Baer 1524.B.b.1

Plate 29: *'El Arrastre', with
horsewoman and putto*,
11 April 1968 VI
Etching. Plate: 315 × 415 mm
Sheet: 550 × 650 mm
2014,7087.29
Bloch 1509; Baer 1525.B.b.1

Plate 30: *Television: ancient
chariot combat*, 11 April 1968 VII
Etching. Plate: 315 × 415 mm
Sheet: 450 × 565 mm
2014,7087.30
Bloch 1510; Baer 1526.B.b.1

Plate 31: *Young girl, looked at by
an old woman and two men
including 'un gitan'*,
12 April 1968 I
Aquatint, etching, drypoint and
scraper. Plate: 320 × 470 mm.
Sheet: 455 × 615 mm
2014,7087.31
Bloch 1511; Baer 1527.B.b.1

Plate 32: *Old man in Vietnamese
hat thinking about the loves of
old men*, 12 April 1968 II
Etching. Plate: 315 × 420 mm.
Sheet: 450 × 565 mm
2014,7087.32
Bloch 1512; Baer 1528.B.b.1

Plate 33: *Woman in bed
dreaming: men and women*,
13 April 1968 I
Aquatint with stop-out varnish
in reserve and scraper.
Plate: 320 × 395 mm.
Sheet: 475 × 570 mm
2014,7087.33
Bloch 1513; Baer 1529.B.b.1

Plate 34: *Television: ancient
chariot race, I*, 13 April 1968 II
Aquatint and etching with
stop-out varnish in reserve and
scraper. Plate: 315 × 390 mm.
Sheet: 475 × 570 mm
2014,7087.34
Bloch 1514; Baer 1530.B.b.1

Plate 35: *Television: ancient
chariot race, II*, 13 April 1968 III
Etching. Plate: 315 × 415 mm.
Sheet: 455 × 565 mm
2014,7087.35
Bloch 1515; Baer 1531.B.b.1

Plate 36: *Painter and model,
rider and 'good guy'*,
13 April 1968 IV
Aquatint and etching with stop-
out varnish in reserve.
Plate: 315 × 415 mm.
Sheet: 450 × 565 mm
2014,7087.36
Bloch 1516; Baer 1532.B.b.1

Plate 37: *Harlequin and various
characters*, 14 April 1968 I
Aquatint and etching with
stop-out varnish in reserve.
Plate: 315 × 390 mm.
Sheet: 475 × 565 mm
2014,7087.37
Bloch 1517; Baer 1533.B.b.1

Plate 38: *Painter thinking of a
large canvas representing three
women*, 14 April 1968 II
Aquatint and etching with
stop-out varnish in reserve.
Plate: 315 × 395 mm.
Sheet: 475 × 565 mm
2014,7087.38
Bloch 1518; Baer 1534.B.b.1

Plate 39: *Painter in front of his
canvas, with a model, thinking
about his subject:
two women …*, 15
April 1968 I, 17 April 1968 II
Aquatint and etching with
stop-out varnish in reserve and
scraper. Plate: 275 × 385 mm.
Sheet: 455 × 540 mm
2014,7087.39
Bloch 1519; Baer 1535.B.b.1

Plate 40: *Around El Greco
and Rembrandt portraits*,
15 April 1968 II, 17, 18, 19 April 1968
Aquatint, drypoint and scraper.
Plate: 225 × 320 mm.
Sheet: 375 × 465 mm
2014,7087.40
Bloch 1520; Baer 1536.B.b.1
(illustrated on p. 116)

Plate 41: *Around El Greco:
portraits with model and fellow*,
15 April 1968 III, 17 April 1968 II
Aquatint, drypoint and scraper.
Plate: 225 × 320 mm.
Sheet: 375 × 465 mm
2014,7087.41
Bloch 1521; Baer 1537.B.b.1

Plate 42: *At the circus: rider,
clown and Pierrot*, 19 April 1968
Aquatint and drypoint with
stop-out varnish in reserve.
Plate: 315 × 390 mm.
Sheet: 475 × 565 mm
2014,7087.42
Bloch 1522; Baer 1538.B.b.1
(illustrated on p. 114)

Plate 43: *Circus: rider, women
and spectators including
a disguised mechanic*,
20 April 1968
Etching. Plate: 315 × 395 mm.
Sheet: 475 × 570 mm
2014,7087.43
Bloch 1523; Baer 1539.B.b.1

Plate 44: *Rider, 'good guy'
and 'musketeer'*, 20 April 1968 II
Aquatint and drypoint with
stop-out varnish in reserve and
scraper. Plate: 315 × 395 mm.
Sheet: 475 × 570 mm
2014,7087.44
Bloch 1524; Baer 1540.B.b.1

Plate 45: *Caricature of General
de Gaulle, and two women*,
21 April 1968 I, 22 April 1968
Aquatint, drypoint and scraper.
Plate: 315 × 390 mm.
Sheet: 475 × 570 mm
2014,7087.45
Bloch 1525; Baer 1541.B.b.1
(illustrated on p. 115)

Plate 46: *Painter with couple
and child*, 21 April 1968 II
Etching. Plate: 280 × 390 mm.
Sheet: 455 × 545 mm
2014,7087.46
Bloch 1526; Baer 1542.B.b.1

Plate 47: *Roman chariot with
old athlete, rider, odalisque and
spectator*, 22 April 1968
Etching. Plate: 280 × 390 mm.
Sheet: 455 × 545 mm
2014,7087.47
Bloch 1527; Baer 1543.B.b.1

Plate 48: *Roman chariot with falling rider, nude woman and spectators*, 23 April 1968
Etching. Plate: 315 × 395 mm.
Sheet: 475 × 570 mm
2014,7087.48
Bloch 1528; Baer 1544.B.b.1

Plate 49: *Old clown with a ravishing person*, 24 April 1968 I
Sugar aquatint.
Plate: 125 × 90 mm.
Sheet: 325 × 250 mm
2014,7087.49
Bloch 1529; Baer 1545.B.b.1

Plate 50: *Painter, model and spectator*, 24 April 1968 II
Sugar aquatint with stop-out varnish in reserve.
Plate: 125 × 90 mm.
Sheet: 325 × 250 mm
2014,7087.50
Bloch 1530; Baer 1546.B.b.1

Plate 51: *Woman on a Roman chariot, Rembrandtesque spectators and kids*, 24 April 1968 III
Sugar aquatint, etching and drypoint with polishing on the plate. Plate: 315 × 390 mm.
Sheet: 475 × 565 mm
2014,7087.51
Bloch 1531; Baer 1547.B.b.1

Plate 52: *Woman and child on a Roman chariot, with an acrobat rider*, 26 April 1968 I
Drypoint. Plate: 280 × 390 mm.
Sheet: 450 × 565 mm
2014,7087.52
Bloch 1532; Baer 1548.B.b.1

Plate 53: *Woman on a Roman chariot, harnessed to a horse, half-human*, 26 April 1968 II
Etching. Plate: 280 × 390 mm.
Sheet: 450 × 565 mm
2014,7087.53
Bloch 1533; Baer 1549.B.b.1

Plate 54: *Roman chariot, ridden by a female athlete, with Cupid and old men*, 26 April 1968 III
Etching. Plate: 280 × 390 mm.
Sheet: 450 × 565 mm
2014,7087.54
Bloch 1534; Baer 1550.B.b.1

Plate 55: *Mythological scene: perhaps Agamemnon's lust for Briseis*, 27 April 1968 I, 28 April 1968
Etching. Plate: 280 × 390 mm.
Sheet: 455 × 545 mm
2014,7087.55
Bloch 1535; Baer 1551.B.b.1

Plate 56: *Fantasy in the genre of the 'Rêve' of Fuseli, with voyeur under the bed*, 28 April 1968 II
Etching and drypoint.
Plate: 280 × 390 mm.
Sheet: 450 × 565 mm
2014,7087.56
Bloch 1536; Baer 1552.B.b.1

Plate 57: *Man stopping a horse in front of a woman*, 29 April 1968 I
Aquatint, etching and scraper.
Plate: 280 × 390 mm.
Sheet: 450 × 565 mm
2014,7087.57
Bloch 1537; Baer 1553.B.b.1

Plate 58: *Gladiator show*, 29 April 1968 II
Etching. Plate: 315 × 395 mm.
Sheet: 475 × 570 mm
2014,7087.58
Bloch 1538; Baer 1554.B.b.1

Plate 59: *Punchinello, with two women*, 30 April 1968
Etching. Plate: 315 × 395 mm.
Sheet: 475 × 570 mm
2014,7087.59
Bloch 1539; Baer 1555.B.b.1

Plate 60: *Punchinello with an acrobat's bicycle, and odalisque with an owl*, 30 April 1968 II
Etching. Plate: 90 × 125 mm.
Sheet: 250 × 325 mm
2014,7087.60
Bloch 1540; Baer 1556.B.b.1

Plate 61: *Circus: Roman chariot and clown*, 1 May 1968 I
Etching. Plate: 90 × 125 mm.
Sheet: 250 × 325 mm
2014,7087.61
Bloch 1541; Baer 1557.B.b.1

Plate 62: *Sailor's dream: women in every port*, 1 May 1968 II, 3 May 1968
Etching. Plate: 220 × 290 mm.
Sheet: 350 × 420 mm
2014,7087.62
Bloch 1542; Baer 1558.B.b.1

Plate 63: *Couple and traveller*, 3 May 1968
Etching. Plate: 220 × 290 mm.
Sheet: 350 × 420 mm
2014,7087.63
Bloch 1543; Baer 1559.B.b.1

Plate 64: *Around the 'Chef-d'œuvre inconnu': painter, model, couple and two painters*, 5, 6, 7, 9 May 1968
Etching, drypoint and scraper.
Plate: 410 × 495 mm.
Sheet: 565 × 645 mm
2014,7087.64
Bloch 1544; Baer 1560.B.b.1
(illustrated on p. 117)

Plate 65: *The workshop with an owl and an official envoy*, 5 May 1968 II
Etching. Plate: 325 × 400 mm.
Sheet: 455 × 545 mm
2014,7087.65
Bloch 1545; Baer 1561.B.b.1

Plate 66: *The portrait*, 6 May 1968
Etching. Plate: 125 × 90 mm.
Sheet: 325 × 250 mm
2014,7087.66
Bloch 1546; Baer 1562.B.b.1

Plate 67: *Old painter, model and spectator*, 7 May 1968 II, 8 May 1968
Etching, drypoint and scraper.
Plate: 125 × 90 mm.
Sheet: 325 × 250 mm
2014,7087.67
Bloch 1547; Baer 1564.B.b.1

Plate 68: *Three women passing the time, with severe spectator*, 7 May 1968
Etching. Plate: 325 × 400 mm.
Sheet: 455 × 545 mm
2014,7087.68
Bloch 1548; Baer 1563.B.b.1

Plate 69: *Musical snack at Celestina's*, 8 May 1968
Etching. Plate: 315 × 420 mm.
Sheet: 450 × 565 mm
2014,7087.69
Bloch 1549; Baer 1565.B.b.1
(illustrated on p. 118)

Plate 70: *'La Célestine': snack in the garden, with young fat bacchus*, 8 May 1968 II
Etching. Plate: 315 × 420 mm.
Sheet: 450 × 565 mm
2014,7087.70
Bloch 1550; Baer 1566.B.b.1

Plate 71: *Young woman in a hat sinning in thought while squinting at a prelate*, 10 May 1968
Etching. Plate: 315 × 420 mm.
Sheet: 450 × 565 mm
2014,7087.71
Bloch 1551; Baer 1567.B.b.1

Plate 72: *Fat courtesan, with an old man and a spectator in costume*, 10 May 1968 II
Etching, drypoint and scraper.
Plate: 190 × 115 mm.
Sheet: 325 × 250 mm
2014,7087.72
Bloch 1552; Baer 1568.B.b.1

Plate 73: *Courtesan in bed, with a visitor*, 10 May 1968 II
Etching. Plate: 410 × 495 mm.
Sheet: 570 × 645 mm
2014,7087.73
Bloch 1553; Baer 1569.B.b.1

Plate 74: *Rembrandtesque visitor to a playful courtesan*, 11 May 1968 I
Etching. Plate: 315 × 415 mm.
Sheet: 455 × 565 mm
2014,7087.74
Bloch 1554; Baer 1570.B.b.1

Plate 75: *Slender painter with women, including a 'little pisser'*, 11 May 1968 III
Etching. Plate: 410 × 495 mm.
Sheet: 570 × 645 mm
2014,7087.75
Bloch 1555; Baer 1571.B.b.1

Plate 76: *Fashions change: two couples*, 12 May 1968 I
Etching. Plate: 190 × 115 mm.
Sheet: 330 × 250 mm
2014,7087.76
Bloch 1556; Baer 1572.B.b.1

Plate 77: *Faun and bacchante, with fauns fighting in the distance*, 12 May 1968 II
Etching. Plate: 190 × 115 mm.
Sheet: 325 × 250 mm
2014,7087.77
Bloch 1557; Baer 1573.B.b.1

Plate 78: *Old faun with a living doll*, 12 May 1968 IV
Etching. Plate: 125 × 90 mm.
Sheet: 325 × 250 mm
2014,7087.78
Bloch 1558; Baer 1574.B.b.1

Plate 79: *Couple, owl and odalisque on horseback (the departure of the Shunamite?)*, 12 May 1968 V
Etching. Plate: 90 × 125 mm.
Sheet: 250 × 325 mm
2014,7087.79
Bloch 1559; Baer 1575.B.b.1

Plate 80: *'La Vie en Rose' ("When … he speaks softly to me …")*, 12 May 1968 VI
Etching. Plate: 275 × 375 mm.
Sheet: 420 × 500 mm
2014,7087.80
Bloch 1560; Baer 1576.B.b.1

Plate 81: *Back to basics: Picasso tourist at the Fuente de Canaletas*, 13 May 1968
Etching. Plate: 410 × 495 mm.
Sheet: 565 × 645 mm
2014,7087.81
Bloch 1561; Baer 1577.B.b.1

Plate 82: *Travelling comedians, with self-portrait in harlequin hat and cockfight*, 13 May 1968 II
Etching. Plate: 275 × 375 mm.
Sheet: 420 × 500 mm
2014,7087.82
Bloch 1562; Baer 1578.B.b.1

Plate 83: *Celestina in action: solicitation*, 14 May 1968 I
Etching. Plate: 90 × 125 mm.
Sheet: 255 × 330 mm
2014,7087.83
Bloch 1563; Baer 1579.B.b.1

Plate 84: *Celestina in action: the pigeon*, 14 May 1968 II
Etching. Plate: 90 × 125 mm.
Sheet: 255 × 325 mm
2014,7087.84
Bloch 1564; Baer 1580.B.b.1

Plate 85: *Staging of 'La Célestine': the gentleman is led towards the hovel*, 14 May 1968 III
Etching with stop-out varnish in reserve on greased plate.
Plate: 295 × 350 mm.
Sheet: 450 × 525 mm
2014,7087.85
Bloch 1565; Baer 1581.B.b.1

Plate 86: *Celestina and her creature lead the gullible and wealthy*, 15 May 1968 I
Aquatint and etching with stop-out varnish in reserve.
Plate: 165 × 205 mm.
Sheet: 285 × 335 mm
2014,7087.86
Bloch 1566; Baer 1582.B.b.1
(illustrated on p.130)

Plate 87: *Theatre or television: cloak and sword*, 15 May 1968 II
Aquatint, drypoint and scraper.
Plate: 295 × 350 mm.
Sheet: 450 × 520 mm
2014,7087.87
Bloch 1567; Baer 1583.B.b.1

Plate 88: *Cloak and sword: pursuit, I*, 15 May 1968 III
Aquatint with stop-out varnish in reserve. Plate: 165 × 205 mm.
Sheet: 280 × 335 mm
2014,7087.88
Bloch 1568; Baer 1584.B.b.1
(illustrated on p.130)

Plate 89: *Cloak and sword: pursuit, II*, 15 May 1968 IV
Aquatint with stop-out varnish in reserve. Plate: 165 × 205 mm.
Sheet: 285 × 335 mm
2014,7087.89
Bloch 1569; Baer 1585.B.b.1
(illustrated on p.131)

Plate 90: *'La Célestine': kidnapping*, 15 May 1968 V
Aquatint, etching and drypoint with stop-out varnish in reserve.
Plate: 165 × 205 mm.
Sheet: 285 × 335 mm
2014,7087.90
Bloch 1570; Baer 1586.B.b.1

Plate 91: *The three musketeers: kidnapping*, 15 May 1968 VI
Aquatint, etching and drypoint with stop-out varnish in reserve.
Plate: 165 × 205 mm.
Sheet: 280 × 335 mm
2014,7087.91
Bloch 1571; Baer 1587.B.b.1

Plate 92: *'La Célestine': pursuit*, 16 May 1968 I
Aquatint and etching with stop-out varnish in reserve.
Plate: 165 × 205 mm.
Sheet: 280 × 335 mm
2014,7087.92
Bloch 1572; Baer 1588.B.b.1

Plate 93: *'La Célestine': escape at dawn*, 16 May 1968 II
Etching with light areas achieved with turpentine on cotton swab.
Plate: 90 × 120 mm.
Sheet: 255 × 325 mm
2014,7087.93
Bloch 1573; Baer 1589.B.b.1

Plate 94: *'A Thousand and One Nights' and 'La Célestine': the young slave*, 16 May 1968 III
Etching with light areas achieved with turpentine on cotton swab.
Plate: 90 × 125 mm.
Sheet: 250 × 325 mm
2014,7087.94
Bloch 1574; Baer 1590.B.b.1
(illustrated on p.120)

Plate 95: *Young girl, Celestina and little master*, 16 May 1968 IV
Etching with light areas achieved with turpentine on cotton swab.
Plate: 90 × 125 mm.
Sheet: 250 × 325 mm
2014,7087.95
Bloch 1575; Baer 1591.B.b.1

Plate 96: *Horseman and his valet, and young girl dressed in a mantle*, 16 May 1968 V
Etching with turpentine on cotton swab.
Plate: 90 × 125 mm.
Sheet: 250 × 325 mm
2014,7087.96
Bloch 1576; Baer 1592.B.b.1

Plate 97: *'Musketeer' seated with a young boy, talking about his life*, 16 May 1968 VI
Etching, drypoint and scraper with turpentine on cotton swab.
Plate: 335 × 495 mm.
Sheet: 500 × 655 mm
2014,7087.97
Bloch 1577; Baer 1593.B.b.1

Plate 98: *Abduction, with Celestina, ruffian, girl, and lord with his valet*, 17 May 1968 I
Aquatint with stop-out varnish in reserve. Plate: 295 × 350 mm.
Sheet: 450 × 520 mm
2014,7087.98
Bloch 1578; Baer 1594.B.b.1

Plate 99: *'La Célestine': escape under the moon*, 18 May 1968 I
Aquatint with stop-out varnish in reserve and scraper.
Plate: 295 × 350 mm.
Sheet: 450 × 520 mm
2014,7087.99
Bloch 1579; Baer 1595.B.b.1

Plate 100: *Couple with Cupid, visitors and spectator*, 19 May 1968 I
Aquatint, drypoint and scraper.
Plate: 295 × 350 mm.
Sheet: 455 × 525 mm
2014,7087.100
Bloch 1580; Baer 1596.B.b.1

Plate 101: *Celestina presenting her two residents to two clients*, 21 May 1968 I
Etching and scraper.
Plate: 90 × 120 mm.
Sheet: 255 × 325 mm
2014,7087.101
Bloch 1581; Baer 1597.B.b.1

Plate 102: *'La Célestine': flight*, 21 May 1968 II
Etching. Plate: 90 × 125 mm.
Sheet: 250 × 325 mm
2014,7087.102
Bloch 1582; Baer 1598.B.b.1

Plate 103: *Couple in carriage and poor pedestrian*, 21 May 1968 III
Etching. Plate: 90 × 125 mm.
Sheet: 250 × 325 mm
2014,7087.103
Bloch 1583; Baer 1599.B.b.1

Plate 104: *Young couple, old couple, spectator, with a carriage in the background*, 21 May 1968 IV
Mezzotint and scraper.
Plate: 315 × 415 mm.
Sheet: 455 × 565 mm
2014,7087.104
Bloch 1584; Baer 1600.B.b.1

Plate 105: *Storm, kidnapping, pursuit*, 23 May 1968 I
Etching and drypoint.
Plate: 235 × 330 mm.
Sheet: 365 × 475 mm
2014,7087.105
Bloch 1585; Baer 1601.B.b.1

Plate 106: *'Mamluk' kidnapping a woman, attacked by a 'musketeer'*, 23 May 1968 II
Etching, drypoint and scraper.
Plate: 235 × 330 mm.
Sheet: 365 × 475 mm
2014,7087.106
Bloch 1586; Baer 1602.B.b.1

Plate 107: *Celestina and girl, with a cat and a young customer*, 24 May 1968 I
Sugar aquatint on greased plate.
Sheet: 250 × 325 mm
2014,7087.107
Bloch 1587; Baer 1603.B.b.1

Plate 108: *Celestina, girl and old client*, 24 May 1968 II
Sugar aquatint on partially greased plate.
Plate: 90 × 125 mm.
Sheet: 250 × 325 mm
2014,7087.108
Bloch 1588; Baer 1604.B.b.1
(illustrated on p.120)

Plate 109: *Theatre: around the Rembrandt*, 25 May 1968 I
Sugar aquatint on partially greased plate.
Plate: 295 × 350 mm.
Sheet: 450 × 520 mm
2014,7087.109
Bloch 1589; Baer 1605.B.b.1

Plate 110: *Patron and his entourage visiting the old painter's workshop*, 25 May 1968 II
Sugar aquatint and drypoint with scraper.
Plate: 235 × 330 mm.
Sheet: 365 × 475 mm
2014,7087.110
Bloch 1590; Baer 1606.B.b.1

Plate 111: *Celestina presents her ward, with a child with an olive branch*, 25 May 1968 III
Sugar aquatint on greased plate. Plate: 235 × 330 mm.
Sheet: 365 × 470 mm
2014,7087.111
Bloch 1591; Baer 1607.B.b.1

Plate 112: *Gentleman visiting Celestina's*, 26 May 1968 I
Sugar aquatint on greased plate. Plate: 60 × 120 mm.
Sheet: 250 × 325 mm
2014,7087.112
Bloch 1592; Baer 1608.B.b.1

Plate 113: *Old beau saluting a lowly ward of Celestina*, 26 May 1968 II
Sugar aquatint and drypoint on partially greased plate.
Plate: 60 × 120 mm.
Sheet: 250 × 325 mm
2014,7087.113
Bloch 1593; Baer 1609.B.b.1

Plate 114: *Young man making his declaration, in the presence of the authorities*, 26 May 1968 III
Sugar aquatint on greased plate. Plate: 235 × 330 mm.
Sheet: 365 × 470 mm
1993,1003.1
Bloch 1594; Baer 1610.B.b.1

Plate 114: *Young man making his declaration, in the presence of the authorities*, 26 May 1968 III
Sugar aquatint on greased plate. Plate: 235 × 330 mm.
Sheet: 365 × 470 mm
2014,7087.114
Bloch 1594; Baer 1610.B.b.1

Plate 115: *Spanish notables visiting a brothel decorated with armour*, 26 May 1968 IV
Etching. Plate: 410 × 495 mm.
Sheet: 570 × 645 mm
2014,7087.115
Bloch 1595; Baer 1611.B.b.1

Plate 116: *Painter, model and visitor*, 27 May 1968
Sugar aquatint on greased plate. Plate: 60 × 120 mm.
Sheet: 250 × 325 mm
2014,7087.116
Bloch 1596; Baer 1612.B.b.1

Plate 117: *Duel, with nude spectator*, 27 May 1968
Sugar aquatint on greased plate. Plate: 60 × 120 mm.
Sheet: 250 × 325 mm
2014,7087.117
Bloch 1597; Baer 1613.B.b.1

Plate 118: *A maja posing on a pedestal*, 27 May 1968
Sugar aquatint on partially greased plate.
Plate: 120 × 60 mm.
Sheet: 325 × 250 mm
2014,7087.118
Bloch 1598; Baer 1614.B.b.1

Plate 119: *The serenade*, 27 May 1968
Sugar aquatint on partially greased plate.
Plate: 120 × 60 mm.
Sheet: 325 × 250 mm
2014,7087.119
Bloch 1599; Baer 1615.B.b.1

Plate 120: *Nude man sitting cross-legged, and two women*, 27 May 1968
Sugar aquatint and drypoint on greased plate.
Plate: 85 × 60 mm.
Sheet: 325 × 250 mm
2014,7087.120
Bloch 1600; Baer 1616.B.b.1

Plate 121: *Odalisque*, 29 May 1968 I
Sugar aquatint and drypoint on partially greased plate.
Plate: 85 × 60 mm.
Sheet: 325 × 250 mm
2014,7087.121
Bloch 1601; Baer 1620.B.b.1

Plate 122: *Maja and Celestina*, 27 May 1968 I
Sugar aquatint and drypoint on partially greased plate.
Plate: 120 × 60 mm.
Sheet: 325 × 250 mm
2014,7087.122
Bloch 1602; Baer 1617.B.b.1

Plate 123: *Celestina, Maja and male accomplice*, 27 May 1968 II
Sugar aquatint and drypoint on partially greased plate.
Plate: 120 × 60 mm.
Sheet: 325 × 250 mm
2014,7087.123
Bloch 1603; Baer 1618.B.b.1

Plate 124: *Old man thinking about his life: gallant youth, mature age of famous painter, work created in a slum, now enthroned under a canopy*, 28 May 1968
Sugar aquatint on partially greased plate with stop-out varnish. Plate: 490 × 335 mm.
Sheet: 655 × 465 mm
2014,7087.124
Bloch 1604; Baer 1619.B.b.1

Plate 125: *Maja in a long dress*, 29 May 1968 II
Sugar aquatint and drypoint on partially greased plate.
Plate: 120 × 60 mm.
Sheet: 325 × 250 mm
2014,7087.125
Bloch 1605; Baer 1621.B.b.1

Plate 126: *Maja in a short dress*, 29 May 1968 III
Sugar aquatint and drypoint on partially greased plate.
Plate: 120 × 60 mm.
Sheet: 325 × 250 mm
2014,7087.126
Bloch 1606; Baer 1622.B.b.1

Plate 127: *Maja in a torn dress*, 29 May 1968 IV
Sugar aquatint and drypoint on partially greased plate.
Plate: 120 × 60 mm.
Sheet: 325 × 250 mm
2014,7087.127
Bloch 1607; Baer 1623.B.b.1

Plate 128: *Filming: shot with two women*, 30 May 1968 I
Aquatint, drypoint and scraper.
Plate: 60 × 120 mm.
Sheet: 250 × 328 mm
2014,7087.128
Bloch 1608; Baer 1624.B.b.1

Plate 129: *Filming: American scene*, 30 May 1968 II
Aquatint and scraper.
Plate: 60 × 80 mm.
Sheet: 250 × 325 mm
2014,7087.129
Bloch 1609; Baer 1625.B.b.1

Plate 130: *Old acrobat arriving with his broken wheel, in a mocking and contemptuous male crowd*, 30 May 1968 III
Etching. Plate: 195 × 255 mm.
Sheet: 325 × 400 mm
2014,7087.130
Bloch 1610; Baer 1626.B.b.1

Plate 131: *Calisto and Melibea in the orchard*, 31 May 1968 I
Etching. Plate: 200 × 255 mm.
Sheet: 330 × 400 mm
2014,7087.131
Bloch 1611; Baer 1627.B.b.1

Plate 132: *Young girl fleeing, with Celestina and a young man*, 31 May 1968 II
Etching with light areas achieved with turpentine on cotton swab.
Plate: 200 × 255 mm.
Sheet: 330 × 400 mm
2014,7087.132
Bloch 1612; Baer 1628.B.b.1

Plate 133: *From a young woman's instructions*, 31 May 1968 III
Etching, drypoint, engraving and scraper.
Plate: 200 × 255 mm.
Sheet: 330 × 400 mm
2014,7087.133
Bloch 1613; Baer 1629.B.b.1

Plate 134: *Meninas and gentlemen in the sierra*, 1 June 1968 I
Sugar aquatint on greased plate. Plate: 335 × 490 mm.
Sheet: 505 × 655 mm
2014,7087.134
Bloch 1614; Baer 1630.B.b.1
(illustrated on p. 129)

Plate 135: *Sex in the old and modern way*, 1 June 1968 II
Etching.
Plate: 410 × 495 mm.
Sheet: 570 × 645 mm
2014,7087.135
Bloch 1615; Baer 1631.B.b.1

Plate 136: *Gentleman and maja*, 2 June 1968 I
Sugar aquatint, drypoint and scraper. Plate: 85 × 60 mm.
Sheet: 325 × 250 mm
2014,7087.136
Bloch 1616; Baer 1632.B.b.1

Plate 137: *Small crouching girl and courtesan*, 2 June 1968 II
Sugar aquatint and drypoint on partially greased plate.
Plate: 85 × 60 mm.
Sheet: 325 × 250 mm
2014,7087.137
Bloch 1617; Baer 1633.B.b.1

Plate 138: *Variation on the theme of Don Quixote and Dulcinea*, 2 June 1968 III
Sugar aquatint and drypoint on greased plate.
Plate: 220 × 290 mm.
Sheet: 350 × 420 mm
2014,7087.138
Bloch 1618; Baer 1634.B.b.1

Plate 139: *Complications after kidnapping*, 3 June 1968 I
Etching and aquatint with sandpaper and stop-out varnish in reserve. Plate: 220 × 290 mm.
Sheet: 350 × 420 mm
2014,7087.139
Bloch 1619; Baer 1635.B.b.1

Plate 140: *Paunchy customer at Celestina's*, 3 June 1968 II
Etching. Plate: 220 × 290 mm.
Sheet: 350 × 420 mm
2014,7087.140
Bloch 1620; Baer 1636.B.b.1

Plate 141: *Childhood memories: street party, with 'good guy' and 'El Gigante'*, 4 June 1968 I
Sugar aquatint on partially greased plate.
Plate: 220 × 290 mm.
Sheet: 350 × 420 mm
2014,7087.141
Bloch 1621; Baer 1637.B.b.1
(illustrated on p. 132)

Plate 142: *Memories: circus, with 'El Gigante' and self-portrait as a baby-old man*, 4 June 1968 II
Aquatint, etching, drypoint and scraper. Plate: 490 × 335 mm.
Sheet: 655 × 465 mm
2014,7087.142
Bloch 1622; Baer 1638.B.b.1

Plate 143: *Portrait of a sad 'musketeer'*, 7 June 1968 I
Aquatint with stop-out varnish in reserve. Plate: 495 × 410 mm.
Sheet: 675 × 565 mm
2014,7087.143
Bloch 1623; Baer 1639.B.b.1

Plate 144: *'Musketeer' in profile, with spear fight around a young woman*, 7 June 1968 II
Aquatint with stop-out varnish in reserve. Plate: 410 × 495 mm.
Sheet: 565 × 645 mm
2014,7087.144
Bloch 1624; Baer 1640.B.b.1

Plate 145: *Horseman and his valet, Celestina and maja*, 7 June 1968 III
Sugar aquatint on partially greased plate.
Plate: 60 × 85 mm.
Sheet: 250 × 325 mm
2014,7087.145
Bloch 1625; Baer 1641.B.b.1

Plate 146: *Reiter kidnapping a woman on behalf of a horseman*, 9 June 1968 I
Sugar aquatint on partially greased plate.
Plate: 60 × 85 mm.
Sheet: 250 × 325 mm
2014,7087.146
Bloch 1626; Baer 1642.B.b.1

Plate 147: *Kidnapping, on foot, with Celestina*, 9 June 1968 II
Sugar aquatint on partially greased plate.
Plate: 60 × 85 mm.
Sheet: 250 × 325 mm
2014,7087.147
Bloch 1627; Baer 1643.B.b.1
(illustrated on p. 121)

Plate 148: *Kidnapping on horseback*, 9 June 1968 III
Sugar aquatint on partially greased plate.
Plate: 60 × 85 mm.
Sheet: 250 × 325 mm
2014,7087.148
Bloch 1628; Baer 1644.B.b.1
(illustrated on p. 121)

Plate 149: *'My God, what a man, how small …'*, 9 June 1968 IV
Sugar aquatint on partially greased plate.
Plate: 60 × 85 mm.
Sheet: 250 × 325 mm
2014,7087.149
Bloch 1629; Baer 1645.B.b.1

Plate 150: *Little old man flattered by Celestina*, 9 June 1968 V
Sugar aquatint on partially greased plate.
Plate: 60 × 85 mm.
Sheet: 250 × 325 mm
2005,0228.3. Funded by an anonymous donor
Bloch 1630; Baer 1646.B.b.1

Plate 150: *Little old man flattered by Celestina*, 9 June 1968 V
Sugar aquatint on partially greased plate.
Plate: 60 × 85 mm.
Sheet: 250 × 325 mm
2014,7087.150
Bloch 1630; Baer 1646.B.b.1

Plate 151: *Visitor with a Bourbon nose at Celestina's*, 9 June 1968 VI
Sugar aquatint on partially greased plate.
Plate: 60 × 85 mm
Sheet: 250 × 325 mm
2014,7087.151
Bloch 1631; Baer 1647.B.b.1

Plate 152: *Don Quixote meeting Dulcinea*, 9 June 1968 VII
Sugar aquatint and sandpaper.
Plate: 225 × 320 mm.
Sheet: 365 × 470 mm
2014,7087.152
Bloch 1632; Baer 1648.B.b.1

Plate 153: *Orgy at the girl's, with spectators from 'The Burial of Count d'Orgaz'*, 10 June 1968 I
Etching. Plate: 375 × 275 mm.
Sheet: 550 × 430 mm
2014,7087.153
Bloch 1633; Baer 1649.B.b.1

Plate 154: *Woman taking a nap, surrounded by spectators*, 10 June 1968 II
Etching. Plate: 225 × 290 mm.
Sheet: 350 × 420 mm
2014,7087.154
Bloch 1634; Baer 1650.B.b.1

Plate 155: *Young woman and old husband, in the distance the lover rides in a garden*, 13 June 1968 I
Sugar aquatint on partially greased plate.
Plate: 85 × 60 mm
Sheet: 250 × 325 mm
2014,7087.155
Bloch 1635; Baer 1651.B.b.1

Plate 156: *Maja and horseman*, 13 June 1968 II
Sugar aquatint.
Plate: 60 × 85 mm
Sheet: 250 × 325 mm
2014,7087.156
Bloch 1636; Baer 1652.B.b.1

Plate 157: *Painter, or writer, with two women*, 13 June 1968 III
Sugar aquatint.
Plate: 60 × 120 mm.
Sheet: 250 × 325 mm
2014,7087.157
Bloch 1637; Baer 1653.B.b.1

Plate 158: *Two women, with voyeurs*, 13 June 1968 IV
Etching and scraper or knife
Plate: 225 × 290 mm.
Sheet: 350 × 420 mm
2014,7087.158
Bloch 1638; Baer 1654.B.b.1

Plate 159: *Venus and Cupid in the style of the 16th century*, 15 June 1968 I
Etching. Plate: 410 × 495 mm.
Sheet: 560 × 645 mm
2014,7087.159
Bloch 1639; Baer 1655.B.b.1

Plate 160: *Venus and Cupid in the 'noble savage' style*, 15 June 1968 II
Etching. Plate: 410 × 495 mm.
Sheet: 565 × 645 mm
2014,7087.160
Bloch 1640; Baer 1656.B.b.1

Plate 161: *Variation on Don Quixote and Dulcinea: travelling actors' stop*, 15 June 1968 III
Sugar aquatint on greased plate. Plate: 335 × 495 mm.
Sheet: 500 × 650 mm
2014,7087.161
Bloch 1641; Baer 1657.B.b.1
(illustrated on p. 127)

Plate 162: *Horseman visiting a girl, with Celestina and a small dog*, 16 June 1968
Sugar aquatint on partially greased plate.
Plate: 100 × 160 mm.
Sheet: 250 × 325 mm
2014,7087.162
Bloch 1642; Baer 1658.B.b.1

Plate 163: *Sex worker and aging men*, 19 June 1968 I
Etching. Plate: 210 × 150 mm.
Sheet: 345 × 280 mm
2014,7087.163
Bloch 1643; Baer 1659.B.b.1

Plate 164: *Sex worker and sailors*, 19 June 1968 II
Etching. Plate: 210 × 150 mm.
Sheet: 345 × 285 mm
2014,7087.164
Bloch 1644; Baer 1660.B.b.1

Plate 165: *Fat courtesan and old beau*, 19 June 1968 III
Etching. Plate: 210 × 150 mm.
Sheet: 330 × 285 mm
2014,7087.165
Bloch 1645; Baer 1661.B.b.1

Plate 166: *Gladiator games*, 20 June 1968 I
Etching. Plate: 150 × 210 mm.
Sheet: 285 × 345 mm
2014,7087.166
Bloch 1646; Baer 1664.B.b.1

Plate 167: *Painter painting the breast of his model*, 19 June 1968 IV
Etching. Plate: 125 × 90 mm.
Sheet: 327 × 250 mm
2014,7087.167
Bloch 1647; Baer 1662.B.b.1

Plate 168: *Fat sex worker on the knees of a bearded man*, 19 June 1968 V
Etching. Plate: 125 × 90 mm.
Sheet: 325 × 250 mm
2014,7087.168
Bloch 1648; Baer 1663.B.b.1

Plate 169: *Greek flautist and dancer*, 20 June 1968 II
Etching. Plate: 90 × 125 mm.
Sheet: 250 × 325 mm
2014,7087.169
Bloch 1649; Baer 1665.B.b.1

Plate 170: *Faun flautist and bacchantes*, 20 June 1968 III
Etching. Plate: 90 × 125 mm.
Sheet: 250 × 325 mm
2014,7087.170
Bloch 1650; Baer 1666.B.b.1

Plate 171: *Painter and model on a bed*, 20 June 1968 IV
Drypoint. Plate: 90 × 125 mm.
Sheet: 250 × 325 mm
2014,7087.171
Bloch 1651; Baer 1667.B.b.1

Plate 172: *Young woman dropping her dress*, 20 June 1968 V
Aquatint and drypoint on greased plate.
Plate: 210 × 150 mm.
Sheet: 345 × 285 mm
2014,7087.172
Bloch 1652; Baer 1668.B.b.1

Plate 173: *Sex worker and Reiter*, 20 June 1968 VI
Sugar aquatint on greased plate. Plate: 210 × 150 mm.
Sheet: 345 × 280 mm
2014,7087.173
Bloch 1653; Baer 1669.B.b.1

Plate 174: *Nude couple posing*, 21 June 1968 I
Sugar aquatint on greased plate. Plate: 125 × 90 mm.
Sheet: 325 × 250 mm
2014,7087.174
Bloch 1654; Baer 1670.B.b.1

Plate 175: *Fat sex worker and 'musketeer'*, 21 June 1968 II
Sugar aquatint on greased plate. Plate: 125 × 90 mm.
Sheet: 325 × 250 mm
2014,7087.175
Bloch 1655; Baer 1671.B.b.1

Plate 176: *Young sex worker and 'musketeer'*, 21 June 1968 IV
Sugar aquatint on greased plate. Plate: 210 × 150 mm.
Sheet: 350 × 285 mm
2014,7087.176
Bloch 1656; Baer 1673.B.b.1

Plate 177: *Couple and little
valet framed by a door*,
21 June 1968 III
Sugar aquatint on greased
plate. Plate: 125 × 90 mm.
Sheet: 325 × 250 mm
2014,7087.177
Bloch 1657; Baer 1672.Bb1

Plate 178: *Big couple, and small
dog, Poilus*, 22 June 1968 I
Etching. Plate: 125 × 90 mm.
Sheet: 325 × 250 mm
2014,7087.178
Bloch 1658; Baer 1674.B.b.1

Plate 179: *Ancillary lovers*,
22 June 1968 II
Sugar aquatint on partially
greased plate.
Plate: 210 × 150 mm.
Sheet: 350 × 285 mm
2014,7087.179
Bloch 1659; Baer 1675.B.b.1

Plate 180: *Young boy dreaming:
women!*, 22 June 1968 IV
Sugar aquatint, drypoint and
scraper on greased plate.
Plate: 495 × 655 mm.
Sheet: 565 × 675 mm
2014,7087.180
Bloch 1660; Baer 1676.B.b.1

Plate 181: *Fat sex worker and
man with a Rembrandtesque
beret and a French bulldog*,
23 June 1968 I
Etching. Plate: 125 × 90 mm.
Sheet: 325 × 250 mm
2014,7087.181
Bloch 1661; Baer 1677.B.b.1

Plate 182: *Young woman in
a shirt, faun and goat's head*, 23
June 1968 II
Etching and drypoint.
Plate: 210 × 150 mm.
Sheet: 350 × 285 mm
2014,7087.182
Bloch 1662; Baer 1678.B.b.1

Plate 183: *Fat courtesan greeted
by three linear gentlemen*, 25
June 1968 I
Etching. Plate: 210 × 150 mm.
Sheet: 345 × 285 mm
2014,7087.183
Bloch 1663; Baer 1679.B.b.1

Plate 184: *Young woman
showing herself to two prostrate
grotesque courtiers*, 25 June
1968 II
Etching. Plate: 125 × 90 mm.
Sheet: 325 × 250 mm
2014,7087.184
Bloch 1664; Baer 1680.B.b.1

Plate 185: *Young courtesan
with a gentleman, a sculptor and
a flirtatious old man*,
25 June 1968 III
Etching. Plate: 125 × 90 mm.
Sheet: 325 × 250 mm
2014,7087.185
Bloch 1665; Baer 1681.B.b.1

Plate 186: *On the beach.
Woman with mirror and two
bathers*, 25 June 1968 IV
Etching. Plate: 410 × 495 mm.
Sheet: 560 × 645 mm
2014,7087.186
Bloch 1666; Baer 1682.B.b.1

Plate 187: *Kid slipping into
a hamman on a day reserved for
women*, 25 June 1968 V,
17 July 1968 I
Etching and drypoint.
Plate: 500 × 650 mm.
Sheet: 630 × 800 mm
2014,7087.187
Bloch 1667; Baer 1683.B.b.1

Plate 188: *Painter painting
the neck of his young model*, 26
June 1968 I
Sugar aquatint on greased
plate. Plate: 90 × 125 mm.
Sheet: 250 × 325 mm
2014,7087.188
Bloch 1668; Baer 1684.B.b.1

Plate 189: *Three 'musketeers'
greeting a woman in bed*,
26 June 1968 II
Sugar aquatint on greased
plate. Plate: 90 × 125 mm.
Sheet: 250 × 325 mm
2014,7087.189
Bloch 1669; Baer 1685.B.b.1

Plate 190: *Celestina, her
protégé, and a young
gentleman*, 26 June 1968 III
Sugar aquatint on greased
plate. Plate: 90 × 125 mm.
Sheet: 250 × 325 mm
2014,7087.190
Bloch 1670; Baer 1686.B.b.1

Plate 191: *Exchange of looks*,
26 June 1968 IV
Sugar aquatint, drypoint and
scraper. Plate: 150 × 210 mm.
Sheet: 280 × 345 mm
2014,7087.191
Bloch 1671; Baer 1687.B.b.1

Plate 192: *Visitor, with his dog,
at a young woman's, with
Celestina*, 26 June 1968 V
Sugar aquatint and drypoint
(for dog) on greased plate.
Plate: 150 × 210 mm.
Sheet: 285 × 345 mm
2014,7087.192
Bloch 1672; Baer 1688.B.b.1

Plate 193: *Pensive man at a
young woman's, with Celestina*,
26 June 1968 VI
Sugar aquatint, drypoint and
scraper on greased plate.
Plate: 150 × 210 mm.
Sheet: 285 × 350 mm
2014,7087.193
Bloch 1673; Baer 1689.B.b.1

Plate 194: *Portrait of one of
the characters from 'The Burial
of Count d'Orgaz', in tears*,
29 June 1968 I
Etching. Plate: 210 × 150 mm.
Sheet: 350 × 285 mm
2014,7087.194
Bloch 1674; Baer 1690.B.b.1

Plate 195: *Man, woman and
child. Study for the El Greco
portrait*, 29 June 1968 II
Etching and drypoint.
Plate: 210 × 150 mm.
Sheet: 345 × 285 mm
2014,7087.195
Bloch 1675; Baer 1691.B.b.1

Plate 196: *'The Burial of Count
d'Orgaz', after Picasso*,
30 June 1968 I
Sugar aquatint, etching and
scraper. Plate: 280 × 390 mm.
Sheet: 450 × 545 mm
2014,7087.196
Bloch 1676; Baer 1692.B.b.1
(illustrated on p. 126)

Plate 197: *Moving, or
revolutionary cart*,
30 June 1968 II
Sugar aquatint and etching.
Plate: 280 × 390 mm.
Sheet: 455 × 545 mm
2014,7087.197
Bloch 1677; Baer 1693.B.b.1

Plate 198: *Don Quixote, Sancho
and a 'musketeer', watching
Dulcinea on a cart pulled by a
masked man*, 3 July 1968 I
Sugar aquatint on greased
plate. Plate: 150 × 210 mm.
Sheet: 280 × 345 mm
2014,7087.198
Bloch 1678; Baer 1694.B.b.1

Plate 199: *Rembrandtesque
man sitting among girls*,
4 July 1968 I
Sugar aquatint on greased
plate. Plate: 150 × 210 mm.
Sheet: 280 × 345 mm
2014,7087.199
Bloch 1679; Baer 1695.B.b.1

Plate 200: *Painter or sculptor
thinking about a warrior
woman, with 'musketeer',
Cupid and small characters*,
5 July 1968 I
Sugar aquatint on greased
plate. Plate: 210 × 150 mm.
Sheet: 350 × 285 mm
2014,7087.200
Bloch 1680; Baer 1696.B.b.1

Plate 201: *Swinging curly-haired
man, with odalisques, putto
and Spaniard in profile*,
5 July 1968 II
Sugar aquatint, drypoint and
scraper. Plate: 280 × 390 mm.
Sheet: 455 × 540 mm
2014,7087.201
Bloch 1681; Baer 1697.B.b.1

Plate 202: *Celestina, maja and
grotesques*, 8 July 1968 I
Sugar aquatint.
Plate: 150 × 210 mm.
Sheet: 285 × 350 mm
2014,7087.202
Bloch 1682; Baer 1698.B.b.1

Plate 203: *Rider, child and
juggler with his balls*,
8 July 1968 II
Sugar aquatint.
Plate: 150 × 210 mm.
Sheet: 285 × 350 mm
2014,7087.203
Bloch 1683; Baer 1699.B.b.1

Plate 204: *Painter painting
on his model*, 15 July 1968 I
Etching. Plate: 410 × 495 mm.
Sheet: 565 × 645 mm
2014,7087.204
Bloch 1684; Baer 1700.B.b.1

Plate 205: *Pastoral
Poussinesque scene on the
theme of Pan and Syrinx*,
15 July 1968 II
Etching. Plate: 410 × 495 mm.
Sheet: 565 × 645 mm
2014,7087.205
Bloch 1685; Baer 1701.B.b.1

Plate 206: *Thinking of Goya:
women in prison*, 16 July 1968 I
Sugar aquatint on greased
plate. Plate: 315 × 395 mm.
Sheet: 475 × 565 mm
2014,7087.206
Bloch 1686; Baer 1702.B.b.1
(illustrated on p. 128)

Plate 207: *Celestina, maja and
two gentlemen*, 17 July 1968 II
Sugar aquatint on greased
plate. Plate: 150 × 225 mm.
Sheet: 250 × 325 mm
2014,7087.207
Bloch 1687; Baer 1703.B.b.1

Plate 208: *Serenade on the flute*, 17 July 1968 III
Sugar aquatint on greased plate. Plate: 150 × 225 mm.
Sheet: 250 × 325 mm
2014,7087.208
Bloch 1688; Baer 1704.B.b.1

Plate 209: *Lunch on the Rembrandtesque grass, with maja and Celestina*, 20 July 1968 III
Sugar aquatint on greased plate. Plate: 175 × 225 mm.
Sheet: 310 × 365 mm
2014,7087.209
Bloch 1689; Baer 1707.B.b.1

Plate 210: *Seated man with pipe, maja and Celestina*, 20 July 1968 I
Sugar aquatint on greased plate. Plate: 60 × 85 mm.
Sheet: 250 × 325 mm
2014,7087.210
Bloch 1690; Baer 1705.B.b.1

Plate 211: *Conversation*, 20 July 1968 II
Sugar aquatint on greased plate. Plate: 60 × 85 mm.
Sheet: 250 × 325 mm
2014,7087.211
Bloch 1691; Baer 1706.B.b.1

Plate 212: *Jacqueline as 'nude maja' with Celestina and two 'musketeers'*, 20 July 1968 IV
Sugar aquatint on greased plate. Plate: 175 × 225 mm.
Sheet: 315 × 365 mm
2014,7087.212
Bloch 1692; Baer 1708.B.b.1

Plate 213: *Painter and model in gaiters dancing, with spectator*, 21 July 1968 I
Etching. Plate: 90 × 115 mm.
Sheet: 250 × 325 mm
2014,7087.213
Bloch 1693; Baer 1709.B.b.1

Plate 214: *Couple (royal?) posing for a painter in court attire*, 23 July 1968 I
Etching. Plate: 90 × 115 mm.
Sheet: 250 × 325 mm
2014,7087.214
Bloch 1694; Baer 1710.B.b.1

Plate 215: *Spanish painter painting the portrait of a nude woman, in the form of a bearded man with a strawberry*, 25 July 1968 I
Etching. Plate: 90 × 120 mm.
Sheet: 250 × 325 mm
2014,7087.215
Bloch 1695; Baer 1711.B.b.1

Plate 216: *Punchinello and dwarf, Roman and old man in front of a dancing odalisque*, 25 July 1968 II
Etching. Plate: 150 × 225 mm.
Sheet: 250 × 325 mm
2014,7087.216
Bloch 1696; Baer 1712.B.b.1

Plate 217: *Couple in the fields, with a putto crowned with flowers*, 26 July 1968 I
Etching. Plate: 320 × 315 mm.
Sheet: 495 × 455 mm
2014,7087.217
Bloch 1697; Baer 1713.B.b.1

Plate 218: *Couple thinking about a threesome*, 26 July 1968 II
Drypoint and scraper.
Plate: 150 × 225 mm.
Sheet: 250 × 325 mm
2014,7087.218
Bloch 1698; Baer 1714.B.b.1

Plate 219: *Gentleman, ashamed woman and Reiter*, 27 July 1968 I
Etching and knife.
Plate: 150 × 225 mm.
Sheet: 250 × 325 mm
2014,7087.219
Bloch 1699; Baer 1715.B.b.1

Plate 220: *Kidnapping, I*, 27 July 1968 II
Drypoint and scraper or knife.
Plate: 150 × 225 mm.
Sheet: 280 × 360 mm
2014,7087.220
Bloch 1700; Baer 1716.B.b.1

Plate 221: *Kidnapping, II*, 27 July 1968 III
Etching. Plate: 315 × 315 mm.
Sheet: 490 × 455 mm
2014,7087.221
Bloch 1701; Baer 1717.B.b.1

Plate 222: *Man with two nude women*, 27 July 1968 IV
Aquatint and scraper.
Plate: 315 × 395 mm.
Sheet: 475 × 565 mm
2014,7087.222
Bloch 1702; Baer 1718.B.b.1

Plate 223: *Kidnapping, III*, 28 July 1968 I
Aquatint. Plate: 315 × 315 mm.
Sheet: 495 × 455 mm
2014,7087.223
Bloch 1703; Baer 1719.B.b.1

Plate 224: *Duel at sunrise*, 29 July 1968 I
Etching with sandpaper.
Plate: 150 × 225 mm.
Sheet: 280 × 380 mm
2014,7087.224
Bloch 1704; Baer 1720.B.b.1

Plate 225: *Rembrandtesque man with pipe and courtesan*, 29 July 1968 II
Etching. Plate: 220 × 145 mm.
Sheet: 265 × 280 mm
2014,7087.225
Bloch 1705; Baer 1721.B.b.1

Plate 226: *Maja and putto, horseman and small voyeur*, 31 July 1968 I
Etching. Plate: 175 × 225 mm.
Sheet: 315 × 365 mm
2014,7087.226
Bloch 1706; Baer 1722.B.b.1

Plate 227: *Country scene, with bearded man crowned with flowers by a putto, and women*, 31 July 1968 II
Etching. Plate: 175 × 225 mm.
Sheet: 315 × 365 mm
2014,7087.227
Bloch 1707; Baer 1723.B.b.1

Plate 228: *Man leaning and kneeling on a chair in front of (or thinking about) a woman*, 1 August 1968 I
Etching, scraper and drypoint with sandpaper.
Plate: 225 × 180 mm.
Sheet: 375 × 315 mm
2014,7087.228
Bloch 1708; Baer 1724.B.b.1

Plate 229: *Pastoral scene: lovers, flautist and watermelon eater*, 1 August 1968 II
Etching. Plate: 175 × 225 mm.
Sheet: 310 × 360 mm
2014,7087.229
Bloch 1709; Baer 1725.B.b.1

Plate 230: *Bather and putto flautist, with men in beach outfits*, 1 August 1968 III
Etching, aquatint and scraper.
Plate: 175 × 260 mm.
Sheet: 280 × 380 mm
2014,7087.230
Bloch 1710; Baer 1726.B.b.1

Plate 231: *Painter at work, with an ugly model*, 1 August 1968 IV
Etching. Plate: 220 × 150 mm.
Sheet: 325 × 250 mm
2014,7087.231
Bloch 1711; Baer 1727.B.b.1

Plate 232: *Two women, one in a harness, an owl, Don Quixote, a gentleman from 'The Burial of Count d'Orgaz' and a conquistador*, 2 August 1968 II
Etching. Plate: 175 × 260 mm.
Sheet: 280 × 380 mm
2014,7087.232
Bloch 1712; Baer 1730.B.b.1

Plate 233: *Stop for travelling actors, with owl, and jester embracing a woman*, 2 August 1968 I
Etching and drypoint.
Plate: 315 × 315 mm.
Sheet: 250 × 325 mm
2014,7087.233
Bloch 1713; Baer 1729.B.b.1

Plate 234: *Painter with a half-recumbent model*, 2 August 1968 III
Aquatint with stop-out varnish in reserve on a greased plate.
Plate: 175 × 260 mm.
Sheet: 250 × 325 mm
2014,7087.234
Bloch 1714; Baer 1731.B.b.1

Plate 235: *Bearded painter in dressing gown, with two nude women and a visitor*, 2 August 1968 IV
Sugar aquatint on greased plate. Plate: 175 × 260 mm.
Sheet: 250 × 325 mm
2014,7087.235
Bloch 1715; Baer 1732.B.b.1

Plate 236: *Woman in hat and carnation, with turbaned man, clown, putto and spectator*, 3 August 1968 I
Etching. Plate: 175 × 260 mm.
Sheet: 280 × 380 mm
2014,7087.236
Bloch 1716; Baer 1733.B.b.1

Plate 237: *Desert belly dance, with paunchy spectator*, 3 August 1968 II
Etching. Plate: 175 × 260 mm.
Sheet: 280 × 380 mm
2014,7087.237
Bloch 1717; Baer 1734.B.b.1

Plate 238: *Oasis with flautist and dancers*, 3 August 1968 III
Etching. Plate: 175 × 260 mm.
Sheet: 280 × 380 mm
2014,7087.238
Bloch 1718; Baer 1735.B.b.1

Plate 239: *Old man seated with a woman, and dancer*, 3 August 1968 IV
Etching. Plate: 175 × 265 mm.
Sheet: 285 × 380 mm (irregular)
2001,1125.28. Presented by an anonymous donor
Bloch 1719; Baer 1736.B

Plate 239: *Old man seated with a woman, and dancer*, 3 Aug 1968 IV
Etching. Plate: 175 × 265 mm.
Sheet: 280 × 350 mm
2014,7087.239
Bloch 1719; Baer 1736.B.b.1

Plate 240: *Old Rembrandtesque
painter painting bacchantes*,
4 August 1968 I
Sugar aquatint and drypoint
on greased plate.
Plate: 195 × 325 mm.
Sheet: 330 × 455 mm
2014,7087.240
Bloch 1720; Baer 1737.B.b.1

Plate 241: *Man of the forest in
front of a painting representing a
bacchante*, 4 August 1968 II
Etching. Plate: 175 × 265 mm.
Sheet: 280 × 370 mm
2014,7087.241
Bloch 1721; Baer 1738.B.b.1

Plate 242: *Around the
'Turkish Bath' of Ingres*,
4 August 1968 III
Etching. Plate: 200 × 325 mm.
Sheet: 330 × 455 mm
2014,7087.242
Bloch 1722; Baer 1739.B.b.1

Plate 243: *Canvas representing
bacchantes, and spectators,
including one with a
Rembrandtesque hat*,
4 August 1968 IV
Etching. Plate: 200 × 325 mm.
Sheet: 325 × 455 mm
2014,7087.243
Bloch 1723; Baer 1740.B.b.1

Plate 244: *Naked in boots*,
4 August 1968 V
Etching. Plate: 225 × 150 mm.
Sheet: 380 × 280 mm
2014,7087.244
Bloch 1724; Baer 1741.B.b.1

Plate 245: *Painter and penitent
monk, owl guitarist, and little
spectator*, 4 August 1968 VI,
5 August 1968
Etching. Plate: 260 × 175 mm.
Sheet: 415 × 300 mm
2014,7087.245
Bloch 1725; Baer 1742.B.b.1

Plate 246: *Bearded man with a hat
adorned with a bell*, 5 August 1968 I
Etching. Plate: 80 × 60 mm.
Sheet: 325 × 250 mm
2014,7087.246
Bloch 1726; Baer 1743.B.b.1

Plate 247: *Young Spanish lady*,
5 August 1968 II
Etching. Plate: 80 × 60 mm.
Sheet: 325 × 250 mm
2014,7087.247
Bloch 1727; Baer 1744.B.b.1

Plate 248: *Celestina introducing
a gentleman to a young woman*,
5 August 1968 III
Etching. Plate: 60 × 85 mm.
Sheet: 250 × 325 mm
2014,7087.248
Bloch 1728; Baer 1745.B.b.1

Plate 249: *Blonde woman
with flower, Celestina and
'musketeer'*, 5 August 1968 IV
Etching. Plate: 60 × 85 mm.
Sheet: 250 × 325 mm
2014,7087.249
Bloch 1729; Baer 1746.B.b.1

Plate 250: *Nightmare*,
5 August 1968 V
Sugar aquatint and scraper
on greased plate.
Plate: 200 × 320 mm.
Sheet: 325 × 455 mm
2014,7087.250
Bloch 1730; Baer 1747.B.b.1

Plate 251: *Painter in front of one
of Raphael's 'Three Graces' and
a forest man in a party hat*, 5
August 1968 VI
Etching. Plate: 315 × 315 mm.
Sheet: 490 × 450 mm
2014,7087.251
Bloch 1731; Baer 1748.B.b.1

Plate 252: *Portrait of an aging
'musketeer' with a blotchy face*,
6 August 1968 I
Etching. Plate: 140 × 110 mm.
Sheet: 325 × 250 mm
2014,7087.252
Bloch 1732; Baer 1749.B.b.1

Plate 253: *A nod to Velázquez:
Infanta in three-quarters*,
6 August 1968 II
Etching. Plate: 140 × 110 mm.
Sheet: 325 × 250 mm
2014,7087.253
Bloch 1733; Baer 1750.B.b.1

Plate 254: *Young puppet lord
with Reiter, and two nude
women*, 7 August 1968 I
Etching. Plate: 225 × 265 mm.
Sheet: 330 × 405 mm
2014,7087.254
Bloch 1734; Baer 1751.B.b.1

Plate 255: *The siesta: couple*,
7 August 1968 II
Etching. Plate: 150 × 210 mm.
Sheet: 280 × 355 mm
2014,7087.255
Bloch 1735; Baer 1752.B.b.1

Plate 256: *The siesta: two
women*, 7 August 1968 III
Etching. Plate: 150 × 210 mm.
Sheet: 280 × 355 mm
2014,7087.256
Bloch 1736; Baer 1753.B.b.1

Plate 257: *Rembrandtesque
man with pipe*, 8 August 1968 I
Etching. Plate: 210 × 150 mm.
Sheet: 350 × 285 mm
2014,7087.257
Bloch 1737; Baer 1754.B.b.1

Plate 258: *Woman at her toilet
and man in a Rembrandtesque
hat*, 8 August 1968 II
Etching. Plate: 210 × 150 mm.
Sheet: 345 × 385 mm
2014,7087.258
Bloch 1738; Baer 1755.B.b.1

Plate 259: *Woman acrobat with
glitter makeup and spectators*,
8 August 1968 III, 9 August 1968
Etching. Plate: 195 × 325 mm.
Sheet: 330 × 455 mm
2014,7087.259
Bloch 1739; Baer 1756.B.b.1

Plate 260: *Old retired privateer
smoking his pipe*,
9 August 1968 I
Etching. Plate: 220 × 175 mm.
Sheet: 375 × 310 mm
2014,7087.260
Bloch 1740; Baer 1757.B.b.1

Plate 261: *Old paunchy sailor
with pipe and contemptuous
young sex worker*,
9 August 1968 II
Etching. Plate: 325 × 200 mm.
Sheet: 475 × 330 mm
2014,7087.261
Bloch 1741; Baer 1758.B.b.1

Plate 262: *Young woman pulling
the moustache of a gentleman
twisting his bangle*, 9 August
1968 III
Etching. Plate: 265 × 210 mm.
Sheet: 420 × 325 mm
2014,7087.262
Bloch 1742; Baer 1759.B.b.1

Plate 263: *Handsome Spanish
gentleman and bearded lady
(or woman 'wearing' a bearded
male head)*, 10 August 1968 I
Sugar aquatint, drypoint and
scraper on greased plate.
Plate: 325 × 200 mm.
Sheet: 375 × 425 mm
2014,7087.263
Bloch 1743; Baer 1760.B.b.1

Plate 264: *Portrait of a
bourgeois Dutch man*,
10 August 1968 II
Etching. Plate: 85 × 60 mm.
Sheet: 325 × 250 mm
2014,7087.264
Bloch 1744; Baer 1761.B.b.1

Plate 265: *Portrait of a
bourgeois Dutch woman
wearing a bonnet*,
10 August 1968 III
Etching.
Plate: 120 × 90 mm.
Sheet: 325 × 250 mm
2014,7087.265
Bloch 1745; Baer 1762.B.b.1

Plate 266: *The servant
(from the previous two)*,
10 August 1968 IV
Etching. Plate: 140 × 110 mm.
Sheet: 325 × 250 mm
2014,7087.266
Bloch 1746; Baer 1763.B.b.1

Plate 267: *Old painter with
an adolescent girl*,
10 August 1968 VII
Etching. Plate: 120 × 90 mm.
Sheet: 325 × 250 mm
2014,7087.267
Bloch 1747; Baer 1766.B.b.1

Plate 268: *The excess of the
painter*, 10 August 1968 VI
Etching. Plate: 135 × 110 mm.
Sheet: 325 × 250 mm
2014,7087.268
Bloch 1748; Baer 1765.B.b.1

Plate 269: *Young sex worker
and old man with bulging eyes*,
10 August 1968 V
Etching. Plate: 85 × 60 mm.
Sheet: 325 × 250 mm
2014,7087.269
Bloch 1749; Baer 1764.B.b.1

Plate 270: *Man with pipe, young
nude woman and small dog*,
12 August 1968 I
Sugar aquatint and scraper with
sandpaper. Plate: 90 × 120 mm.
Sheet: 250 × 325 mm
2014,7087.270
Bloch 1750; Baer 1767.B.b.1

Plate 271: *Gentleman with
pipe and nude maja*,
12 August 1968 II
Etching, black areas achieved
using sandpaper.
Plate: 90 × 120 mm.
Sheet: 250 × 325 mm
2014,7087.271
Bloch 1751; Baer 1768.B.b.1

Plate 272: *Young woman and
'musketeer'*, 13 Aug 1968 I,
15 August 1968
Sugar aquatint and etching
on partially greased plate.
Plate: 90 × 115 mm.
Sheet: 250 × 325 mm
2014,7087.272
Bloch 1752; Baer 1769.B.b.1

Plate 273: *'Musketeer' blowing
a puff of pipe smoke into
a young woman's face*,
13 August 1968 II,
15 August 1968
Sugar aquatint and drypoint.
Plate: 90 × 115 mm.
Sheet: 250 × 325 mm
2014,7087.273
Bloch 1753; Baer 1770.B.b.1

Plate 274: *Man with pipe and cane, and young nude woman*, 13 August 1968 III, 15 August 1968 II
Sugar aquatint and drypoint on partially greased plate.
Plate: 90 × 115 mm.
Sheet: 250 × 325 mm
2014,7087.274
Bloch 1754; Baer 1771.B.b.1

Plate 275: *Young woman and smoker*, 13 August 1968 IV, 15 August 1968
Sugar aquatint, drypoint and scraper on partially greased plate. Plate: 90 × 115 mm.
Sheet: 250 × 325 mm
2014,7087.275
Bloch 1755; Baer 1772.B.b.1

Plate 276: *In the garden: odalisque in slippers and hat, with flowers, and Ingresque spectator*, 14 August 1968 I
Etching. Plate: 195 × 325 mm.
Sheet: 330 × 455 mm
2014,7087.276
Bloch 1756; Baer 1774.B.b.1

Plate 277: *Nude woman sitting cross-legged and grotesque man with hand on heart*, 13 August 1968 V
Etching. Plate: 155 × 210 mm.
Sheet: 285 × 350 mm
2014,7087.277
Bloch 1757; Baer 1773.B.b.1

Plate 278: *Woman with a flower on a 'deckchair'*, 14 August 1968 II
Etching. Plate: 200 × 325 mm.
Sheet: 315 × 455 mm
2014,7087.278
Bloch 1758; Baer 1775.B.b.1

Plate 279: *Acrobat model and draughtsman*, 15 August 1968
Etching. Plate: 90 × 120 mm.
Sheet: 250 × 325 mm
2014,7087.279
Bloch 1759; Baer 1776.B.b.1

Plate 280: *Big sex worker, witch with an owl and traveller in clogs*, 15 August 1968 I
Etching. Plate: 155 × 210 mm.
Sheet: 285 × 350 mm
2014,7087.280
Bloch 1760; Baer 1777.B.b.1

Plate 281: *Tree in the storm, with flight towards a church*, 15 August 1968 III
Sugar aquatint and drypoint on greased plate.
Plate: 200 × 325 mm.
Sheet: 315 × 450 mm
2014,7087.281
Bloch 1761; Baer 1778.B.b.1
(illustrated on p. 132)

Plate 282: *As long as we get drunk …*, 18 August 1968 I
Etching. Plate: 120 × 90 mm.
Sheet: 325 × 250 mm
2014,7087.282
Bloch 1762; Baer 1779.B.b.1

Plate 283: *Television: floor gymnastics, with spectators*, 18 August 1968 II
Etching. Plate: 210 × 155 mm
Sheet: 350 × 280 mm
2014,7087.283
Bloch 1763; Baer 1780.B.b.1

Plate 284: *Opium smoker, woman in slippers on her bed and small dog*, 18 August 1968 III
Etching. Plate: 155 × 210 mm.
Sheet: 280 × 350 mm
2014,7087.284
Bloch 1764; Baer 1781.B.b.1

Plate 285: *Two women frolicking on a beach mat*, 18 August 1968 IV
Etching. Plate: 200 × 325 mm.
Sheet: 315 × 450 mm
2014,7087.285
Bloch 1765; Baer 1782.B.b.1

Plate 286: *Two fat nude women and a voyeur*, 18 August 1968 V
Etching. Plate: 155 × 210 mm.
Sheet: 325 × 455 mm
2014,7087.286
Bloch 1766; Baer 1783.B.b.1

Plate 287: *Rembrandtesque man and two nude women*, 18 August 1968 VI
Etching. Plate: 155 × 210 mm.
Sheet: 280 × 350 mm
2014,7087.287
Bloch 1767; Baer 1784.B.b.1

Plate 288: *Woman seducing a pensive man*, 19 August 1968 I
Etching. Plate: 280 × 390 mm.
Sheet: 450 × 545 mm
2014,7087.288
Bloch 1768; Baer 1785.B.b.1

Plate 289: *A nod to the 'Turkish Bath': women taking a nap in the sun*, 20 August 1968 I
Etching. Plate: 280 × 390 mm.
Sheet: 450 × 545 mm
2014,7087.289
Bloch 1769; Baer 1786.B.b.1

Plate 290: *A nod to the 'Turkish Bath': women sunbathing at the pool*, 21, 22 August 1968
Etching. Plate: 280 × 390 mm.
Sheet: 450 × 545 mm
2014,7087.290
Bloch 1770; Baer 1787.B.b.1

Plate 291: *Circus rider, Rembrandtesque man and unshaven spectator*, 22 August 1968 II
Etching. Plate: 280 × 390 mm.
Sheet: 450 × 545 mm
2014,7087.291
Bloch 1771; Baer 1788.B.b.1

Plate 292: *Four porters bringing a young woman on a stretcher to a gentleman*, 23 August 1968 I
Etching. Plate: 280 × 390 mm.
Sheet: 450 × 545 mm
2014,7087.292
Bloch 1772; Baer 1789.B.b.1

Plate 293: *Painter, model in straw hat and gentleman*, 23 August 1968 II
Etching. Plate: 280 × 390 mm.
Sheet: 450 × 545 mm
2014,7087.293
Bloch 1773; Baer 1790.B.b.1

Plate 294: *Gentleman's daydream: surprise, as a voyeur, the painter painting on his model*, 24 August 1968 I
Etching and drypoint.
Plate: 165 × 210 mm.
Sheet: 285 × 335 mm
2014,7087.294
Bloch 1774; Baer 1791.B.b.1

Plate 295: *Opium reveries: smoker in papal cap discovering the mystery of the Trinity in a woman's breasts and dove, with jester in triangular hat behind*, 28 August 1968 I
Etching. Plate: 165 × 205 mm.
Sheet: 280 × 335 mm
2014,7087.295
Bloch 1775; Baer 1792.B.b.1

Plate 296: *Raphael and La Fornarina, I*, 29 August 1968 I
Etching. Plate: 280 × 390 mm.
Sheet: 450 × 545 mm
2014,7087.296
Bloch 1776; Baer 1793.B.b.1
(illustrated on p. 122)

Plate 297: *Raphael and La Fornarina, II: with a hidden voyeur*, 29 August 1968 II
Etching. Plate: 280 × 390 mm.
Sheet: 450 × 545 mm
2014,7087.297
Bloch 1777; Baer 1794.B.b.1

Plate 298: *Raphael and La Fornarina, III: with the Pope as a hidden voyeur*, 31 August 1968 I
Etching. Plate: 165 × 205 mm.
Sheet: 280 × 335 mm
2014,7087.298
Bloch 1778; Baer 1795.B.b.1

Plate 299: *Raphael and La Fornarina, IV: with the Pope drawing the curtain*, 31 August 1968 II
Etching. Plate: 235 × 330 mm.
Sheet: 375 × 470 mm
2014,7087.299
Bloch 1779; Baer 1796.B.b.1

Plate 300: *Raphael and La Fornarina, V: with voyeur pulling back the curtain*, 31 August 1968 III
Etching. Plate: 410 × 495 mm.
Sheet: 565 × 645 mm
2014,7087.300
Bloch 1780; Baer 1797.B.b.1

Plate 301: *Raphael and La Fornarina, VI: finally alone!*, 1 September 1968 I
Etching. Plate: 295 × 510 mm.
Sheet: 440 × 655 mm
2014,7087.301
Bloch 1781; Baer 1798.B.b.1

Plate 302: *Raphael and La Fornarina, VII: the Pope is there, sitting*, 1 September 1968 II
Etching. Plate: 295 × 510 mm.
Sheet: 445 × 655 mm
2014,7087.302
Bloch 1782; Baer 1799.B.b.1

Plate 303: *Raphael and La Fornarina, VIII: the Pope enters, with a soft smile*, 1 September 1968 III
Etching. Plate: 145 × 210 mm.
Sheet: 280 × 348 mm
2014,7087.303
Bloch 1783; Baer 1800.B.b.1

Plate 304: *Raphael and La Fornarina, IX: the Pope arrives*, 1 September 1968 IV
Etching. Plate: 145 × 210 mm.
Sheet: 283 × 346 mm
2014,7087.304
Bloch 1784; Baer 1801.B.b.1
(illustrated on p. 123)

Plate 305: *Raphael and La Fornarina, X: the Pope had his chair brought*, 2 September 1968 I
Etching. Plate: 145 × 210 mm.
Sheet: 380 × 350 mm
2014,7087.305
Bloch 1785; Baer 1802.B.b.1

Plate 306: *Raphael and La Fornarina, XI: the Pope is speechless in his chair*, 2 September 1968 II
Etching. Plate: 145 × 205 mm.
Sheet: 280 × 345 mm
2014,7087.306
Bloch 1786; Baer 1803.B.b.1

Plate 307: *Raphael and
La Fornarina, XII: in his chair,
the Pope feels cuckolded*,
2 September 1968 III
Etching. Plate: 145 × 210 mm.
Sheet: 285 × 350 mm
2014,7087.307
Bloch 1787; Baer 1804.B.b.1

Plate 308: *Raphael and
La Fornarina, XIII: in his chair,
the Pope sticks out his tongue*,
3 September 1968 I
Etching. Plate: 150 × 210 mm.
Sheet: 285 × 350 mm
2014,7087.308
Bloch 1788; Baer 1805.B.b.1

Plate 309: *Raphael and
La Fornarina, XIV: the Pope
has slipped away*,
3 September 1968 II
Etching. Plate: 145 × 210 mm.
Sheet: 285 × 350 mm
2014,7087.309
Bloch 1789; Baer 1806.B.b.1

Plate 310: *Raphael and
La Fornarina, XV: the Pope
is back, on his pot*,
4 September 1968 I
Etching. Plate: 145 × 210 mm.
Sheet: 285 × 350 mm
2014,7087.310
Bloch 1790; Baer 1807.B.b.1

Plate 311: *Raphael and
La Fornarina, XVI: the Pope
is back, on his pot, pensive*,
4 September 1968 II
Etching. Plate: 145 × 210 mm.
Sheet: 280 × 347 mm
2014,7087.311
Bloch 1791; Baer 1808.B.b.1

Plate 312: *Raphael and
La Fornarina, XVII: on his pot, a
cardinal, tickled, laughs*,
4 September 1968 III
Etching. Plate: 145 × 210 mm.
Sheet: 285 × 350 mm
2014,7087.312
Bloch 1792; Baer 1809.B.b.1

Plate 313: *Raphael and
La Fornarina, XVIII: the
Pope has a funny hairstyle*,
4 September 1968 IV
Etching. Plate: 145 × 210 mm.
Sheet: 285 × 350 mm
2014,7087.313
Bloch 1793; Baer 1810.B.b.1

Plate 314: *Raphael and
La Fornarina, XIX: Pope on
his pot, with tiara and muff;
Michelangelo is
hidden under the bed*,
5 September 1968 I
Etching. Plate: 145 × 210 mm.
Sheet: 285 × 350 mm
2014,7087.314
Bloch 1794; Baer 1811.B.b.1

Plate 315: *Raphael and
La Fornarina, XX: the Pope is
leaving*, 7 September 1968 I
Etching. Plate: 145 × 210 mm.
Sheet: 285 × 350 mm
2014,7087.315
Bloch 1795; Baer 1812.B.b.1

Plate 316: *Raphael and
La Fornarina, XXI: Michelangelo
is hidden under the bed*,
8 September 1968 I
Etching. Plate: 145 × 210 mm.
Sheet: 280 × 350 mm
2014,7087.316
Bloch 1796; Baer 1813.B.b.1

Plate 317: *Raphael and
La Fornarina, XXII: Michelangelo
under the bed; enter Piero
Crommelynck*,
8 September 1968 II
Etching. Plate: 145 × 210 mm.
Sheet: 280 × 345 mm
2014,7087.317
Bloch 1797; Baer 1814.B.b.1
(illustrated on p. 123, detail
p. 108)

Plate 318: *Raphael and
La Fornarina, XXIII: alone,
hugging each other on the
ground*, 8 September 1968 III
Etching. Plate: 145 × 210 mm.
Sheet: 280 × 355 mm
2014,7087.318
Bloch 1798; Baer 1815.B.b.1

Plate 319: *Raphael and
La Fornarina, XXIV: with
a voyeur in a two-cornered hat,
and two pigeons*,
9 September 1968 I
Etching. Plate: 145 × 210 mm.
Sheet: 285 × 350 mm
2014,7087.319
Bloch 1799; Baer 1816.B.b.1

Plate 320: *Couple of lovers
(Raphael and La Fornarina:
end)*, 9 September 1968 II
Etching. Plate: 145 × 210 mm.
Sheet: 280 × 350 mm
2014,7087.320
Bloch 1800; Baer 1817.B.b.1

Plate 321: *Writing with his
muse, working on a tale like
'A Thousand and One Nights',
about a cabalist with an owl,
a young man and a hetaera*,
18 September 1968 I
Etching. Plate: 145 × 210 mm.
Sheet: 280 × 350 mm
2014,7087.321
Bloch 1801; Baer 1818.B.b.1

Plate 322: *Young woman in bed,
Celestina and gentleman*, 18
September 1968 II
Etching. Plate: 145 × 210 mm.
Sheet: 285 × 350 mm
2014,7087.322
Bloch 1802; Baer 1819.B.b.1

Plate 323: *Young woman and
gentleman: Egyptian sculpture
with painted base*,
18 September 1968 III
Etching. Plate: 205 × 265 mm.
Sheet: 325 × 400 mm
2014,7087.323
Bloch 1803; Baer 1820.B.b.1

Plate 324: *Painter and model
hiding her face*, 19 September
1968 I
Etching. Plate: 210 × 265 mm.
Sheet: 325 × 410 mm
2014,7087.324
Bloch 1804; Baer 1821.B.b.1

Plate 325: *Painter painting
a Venus with little dog*,
19 September 1968 II
Etching. Plate: 210 × 265 mm.
Sheet: 330 × 400 mm
2014,7087.325
Bloch 1805; Baer 1822.B.b.1

Plate 326: *Fat man lowering
his pants in the circus ring*,
19 September 1968 III
Etching. Plate: 210 × 265 mm.
Sheet: 330 × 405 mm
2014,7087.326
Bloch 1806; Baer 1823.B.b.1

Plate 327: *Field painters: around
the 19th century and Courbet*,
20 September 1968 I
Sugar aquatint on greased
plate. Plate: 210 × 265 mm.
Sheet: 330 × 405 mm
2014,7087.327
Bloch 1807; Baer 1824.B.b.1
(illustrated on p. 124)

Plate 328: *Field painters: lunch
on the Impressionist grass*,
21 September 1968 I
Sugar aquatint on greased
plate. Plate: 210 × 265 mm.
Sheet: 330 × 400 mm
2014,7087.328
Bloch 1808; Baer 1825.B.b.1

Plate 329: *Celestina, client
and little faceless nude maja*,
21 September 1968 II
Sugar aquatint on greased plate
(worked with varnish on the
sleeve). Plate: 205 × 270 mm.
Sheet: 330 × 405 mm
2014,7087.329
Bloch 1809; Baer 1826.B.b.1

Plate 330: *Man seated next
to a woman combing her hair,
with two painters behind*,
21 September 1968 III,
24 September 1968
Sugar aquatint, drypoint and
scraper. Plate: 205 × 270 mm.
Sheet: 330 × 405 mm
2014,7087.330
Bloch 1810; Baer 1827.B.b.1

Plate 331: *Egyptian and women*,
21 September 1968 IV
Etching. Plate: 205 × 270 mm.
Sheet: 330 × 405 mm
2014,7087.331
Bloch 1811; Baer 1828.B.b.1

Plate 332: *Matamore dressed
in his Sunday best behind the
scenes of a circus*,
21 September 1968 V
Etching. Plate: 210 × 265 mm.
Sheet: 330 × 405 mm
2014,7087.332
Bloch 1812; Baer 1829.B.b.1

Plate 333: *Medieval man at
the circus*, 25 September 1968 I
Etching. Plate: 210 × 265 mm.
Sheet: 330 × 400 mm
2014,7087.333
Bloch 1813: Baer 1830.B.b.1

Plate 334: *Biblical scene (David
and Bathsheba?),
with jester in two-cornered hat*,
25 September 1968 II
Etching. Plate: 205 × 265 mm.
Sheet: 325 × 410 mm
2014,7087.334
Bloch 1814; Baer 1831.B.b.1

Plate 335: *Old jester
contemplating acrobats, I*,
25 September 1968 III
Etching. Plate: 210 × 260 mm.
Sheet: 325 × 405 mm
2014,7087.335
Bloch 1815; Baer 1832.B.b.1

Plate 336: *Theatre: farewell to
the rider*, 26 September 1968 I
Aquatint with stop-out varnish
in reserve.
Plate: 225 × 320 mm.
Sheet: 380 × 470 mm
2014,7087.336
Bloch 1816; Baer 1833.B.b.1

Plate 337: *Old jester
contemplating acrobats, II*,
26 September 1968 II
Aquatint with stop-out varnish
in reserve. Plate: 210 × 265 mm.
Sheet: 330 × 405 mm
2014,7087.337
Bloch 1817; Baer 1834.B.b.1

Plate 338: *Television: Quaker,
little red, horsewoman …*,
26 September 1968 III
Etching. Plate: 205 × 270 mm.
Sheet: 330 × 405 mm
2014,7087.338
Bloch 1818; Baer 1835.B.b.1

Plate 339: *Morning: pipe,
woman and chocolate*,
26 September 1968 IV
Sugar aquatint on partially
greased plate.
Plate: 205 × 270 mm.
Sheet: 325 × 405 mm
2014,7087.339
Bloch 1819; Baer 1836.B.b.1

Plate 340: *Three old friends
visiting: Mr Smokes, Mrs
Watches*, 27 September 1968 I
Aquatint and scraper.
Plate: 205 × 265 mm.
Sheet: 330 × 400 mm
2014,7087.340
Bloch 1820; Baer 1837.B.b.1

Plate 341: *Man in hat drawing
next to a woman offering
herself*, 27 September 1968 II
Aquatint, drypoint and scraper.
Plate: 205 × 265 mm.
Sheet: 325 × 405 mm
2014,7087.341
Bloch 1821; Baer 1838.B.b.1

Plate 342: *The bust of the
dead painter is crowned by the
academy: the widow mocks*,
28 September 1968 I
Etching. Plate: 205 × 265 mm.
Sheet: 330 × 405 mm
2014,7087.342
Bloch 1822; Baer 1839.B.b.1

Plate 343: *Hollywood
blockbuster, with spectators*,
29 September 1968 I,
2 October 1968
Etching and drypoint.
Plate: 205 × 270 mm.
Sheet: 330 × 405 mm
2014,7087.343
Bloch 1823; Baer 1840.B.b.1

Plate 344: *Around the 'Chef-
d'œuvre inconnu': Porbus and
the young Poussin at Frenhofer's*,
30 September 1968 I
Aquatint and scraper.
Plate: 205 × 325 mm.
Sheet: 380 × 470 mm
2014,7087.344
Bloch 1824; Baer 1841.B.b.1

Plate 345: *Celestina, maja or
Olympia naked, with Manet and
Marcellin Desboutin: couple of
spectators in the background*
1 October 1968 I
Sugar aquatint with scraper on
greased plate.
Plate: 205 × 325 mm.
Sheet: 365 × 470 mm
2014,7087.345
Bloch 1825; Baer 1842.B.b.1
(illustrated on p. 119)

Plate 346: *Painter with a sulking
model*. 4 October 1968 I
Etching.
Plate: 230 × 325 mm.
Sheet: 360 × 470 mm
2014,7087.346
Bloch 1826; Baer 1843.B.b.1

Plate 347: *Serenade at sunset
in a Monet-style undergrowth*,
5 October 1968 I
Sugar aquatint on greased
plate. Plate: 230 × 325 mm.
Sheet: 360 × 470 mm
2014,7087.347
Bloch 1827; Baer 1844.B.b.1
(illustrated on p. 125)

*Brothel. Chatter, with parrot,
Celestina, and the portrait
of Degas* from *156 Suite*,
4 April 1971
Etching. Plate: 366 × 492 mm.
Sheet: 500 × 650 mm
1993,1003.2
Bloch 1964; Baer 1973.Ba
(illustrated on pp. 134–5)

DRAWINGS

Nude girl, c. 1905
Pen and grey ink on paper.
321 × 215 mm
1926,0313.31. Presented by the
Contemporary Art Society

Study for *Les Demoiselles
d'Avignon*, 1906–7
Red, orange and pink bodycolour
and watercolour on paper.
626 × 460 mm
1996,0216.3. Purchased with
a contribution from Art Fund
(as the National Art Collections
Fund) (illustrated on p. 13)

*Portrait of Enrico Cecchetti,
ballet master of La Scala,
Milan*, 1925
Pencil on paper. 340 × 60 mm
2024,7043.1. Bequeathed by
Karsten Schubert

Leaping bulls from the Institute
of Contemporary Art Visitors'
Book, 1950
Watercolour and coloured inks.
251 × 402 mm
1975,0726.4.2–3. Presented
by Roland Penrose
(illustrated on p. 93)

Bathers, 1961
Pencil on paper. 330 × 502 mm
2024,7043.2. Bequeathed by
Karsten Schubert

GLOSSARY OF PRINTMAKING TERMS

The main printmaking techniques and terms referred to in this publication are described below. Fuller explanations are given in Antony Griffiths, *Prints and Printmaking: An Introduction to the History and Techniques* (1st pub. 1980), 2nd edn, London: The British Museum Press, 1996, reprinted with revisions 2010; and Paul Goldman, *Looking at Prints, Drawings and Watercolours: A Guide to Technical Terms* (1st pub. 1988), 2nd edn, London: The British Museum Press, 2006.

AQUATINT

A variety of etching used to create tone, originally to imitate the effect of a watercolour wash. Within a dust-box, fine resin particles are shaken and allowed to fall as a thin layer on to a metal plate; this is then heated until the resin melts and fuses to the surface, forming a porous ground. During immersion in an acid bath, the acid bites into the minute channels around each resin particle. These hold sufficient ink to print as an even tone. Highlights can be obtained by 'stopping out' with an acid-resistant varnish (see under *etching*) and also by directly working the aquatinted plate with a *scraper*.

DRYPOINT

The line is drawn directly into a metal plate with a sharp point held like a pencil, which throws up a metal burr along the incision. Ink is retained in the burr, producing a rich feathery line when printed. Because the burr wears down easily under pressure from the press, only a few impressions showing the full richness of the drypoint line can be pulled. The plate is sometimes steel-faced to protect the burr from wearing and so allow a larger number of impressions to be printed.

ENGRAVING

Lines are cut cleanly and directly into the bare metal plate using a V-shaped tool called a *burin*.

ETCHING

A needle is used to draw freely through a hard, waxy acid-resistant ground covering the metal plate. The exposed metal is then 'bitten' by acid, creating the lines. This is done by immersing the plate in an acid bath; the longer the acid bites, the deeper the lines become and the darker they print. The plate can be bitten to different depths by 'stopping out' the lighter lines with a varnish before returning the plate to the bath. The ground is then cleaned off before printing.

GREASED PLATE

Metal plates are usually de-greased to prepare them for aquatint processes. This step can be skipped, or grease can be added intentionally, which will result in the applied ground not holding evenly. This unevenness produces grey tones in subsequent impressions.

IMPRESSION

A single printing from a plate, stone or block.

INTAGLIO PRINTMAKING

The traditional hand-drawn techniques of *etching*, *aquatint*, *drypoint* and *engraving* are all intaglio processes. The methods of printing are the same, but the result of each technique is different. The basic principle is that the line is incised into the metal plate, which is usually copper or zinc. Ink is rubbed with a dabber into the recessed lines and the surface of the plate wiped clean. Printing is achieved by placing a sheet of dampened paper over the inked plate, which is then passed through the press under heavy pressure. Characteristic of intaglio printmaking is the plate mark impressed into the paper.

LINOCUT

A sheet of linoleum is cut with chisels and gouges so that the areas to be inked stand in relief. Ink is rolled onto the surface of the block, which is printed onto a sheet of paper, either using a press or by rubbing the back of the paper by hand or with a spoon.

LITHOGRAPH

An image is drawn on the printing surface (usually a stone or zinc plate) with a greasy medium, such as crayon or a lithographic ink known as tusche. The printing surface is dampened so that when greasy ink is applied it adheres only to the drawn image and is repelled by the water elsewhere. The image is printed onto paper using a flat-bed press.

PLATE TONE (SOMETIMES CALLED SURFACE TONE)

An effect obtained by incompletely wiping the printing plate so as to leave a film of ink on the surface.

PROOF

An impression outside the edition, usually pulled during the process of working on the plate and sometimes called a *trial proof*.

SCRAPER

A sharp, knife-like tool traditionally used to scrape away unwanted lines or grooves on the metal plate.

STATE

While the artist works on the plate, proofs are taken which record the different stages, or *states*, in the development of the print.

SUGAR AQUATINT (SOMETIMES CALLED SUGAR-LIFT AQUATINT)

A type of *aquatint* which allows the artist to produce the design in positive brushstrokes. After the plate has been prepared with resin, the image is brushed on to the plate using a special fluid containing sugar. When almost dry the plate is covered with an acid-resistant 'stopping-out' varnish and immersed in a bath of warm water. As the sugar swells in the water it causes the varnish to lift, revealing the artist's original resin-covered drawing. The plate is now ready to be 'bitten' by acid in the usual way, while the 'stopping-out' varnish protects the non-drawn areas of the plate.

TRANSFER LITHOGRAPH

A lithograph that begins as a drawing on transfer paper, which is then transferred onto a stone printing surface.

ACKNOWLEDGEMENTS

This exhibition has been made possible with contributions from Frederick Mulder Ltd, ARTscapades, The Michael Marks Charitable Trust, the P F Charitable Trust and the IFPDA Foundation. The breadth of the Museum's Picasso holdings are in large part due to the generosity of Hamish Parker. We extend our thanks to him again for his support for this publication and to the Charities Aid Foundation for facilitating his gifts.

This publication and accompanying exhibition have been collaborative projects, involving many colleagues across the British Museum. In the department of Prints and Drawings, I owe special thanks to Hugo Chapman, Jennifer Ramkalawon, Isabel Seligman, Olenka Horbatsch and Sarah Vowles, and former members of the department Stephen Coppel, Antony Griffiths and Frances Carey. The assistance of Genevra Higginson, the 2024 Michael Bromberg Research Fellow, has been invaluable. My special thanks also go to the Publishing team, especially Claudia Bloch, Lydia Cooper, Beata Kibil and Nathaniel Balch.

In Advancement, I am grateful to Evelyn Curtin, Jennifer Ebrey, Alice Parr, Gina Grassi, Lucy Holmes and Alice Macrae; in other curatorial departments, Thomas Harrison, Jill Cook, Alexandra Villing and Judy Rudoe; in Collection Management, Valeria Di Tommaso, Jadene Imbusch, Lizzie Barratt, Anna Chamberlain, Hebe Halstead, Lynne Darwood, Hannah James, Alex Truscott and Jim Peters; in Conservation, Samantha Taylor, Christina Angelo and Keeley Wilson; in Photography, Joanna Fernandes, Bradley Timms, Marco Borsato and Isabel Marshall; in Exhibitions, Rosalind Winton, Ruth Cribb, Rebekah Manning, Lydia Fellgett, Deklan Kilfeather, Evelin Arweck and Ann Lumley; in Design, Vicci Ward, Helen Adrados and Aaron Jones; in Interpretation, Stuart Frost, Natalie Buy and Maria Blyzinsky; in Marketing, Sean McParland and Helen Atkinson; in Press, Jane Parsons and Matthew Hutt; in Learning and National Partnerships, Shani Crawford, Jaime Prada and Hilary Williams and in the Directorate, Nicholas Cullinan, Jill Maggs, Carl Heron and Jane Portal. I would also like to thank Rob King, Julia Bettinson and Harry King from Altaimage; Phoebe Colley, copyeditor; Amanda Speake, indexer; and Sandra Zellmer for her thoughtful design of the book. I am very grateful to those outside the Museum who have provided help and support, including Anne-Françoise Gavanon, Frederick Mulder, Elizabeth Cowling and James Curran. And finally, I am immensely grateful to Hamish Parker, without whom this project would not have been possible.

CREDITS

The publisher would like to thank the copyright holders for granting permission to reproduce the copyrighted material included. Every attempt has been made to trace accurate ownership of copyrighted material in this book. Any errors or omissions will be corrected in subsequent editions provided notification is sent to the publisher.

Further information about the Museum and its collection can be found at britishmuseum.org. Registration numbers for British Museum objects are included in the checklist on pages 138–157. Unless otherwise stated, copyright in photographs belongs to the institution mentioned in the caption. All images of British Museum objects are © 2024 The Trustees of the British Museum, courtesy the Department of Photography and Imaging.

All works by Pablo Picasso © Succession Picasso/DACS, London 2024

fig. 1: Photo by Tony Vaccaro/ Getty Images
fig. 2: © Succession Picasso/ DACS, London 2024/ Bridgeman Images
fig. 4: © ADAGP, Paris and DACS, London 2024
fig. 6: © Succession Picasso/ DACS, London 2024/ Bridgeman Images
fig. 10: Photo: © Fundació Museu Picasso de Barcelona
figs 13–14: Photo: National Gallery of Art, Washington © 2024 Estate of Pablo Picasso/Artists Rights Society (ARS), New York
figs 16–17: Photo Edward Quinn, © edwardquinn.com

Sources for translations of quotations:
p. 20: © Hans Bollger, *Picasso's Vollard Suite*, London: Thames & Hudson, 1956 and 1977, reprinted 1994. Translated from Daniel-Henry Kahnweiler, 'Huit entretiens avec Picasso', *Le Point*, vol. 7, no. 42 (October 1952), Verlag Gerd Hatje.
p. 21: © Daniel-Henry Kahnweiler with Francis Crémieux, *My Galleries and Painters*, trans. Helen Weaver, London: Thames & Hudson, 1971 (originally published 1961, Gallimard).
pp. 27, 109: From FOREVER PICASSO by Robert Otero. Copyright © Harry N. Abrams, Inc., New York. Used by permission of ABRAMS, an imprint of Harry N. Abrams, Inc., New York. All rights reserved.
p. 31: Quoted in Jean-Paul Crespelle, *La vie quotidienne à Montmartre au temps de Picasso, 1900–1910*, New York: Hachette, 1978, p. 11 (translated by author).
p. 43: Quoted in Dor de La Souchère, *Picasso in Antibes*, trans. Walter John Strachan, London: Lund Humphries, 1960, p. 54.
p. 77: © Tate 1988, *Picasso 1953–1972: Painting as Model* by David Michel Leiris Etc. Sylvester. Reproduced by permission of the Tate Trustees. First published in French as 'Picasso 1953–1973 : la peinture comme modèle' in the exhibition catalogue *Le dernier Picasso 1953–1972*, Éditions du Centre Pompidou, Paris, 1988.
p. 97: Quoted in 'Picasso speaks', *The Arts*, New York, May 1923, quoted in Elizabeth Cowling and Jennifer Mundy, *On Classic Ground: Picasso, Leger, de Chirico and the New Classicism, 1910–1930* (Tate, 1990), p. 201.